In Search of the Spirit:
Selected Works, Volume Two

In Search of the Spirit:
Selected Works, Volume Two

The Spirit and Early Jewish Literature

JOHN R. LEVISON

CASCADE Books • Eugene, Oregon

IN SEARCH OF THE SPIRIT: SELECTED WORKS, VOLUME TWO
The Spirit and Early Jewish Literature

Copyright © 2024 John R. Levison. All rights reserved. Except for brief quotations in critical publications or reviews, no part of this book may be reproduced in any manner without prior written permission from the publisher. Write: Permissions, Wipf and Stock Publishers, 199 W. 8th Ave., Suite 3, Eugene, OR 97401.

Cascade Books
An Imprint of Wipf and Stock Publishers
199 W. 8th Ave., Suite 3
Eugene, OR 97401

www.wipfandstock.com

PAPERBACK ISBN: 978-1-7252-9055-6
HARDCOVER ISBN: 978-1-7252-9056-3
EBOOK ISBN: 978-1-7252-9057-0

Cataloguing-in-Publication data:

Names: Levison, John R., author.

Title: In search of the Spirit: selected works, volume 2 : the Spirit and early Jewish literature / John R. Levison.

Description: Eugene, OR: Cascade Books, 2024. | Includes bibliographical references and index.

Identifiers: ISBN 978-1-7252-9055-6 (paperback). | ISBN 978-1-7252-9056-3 (hardcover). | ISBN 978-1-7252-9057-0 (ebook).

Subjects: LCSH: Holy Spirit (Judaism)—History of doctrines. | Philo, of Alexandria. | Josephus. | Dead Sea Scrolls. | Jewish religious literature.

Classification: BM176 L380 2024 (print). | BM176 (ebook).

09/10/24

To
Ron Herms
Loren Stuckenbruck
Archie Wright

Contents

Permisssions | ix
Acknowledgments | xi
Abbreviations | xiii
Introduction | xxi

1. Did the Spirit Withdraw from Israel? An Evaluation of the Earliest Jewish Data | 1
2. Judith 16:14 and the Creation of Woman | 24
3. The Two Spirits in Qumran Theology | 27
4. Inspiration and the Divine Spirit in the Writings of Philo Judaeus | 53
5. Ascent and Inspiration in the Writings of Philo Judaeus | 100
6. The Prophetic Spirit as an Angel According to Philo | 128
7. Prophetic Inspiration in Pseudo-Philo's Liber Antiquitatum Biblicarum | 148
8. The Debut of the Divine Spirit in Josephus's *Antiquities* | 177
9. The Angelic Spirit in Early Judaism | 193
10. Retrospect and Prospect | 230

Bibliography | 271
Index of Modern Authors | 281
Index of Ancient Documents | 285

Permissions

Unless otherwise noted, Scripture quotations, including of the Apocrypha, are taken from the New Revised Standard Version Bible, copyright © 1989 National Council of the Churches of Christ in the United States of America. Used by permission. All rights reserved worldwide.

Scripture quotations marked (JB) are taken from the Jerusalem Bible, published and copyright © 1966, 1967, and 1968 by Daron, Longman & Todd Ltd. and Doubleday and Co. Inc. and used by permission of the publishers.

Scripture quotations marked (NEB) are taken from the English Bible, copyright © Cambridge University Press and Oxford University Press, 1961, 1970. All rights reserved.

Scripture quotations marked (NJB) are taken from the New Jerusalem Bible, published and copyright © 1985 by Darton, Longman & Todd Ltd and Les Editions du Cerf, and used by permission of the publishers.

Acknowledgments

Funding that has provided sustained periods of research to write the articles and chapters in these volumes was provided by the National Endowment for the Humanities, the Alexander von Humboldt Foundation, the National Humanities Center, the International Catacomb Society, and the W. J. A. Power Chair of Old Testament Interpretation and Biblical Hebrew at Perkins School of Theology, Southern Methodist University.

Chapter 1 was previously published as "Did the Spirit Withdraw from Israel? An Evaluation of the Earliest Jewish Data," *NTS* 43 (1997) 35–57. Copyright © 1997 John R. Levison. Reprinted with permission.

Chapter 2 was previously published as "Judith 16:14 and the Creation of Woman," *JBL* 114 (1995) 467–69. Reprinted by permission.

Chapter 3 was previously published as "The Two Spirits in Qumran Theology," in *The Dead Sea Scrolls and the Qumran Community*, vol. 2 of *The Bible and the Dead Sea Scrolls*, edited by James H. Charlesworth (Waco: Baylor University Press, 2006), 169–94. Copyright © 2006 Baylor University Press. Reprinted by arrangement with Baylor University Press. All rights reserved.

Chapter 4 was previously published as "Inspiration and the Divine Spirit in the Writings of Philo Judaeus," *JSJ* 26 (1995) 271–323. Reprinted by permission of Brill.

Chapter 5 was previously published as "Ascent and Inspiration in the Writings of Philo Judaeus," in *Apocalypticism and Mysticism in Ancient Judaism and Early Christianity*, edited by John J. Collins et al. (Berlin: de Gruyter, 2018), 129–54.

ACKNOWLEDGMENTS

Chapter 6 was previously published as "The Prophetic Spirit as an Angel According to Philo," *HTR* 88 (1995) 189–207. Copyright © 1995 by the President and Fellows of Harvard College. Reprinted with permission.

Chapter 7 was previously published as "Prophetic Inspiration in Pseudo-Philo's *Liber Antiquitatum Biblicarum*," *JQR* 85 (1995) 297–329. Copyright © 1995 by the Center for Judaic Studies University of Pennsylvania. Used with permission.

Chapter 8 was previously published as "The Debut of the Divine Spirit in Josephus's *Antiquities*," *HTR* 87 (1994) 123–38. Copyright © 1994 by the President and Fellows of Harvard College. Reprinted with permission.

Chapter 9 was previously published as "The Angelic Spirit in Early Judaism," in *Society of Biblical Literature 1995 Seminar Papers* (Atlanta: Scholars, 1995), 464–93. SBLSPS 34. Reprinted by permission.

Chapter 10 was previously published as "Retrospect" and "Prospect," in *The Spirit in First Century Judaism* (Leiden: Brill, 1997), 217–59. AGJU 29. Reprinted by permission of Brill.

Abbreviations

ANCIENT

Abr.	*De Abrahamo*
Aet.	*De aeternitate mundi*
Ag. Ap.	*Against Apion*
Agr.	*De agricultura*
Amat.	*Amatorius*
Ant.	*Jewish Antiquities*
Apol.	*Apologia*
b. B. Bat.	Babylonian Talmud Baba Batra
b. Sanh.	Babylonian Talmud Sanhedrin
b. Soṭah	Babylonian Talmud Soṭah
b. Yoma	Babylonian Talmud Yoma
2 Bar.	2 Baruch (Syriac Apocalypse)
Cels.	*Contra Celsum*
Cher.	*De cherubim*
1 Chr	1 Chronicles
2 Chr	2 Chronicles
Conf.	*De confusione linguarum*
Contempl.	*De vita contemplativa*
Dan	Daniel

ABBREVIATIONS

Decal.	*De decalogo*
Def. orac.	*De defectu oraculorum*
Dem.	*De Demosthene*
De or.	*De oratore*
Det.	*Quod deterius potiori insidari soleat*
Deus	*Quod Deus sit immutabilis*
Deut	Deuteronomy
Diatr.	*Diatribai (Dissertationes)*
Dic. exercit.	*De dicendi exercitatione (Or. 18) (Training for Public Speaking)*
Div.	*De divinatione*
1 *En.*	1 Enoch (Ethiopic Apocalypse)
Enn.	*Enneades*
Ep.	*Epistulae Morales*
Euthyd.	*Euthydemus*
Euthyphr.	*Euthyphro*
Exod	Exodus
Ezek	Ezekiel
Fug.	*De fuga et inventione*
Gen	Genesis
Gen. Socr.	*De genio Socratis (On the Genius of Socrates)*
Geogr.	*Geographica*
Gig.	*De gigantibus (On Giants)*
Hab	Habakkuk
Hab.	*De habitu (Or. 72)*
Hag	Haggai
Her.	*Quis rerum divinarum heres sit (Who Is the Heir?)*
Herm. Mand.	Shepherd of Hermas, Mandate(s)
Hom. 1 Cor.	*Homiliae in epistulam i ad Corinthios*
Hos	Hosea
Inst.	*Divinarum institutionum libri VII* (Lactantius)
Inst.	*Institutio oratoria* (Quintilian)
Ios.	*De Iosepho*
Iph. taur.	*Iphigenia taurica*
Isa	Isaiah

Is. Os.	*De Iside et Osiride*
Jdt	Judith
Jer	Jeremiah
Josh	Joshua
Jub.	Jubilees
Judg	Judges
J.W.	*Jewish War*
1 Kgs	1 Kings
2 Kgs	2 Kings
LAB	Liber antiquitatum biblicarum (Pseudo-Philo)
Lam	Lamentations
Leg.	*Legum allegoriae*
Legat.	*Legatio ad Gaium*
Lev Rab.	Leviticus Rabbah
Lives	*Lives of Eminent Philosophers*
1 Macc	1 Maccabees
Mek.	Mekilta
Mem.	*Memorabilia*
Migr.	*De migratione Abrahami*
Mixt.	*De mixtione*
Mos.	*De vita Mosis*
m. Soṭah	Mishnah Soṭah
Mut.	*De mutatione nominum*
Nat. d.	*De natura deorum*
Neh	Nehemiah
Num	Numbers
Opif.	*De opificio mundi* (*On the Creation of the World*)
Phaedr.	*Phaedrus*
Phoen.	*Phoenissae*
Plant.	*De plantatione* (*Concerning Noah's Work as a Planter*)
Post.	*De posteritate Caini*
Praem.	*De praemiis et poenis* (*On Rewards and Punishments*)
Pr Azar	Prayer of Azariah
Prob.	*Quod omnis probus liber sit*
Ps(s)	Psalm(s)

ABBREVIATIONS

Ps-Justin	Pseudo-Justinus
QE	*Quaestiones et solutiones in Exodum*
QG	*Quaestiones et solutiones in Genesin*
1QH	Hodayot or Thanksgiving Hymns[1]
1QM	Milḥamah or War Scroll
1QS	Serek Hayaḥad or Rule of the Community
4QShira	Shirot[a] or Songs of the Sage[a] (4Q510)
Quaest. plat.	*Quaestiones platonicae*
3 Regn.	*De regno iii (Or. 3) (Kingship 3)*
Resp.	*Respublica (Republic)*
Rhet. Her.	Rhetorica ad Herennium
Sacr.	*De sacrificiis Abelis et Caini*
1 Sam	1 Samuel
2 Sam	2 Samuel
Sib. Or.	Sibylline Oracles
Sir	Sirach/Ecclesiasticus
Somn.	*De somniis*
Spec.	*De specialibus legibus (On the Special Laws)*
Subl.	*De sublimitate*
Symp.	*Symposium*
T. Ab.	Testament of Abraham
T. Ash.	Testament of Asher
T. Benj.	Testament of Benjamin
T. Gad	Testament of Gad
Theaet.	*Theaetetus*
Tim.	*Timaeus*
T. Jud.	Testament of Judah
T. Levi	Testament of Levi
t. Pesaḥ.	Tosefta Pesaḥim
t. Soṭah	Tosefta Soṭah

1. Throughout this volume, I have preserved references to columns and lines in the Qumran Hymns (1QH) found in Eleazar Sukenik's edition, *The Dead Sea Scrolls of the Hebrew University*. More recent reconstruction of the scroll, with differing columns and lines, can be found in Schuller and Newsom, *The Hodayot*. To convert Sukenik's reconstruction of columns and lines to Schuller and Newsom's, readers can consult the helpful chart Schuller and Newsom provide on pp. 4–6 of their edition.

Tusc.	*Tusculanae disputationes*
Virt.	*De virtutibus*
Wis	Wisdom of Solomon
y. Šeb.	Jerusalem Talmud Šebiʾit
y. Soṭah	Jerusalem Talmud Soṭah
Zech	Zechariah

MODERN

AB	Anchor Bible
ABD	*The Anchor Bible Dictionary*. Edited by David Noel Freedman. 6 vols. New York: Doubleday, 1992
AGJU	Arbeiten zur Geschichte des antiken Judentums und des Urchristentums
AHw	*Akkadisches Handwörterbuch*. Wolfram von Soden. 3 vols. Wiesbaden, 1965–81
ALGHJ	Arbeiten zur Literatur und Geschichte des hellenistischen Judentums
ANF	*Ante-Nicene Fathers*
ANRW	*Aufstieg und Niedergang der römischen Welt: Geschichte und Kultur Roms im Spiegel der neueren Forschung*. Part 2, *Principat*. Edited by Hildegard Temporini and Wolfgang Haase. Berlin: de Gruyter, 1972–
AR	*Archiv für Religionswissenschaft*
BBB	Bonner biblische Beiträge
BCE	before the Common Era
BFCT	Beiträge zur Förderung christlicher Theologie
BJS	Brown Judaic Studies
BZNW	Beihefte zur Zeitschrift für die neutestamentliche Wissenschaft
ca.	circa
CAD	*The Assyrian Dictionary of the Oriental Institute of the University of Chicago*. 26 vols. Chicago: The Oriental Institute of the University of Chicago, 1956–20011
CBQMS	The Catholic Biblical Quarterly Monograph Series

ABBREVIATIONS

CD	Cairo Genizah copy of the Damascus Document
CE	Common Era
CRINT	Compendia Rerum Iudaicarum ad Novum Testamentum
DSS	Dead Sea Scrolls
e.g.	*exempli gratia*, for example
ETL	*Ephemerides Theologicae Lovanienses*
FRLANT	Forschungen zur Religion und Literatur des Alten und Neuen Testaments
HTR	*Harvard Theological Review*
HUCA	*Hebrew Union College Annual*
IDB	*The Interpreter's Dictionary of the Bible*. Edited by George Arthur Buttrick. 4 vols. New York: Abingdon, 1962
JB	Jerusalem Bible
JBL	*Journal of Biblical Literature*
JJS	*Journal of Jewish Studies*
JQR	*Jewish Quarterly Review*
JSHRZ	*Jüdische Schriften aus hellenistisch-römischer Zeit*
JSJ	*Journal for the Study of Judaism in the Persian, Hellenistic, and Roman Periods*
JSP	*Journal for the Study of the Pseudepigrapha*
JSPSup	Journal for the Study of the Pseudepigrapha Supplement Series
JTS	*Journal of Theological Studies*
LCL	Loeb Classical Library
LHBOTS	Library of Hebrew Bible/Old Testament Studies
LXX	Septuagint (the Greek OT)
n(n)	note(s)
NAWG	Nachrichten (von) der Akademie der Wissenschaften in Göttingen
NEB	New English Bible
NJB	New Jerusalem Bible
NovT	*Novum Testamentum*
NovTSup	Supplements to Novum Testamentum
NPNF²	*Nicene and Post-Nicene Fathers*, Series 2
NRSV	New Revised Standard Version

NTL	New Testament Library
NTS	*New Testament Studies*
OTL	Old Testament Library
OTP	*The Old Testament Pseudepigrapha.* Edited by James H. Charlesworth. 2 vols. New York: Doubleday, 1983, 1985
p(p).	page(s)
PAAJR	*Proceedings of the American Academy of Jewish Research*
PG	Patrologia Graeca [= *Patrologiae Cursus Completus: Series Graeca*]. Edited by Jacques-Paul Migne. 162 vols. Paris, 1857–86
PTS	Patristische Texte und Studien
PTSDSSP	Princeton Theological Seminary Dead Sea Scrolls Project
RevQ	*Revue de Qumran*
RHR	*Revue de l'histoire des religions*
SANT	Studien zum Alten und Neuen Testaments
SBLDS	Society of Biblical Literature Dissertation Series
SBLSP	Society of Biblical Literature Seminar Papers
SC	Sources chrétiennes. Paris: Cerf, 1943–
SPhiloA	Studia Philonica Annual
SSEJC	Studies in Scripture in Early Judaism and Christianity
ST	*Studia Theologica*
SUNT	Studien zur Umwelt des Neuen Testaments
SVTP	Studia in Veteris Testamenti Pseudepigraphica
TDNT	*Theological Dictionary of the New Testament.* Edited by Gerhard Kittel and Gerhard Friedrich. Translated by Geoffrey W. Bromiley. 10 vols. Grand Rapids: Eerdmans, 1964–76
TDOT	*Theological Dictionary of the Old Testament.* Edited by G. Johannes Botterweck and Helmer Ringgren. Translated by John T. Willis et al. 17 vols. Grand Rapids: Eerdmans, 1974–2021
v(v).	verse(s)
viz.	*videlicet*, namely
VT	*Vetus Testamentum*
VTSup	Supplements to Vetus Testamentum
WBC	Word Biblical Commentary

ABBREVIATIONS

WUNT	Wissenschaftliche Untersuchungen zum Neuen Testament
ZTK	*Zeitschrift für Theologie und Kirche*

Introduction

In this three-volume set, *In Search of the Spirit*, you will encounter my approach to the study of the spirit in antiquity. The first volume is devoted to the spirit in biblical literature and the last to my engagement with scholars, while this volume is taken up with my study of the spirit in early Jewish literature. You will discover on the first page of the first article in this volume the entrenched but errant perspective that ancient Jews believed the spirit had departed from Israel with the death of the last canonical prophet. As Hermann Gunkel, who inaugurated the modern study of the spirit in the ancient world, expressed it, Judaism at the time of Jesus was "bereft of the Spirit."[1]

This volume is, it is fair to say, my final effort to ensure that this perspective is put to rest once and for all. Such a view of early Judaism, though a convenient foil for New Testament pneumatology, is untenable in light of extant data. On the one hand, the smattering of early Jewish texts cited to undergird the view that prophecy had ceased—or, to put the matter another way, the spirit had withdrawn—cannot bear the weight of that perspective. On the other hand, myriad texts put the lie to this perspective, from the Dead Sea Scrolls to the Liber antiquitatum biblicarum, from the commentaries of Philo of Alexandria to the histories of Flavius Josephus, from Sirach to the Wisdom of Solomon, all of which contain significant references to inspiration by the spirit.

When I wrote my first article on the spirit during a National Endowment for the Humanities summer seminar for college teachers, led by Louis Feldman, I knew none of this. I simply wrote a paper on the topic of the seminar, the Greek encounter with Judaism in the Hellenistic era. I don't even have the foggiest recollection of why I wrote on the Liber antiquitatum

---

1. Gunkel, *Influence of Holy Spirit*, 6.

biblicarum. But write I did—and happily so. That paper opened such a vein of curiosity, prompted by unexpected findings, that I continued to write on inspiration in antiquity for thirty years, during which time I came to marvel at the erudition of scholars such as Henry Swete, Hermann Gunkel, Paul Volz, Hans Leisegang, I. Heinemann, Friedrich Büchsel, Heinrich von Baer, and Gérard Verbeke, to name a few. These authors, some of whom wrote as proponents or opponents of the history of religions school a century or more ago, captured my attention. Three of them, in particular, became my guides in search of the spirit, though each had died before I was born.

I wrestled and resonated, in particular, with the life and legacy of Hermann Gunkel. Not in terms of his stature, of course, but in other more modest ways. Gunkel began by studying the New Testament but ended by working primarily in Old Testament studies; I entered the Duke University doctoral program to study the New Testament and now find myself in a chair devoted to the interpretation of the Old Testament. Gunkel focused upon the experience—the effects or *Wirkungen*—of the spirit; readers of my publications, especially books, essays, and blogs intended for a wide audience, such as *Fresh Air: The Holy Spirit for an Inspired Life*, *Forty Days with the Holy Spirit*, and *Seven Secrets of the Spirit-Filled Life*, need not look far to discern a keen interest, not just in how ancient authors *thought* about the holy spirit, but how they *experienced* that spirit, as well.

Yet I am compelled, too, to resist Gunkel's appraisal of early Judaism. Gunkel contended, quite fittingly, "We must therefore view Judaism as the real matrix of the gospel . . . but without denying the influence of a reading of the Old Testament."[2] Yet the character of Judaism into which Jesus was born was dreary and dismal. "But what a powerful impression the pneuma must have made when its fullness appeared to a Judaism bereft of the Spirit," he supposed.[3] While I celebrate Gunkel's effort to see Judaism as "the real matrix of the gospel," I am compelled by the texts themselves to reject his appraisal of Judaism as "bereft of the Spirit."

Over the last few decades, I have come as well to admire the tenacity of Hans Leisegang, the son of a rural pastor who corrected his magisterial first book on the spirit under the severe constraints of the First World War. "It was not easy to make the corrections outdoors," he reminisced, "in rain and sunshine, in quarters loud with the noise of comrades, and finally to write with my left hand in a military hospital."[4] Later in life, Leise-

---

2. Gunkel, *Influence of Holy Spirit*, 5–6.
3. Gunkel, *Influence of Holy Spirit*, 6.
4. Leisegang, *Heilige Geist*, iv. For biographical details, consult Mesch, *Hans Leisegang*.

gang would resist National Socialism and, in 1934, be put in prison for six months. Restored to his academic post in Jena only after the Second World War, he found himself again compelled to resist a totalitarian regime, as he refused to become a delegate for the Soviet Volkskongreß. When the Soviet-controlled student council manipulated a meeting to expel him, they failed; he received 1,097 student votes of support, 282 of rejection, and 113 abstentions—all of this in a noxious atmosphere in which those who supported him essentially declared their opposition to the Soviet Party. Consequently, though he had already been offered the position of rector at the Free University in Berlin, along with a chair in philosophy, Leisegang opted to stay in Jena, because, as he saw it, his students there needed him more than those in Berlin. Nonetheless, the Soviet minister of culture at the time accused him of yelling at her in private conversation—*bawling* at her, as she put it—and he was summarily dismissed. So Hans Leisegang and his family headed to Berlin, where he would die, a few years later, in 1951.

Leisegang asked the pivotal question, "Is the teaching of the Holy Spirit of Greek or Oriental origin?"[5] He answered that the Old Testament exerted influence on early Christianity through a form of Judaism that was highly Greek in orientation: "Perhaps even the theologians and learned of the Hellenistic era approached the Old Testament with a concept of the Holy Spirit already fully worked out in Hellenism, and they believed to have found it afresh in the *pneuma hagion* of the Septuagint."[6] To create a bridge between Greek conceptions of *pneuma* and the more developed ones of Christianity, Leisegang plumbed the writings of Philo of Alexandria. Philo provided a sort of middle point, his interpretations lying at the nexus of Greek, Jewish, and Christian cultures. Yet Leisegang went further by attempting to peel the putative Jewish veneer from Philo's writings to probe the Greek conceptions that lay at their core. "Philo's perspectives had such deep roots in popular Greek beliefs," he supposed, "that he already took over popular conceptions thoroughly drenched in Greek philosophy."[7]

As with Gunkel, I demur, because I deem the dichotomy between Greek and Jewish elements to be a false one. It is not possible—or desirable—either to peel off the veneer from Philo's Greek thought to discover his Jewish core or to peel off the veneer of Philo's Jewish thought to discover his Greek core. The Greek and Jewish dimensions of Philo's thought suffuse one another in a symbiotic relationship that illumines the whole of his oeuvre. Nevertheless, while I cannot ultimately accept Leisegang's attempt to

5. Leisegang, *Heilige Geist*, 10–11.
6. Leisegang, *Heilige Geist*, 11.
7. Leisegang, *Heilige Geist*, 11–12.

distinguish a Greek core from a Jewish veneer, I value his magisterial effort to identify those Greek aspects that give the writings of Philo their brilliant hue and unique tenor.

In the chapters and articles to come, you will discern the influence of a third scholar, Paul Volz, whose analysis of the spirit provides a trenchant corrective to Hermann Gunkel's assessment of Judaism as "bereft of the Spirit." As I noted in the introduction to the first volume, Volz contended that "the habit of comparing a form of Judaism that is coming to an end with a youthful form of Christianity has led regularly to a misunderstanding of the former. This is historically unsuitable and, moreover, it is far more probable that the new religion arose out of a period of religious stirring and deep feeling rather than out of a torpid and dying one."[8] A few years ago, in *The Holy Spirit before Christianity*, I distinguished my views from Volz's on the matter of the spirit as a hypostasis, but that is little more than a scholarly quibble.[9] His work, represented by this quotation, is prescient, reliable, and robust, and I have spent many hours reading and reflecting contentedly upon his splendid *Der Geist Gottes und die verwandten Erscheinungen im Alten Testament und im anschließenden Judentum*.

These three authors raised vital questions for our study of the spirit in early Jewish antiquity during the Greco-Roman era. How did people experience, and not just think about, this spirit? In the context of the Greek encounter with Judaism during the Hellenistic era, what elements were adopted to generate ancient pneumatologies? And is it more likely that Christianity rose from arid soil or from a form of Judaism that embraced the exigencies and experiences of inspiration? These do not circumscribe the totality of questions they raised or the entirety of questions we must ask of antiquity, but they do provide pivotal points of departure for scholarship in search of the spirit.

---

8. Volz, *Geist Gottes*, 144.
9. Levison, *Holy Spirit before Christianity*, 87–98.

I

Did the Spirit Withdraw from Israel?

An Evaluation of the Earliest Jewish Data[1]

1. INTRODUCTION

The view that the Holy Spirit as the source of prophecy was believed by Jews during the Tannaitic period to have withdrawn from Israel, to return only in the eschatological future, is built upon a pastiche of texts: Ps 74:9; 1 Macc 4:46; 9:27; 14:41; Josephus's *Ag. Ap.* 1.37–41; 2 Bar. 85:3; Pr Azar 15; t. Soṭah 13.2–4. On the basis of such texts, E. Sjöberg referred to "a widespread theological conviction"[2] about the withdrawal of the Holy Spirit, and J. Vos to "die verbreitete Tradition."[3] C. K. Barrett quoted G. F. Moore approvingly: "The Holy Spirit is the Spirit of prophecy . . . The Holy Spirit is so specifically prophetic inspiration that when Haggai, Zechariah, and Malachi, the last prophets, died, the Holy Spirit departed from Israel."[4] W. D. Davies suggested cautiously, after a thorough analysis of the data, "We may now assume that Paul was reared within a Judaism which, to use very moderate language, tended to relegate the activity of the Holy Spirit to the

---

1. I would like to thank Louis H. Feldman for reading a draft of this manuscript and providing perceptive comments, as well as Eric M. Meyers and Rebecca Gray for insightful conversations.

2. Sjöberg, "πνεῦμα, πνευματικός," 385.

3. Vos, *Traditionsgeschichtliche Untersuchungen*, 72.

4. Barrett, *Holy Spirit*, 108–9.

past."[5] G. W. H. Lampe generalized, "In the main, the Spirit continues to be thought of as being, pre-eminently, the Spirit of prophecy, manifested in the distant past in such great figures as Elijah (Ecclus. 48.12) or Isaiah (vs. 24), but which was now no longer present in Israel."[6] J. Jeremias subtitled section 9 of his *New Testament Theology* "The Return of the Quenched Spirit," and summarized this view: "With the death of the last writing prophets, Haggai, Zechariah and Malachi, *the spirit was quenched* because of the sin of Israel. After that time, it was believed, God still spoke only through the 'echo of his voice' . . . a poor substitute."[7] D. Hill wrote, "There can be no doubt that, long before the turn of the eras, the Jews believed that prophecy as such had ceased in Israel and that the prophetic Spirit had withdrawn."[8] J. D. G. Dunn cited these texts, adding Zech 13.2-6, to support the view that "with the rabbis the belief becomes very strong that Haggai, Zechariah and Malachi were the last of the prophets and that thereafter the Spirit had been withdrawn."[9] Recent adherents of this view include F. W. Horn and G. Fee. Horn has contended that the references in 1 Maccabees, 2 Bar. 85:3 (and parallels in b. Sanh. 11a and b. Soṭah 49ab), and *Ag. Ap.* 1.37-41, as well as the absence of references to the Spirit in 1 and 2 Enoch, Daniel, 4 Ezra, and Syriac Apocalypse of Baruch, constitute evidence "des allgemeinen Bewußtseins der Prophetenlosigkeit oder Geistlosigkeit"[10] that many New Testament texts presuppose (e.g., Mark 1:8; 3:28-29; John 7:39; 20:22; Acts 19:2).[11] Most recently, Fee has asserted, "Noticeably missing in the intertestamental literature . . . is the sense that the Spirit speaks through any contemporary 'prophet.' This is almost certainly the result of the growth of a tradition called 'the quenched Spirit,' which begins in the later books of the Old Testament and is found variously during the Second Temple period."[12]

The purpose of this essay is to challenge this consensus by reexamining early Jewish texts that putatively support it. For the non-rabbinic texts (Ps

---

5. Davies, *Paul and Rabbinic Judaism*, 215. This statement follows a serious analysis of other data that indicate the continued working of the Holy Spirit (208-15). Professor Davies has communicated to me in private conversation that he no longer espouses this position, upon which he wrote a half century ago.

6. G. W. H. Lampe, "Holy Spirit," *IDB* 2:630.

7. Jeremias, *New Testament Theology*, 81.

8. Hill, *New Testament Prophecy*, 21.

9. Dunn, *Christology in the Making*, 135. See also Dunn, *Baptism in the Holy Spirit*, 27, where he states that at the baptism of Jesus "the long drought of knowing the Spirit comes to an end."

10. Horn, *Angeld des Geistes*, 31.

11. Horn, *Angeld des Geistes*, 31. For the discussion in its entirety, see 26-32.

12. Fee, *Empowering Presence*, 914.

74:9; Pr Azar 15; 1 Macc 4:46; 9:27; 14:41; *Ag. Ap.* 1.37–41; 2 Bar. 85:3), this task has already been accomplished by several scholars, most notably R. Meyer, R. Leivestad, D. E. Aune, and F. Greenspahn, who have steadily chipped away at this position;[13] in the following section, I shall garner important elements from their discussions, adding a few observations of my own. The third section proceeds further by proffering a fresh analysis of t. Soṭah 13.2–4 in its literary context because t. Soṭah 13.2–4, although it is recognized as the "classic statement"[14] and "classic formula"[15] of the view that the Holy Spirit withdrew and would return in the eschatological future, has received none of the critical attention that the non-rabbinic sources have.

2. THE CEASING OF PROPHECY REEXAMINED

Although the non-rabbinic texts contain no reference to the Holy Spirit, the relationship between prophecy and the Spirit is thought by scholars who deal with this issue to be sufficiently secure to permit the implication that the Spirit withdrew when prophecy ceased. These data, therefore, must be examined. Despite the confidence with which these data are thought to support the dogma of the withdrawn Spirit, J. Barton's observation that the evidence is "somewhat obscure and difficult to interpret"[16] is closer to the truth of the matter. The following synthesis should demonstrate adequately that the so-called dogma of the withdrawn Spirit is built upon uncertain and ambiguous ancient texts that do not even refer to the ceasing of prophecy.

A. Psalm 74:9

> We do not see our emblems;
> there is no longer any prophet,
> and there is no one among us who knows how long.

The recognition that this psalm is probably to be dated some time during the exile, after the destruction of Jerusalem in 587 BCE,[17] may be considered enough evidence to discount its use as postexilic evidence for the view

---

13. Meyer, "Prophecy and Prophets"; Leivestad, "Dogma"; Aune, *Prophecy in Early Christianity*, 103–6; Greenspahn, "Why Prophecy Ceased."

14. Lampe, *IDB* 2:630.

15. Barton, *Oracles of God*, 115.

16. Barton, *Oracles of God*, 108. Aune contends more stridently, "The evidence . . . flatly contradicts that view" (*Prophecy in Early Christianity*, 103).

17. See Kirkpatrick, *Book of Psalms*, 439–42; Tate, *Psalms 51–100*, 247.

that prophecy ceased; the psalm may not look to the distant past. In its historical context, whether exilic or Maccabean, the psalm reflects a situation in which the prophets who predicted salvation are silenced by events and those who, like Jeremiah and Ezekiel, predicted correctly, continue to experience opprobrium. In this historical context, prophets have not ceased to exist but have fallen into disrepute (cf. Lam 2:14).[18]

Regardless of date, the literary form of the psalm undermines its value as evidence that prophecy ceased. It is a community lament, which exaggerates the horrors of the community's situation in order to solicit God's help. One could argue analogously from the equally exaggerated lament in Lam 2:6, "the LORD has abolished in Zion festival and sabbath," that the Sabbath ceased with the destruction of Jerusalem; such an inference would of course be incorrect.[19] Neither the historical context nor the literary form of Ps 74, then, permits its use as evidence that a belief in the end of prophecy emerged during the postexilic and rabbinic periods.

B. Prayer of Azariah 15[20]

> In our day we have no ruler, or prophet, or leader,
> no burnt offering, or sacrifice, or oblation, or incense,
> no place to make an offering before you and to find mercy.

Although probably written much later than the situation it purports to describe, this text is part of a lament that depicts the anarchy that followed upon the destruction of Jerusalem in 587 BCE. As in Ps 74, a community lament, we have to do here with "eine Klage über Mangel an Propheten" and "keine dogmatische Idee einer prophetenlosen Epoche."[21] At any rate, the elements of the immediate context, such as sacrifices and rulers, were in fact restored to Israel following the exile, so that it would require a blatant disregard for context to extrapolate a dogma of the ceasing of prophecy from the brief mention of the lack of prophets "in our day."

---

18. Meyer, "Prophecy and Prophets," 814; Aune, *Prophecy in Early Christianity*, 105; Greenspahn, "Why Prophecy Ceased," 40.
19. Barton, *Oracles of God*, 107.
20. Theodotian Dan 3:38.
21. Leivestad, "Dogma," 292.

C. 1 Maccabees

> And they thought it best to tear it down, so that it would not be a lasting shame to them that the Gentiles had defiled it. So they tore down the altar, and stored the stones in a convenient place on the temple hill until a prophet should come to tell what to do with them. (4:46)

> So there was great distress in Israel, such as had not been since the time that prophets ceased to appear among them. (9:27)

> The Jews and their priests have resolved that Simon should be their leader and high priest forever, until a trustworthy prophet should arise. (14:41)

These passages have often been understood to support a view that prophecy ceased in the distant past (9:27) and would be renewed in the eschatological future (4:46; 14:41).[22] Such an interpretation, however, is based upon a misconstrual of these texts.

First Maccabees 9:27 ought not to be interpreted as a reference to the ceasing of prophecy in the distant past, notwithstanding modern translations such as NRSV (above) and NEB ("since the day when prophets ceased to appear among them"). The basis for rejecting this interpretation is simple. In 1 Maccabees, the temporal prepositional phrase ἀφ' οὗ (from which time) consistently is followed immediately by clarification that permits the reader to identify this point in time. According to the sentence that follows 1 Macc 9:27, the friends of Judas gathered and said to Jonathan (9:29):

> Ἀφ' οὗ ὁ ἀδελφός σου Ιουδας τετελεύτηκεν
> Since the time your brother Judas died[23]

The particular point in time left indefinite by the words ἀφ' οὗ is specified immediately as the day Judas died, from which point no one has arisen to oppose the enemies. A similar formulation characterizes 1 Macc 12:10:

> ἀφ' οὗ ἀπεστείλατε πρὸς ἡμᾶς
> From the time you wrote to us

Here the particular moment in time left indefinite by the words ἀφ' οὗ is specified immediately as the day on which a letter was written, from which

---

22. See, for example, Goldstein, *I Maccabees*, 12-13; Horn, *Angeld des Geistes*, 29-30.
23. The translations of 1 Macc 9:29; 12:10; 12:22; 16:24 are my own.

point the passing of time is counted. In 1 Macc 12:22, King Arius writes a letter to Onias in which he says,

> καὶ νῦν ἀφ' ἐγνωμεν ταῦτα
> And now from the time we have known these things

Once again, the particular moment in time left indefinite by the words ἀφ' οὗ is specified immediately as the day on which Arius and the Spartans realized these things, namely, that they and the Jews are brothers of the family of Abraham (12:21), from which point they are to write to one another and to hold livestock and property in common. The final formulation analogous to 1 Macc 9:27 occurs in the concluding sentence of the book of 1 Maccabees (16:24):

> ἀφ' οὗ ἐγενήθη ἀρχιερεὺς μετὰ τὸν πατέρα αὐτοῦ
> From the time he became high priest after his father

Once more, the particular moment in time left indefinite by the words ἀφ' οὗ is specified as the day of John Hyrcanus's accession to the high priesthood, from which point his acts and achievements, as recorded in his annals, are said to begin. In 1 Macc 9:27, we encounter a clause that should be translated consistently with these related formulations:

> ἀφ' ἧς ἡμέρας οὐκ ὤφθη προφήτης αὐτοῖς
> From the day a prophet did not appear to them

Here the particular moment in time left indefinite by the words ἀφ' ἧς ἡμέρας is specified as the day on which a prophet did not appear (οὐκ ὤφθη προφήτης), from which point the absence of comparable distress is dated. From that day until now, no such distress afflicted Israel.[24]

In each of these instances, what immediately follows ἀφ' οὗ/ἧς ἡμέρας specifies a particular moment in time, such as the failure of a prophet to appear on a day of distress, the death of Judas, the recognition of a relationship between Spartans and Jews, or the accession of John Hyrcanus. What begins at that moment is something else, such as the relative absence of distress, the absence of a military leader, the beginning of camaraderie, or achievements. The translation of 1 Macc 9:27, therefore, to indicate "the disappearance of prophecy among them" (NJB) is due to a confusion of the events of a particular moment in time and the events that took place thereafter. In 1 Macc 9:27, the detail that a prophet did not appear enables the readers to

---

24. This interpretation is borne out by the simplicity of the language of 1 Macc 9:27. The verb ὤφθη, which refers elsewhere in 1 Maccabees to the appearances of Judas (4:6) and a military detachment (4:19), is employed similarly here of the nonappearance of a prophet at a particular point in time rather than to the *ceasing* of prophecy for all time.

identify the particular day of distress to which the author refers, from which point relative tranquility can be dated.²⁵

Once we have dispensed with 1 Macc 9:27 as one leg of the alleged ceasing of prophecy, it is not difficult to dispense with the other leg—the expectation of an eschatological prophet—which is based upon 1 Macc 4:46 and 14:41. The first of these texts refers to an as yet unidentified prophet in the near future who will instruct the priests about where to place the defiled stones. The decision the priests make is practical, "a realistic interim decision taken on the understanding that a prophetic word might well occur in the not-too-distant future."²⁶

The last reference, 1 Macc 14:41, refers to a prophet who is expected to legitimate the Hasmonean dynasty. The task of this prophet is, as is a prophet's task in 4:46, concrete, integrally tied to theocracy and temple.²⁷ Although this reference to a prophet with final authority represents "a way of stopping short of completely idealizing the Hasmonean program of restoration and reconstruction,"²⁸ it also suits the pro-Hasmonean perspective of 1 Maccabees. First Maccabees 14:27-45 is particularly pro-Hasmonean, for it contains what the Jews wrote on bronze tablets, placed on pillars on Mount Zion, to "thank Simon and his sons" (14:25). It suits the Hasmonean cause to stress that, at least at the present moment, there is no prophet—or perhaps no need for one—who might, like the ancient prophets, challenge Hasmonean authority. Moreover, the implication of this statement, that this future prophet would support the Hasmonean cause, comprises further propaganda for the Hasmonean program.

The expectation of a prophet to instruct and legitimate in 4:46 and 14:41 reflects, therefore, the expectation that a prophet would in fact appear in order to fulfil concrete functions. The need to wait for this prophet is analogous to the situation in Ezra 2:63, where the governor tells those excluded from the priesthood "not to partake of the most holy food, until there should be a priest to consult Urim and Thummim."²⁹

---

25. Josephus omits this reference to a prophet in his version: "After this calamity had befallen the Jews, which was greater than any they had experienced since their return from Babylon" (*Ant.* 13.5).

26. Barton, *Oracles of God*, 107.

27. Meyer feels justified in identifying this prophet with John Hyrcanus, who occupies the climactic position in 1 Maccabees and is accorded prophetic status by Josephus ("Prophecy and Prophets," 815). On Josephus's interpretation of John Hyrcanus, see Gray, *Prophetic Figures*, 16-23.

28. Aune, *Prophecy in Early Christianity*, 104; Leivestad, "Dogma," 295-96.

29. Greenspahn, "Why Prophecy Ceased," 39-40.

These references to future prophets can support the dogma of the permanent ceasing of prophecy only if the awaited prophets are one and the same eschatological figure who would bring about the restoration of prophecy which had ceased in the distant past. This identification is unlikely. First, we have seen already that the tasks of these prophets are concrete, implying continuity with the present world order. Second, these statements are presented as historical observations. They contain no allusion to figures such as the prophet of Deut 18:15–18, to prophetic texts that predict the outpouring of the Spirit (e.g., Joel 2:28–29), or even to the canonical prophets, as Josephus does in *Ag. Ap.* 1.37–41. Third, the overall perspective of 1 Maccabees is theocratic, centered upon the Hasmonean dynasty, rather than eschatological. If these prophets are to be identified with one eschatological prophet, the references must indicate this, since 1 Maccabees does not itself contain a significant eschatological component that allows us to infer an eschatological dimension in these statements. First Maccabees 4:46 and 14:41 contain no such indications.

These three references to prophets in 1 Maccabees do not, then, comprise a link in the alleged chain of the early Jewish conviction that prophecy had ceased. First Maccabees 9:27 refers to a particular day of distress on which a prophet failed to appear. First Maccabees 4:46 refers to a prophet who would clarify a question about stones of the altar. First Maccabees 14:41 refers to a prophet who would clarify the status of the priest-ruler in a context rife with pro-Hasmonean sentiment.

D. Josephus's *Ag. Ap.* 1.37–41

Two centuries separate 1 Maccabees from Josephus's *Contra Apionem*, which contains the next putative reference to the ceasing of prophecy. The breadth of this gap alone should raise caution about merging these two writings into a single dogmatic whole, even if 1 Maccabees supported this dogma, which, as we saw, it does not.

> From Artaxerxes to our own time the complete history has been written, but has not been deemed worthy of equal credit with the earlier records, because of the inaccurate succession of the prophets. (*Ag. Ap.* 1.41)[30]

---

30. Translation and quotation from LCL (Thackeray). I replace the LCL translation "failure of the exact" with "inaccurate," following the suggestion of Louis H. Feldman in a letter of Nov. 1, 1994. Greek διὰ τὸ μὴ γενέσθαι τὴν τῶν προφητῶν ἀκριβῆ διαδοχήν.

The fundamental reason why this text cannot be included as evidence of a dogma of the ceasing of prophecy is that Josephus "speaks not of the cessation of prophecy as such but rather of the failure of the exact succession of the prophets."[31]

The motivation for this statement arises from the difference in the quality of literary sources before and after the reign of Artaxerxes.[32] For the prior period from the death of Moses until the advent of Artaxerxes there exists, in Josephus's opinion, reliable history. The reason he offers is that prophets were present to record "a clear account of the events of their own time just as they occurred" (1.37), that is, these "prophets subsequent to Moses wrote the history of the events of their own times in thirteen books" (1.40). In contrast, history for the subsequent period, from Artaxerxes's to Josephus's day, "has not been deemed worthy of equal credit with the earlier records" (1.41). He attributes the inferiority of histories of this period to "the failure of the exact succession of the prophets" (1.41), that is, the absence in some generations of prophets who could give "a clear account of the events of their own time just as they occurred," as they had done prior to Artaxerxes.

The reference to an "inaccurate succession of the prophets," therefore, is motivated by the need to explain why sources for the final period of Jewish history are inferior. Josephus neither implies that prophecy ceased nor gives the slightest hint that this is due to the withdrawal of the Spirit. On the contrary, inspired prophets continued to record history in the period after Artaxerxes but with less regularity than formerly.[33]

---

31. Feldman, "Prophets and Prophecy," 400; Aune, *Prophecy in Early Christianity*, 106; Greenspahn, "Why Prophecy Ceased," 40.

32. Gray, *Prophetic Figures*, 8–16.

33. Several other elements support the view that Josephus believed prophecy to have continued. First, the fact that Josephus refers to Cleodemus the Prophet (*Ant.* 1.240–241) and to John Hyrcanus as a prophet (*J.W.* 1.68–69; *Ant.* 13.299–300) would seem to indicate that prophecy had not ceased, although one cannot be certain because the reference to Cleodemus is taken by Josephus from Alexander Polyhistor, who may have used the term loosely, and the reference to John Hyrcanus may have been influenced by the fact that Josephus was descended from the Hasmoneans. See Feldman, "Prophets and Prophecy," 400–407; Gray, *Prophetic Figures*, 8–23. Second, Gray discusses dreams and predictions after the time of John Hyrcanus as evidence that prophecy continued (26–34). Third, Gray devotes successive significant chapters to Josephus's view of himself, the Essenes, the "sign prophets" (e.g., Theudas, *Ant.* 20.97–99), and other prophetic figures in part to demonstrate the thesis that "the belief that prophecy had ceased should not be understood as a hard-and-fast dogma, but rather as one expression of a wider nostalgia for the distant past" (167).

E. 2 Baruch 85:3

> But now, the righteous have been assembled, and the prophets are sleeping.[34]

This statement is part of Baruch's final letter, written (in its narrative context) in the final days of human existence, when "the youth of this world has passed away, and the power of creation is already exhausted, and the coming of the times is very near and has passed by" (85:10). His instructions are straightforward: "Therefore, before his judgment exacts his own and truth of that which is its due, let us prepare ourselves" (85:9). The responsibility for this preparation lies with each individual,[35] and the conviction that there are no prophets left upon whom one can depend for intercession lends further urgency to the author's appeal for preparation:

> There will not be an opportunity to repent anymore . . . nor sending up petition . . . nor opportunity of repentance . . . nor supplicating for offenses, nor prayers of the fathers, nor intercessions of the prophets, nor help of the righteous. (85:12)

This last-minute scenario applies to no other era in human history than its final moments. Prayers, repentance, the presence of prophets and righteous people—elements that once characterized human existence and provided hope for salvation—are gone, worthless in the face of impending judgment.

In this context, the sleeping of the prophets neither presupposes nor promotes a view that sometime in history, perhaps at the destruction of the temple or following the reign of Artaxerxes, prophecy ceased. The author's concern rather is to convince his readers that, from the standpoint of the final moments before judgment, the individual can no longer rely, as he or she once did in the normal course of human life, upon the merits of ancestors, prophets, or the righteous.

We should note as well that the primary function of prophets in 2 Bar. 85:3 is intercession. In this respect, they are included alongside ancestors and the righteous. There is no implication that their absence is attributable

---

34. Translations of 2 Baruch by A. F. J. Klijn in Charlesworth, *Old Testament Pseudepigrapha*, 1:621–52.

35. This conviction is encapsulated in 54:15: "Although Adam sinned first and has brought death upon all who were not in his own time, yet each of them who has been born from him has prepared for himself the coming torment. And further, each of them has chosen for himself the coming glory."

F. Summary

This survey confirms Greenspahn's observation that "intertestamental authors may have sensed an absence of prophets—something noted in other periods as well (1 Sam 3:1)—but they simply did not state that prophecy had come to an end, temporarily or otherwise."[37] Equally apparent is that the sorts of prophecy envisaged by these authors comprise a wide variety and therefore point away from the adherence to a single dogma of the ceasing of prophecy. Prophets are depicted as predictors (Ps 74:9), leaders (Pr Azar 15), decision-makers and legitimators of a theocracy (1 Macc 4:46; 14:41), writers of history (*Ag. Ap.* 1.41), and intercessors (2 Bar. 85:3). If a single conviction that prophecy ceased unites these statements, we may ask which sort provides the common denominator. And finally, we may recall that the syntax of 1 Macc 9:27, a central text in the alleged dogma of the ceasing of prophecy in the distant past, has been misconstrued, with the result that an event at one point in time—the failure of a prophet to appear *on* a day of distress—has been interpreted to mean that prophecy *from* that day has ceased.

Although this synthesis demonstrates how inadequate the use of these individual texts is, how liable to misinterpretation they are, and how uncertain their relation to each other is, nonetheless the interpretation of another significant text, perhaps the most important of all, has been perpetually assumed. Despite the trenchant critique of the so-called dogma of the ceasing of prophecy that the studies surveyed here offer, they leave unexamined the assumption that t. Soṭah 13.2–4 confirms the belief in the withdrawal of the Holy Spirit and a correlative ceasing of prophecy.

3. TOSEFTA SOṬAH 13.2–4[38]

When Haggai, Zechariah, and Malachi, the last of the prophets, died, the Holy Spirit ceased in [from] Israel. Nevertheless, a

---

36. Meyer, "Prophecy and Prophets," 815.

37. Greenspahn, "Why Prophecy Ceased," 40.

38. Before embarking upon our analysis, we ought to recognize the perennial problem of dating rabbinic material. Strack and Stemberger place the final redaction of the Tosefta in the later third or fourth centuries (*Introduction to the Talmud*, 176). Its

Bath Qol was heard by them: It once happened that the sages entered a house in Jericho and they heard a Bath Qol, saying, "There is a man here who is worthy of the Holy Spirit, but there is no one in his generation righteous." Thereupon, they set their eyes upon Hillel . . . Again . . . they heard a Bath Qol saying, "There is a man here who is worthy of the Holy Spirit, but there is no one in his generation righteous." Thereupon, they set their eyes upon Samuel the Small.[39]

This text is assumed to encapsulate the dogma of the withdrawal of the prophetic Spirit from Israel during the postexilic period, so much so that even those scholars who reject the use of the other (non-rabbinic) texts admit that the t. Soṭah expresses the conviction that the Spirit withdrew when the last canonical prophets died. R. Meyer, for example, after giving grounds for rejecting Ps 74:9; Pr Azar 15; 1 Macc 4:46; 9:27; 14:41; and *Ag. Ap.* 1.37–41 as components of a tradition according to which prophecy was believed to have ceased, is compelled to write: "Things are different in the sphere of Rabbinic tradition. Here one finds sophisticated theological deliberation aimed at restricting the rise of legitimate prophecy to an ideal classical period in the past."[40] The meaning of this saying and the cases of Hillel and Samuel the Small are understood unanimously by modern scholars: with the end of the succession of the canonical prophets, the Holy Spirit was replaced by an inferior *bath qol*. The cases of Hillel and Samuel the Small are evidence: the *bath qol* informs the sages who are gathered together that both of these rabbis are worthy of the Spirit but cannot receive it because of the evil generations to which they belong.[41]

---

reliability as a source for understanding the first century CE, therefore, is dependent in part upon the existence of prior texts which share its perspective. I have attempted to demonstrate in part 2 that no such firm evidence of this viewpoint antedates the Tosefta itself. Therefore, even if t. Soṭah 13.2–4 supported the alleged dogma of the permanent withdrawal of the prophetic Spirit, its usefulness for interpreting the New Testament would be limited.

39. Unpublished translation of E. M. Meyers. Other translations of the Tosefta, unless otherwise specified, are from Neusner, *Tosefta*. Hebrew citations and the translations of Meyers and myself are based upon Zuckermandel, *Tosephta*.

40. Meyer, "Prophecy and Prophets," 816. Similarly Horn, "Holy Spirit," 263–64.

41. Marmorstein infers from a saying of Rabbi Akiba, who taught that during the thirty-eight years of Israel's punishment, Moses received no divine address, meeting with the shekhinah, or any visit from the Holy Spirit: "For this reason and not on any personal ground it was said that Hillel would have been worthy of the Holy Spirit had not the sinfulness of his age robbed him of its possession" ("Holy Spirit," 126). We should observe, however, that the *bath qol* in t. Soṭah 13.2–4 is a mode of divine revelation; clearly the generation is not so evil that the sages cannot collectively hear the divine voice. The caveat proffered in 13.3 that, despite the withdrawal of the

A. The Principle of Intermittence in t. Soṭah 10.1

The most damaging aspect of this interpretation is that it disregards the literary context of t. Soṭah 13.2–4 and, therefore, violates the straightforward principle t. Soṭah 13.2–4 is intended to illustrate:

> When a righteous person comes into the world, good comes into the world . . . and retribution departs from the world; and when the righteous person leaves the world, retribution comes into the world and goodness departs from the world. (10.1)[42]

The compiler illustrates this principle by means of a historical survey which extends from Noah to the Sanhedrin (10.1—15.7). So long as Noah was in the world, he brought comfort to the world. Methuselah even withheld judgment beyond the span of his life, during the seven days in which he was mourned (10.1–3).

The leitmotiv of the ancestral period is famine (10.5–10). While Abraham lived, there was plenty; when he died, there was famine. After Abraham died, the wells were stopped up and famine spread until Isaac lived and the wells once again gushed. Before Jacob travelled to Egypt, there had been famine; when he was in Egypt, there was seed and harvest, although after his death, famine returned. Similarly, Potiphar was not blessed until Joseph went to Egypt; and Israel was blessed as long as Joseph lived but was threatened by Egypt's new ruler after he died.

A related leitmotiv characterizes the exodus. While Miriam lived, the well provided water; when she died, it dried up. While Aaron lived, a pillar of cloud led Israel; when he died, people made war against Israel. While Moses lived, there was manna; when he died, manna ceased (11.1–2, 10).[43]

The principle of 10.1 is adopted again in the discussion of Elijah and Elisha (12.5–6). Before Elijah disappeared, the Holy Spirit was commonplace in Israel; after his departure, it departed from the sons of the prophets. While Elisha lived, no Arameans threatened Israel; when he died, bands of Moabites invaded their land.

Spirit, God continued to communicate by means of the *bath qol*, is an attempt to rebut the implication that God failed to communicate. Therefore, the analogy Marmorstein draws between this text and Akiba's statement about Moses is unsuitable; there is here communication—significant communication which confirms the presence of rabbis worthy of the Holy Spirit.

42. Translation mine.

43. T. Soṭah 11.10 in Zuckermandel, *Tosephta*, is 11.8 in Neusner's translation (*Tosefta*).

The inescapable lesson of these illustrations is the principle of t. Soṭah 10.1: goodness enters the world with the righteous and departs with their death. So long as there is a righteous one alive, Israel can be blessed (e.g., by harvest). When the righteous one departs, however, Israel falls prey to evil (e.g., famine).

In t. Soṭah 14, this principle is expressed negatively by means of a description of generations devoid of the presence of a righteous person. During these generations, the glory of the Torah ceases, the shekhinah withdraws, etc.

In t. Soṭah 15.3–5, this survey reaches its apex with a list in which the death of significant rabbis signals a variety of losses. The good that characterized their generation while they lived is lost at their death. For instance, when Rabbi Eliezer died, the glory of the Torah ceased. When Rabbi Akiba died, the springs of wisdom ceased. When Rabbi Ḥanina b. Dosa died, miracle workers ceased. The survey concludes that, when Rabbi died, troubles became twofold.

The references to the latter prophets in t. Soṭah 13.2 ought also to be interpreted within this larger context in relationship to the principle that when the righteous are in the world, good comes, and when the righteous depart, evil enters the world. The statement about the deaths of Haggai, Zechariah, and Malachi quintessentially reinforces the principle of t. Soṭah 10.1: with their deaths, the Spirit withdrew. References to Simeon the Righteous (13.7), following mention of Hillel and Samuel the Small, also underscore the principle of 10.1. While Simeon the Righteous lived, the western lamp was lit, the altar fire burned perpetually, and the showbread and two loaves provided miraculous nourishment; when Simeon the Righteous died, the western lamp was often extinguished, the altar fire grew weak, and the priestly food, what little there was, was eaten by gluttons.

According to a contextual interpretation of t. Soṭah 13.2–4, therefore, the references to the latter prophets, Hillel, and Samuel the Small should be understood according to the principle that is introduced in 10.1 and illustrated throughout the subsequent six chapters of Tosefta Soṭah, that the presence of the righteous in the world brings the presence of good, while their absence brings the loss of good and entry of evil. Understood within this literary context, the withdrawal of the Holy Spirit at the death of Haggai, Zechariah, and Malachi is a formidable affirmation that their lives made the presence of the Holy Spirit possible, while their death brought the loss of this particular good. Again within this literary context, the references to the worthiness of Hillel and Samuel the Small should be interpreted, not as evidence that they did *not* possess the Holy Spirit but as evidence that the Holy Spirit, which withdrew with the death of Haggai, Zechariah, and Malachi, has now returned because these righteous men are worthy. They are rabbis—"righteous"—whose worthiness of the Holy Spirit is so apparent that those gathered lift their eyes automatically to these figures.[44]

B. The Language of Impermanence in t. Soṭah 10–15

This interpretation of the references to the return of the Holy Spirit to Hillel and Samuel the Small is entirely consistent with t. Soṭah 13.2 when it is interpreted within the larger context. From the perspective of its context in the tractate, the withdrawal of the Holy Spirit ought to be interpreted as a temporary phenomenon.

First of all, the compiler does not write "when prophecy ceased, the Holy Spirit withdrew," but "when the latter prophets, Haggai, Zechariah, and Malachi, died, the Holy Spirit withdrew." This particular form recurs throughout t. Soṭah 10–15, particularly in its climax in 15.3–5 (cf. m. Soṭah 9.15) in which the compiler lists what was lost to the world with the death of certain rabbis:

> When R. Eliezer died, the glory of the Torah ceased.
> When R. Joshua died, men of counsel ceased, and reflection ended in Israel.
> When R. Akiba died, the arms of Torah were taken away, and the springs of wisdom ceased.
> When R. Eleazar b. Azariah died, the crown of wisdom ceased, for, "The crown of the wise is their riches."
> When Ben Azzai died, conscientious students ceased.
> When Ben Zoma died, exegetes died.
> When R. Hanina b. Dosa died, wonder-workers died out in Israel.
> When Abba Yose b. Qitnit of Qatanta died, piety became small in Israel . . .
> When Rabban Simeon b. Gamaliel died, locusts came and troubles increased.
> When Rabbi died, troubles were doubled.

The purpose of this litany is to extol the particular characteristics of each rabbi by describing what the world lost at their death. In other words, the formula "When X died . . . Y [good] ceased/died/ or Z [evil] increased" is a eulogy in which individual rabbis are remembered for their most significant contributions. It would be absurd to historicize this formula, here in t. Soṭah 15.3–5 as well as in m. Soṭah 9.15, to mean that, with the death

---

44. See also the similar prediction of Simeon the Righteous in t. Soṭah 13.5.

of a particular rabbi, the characteristic for which he was renowned ceased forever and entirely from the world. Rabbinic eulogies tended to exaggerate. For example, if springs of wisdom and the arms of Torah ceased with the death of Akiba or interpreters with the death of Ben Zoma, how could Rabbi, a fifth-generation Tanna, have compiled the Mishna?

The problem that arises if this formula be taken to indicate a permanent loss, in the sense that the withdrawal of the Holy Spirit in t. Soṭah 13.2–4 customarily is, can be easily illustrated by comparing t. Soṭah 14.3, 14.8, and 15.3. According to the first text, the "glory of Torah ceased" when pleasure-seekers multiplied. According to the second text, the "glory of Torah ceased" when those who drew out their spit multiplied and the disciples became few in number. According to the third text, if a textual variant is accepted that reads "glory" rather than "book," the "glory of Torah ceased" when Rabbi Eliezer died. Quite obviously, the "glory of Torah" could not have disappeared permanently three times. The first two statements rather are ways of emphasizing the depth of evil that led to a temporary loss of commitment to Torah, which transpired when there was none sufficiently righteous to bring about the return of this glory. The third statement emphasizes the greatness of Eliezer: when he died, the book or glory of Torah ceased.

A similar viewpoint is evident in the two passages that refer to the Holy Spirit in t. Soṭah 12.5 and 13.2–4. According to 12.5, the Holy Spirit was present to a great degree before Elijah disappeared, while after his disappearance, the so-called sons of the prophets lost this Spirit. According to t. Soṭah 13.2, of course, the Spirit must have returned, although t. Soṭah 12.5 never expresses explicitly this conviction. It is simply not possible for the Holy Spirit to have ceased twice.[45]

The occurrence of a similar formula in t. Soṭah 13.2–4 should not be interpreted otherwise. The saying begins similarly to others, whether they concern Miriam or Rabbi Eliezer: "When the latter prophets died, Haggai, Zechariah, and Malachi . . ." This introduction eulogizes these prophets by placing them in a line of righteous, from Noah to the Sanhedrin, whose presence brought good into the world. The saying concludes, "the Holy Spirit withdrew from Israel." This conclusion indicates that they were known

---

45. The formula employed to describe what was lost or what evil entered with the death of certain rabbis characterizes also the survey of the biblical characters, though it differs, as we might expect, from its rabbinic counterparts in being followed by the question, "What is said" and an explanation by means of a biblical citation, which demonstrates that the death of a great biblical figure resulted in the loss of blessing: "When Abraham had died, what is said?" or "When Miriam died, what is said?" In each instance, as we have seen, the loss is temporary, and it is alleviated when another righteous person appears.

particularly for their possession of the Holy Spirit. In other instances, this is the glory of Torah, good students, and exegetes. In this instance, these latter prophets, and perhaps by implication other prophets before them, are eulogized for their possession of the Holy Spirit.

The principle of 10.1, as it is applied throughout chapters 10–15, invests these eulogies with a chronological dimension: what is lost with the death of one righteous person can be restored with the presence of another righteous person (e.g., famine in the ancestral age). From the perspective of this principle and the numerous illustrations in its context, the loss of the Holy Spirit in t. Soṭah 13.2 ought to be interpreted as a temporary phenomenon that awaits *a righteous person who would allow good to reenter the world*. Who other than Hillel should be deemed sufficiently righteous so early in the rabbinic period as to merit the return of the Holy Spirit? He is the natural successor to the prophets, the righteous one worthy to allow the Holy Spirit reentry to the community of sages. It cannot be unintentional that he is described in t. Soṭah 13.3 as a "disciple of Ezra," a designation that places Hillel securely in the succession detailed in 'Abot 1.1:

> Moses received the Law from Sinai and committed it to Joshua, and Joshua to the elders, and the elders to the Prophets; and the Prophets committed it to the men of the Great Synagogue.[46]

The *bath qol* that maintained God's communication during this postexilic period now announces that there is one worthy of the Holy Spirit, and this one righteous individual is sufficient, according to the principle of 10.1, to allow the Holy Spirit again to be present. That his disciple, Samuel the Small, a lesser figure than Hillel, is also worthy is evident in Samuel's ability to predict, like the prophets, the evil that, according to the principle of 10.1, will take place after his death. Even Sjöberg, who otherwise argues strenuously that the Holy Spirit was believed to have ceased, admits that such a prediction indicates that Samuel "received some inspiration through the Holy Spirit."[47]

The withdrawal of the Holy Spirit with the death of the latter prophets, therefore, should be understood as a temporary lapse in the presence of the Holy Spirit until another person sufficiently righteous should appear, namely Hillel. This interpretation is confirmed by both the principle that provides the thread of t. Soṭah 10–15 and the meaning of the oft-repeated formula we have discussed: the death of a righteous person leads to the loss of good or the presence of evil until another righteous person should emerge whose

---

46. Translation from Danby, *Mishnah*, 446.
47. Sjöberg, "πνεῦμα, πνευματικός," 368n296.

presence brings good. In this case, the latter prophets are identified as those who possessed the Holy Spirit and whose death occasioned the withdrawal of the Holy Spirit. Hillel and Samuel the Small are identified as those whose worthiness makes possible the return of the Holy Spirit.

We may add one corroborative piece of evidence from the context of t. Soṭah 13.2–4 to demonstrate that the withdrawal of the Holy Spirit following the death of the latter prophets is not intended to describe a permanent withdrawal of the Holy Spirit. In two instances, when a permanent loss is described, its permanence is made explicit.

In the first instance (11.10; Neusner, 11.8), the compiler reiterates the principle of 10.1, that the presence of a righteous person brings blessing, their death evil, and a righteous successor the return of blessing.

> On their account were three gifts given to them: the pillar of cloud, manna, and the well—the well through the merit of Miriam, the pillar of cloud through the merit of Aaron, and the manna through the merit of Moses.
> When Miriam died, the well ceased [נסתלקה], but it came back [חזרה] through the merit of Moses and Aaron.
> When Aaron died, the pillar of cloud ceased [נסתלק], but both of them came back [חזרו] through the merit of Moses.
> When Moses died, all three of them came to an end [נסתלקו] *and never came back* [ולא חזרו], as it is said, "In one month I destroyed the three shepherds." (Zech 11.8)

Significant from our standpoint is that the assumption of these sayings is the ephemeral nature of loss. In contrast, when the loss is permanent, as it becomes with the death of Moses, this permanence must be stated explicitly, both by the addition of the words "and never came back" and the biblical citation of Zech 11:8. In contrast, the loss of the Holy Spirit in 13.2 is not said explicitly to be permanent and ought, therefore, to be interpreted along the lines of the principle delineated in t. Soṭah 10.1.

The second instance of a permanent effect concerns the temple (15.2). In this case, the language is similar to m. Soṭah 9.12:

> Rabban Simeon b. Gamaliel says in the name of R. Joshua, "*From the day* [מיום] on which the temple was destroyed, *there is no day* [אין יום] on which there is no curse, and dew has not come down as a blessing, and the good taste of produce is gone."

The point is made emphatically: "And the one (i.e., curse) stands after the other" (וראשון ראשון עומר).[48] Once again, this statement says explicitly what

---

48. Translation mine.

cannot be assumed: the evil that followed the destruction of the temple is permanent. From this vantage point, the destruction of the temple incurred irreparable losses. In contrast to the phraseology of this case, the reference to the withdrawal of the Holy Spirit in t. Soṭah 13.2 contains no indication that the withdrawal was permanent; on the contrary, the *bath qol* that replaced it says to the gathered rabbis that Hillel and Samuel the Small are worthy of the Holy Spirit although their generations are not.

C. The Advantage of This Interpretation

Tosefta Soṭah 13.2-4, understood in the context of the principle and formulae that dominate t. Soṭah 10-15, can be neatly summarized. The result of the death of the latter prophets was the withdrawal of the Holy Spirit from Israel. Despite the absence of the Holy Spirit, God continued to communicate with Israel by means of the *bath qol*. When a righteous person worthy of the Holy Spirit emerged, this *bath qol* announced the return of the Holy Spirit.

This interpretation has the important advantage of alleviating a tension in early Jewish sources between an alleged dictum that contends that the Holy Spirit has permanently withdrawn and numerous references to the current activity of the Spirit. Quite apart from claims to the Spirit at Qumran,[49] Philo's autobiographical accounts of inspiration by the Spirit,[50] and instances in which early Jewish authors demonstrate an interest in matters of the Spirit by inserting references to the Spirit in their versions of the Bible,[51] there are also several instances in rabbinic literature in which Tannaitic rabbis accomplish something extraordinary by the Holy Spirit.[52] For example, Rabbis Akiba,[53] Meir,[54] and Simeon ben Yoḥai[55] "saw in the Holy Spirit" something that could not otherwise be known, such as experiences of their students that took place elsewhere. It is reported of Rabban Gamaliel

---

49. E.g., 1QH 12.11-12; 13.19; 14.25.

50. Philo, *Spec.* 3.1-6; *Cher.* 27-29; *Somn.* 2.252. On these, see Levison, "Inspiration and Divine Spirit."

51. E.g., Josephus, *Ant.* 4.108, 118-119; 8.114; on these, see Levison, "Josephus' Interpretation." See also Pseudo-Philo, LAB 27.9-10; on this, see Levison, "Prophetic Inspiration."

52. For important overviews, see Marmorstein, "Holy Spirit," 132-35; Schäfer, *Vorstellung vom heiligen Geist*, 116-34, esp. 121-23; Parzen, "Ruaḥ Haḳodesh."

53. Lev Rab. 21.8.

54. y. Soṭah 1.4.

55. y. Šeb. 9.1.

that he "met" someone "in the Holy Spirit" because he miraculously knew his name.[56]

Contemporary scholars have proposed a variety of solutions to explain the tension between t. Soṭah 13.2–4, as it is customarily interpreted, and these sorts of texts, which assume the ongoing activity of the Holy Spirit. According to F. Büchsel, this passage "ist kein dogmatischer Lehrsatz, sondern ein Ausdruck des rabbinischen Situationsbewusstseins: 'die Zeit hat es nicht verdient.'"[57] E. Schweizer understands t. Soṭah 13.2–4 as an expression of "official theology" and the experiences of the Holy Spirit as unsanctioned.[58] Schäfer understands t. Soṭah 13.2–4 as an expression of "nationales Charisma" and the others as instances of "*individuelles Charisma.*"[59] Leivestad considers it to be "nur ein beschränktes Dogma," which permits the recurrence of prophecy "wenn eine Generation würdig wäre."[60] Aune contends that this view has a "theoretical character," which, at any rate, is "only one view among many."[61]

Other scholars have proposed various historical impulses to explain this presumed unexpected restriction of the Holy Spirit in t. Soṭah 13.2–4 in an early rabbinic period otherwise open to the presence of the Holy Spirit. R. Meyer links the restriction of legitimate prophecy to an ideal classical period with "the development of the synagogal concept of the Canon."[62] E. A. Urbach regards the theory of t. Soṭah 13.2–4, that the Spirit definitively ceased in the distant past, as a response to early Christian claims that the Holy Spirit had been transferred from Jews to Christians. To Christians Jews could respond that the Holy Spirit ceased long before the advent of Christianity.[63] Greenspahn contends instead that the statement that the Holy Spirit had ceased is a polemic "directed against a much broader phenomenon of continuing Jewish prophecy." It is "not an empirical observation as to the absence of prophets, whose existence is clear from numerous sources, but a denigration and even denial of these figures' legitimacy."[64]

---

56. t. Pesaḥ. 1.27.
57. Büchsel, *Geist Gottes*, 118.
58. Schweizer, *Holy Spirit*, 30.
59. Schäfer, *Vorstellung vom heiligen Geist*, 148–49.
60. Leivestad, "Dogma," 290.
61. Aune, *Prophecy in Early Christianity*, 104.
62. Meyer, "Prophecy and Prophets," 816. For criticism of this view, see Barton, *Oracles of God*, 112–15.
63. Urbach, "Matay Paseqah Hanevu'ah?" See summaries and critiques in Schäfer, *Vorstellung vom heiligen Geist*, 144–46; Greenspahn, "Why Prophecy Ceased," 42–43.
64. Greenspahn, "Why Prophecy Ceased," 48–49.

The interpretation proposed here renders all of these solutions unnecessary for the early period of rabbinic Judaism. Indeed, t. Soṭah 13.2–4, understood as an affirmation of the renewal of the Holy Spirit among the rabbis, is remarkably consistent with two Tannaitic statements about the reception of the Holy Spirit. The implication of the twice-repeated statement in 13.3–4, "but there is no one in his generation righteous," is that this renewal is not widespread. The reason is explicit: the unworthiness of the generation. This basis for the limitation of the Holy Spirit is consistent with m. Soṭah 9.10–15, which parallels t. Soṭah 13–15 significantly. In m. Soṭah 9.15, Rabbi Phineas ben Jair says:

> Heedfulness leads to cleanliness, and cleanliness leads to purity, and purity to abstinence, and abstinence leads to holiness, and holiness leads to humility, and humility leads to the shunning of sin, and the shunning of sin leads to saintliness, and saintliness leads to [the gift of] the Holy Spirit, and the Holy Spirit leads to the resurrection of the dead. And the resurrection of the dead shall come through Elijah of blessed memory.

Worthiness is in this mishnaic text the requirement for the reception of the Holy Spirit. Similar is a saying of Rabbi Nehemiah reported in Mekilta de-Rabbi Ishmael, another source of Tannaitic sayings, which applies a principle from Israelite history—the faith of Israel—to his own period:

> For as a reward for the faith with which Israel believed in God, the Holy Spirit rested upon them ... R. Nehemiah says: Whence can you prove that whosoever accepts even one single commandment with true faith is deserving of having the Holy Spirit rest upon them.[65]

In t. Soṭah 13.2–4, the requirement of worthiness is adapted to the principle of 10.1: Hillel and Samuel the Small receive the Holy Spirit because they are worthy, but their generation, due to its unworthiness, does not receive the Holy Spirit.

There is no need, then, to harmonize t. Soṭah 13.2–4 and other rabbinic statements about the Holy Spirit. The view of the Holy Spirit in t. Soṭah 13.2–4 accords remarkably with those of m. Soṭah 9.15 and the Mekilta de-Rabbi Ishmael. In all three, those who are worthy and holy and faithful are capable of receiving the Holy Spirit. In t. Soṭah 13.2–4, these are identified specifically as Hillel and Samuel the Small.[66]

---

65. Mek. Beshallaḥ 7. Translation from Lauterbach, *Mekilta de-Rabbi Ishmael*, 1:252.

66. Parallel texts in b. Soṭah 48b, b. Sanh. 11a, b. Yoma 9b, and y. Soṭah 9.17, where there is likewise no indication that the withdrawal of the Holy Spirit was believed to

4. CONCLUSION

To say with t. Soṭah 13.2–4 that the Holy Spirit ceased temporarily in Israel is compatible with the historical demise of prophecy during the postexilic period. The authority of priests appears to have broadened and the authority of prophets to have rested increasingly upon allusions to prior prophets and Torah.[67] A concomitant nostalgia for the preexilic period, when the monarchy and Solomon's Temple metaphorically dominated the skyline of Jerusalem, naturally exercised an influence over Second Temple Judaism.

We have seen, however, that the desultory references to the absence of prophecy in scattered texts from the exilic period onward simply cannot bear the weight of the so-called early Jewish dogma of the ceasing of prophecy. Most of these texts depict temporary situations of crisis worsened by the absence of prophets. The psalmist laments that no one can predict when the crisis will end (Ps 74:9). The social fabric is destroyed and leaders or the righteous, including prophets, have disappeared, according to Pr Azar 15 and 2 Bar. 85:3. The author of 1 Maccabees compares a contemporary crisis with a day of crisis in the past on which no prophet appeared (9:27). None of these authors assesses the presence of prophecy over a period of time.

Nor can Josephus's *Ag. Ap.* 1.37–41 support the alleged belief that the spirit of prophecy withdrew permanently from Israel. Josephus attributes the inferior quality of the literary sources for Jewish history after the reign of Artaxerxes not to the ceasing of prophecy but rather to "the failure of the exact succession of the prophets." Josephus's motivation is also unique among all of the authors cited to support the ceasing of prophecy in that, in his case alone, a literary problem shapes his depiction of history. Therefore, *Ag. Ap.* 1.37–41 fits uncomfortably into the putative historical development of this dogma.

In the absence of these earlier texts, the basis of the alleged dogma of the withdrawn Spirit during the New Testament era is reduced to a rabbinic text, t. Soṭah 13.2–4, whose composition probably postdates this era by at least two centuries. Equally important, t. Soṭah 13.2–4 supports the dogma that the Holy Spirit withdrew permanently—until an eschatological dénouement—only when it is wrenched from its literary context and interpreted with disregard for the principle enunciated clearly in 10.1, which dominates much of the remainder of the tractate. Interpreted within its literary context, t. Soṭah 13.2–4 is an affirmation that, with the presence once

---

be permanent.

67. See, for example, Meyers, "Crisis of Mid-Fifth Century."

again of the righteous in the first century CE, the Holy Spirit could reappear following its temporary withdrawal after the death of the latter prophets.

To bring our study to a close, we should revisit the survey of New Testament scholarship with which we began, where we may now recognize in retrospect that there exists a startling disparity between the confidence with which much New Testament scholarship has repeated the view that the Holy Spirit was believed to have withdrawn and the weight of evidence that actually supports this view. This observation teaches a clear lesson: when an early Jewish viewpoint, such as the alleged case of the withdrawal of the prophetic Spirit and its eschatological return, provides what appears to be an exceptionally suitable foil for New Testament points of view, New Testament scholars ought to exercise particular suspicion about the possibility of the manipulation of data. This suspicion ought to propel them to a fresh examination of the Jewish data collected to construct such an edifice, if not to demolish it—as I have attempted to do—at least to expose the fissures in its foundation.

2

Judith 16:14 and the Creation of Woman

In a climactic psalm toward the end of the tale of a heroic rescue of Israel by her hand, Judith exclaims:

> Let all your creatures serve you,
> for you spoke, and they were made.
> You sent forth your spirit, and it formed them;
> there is none that can resist your voice. (16:14)

The occurrence here of the verb ᾠκοδόμησεν (Hebrew בנה) is somewhat surprising.[1] F. Zimmermann was so puzzled by the verb that he believed something was wrong and suggested that the Hebrew *Vorlage* was corrupt: "What is plainly required in the verse, however, is the meaning that God sends forth His spirit and gives them *understanding*."[2] According to Zimmermann, the original Hebrew read ותבינם rather than ותבנה. The solution to the apparent awkwardness of this verb, however, lies not in a hypothetical reconstruction but in a profound intertextual echo within the biblical tradition.

---

1. On the question of whether Judith was written originally in Hebrew, see Moore, *Judith*, 66–67.

2. Zimmermann, "Aids for the Recovery," 73.

The prominence of creation language in Jdt 16:14b-c, with its dual emphasis on word and breath, echoes Ps 33:6:

> By the word of the LORD the heavens were made,
> and all their host by the breath of his mouth.[3]

Judith 16:14c also contains an unmistakable allusion to Ps 104:30a (103:30a LXX), one of a group of psalms intended to praise God as creator:

> ἐξαποστελεῖς τὸ πνεῦμά σου (Ps 103:30a LXX)
> ἀπέστειλας τὸ πνεῦμά σου (Jdt 16:14c)

The fuller context, Ps 104:29-30, reads:

> When you hide your face, they are dismayed;
> when you take away their breath, they die and return to their dust.
> When you send forth your spirit, they are created;
> and you renew the face of the ground.

These lines are replete with allusions to Gen 2:7 and 3:19, to the creation and demise of Adam, indicating that the psalmist's conception of the ongoing creation of the inhabitable world is shaped by the creation of the first man.[4]

Not so in the psalm of Judith, where the striking allusion to Ps 104:30a becomes the springboard for a subtle intertextual echo with which Judith reorients the conception of creation. Judith does not continue, as the reader is led to expect by this taut linguistic parallel, with the words of Ps 104:30a, καὶ κτισθήσονται, but instead substitutes for this more natural reading the seemingly awkward expression καὶ ᾠκοδόμησεν (Hebrew ותבנה). The verb בנה invariably refers in the Hebrew Bible to the building of cities, altars, the temple, or nations, but *only once* is בנה employed to depict the creation of living beings—in its first biblical occurrence, Gen 2:22, in which God is said to have taken the rib of Adam and "built" from it the first woman. In other words, the verb בנה is never employed in the Bible to depict living creation *except for the creation of woman* in Gen 2:22.[5]

---

3. The reference to "a new song" in Jdt 16:13 may echo Ps 33:3: "Sing to [the LORD] a new song." See also Ps 144:9.

4. On this widespread interpretation in other writings of Second Temple Judaism, see Levison, *Portraits of Adam*, 148-51.

5. In Amos 9:6, God builds the upper chambers of the physical cosmos. In Ps 78:69, God is said to build the sanctuary like the high heavens. Both of these acts of creation have to do with inanimate creations, analogous to temple and city, rather than to living beings; their creation can, therefore, be understood as an act of building. On the consistent use of בנה to convey building in the Hebrew Bible, see Wagner, "בָּנָה," 166-81. In other ancient Near Eastern languages, cognates of the root בנה may denote creation.

The strong similarity between Jdt 16:14a and Ps 104:30c, therefore, underscores a profound reorientation of the conception of creation. In Ps 104, praise of the creator evokes the image of the creation of the first man, of dust inbreathed and returned again to the ground; in the psalm of Judith, praise of the creator evokes instead the image of the creation of woman, of being built from a single rib into a creation of God.

This refocusing of Ps 104:30 onto the creation of woman suits a book in which Judith is a courageous heroine who single-handedly rescues Israel. The psalm itself is, moreover, a woman's song—begun when women are gathered (15:12); focused on the oppressed (16:4) and the victory they, the "sons of slave girls," bring about (vv. 11–12); claimed for Judith throughout by first-person singular pronouns ("my young men . . . infants . . . children . . . virgins" [16:4]), as well as in the stanza that contains 16:14 ("I will sing to my God a new song" [16:13]); and followed by an encomiastic description of Judith's generosity with booty, lifelong chastity, and magnanimity toward her maid (16:18–25). In this psalm, sung by the prototypical Jewish heroine, the discovery of an intertextual echo of the creation of the first woman is anything but unexpected.

The recognition of this allusion to Gen 2:22 provides in addition a small piece of evidence in the debate about whether Jdt 16:13–17 belongs to the original psalm or is a later interpolation.[6] The subtle allusion to Gen 2:22 suggests that this stanza may not be a later interpolation, for it well suits the emphasis on the defining role of a woman in Jdt 8–16.

See Akkadian "banû," AHw 1:103; CAD 2:87–88. Moreover, the Canaanite god El was regarded as "creator of created things" (bny bnwt); this was, according to J. Gray, "one of his stock epithets in the Ras Shamra texts" (Legacy of Canaan, 33). In my opinion, the late date of Judith (see Moore, Judith, 67–71, on a date in the Hasmonean period) and its distinct allusions to the Bible in this context suggest here primary dependence on the biblical tradition, in which בנה denotes an act of building.

6. Compare Craven, who contends that this stanza is original (Artistry and Faith, 110–12), and Moore, who tends toward the opinion that it is an interpolation (Judith, 255–56).

3

The Two Spirits in Qumran Theology

INTRODUCTION[1]

Nearly two columns of the Rule of the Community (1QS) are devoted to the Master's responsibility "to instruct and teach all the Sons of Light concerning the nature of all the sons of man." These are among the most defining and significant portions of instruction in the entirety of the scrolls, yet the content of this teaching is baffling. Its opaqueness, which tends to obfuscate rather than to clarify human nature, renders a clear definition of "spirit" evasive. This noun, which occurs no less than sixteen times in 1QS 3.13—4.26, is employed in such an array of expressions as "all the kinds of their [sons of man] spirits," "two spirits in which to walk," "all the spirits of his [the angel of darkness] lot," "a spirit of humility and patience," "the spirit of deceit," and the "holy spirit."

---

1. Overviews of research and bibliographies may be found in Lichtenberger, *Studien zum Menschenbild*, 123–24n1; Sekki, *Meaning of Ruaḥ*. Throughout this volume, I have preserved references to columns and lines in the Qumran Hymns (1QH) found in Eleazar Sukenik's edition, *The Dead Sea Scrolls of the Hebrew University*. More recent reconstruction of the scroll, with differing columns and lines, can be found in Schuller and Newsom, *The Hodayot*. To convert Sukenik's reconstruction of columns and lines to Schuller and Newsom's, readers can consult the helpful chart Schuller and Newsom provide on pp. 4–6 of their edition.

In an assiduous and variegated effort to ascertain the conceptions of "spirit" that coalesce in this teaching, two dominant questions have emerged. One is the nature of the notoriously elusive "two spirits." Are they human dispositions or angels or something altogether different? The other question, at the center of which is this teaching in 1QS 3.13—4.26, is whether Qumran pneumatology was consistent or whether various conceptions collided in the centuries-long history of the Qumran community.

The combination of industry and creativity that led to the formulation of these issues and the drive toward their resolution is impressive. Even before a decade had elapsed after the publication of the Community Rule, scholars had with acuity and intellectual breadth forged several approaches to these issues. I have, therefore, opted in this study to revisit in some detail the most paradigmatic of those analyses of the two spirits in Qumran theology to expose their foundational observations and their most compelling arguments.

Because the teaching of the two spirits occurs within the confines of a single text, and because the studies I hope to elucidate contain numerous citations, it may prove useful to begin with a translation of 1QS 3.13—4.26:

> [col. 3] (13) It is for the Master to instruct and teach all the Sons of Light concerning the nature of all the sons of man, (14) with respect to all the kinds of their spirits with their distinctions for their works in their generations and with respect to the visitation of their afflictions together (15) with their times of peace. From the God of knowledge comes all that is occurring and shall occur. Before they came into being he established all their designs; (16) and when they come into existence in their fixed times they carry through their task according to his glorious design. Nothing can be changed. In his hand (are) (17) the judgments of all things; he being the one who sustains them in all their affairs. He created the human for the dominion of (18) the world, designing for him two spirits in which to walk until the appointed time for his visitation, namely the spirits of (19) truth and deceit. In a spring of light emanates the nature of truth and from a well of darkness emerges the nature of deceit. (20) In the hand of the Prince of Lights (is) the dominion of all the Sons of Righteousness; in the ways of light they walk. But in the hand of the Angel of (21) Darkness (is) the dominion of the Sons of Deceit; and in the ways of darkness they walk. By the Angel of Darkness comes the aberration of (22) all the Sons of Righteousness; and all their sins, their iniquities, their guilt, and their iniquitous works (are caused) by his dominion, (23) according to God's mysteries, until his end. And all their afflictions and the appointed times

of their suffering (are caused) by the dominion of his hostility. (24) And all the spirits of his lot cause to stumble the Sons of Light; but the God of Israel and his Angel of Truth help all (25) the Sons of Light. He created the spirits of light and darkness, and upon them he founded every work, (26) [...] every action, and upon their ways (are) [al]l [...]. The one God loves for all [col. 4] (1) [app]ointed times of eternity, taking pleasure in all its doings forever; (concerning) the other he loathes its assembly, and all its ways he hates forever. (2) And these are their ways in the world: to illuminate the heart of man and to level before him all the ways of true righteousness; and to make his heart fear the judgments of (3) God; and a spirit of humility and patience, of great compassion and constant goodness, and of prudence, insight, and wonderful wisdom, which is firmly established in all (4) the works of God, leaning on his great mercy; and a spirit of knowledge in all work upon which he is intent, zeal for righteous precepts, a holy intention (5) with a steadfast purpose; and great affection towards all the Sons of Truth; and a glorious purity, loathing all unclean idols, and walking with reservation (6) by discernment about everything, concealing the truth of the mysteries of knowledge. The (preceding) are the principles of the spirit for the Sons of Truth (in) the world. The visitation of all those who walk in it (will be) healing (7) and great peace in a long life, multiplication of progeny together with all everlasting blessings, endless joy in everlasting life, and a crown of glory (8) together with a resplendent attire in eternal light. (9) But concerning the Spirit of Deceit (these are the principles): greed and slackness in righteous activity, wickedness and falsehood, pride and haughtiness, atrocious disguise and falsehood, (10) great hypocrisy, fury, great vileness, shameless zeal for abominable works in a spirit of fornication, filthy ways in unclean worship, (11) a tongue of blasphemy, blindness of eyes and deafness of ear, stiffness of neck and hardness of heart, walking in all the ways of darkness, and evil craftiness. The visitation of (12) all those who walk in it (will be) many afflictions by all the angels of punishment, eternal perdition by the fury of God's vengeful wrath, everlasting terror (13) and endless shame, together with disgrace of annihilation in the fire of the dark region. And all their times for their generations (will be expended) in dreadful suffering and bitter misery in dark abysses until (14) they are destroyed. (There will be) no remnant nor rescue for them. (15) In these (two spirits are) the natures of all the sons of man, and in their (two) divisions all their hosts of their generations have a share; in their ways they walk, and the entire task of (16) their works (falls) within their divisions according to a man's share, much or little, in all the times of eternity. For God has set them apart until the Endtime; (17) and put eternal enmity between their (two) classes. An abomination to truth (are) the doings of deceit, and an abomination to deceit (are) all the ways of truth. (There is) a fierce (18) struggle between all their judgments, for they do not walk together. But God, in his mysterious understanding and his glorious wisdom, has set an end for the existence of deceit. At the appointed time (19) for visitation he will destroy it forever. Then truth will appear forever (in) the world, which has polluted itself by the ways of ungodliness during the dominion of deceit until (20) the appointed time for judgment which has been decided. Then God will purify by his truth all the works of man and purge for himself the sons of man. He will utterly destroy the spirit of deceit from the veins of (21) his flesh. He will purify him by the Holy Spirit from all ungodly acts and sprinkle upon him the Spirit of Truth like waters of purification, (to purify him) from all the abominations of falsehood and from being polluted (22) by a spirit of impurity, so that upright ones may have insight into the knowledge of the Most High and the wisdom of the sons of heaven, and the perfect in the Way may receive understanding. For those God has chosen for an eternal covenant, (23) and all the glory of Adam shall be theirs without deceit. All false works will be put to shame. Until now the spirits of truth and deceit struggle in the heart of humans, (24) and (so) they walk in wisdom or vileness. According to a man's share in truth shall he be righteous and thus hate deceit, and according to his inheritance in the lot of deceit he shall be evil through it, and thus (25) loathe truth. For God has set them apart until the time of that which has been decided, and the making of the new. He knows the reward of their works for all the end of (26) [appointed tim]es, and he allots them to the sons of man for knowledge of good [... and thus] dec[id]ing the lots for every living being, according to this spirit [...] the visitation.[2]

---

2. Translations from Qimron and Charlesworth, "Rule of the Community (1QS)." Translations of other documents are from García Martínez, *Dead Sea Scrolls Translated* (2nd ed.).

THE TWO SPIRITS: COSMIC BEINGS OR HUMAN DISPOSITIONS?

Within a decade of the publication of the Community Rule, scholars had forged no less than three distinct approaches to the teaching of the two spirits. K. G. Kuhn and A. Dupont-Sommer, drawing upon *external parallels* with Zoroastrianism, interpreted the two spirits primarily as cosmic beings locked in war with one another. In response to that approach, P. Wernberg-Møller sought to demonstrate "on purely *internal grounds*"[3]—from elements within the document itself—that these spirits are two inclinations within each individual human being. O. Seitz, in a less influential but nonetheless significant study, explained the teaching of the two spirits as the product of the *creative exegesis* of 1 Sam 16:14, "And the spirit of the Lord departed from Saul, and an evil spirit from the Lord troubled him." By 1961, then, three approaches to the two spirits had emerged, yielding a disorienting array of interpretations.

The Two Spirits and External Parallels

In articles published in 1950, K. G. Kuhn and A. Dupont-Sommer agreed that the Qumran community had come under Iranian influence.[4] This hypothesis is credible, since Jews had lived for centuries under Persian domination. Two years later, both scholars had discovered in the Community Rule, which contains the teaching of the two spirits (1QS 3.13—4.26), sufficient evidence to reaffirm resoundingly their conviction that Zoroastrian influences had shaped the earliest beliefs of the Qumran community.[5] Both independently cited numerous correspondences between the teaching on the two spirits in 1QS 3-4 and the Gāthās of Zarathustra, which comprises the primary repository of the teachings of Zoroaster, whose influence lay at the headwaters of Iranian religion or Zoroastrianism, centuries prior to

---

3. Wernberg-Møller, "Reconsideration of Two Spirits," 441; emphasis added.

4. André Dupont-Sommer wrote, "If Essenism had earlier been influenced largely by Zoroastrianism [= Iranian religion], whose influence was not wholly eliminated afterwards, the Master of Justice [Teacher of Righteousness] himself brought about its reform under the influence of another mystical movement, Neo-Pythagoreans" (*Dead Sea Scrolls*, 92). Karl G. Kuhn noted that Qumran theology "accords surprisingly with the original preaching of Zarathustra [= Zoroaster]" ("Hebräischen Texte," 211). Kuhn wrote this although, as he explained in a subsequent publication, he had not yet seen the Rule of the Community ("Sektenschriften und iranische Religion," 297, 314).

5. Kuhn, "Sektenschriften und iranische Religion"; Dupont-Sommer, "Instruction sur deux Esprits."

the founding of the community at Qumran. It will serve us well to dwell upon these parallels because they constitute the most cogent defense of the interpretation of the two spirits as cosmic beings locked in war with one another. The most significant correspondences include:

(1) 1QS 3.18: "two spirits in which to walk until the appointed time for his visitation, namely the spirits of truth and of deceit." Both Kuhn and Dupont-Sommer, by observing that the basic opposition between two spirits could not be traced to the Hebrew Bible, freed themselves to contend that this distinction was derived from Zoroastrianism. Dupont-Sommer cited Yasna 45.2, of the Gāthās, as evidence:[6] "Yes, I shall speak of the two fundamental spirits of existence, of which the virtuous one would have thus spoken to the evil one: 'Neither our thoughts nor teachings nor intentions, neither our preferences nor words, neither our actions nor conceptions nor our souls are in accord.'"[7]

(2) Kuhn argued more generally that the tenor of 1QS 3–4, with its eschatological point of reference and an ethical dualism between right actions and evildoing, corresponds quintessentially to the ethical dualism and eschatological resolution of Yasna 30.3–5:

> Yes, there are two fundamental spirits, twins which are renowned to be in conflict. In thought and in word, in action, they are two: the good and the bad. And between these two, the beneficent have correctly chosen, not the maleficent. Furthermore when these two spirits first came together, they created life and death, and how, at the end, the worst existence shall be for the deceitful but the best thinking for the truthful person. Of these two spirits, the deceitful one chose to bring to realization the worst things. (But) the very virtuous spirit . . . chose the truth and (so shall those) who shall satisfy the Wise Lord continuously with true actions.

For Kuhn, in particular, these references to two spirits in a context that contains *fundamental* ethical and eschatological dualisms suggest the influence of Zoroastrianism on 1QS 3.13—4.26.[8]

(3) 1QS 3.24-25: "But the God of Israel and his angel of Truth help all the Sons of Light." Dupont-Sommer discerned a parallel between this affirmation of divine aid for the children of light and Yasna 50.5: "Lord, let wisdom come in the company of truth across the earth! Yes, if ye shall be

---

6. Dupont-Sommer, "Instruction sur deux Esprits," 16–17, 19; on 1QS 3.19, 21.

7. All translations from the Gāthās are by Insler, *Gāthās of Zarathustra*. For a description of the good spirit, see in the Avesta Yasna 47.

8. Kuhn, "Sektenschriften und iranische Religion," 304–5.

pleased with your prophet, reveal Thyself with visible help, mighty through Thy hand, through which he might see us in happiness."[9]

(4) 1QS 4.2: "And these are their [the spirits'] ways in the world." The concept of two ways in relation to two factions of people is discernible, according to Dupont-Sommer, in Yasna 31.2, where, in a context that refers to two factions, the truthful and deceitful, it is said, "If the better course for the soul has not been seen through these words, then let me lead all of you in which way the Wise Lord knows (to exist) that judgment between the two alternatives by which we are going to live in accordance with truth."[10]

(5) 1QS 4.6. The visitation of all those who walk in it [the spirit of truth] (will be) healing." The effect of healing, according to Dupont-Sommer, is frequent in the Gāthās, e.g., Yasna 44.16; 31.19. The good person, "virtuous through truth, watching over the heritage for all, is a world-healer and Thy ally in spirit, Wise One" (44.2).[11]

(6) 1QS 4.15-18: "In these (two spirits are) the natures of all the sons of man, and in their (two) divisions all their hosts of their generations have a share . . . For God has set them apart until the Endtime; and put eternal enmity between their (two) classes . . . But God, in his mysterious understanding and glorious wisdom, has set an end for the existence of deceit." The division of humankind into two distinct groups until eschatological judgment is fundamental to the Gāthās, e.g., Yasna 31.2, 3; 43.12; 47.6; 51.9. Both Kuhn and Dupont-Sommer cited in this regard Yasna 44.15: "Tell me truly, Lord . . . when the two hosts who share no wonts come together, where and to which one shalt Thou grant victory?"[12]

To be able to locate at Qumran a particular text that confirmed the suspicion that the community had been influenced by Iranian theology must have generated considerable enthusiasm. The recurrence of the opposition between two spirits in a context dominated by eschatology and ethical dualism is of considerable import.

Nonetheless, these parallels were challenged because the Gāthās, though they purport to express the convictions of Zoroaster, who lived centuries before the founding of the Qumran community, were actually written

---

9. Dupont-Sommer, "Instruction sur deux Esprits," 21.
10. Dupont-Sommer, "Instruction sur deux Esprits," 22.
11. Dupont-Sommer, "Instruction sur deux Esprits," 25.
12. Dupont-Sommer, "Instruction sur deux Esprits," 28-29; Kuhn, "Sektenschriften und iranische Religion," 305. Dupont-Sommer cited Yasna 43.8, 15; 46.6 as parallels to the "eternal hatred." The ultimate defeat of the evil spirit and victory of the good spirit is, according to Dupont-Sommer, a fundamental doctrine of Zoroastrianism (Yasna 30.8, 10; 43.5) ("Instruction sur deux Esprits," 30).

centuries *after* the demise of the Qumran community.[13] Dupont-Sommer had partially anticipated this critique by marshalling corroborative evidence from Plutarch's description of Zoroastrianism in *De Iside et Osiride*, which was composed prior to ca. 120 CE, in support of the possible influence of Zoroastrianism on the community at Qumran. On the respective origins and enmity of the two spirits in light and darkness (1QS 3.19–21), Dupont-Sommer could refer to Plutarch's description of Zoroastrian gods: "Oromazes [Ahura Mazda], born from the purest light, and Areimanius, born from the darkness, are constantly at war with each other."[14] On the equal divisions of the two spirits (1QS 4.15–16), Dupont-Sommer noted that every time the good god (Ahura Mazda) created other gods, the evil god matched them in number.[15] And on the ultimate defeat of the evil god (1QS 4.18), Dupont-Sommer cited a small portion of Plutarch's description: "But a destined time shall come when it is decreed that Areimanius, engaged in bringing on pestilence and famine, shall by these be utterly annihilated and shall disappear."[16]

These parallels with *De Iside et Osiride* were not entirely adequate to forestall the criticisms of scholars such as F. Nötscher. Nötscher contended that *general* dualisms, such as good and evil, belong to common human perceptions of reality and, therefore, need hardly be traced to early Zoroastrianism, about which almost nothing is known.[17] Many of the parallels that Kuhn and Dupont-Sommer adduced do admittedly fit in this category. Belief in God's aid to the suffering righteous, for example, is hardly limited to Zoroastrianism. H. G. May, moreover, subsequently garnered a wide variety of scriptural texts, such as the cosmic battle between Gog and Magog in Ezek 38–39, to create a believable biblical context for this sort of dualism.[18] Nötscher observed as well that Zoroastrianism underwent changes in the course of a millennium and that the *specific* dualism between light and darkness that is fundamental to Qumran dualism is less characteristic of the Gāthās (the primary evidence for early Zoroastrianism) than of the

---

13. For a concise discussion of Zoroastrianism, see Boyce, "Zoroaster, Zoroastrianism."
14. Dupont-Sommer, "Instruction sur deux Esprits," 18.
15. Dupont-Sommer, "Instruction sur deux Esprits," 29n1.
16. Dupont-Sommer, "Instruction sur deux Esprits," 30.
17. Nötscher, *Zur theologischen Terminologie*, 86–92. Kuhn had already acknowledged this ("Sektenschriften und iranische Religion," 309).
18. May, "Cosmological Reference," 12. He cited as well several instances in which the qualities of God were hypostatized and "thought of as angelic beings" (e.g., Ps 85:11–14) in an attempt to identify a plausible biblical basis for explaining the origins of the two angelic spirits.

later Avesta. This particular dualism, then, can hardly be adduced as an indication of Zoroastrian influence on Qumran theology.

There exists, moreover, another breach in the foundation of Zoroastrian influence. The influence of early Zoroastrianism cannot satisfactorily explain the struggle of the two spirits *within* the human heart (e.g., 1QS 4.23) or the capacity of a child of light to sin. This aspect of 1QS 3–4 compelled Dupont-Sommer, without the ability to appeal to Zoroastrian parallels, to conjecture awkwardly, "The idea seems to be that, if the two spirits *in each person* are unequally apportioned, they are found *together* equally: the two forces, in some manner, are equal."[19]

Kuhn too acknowledged this tension, recognizing that (as he perceived it) in 1QS 3.15—4.19 two *groups* of people are divided under their respective spirits of light and falsehood, which war in cosmic battle with one another, while in 1QS 4.20–23, the spirits of truth and falsehood are said to struggle *within each individual*. He explained this tension in two ways. First, he regarded the tension as a matter of terminology rather than substance, for even in 1QS 3.22, the children of light are led astray in the context of a cosmic battle by the prince of darkness and his coterie of evil spirits. What 1QS 4.20–23 expresses as an anthropological dualism—a struggle within an individual—is much the same as the cosmic dualism of 1QS 3.15–19, in the course of which the righteous are led astray. Kuhn contended, second, that "this terminological distinction lies in this, that the dualism of the two original spirits of truth and evil, from Iranian [Zoroastrian] religion, which was adopted in 1QS 4.20ff. is combined with the Old Testament conceptions of the 'new spirit,' of the 'holy spirit,' of the 'steadfast spirit' which God will place in the heart of the pious" (Ezek 36:25–27; Ps 51:10, 12–14, 19).[20]

In the end, Kuhn's inability to adduce Zoroastrian parallels to explain the presence of an anthropological dualism (the struggle within) in 1QS 3–4 exposes a gap in the hypothesis of Zoroastrian influence. How taut are the parallels if Zoroastrianism cannot adequately explain the anthropological dimension of 1QS 3–4?[21]

---

19. Dupont-Sommer, "Instruction sur deux Esprits," 29; emphasis original.

20. Kuhn, "Sektenschriften und iranische Religion," 301–2n4. Wildberger attempted to strengthen the hypothesis of Zoroastrian influence by identifying the "spirit of impurity" with Belial. He went on, on the basis of 1QS 10.21 ("Belial I will not keep in my heart"), to locate the spirit of impurity or Belial both in the cosmos and "in the heart" of the children of darkness ("Dualismus in den Qumranschriften").

21. Some scholars have refined the Zoroastrian hypothesis by pinpointing a particular form of Zoroastrianism known as Zurvanism. See, for example, Duchesne-Guillemin, "Zervanisme"; Charlesworth, "Critical Comparison," 400–401.

The Two Spirits and Internal Considerations

Into this breach, nearly a decade later, strategically stepped P. Wernberg-Møller,[22] who, "on purely internal grounds" (as opposed to citing external parallels) attempted to redress the balance by contending that the two spirits in 1QS 3–4 are to be understood as two dispositions within all human beings, as the precursor of the rabbinic concept of the two impulses:

> It may thus be doubted whether we have a parallel at all here to the concept in the *Gathas* of the two sharply separated divisions of mankind. The sons of righteousness are, in a way, regarded as a section within the larger whole, the sons of perversion, and as belonging to them. This feeling of solidarity with the rest of mankind is something very characteristic of the anthropology of the Qumran community . . . it comes out very strongly in *1 QS* XI and in *1 QH*; but it also lies behind the instruction before us [in 1QS 3–4].[23]

The focus of 1QS 3–4 is the variety of human spirits produced by the struggle between truth and perversity within the human heart. Although Wernberg-Møller's study is dense, its most cogent evidence may nonetheless be summarized.

(1) 1QS 3.14 refers not to "two kinds" of spirits but to "all the ranks of their spirits." The focus of 1QS 3–4 is not two groups—the number "two" occurs only in 3.18. All human beings are distinguished from one another on the basis of a variety of spiritual states and not because they belong to one of two mutually exclusive groups.[24] Nor does 1QS 3.14–15 have in view an eschatological judgment akin to Zoroastrianism. The vocabulary is similar to 1QS 3.23, in which punishment and grief are *present* realities. The words "punishment," and "recompense," moreover, derive from Hos 9:7, in which they describe Israel's sinful present existence.

(2) 1QS 3.18, which mentions the placement of two spirits in human beings, constitutes an allusion to Gen 2:7. The image therefore is akin to the creative inbreathing of two spirits rather than to the creation of two cosmic spirits, as in Zoroastrianism.[25]

---

22. Independently of Wernberg-Møller, Treves contended that the two spirits are not angels because the reference is to "all varieties"; the allotment of spirits to the single angel of darkness suggests that angels and spirits are not synonyms (1QS 3.24); the spirit is sprinkled (1QS 4.21) and angels are not; in the Hebrew Scriptures, angels do not dwell in human hearts (1QS 4.23) ("Two Spirits").

23. Wernberg-Møller, "Reconsideration of Two Spirits," 428.

24. Wernberg-Møller, "Reconsideration of Two Spirits," 419–20.

25. Wernberg-Møller, "Reconsideration of Two Spirits," 422.

(3) 1QS 3.18-19 corresponds to 4.18-22, particularly the reference to "the time fixed for His [God's] visitation." This parallel "makes it clear that the expression 'spirits of truth and perversion' in 1QS 3.18-19 means two *psychological* qualities." In 1QS 4.18-22, the point is "that perfection is at present, however desirable, not practicable, but it will be so when God will replace the 'perverted' mind by a 'true' and 'holy' disposition [i.e., spirit]."[26] Thus can Wernberg-Møller appeal to 1QS 4.18-22, in which the spirit is that which exists within a human, to elucidate the more obtuse earlier reference.

(4) 1QS 3.13—4.6 in general presents no strict dualism but rather a framework in which God is consistently stronger than the angel of darkness. Once again, the focus is not upon two equal and opposed cosmic spirits.[27]

(5) The lists in 1QS 4.2-14, which contrast "the spirit of meekness, of patience, generous compassion, eternal goodness" and "the spirit of deceit" do not refer to two cosmic spirits with their respective realms of morality. Rather each human, both within and outside the Qumran community, exhibits in varying measure the characteristics of these spirits, and it is the mixture of these characteristics that determines, as in 1QS 3.14, "all the ranks of their spirits." The exegetical basis for this inference is that the sons of truth are referred to twice in the first list, but the sons of perversion are not mentioned at all in either list. The intent of these contrasting lists, therefore, is not to distinguish between the righteousness of the children of light and the evil of the children of darkness, but to depict the nature of all people, who participate to varying degrees in good and evil. The children of darkness do not even come into the picture.[28]

(6) 1QS 4.17-18 describes a fierce struggle, and 4.23 locates this struggle in the human heart: "Until now the spirits of truth and of injustice feud in the heart of man and they walk in wisdom or in folly." The nature of this struggle determines the particular *share* one has in the spirits of truth and perversion.[29]

These observations, among others, formed the basis for Wernberg-Møller's contention—made in direct opposition to K. G. Kuhn and A. Dupont-Sommer:

> The difference between light and darkness, righteousness and sin was, of course, felt to be radical; but the domains of these opposites were not kept strictly apart. Perversion and darkness made inroads upon the realms of truth and light because the

26. Wernberg-Møller, "Reconsideration of Two Spirits," 423; emphasis original.
27. Wernberg-Møller, "Reconsideration of Two Spirits," 425-27.
28. Wernberg-Møller, "Reconsideration of Two Spirits," 429-31.
29. Wernberg-Møller, "Reconsideration of Two Spirits," 433.

sons of righteousness, in spite of their name and election, like the rest of mankind, had two "spirits," two opposing inclinations (III, 18) constantly at war with one another (IV, 23), of which, at the moment, the "perverse" one had the upper hand.[30]

Wernberg-Møller's analysis of 1QS 3-4 served as an important corrective to Kuhn's and Dupont-Sommer's explanation of 1QS 3-4 via Zoroastrianism. His exclusive emphasis upon the anthropological dimension was nonetheless as one-sided as their emphasis upon the cosmic dimension. H. G. May later contended, for example, that even a reference to "all their kinds of spirits" (1QS 3.14) is set in a context replete with references to the spirit of truth and deceit or the prince of light and the angel of darkness,[31] and J. H. Charlesworth justifiably observed that "anyone advocating a psychological rendering of this passage must necessarily explain why here particularly 'Angel of Darkness' or 'Angel of Truth' should be drained of their cosmic force."[32]

The Two Spirits and Biblical Exegesis

Unlike Kuhn, Dupont-Sommer, and Wernberg-Møller, O. Seitz attempted to explain what he perceived to be the coexistence of various dualisms in 1QS 3-4. Seitz uncovered this complexity by discerning a relationship between passages from the Shepherd of Hermas, the Testaments of the Twelve Patriarchs, and the Community Rule, and by tracing their coalescence of conceptions primarily to 1 Sam 16:14: "And the spirit of the Lord departed from Saul, and an evil spirit from the Lord troubled him."[33] This biblical text emerged in Herm. Mand. 5.1.2a, 3-4 in the conviction that

30. Wernberg-Møller, "Reconsideration of Two Spirits," 427.

31. May, "Cosmological Reference," 2.

32. Charlesworth, "Critical Comparison," 398. Charlesworth also observed that 1QS 3.18 is not about the placement of two spirits *within* human beings but the allotment of two spirits *for* human beings to follow. 1QS 3.18 reads ל (as in 2 Sam 12:20) and not ב. In this interpretation, human beings situate themselves in either of the two spirits; the two spirits are not situated within a human being ("Critical Comparison," 396). Nonetheless, other of Wernberg-Møller's observations were subsequently strengthened. For example, his contention that 1QS 3.14 has less to do with two spirits than with varieties of spirits was borne out by Sekki's observation that the closest parallel to this formulation occurs in 1QS 20, where the expression refers to the varieties of spiritual perfection of priests, which are the basis for their rank in the community (*Meaning of Ruaḥ*, 195). 1QS 3.14 suggests that the varieties of spiritualities *within individual members of Qumran* may lie rather more at the forefront of 1QS 3-4 than does the *division of the members from nonmembers based upon the two spirits of 1QS 3.18-19.*

33. Seitz, "Two Spirits in Man." He also discerned adumbrations of the lying spirit

> the holy spirit which dwells in you will be pure ... But if any quick temper enters, at once the holy spirit, being delicate, is pressed for room ... for it is choked by the evil spirit ... being defiled by the quick temper.
>
> Therefore, abstain from quick temper, which is the most evil spirit; but put on patience. (5.2.8)

Seitz noted that 1 Sam 16:14 is unique in Scripture as the text in which God is said to send *both* an evil and a good spirit. Seitz took the verb "choked," which occurs as well in the Septuagint version of 1 Sam 16:14, as further evidence that this discussion in the Shepherd of Hermas is spun exegetically from 1 Sam 16:14 (1 Kgs 16:14 LXX).[34] The centrality, moreover, of "quick temper," suggests the influence of the story of Saul, who was flung into fits of rage when inhabited by the evil spirit.

This antithesis between *two spirits* is similar to the opposition of *two angels* in Herm. Mand. 6.2.1:

> Behold then the works of the angel of evil. First of all he is quick tempered ... whenever this one arises in your heart, recognize him by his works ... Whenever quick temper or bitterness assails you, recognize that he is in you.
>
> Trust the angel of righteousness, but avoid the angel of evil ... For if any man is faithful, and the desire of this angel arises in his heart, that man or woman must commit some sin.

The antithesis between good and evil that is manifest in opposition between two spirits and two angels that "arise in the heart" is evident further in a "psychological dualism" between two desires:

> The evil desire is the daughter of the devil ... But you must put on the desire of righteousness and, armed with the fear of the Lord, resist them [evil desires] ... If you serve the good desire and are subject to her, you will be able to gain dominion over the evil desire and bring her into subjection. (Herm. Mand. 12.2.2–5)

Seitz mustered analogous exegetical activity from the Testaments of the Twelve Patriarchs. A similar antithesis of two spirits is in evidence, according to Seitz, in T. Gad 4:7: "The spirit of hate cooperates with Satan through impatience, but the spirit of love cooperates with the law of God in patience." The *complexity* of antitheses is evident as well in the Testaments of the Twelve Patriarchs.

---

of 1 Kgs 22:21–23 in 1QS 4.9 and Herm. Mand. 3.1, 2, 4 ("Two Spirits in Man," 86).

34. Although Seitz did not cite Pseudo-Philo, LAB, this interpretation is especially evident in LAB 60.1–2, where the evil spirit is said to have *choked* Saul.

> If the soul wills to walk well . . . it does all its deeds in righteousness . . . But if the inclination tends toward evil, . . . it is dominated by Beliar; even it if does something good, he perverts it to evil . . . since the treasure of the inclination is filled with an evil spirit. (T. Ash. 1:6–9)

> The *inclination* of the good man is not under the control of the error of the *spirit of Beliar*, for the *angel of peace* guides his soul. (T. Benj. 6:1)[35]

Precisely this complexity characterizes 1QS 3–4, where the spirits under the dominion of the angel of darkness mislead the children of light (1QS 3.24), and where "the spirits of truth and deceit struggle in the heart of humans" (1QS 4.23). Seitz discerned, as well, a level of psychological (i.e., anthropological) dualism in the reference to inclinations in 1QS 4.4–5—"A holy intention with a steadfast purpose"—which is followed shortly later, in 1QS 5.4–5, by the exhortation: "No man shall wander in the stubbornness of his heart, to err following his heart, his eyes, and the plan of his inclination." Even some of the effects of the two spirits as they act upon this inclination are similar to the Shepherd of Hermas and the Testaments of the Twelve Patriarchs: either patience (1QS 4.3) or quick temper (1QS 4.10).[36]

Seitz included far more exegetical data, as well as frequent relevant references to the rabbinic conception of the two inclinations, to substantiate his view that the teaching of the two spirits could best be understood as the product of creative exegesis. It is nonetheless the correspondences he discerned between the complex coexistence of dualisms in the Shepherd of Hermas, the Testaments of the Twelve Patriarchs, and the Community Rule, alongside the ability to trace them together to 1 Sam 16:14, that constitute Seitz's primary contribution.

Two Spirits: The Via Media

Although most scholars have responded primarily to Wernberg-Møller or to K. G. Kuhn and Dupont-Sommer, they have tended nonetheless to adhere, like Seitz, to an interpretation that acknowledges the coexistence of anthropological and cosmic dualisms in 1QS 3–4. What is indeed striking, despite this superficial consensus, is the *variety of rationales* for these interpretations, as a whirlwind review of select studies should illustrate.

---

35. Seitz, "Two Spirits in Man," 91–92; emphasis added.
36. Seitz, "Two Spirits in Man," 93.

B. Otzen explained 1QS 3-4 as an instance of a late Jewish belief according to which what happens in the world at large is played out in individual human beings. Within each human transpires a psychological dualism (*microcosm*) of spirits, which corresponds to a cosmic-mythological dualism (*macrocosm*) of angels and demons.[37]

E. Schweizer underscored the ethical dimension of 1QS 3-4 by placing it in the context of *the fundamental decision to obey Torah*. Although the formulation of the two spirits is analogous to the rabbinic conception of the two impulses, this understanding of the two spirits does not suffice. Human beings can decide only from God's power; accordingly the two spirits are identified as angels who act in God's power to help and to hinder people in their ethical decisions.[38]

A. R. C. Leaney, like Schweizer, argued that there is in 1QS 3-4 an issue more fundamental than the two spirits; viz., the contrast between *light and darkness*. The association is evident in 1QS 3.18-19: "two spirits . . . the spirits of truth and of deceit. In a spring of light emanates the nature of truth and from a well of darkness emerges the nature of deceit." The particular expressions of this fundamental conviction are, however, confused, for "the writer is not clear whether he wishes to teach that man as such is a combination of a good and a bad spirit or that mankind is divisible into the good (arising from light) and the bad (arising from darkness)."[39]

J. G. Gammie regarded the fundamental element of 1QS 3-4 to be ethical dualism, which he defined as *the division of people into opposing (e.g., good and evil) groups*. According to Gammie, "1QS 3.13—4.26 teaches an ethical dualism which at times is internalized into a psychological dualism and at times externalized or further extended into a modified cosmic dualism."[40]

H. Lichtenberger contended that 1QS 3.13—4.26 deals primarily with *the tension between God's responsibility for creation and the presence of evil among the faithful*. The primary point of 1QS 3.18-19, for example, is that God has created both spirits. The interpretation of the two spirits in 1QS 3.18 as human dispositions that, in the following line, are related to cosmic, mythological elements of light and darkness is secondary to the acknowledgment that God in the beginning created both, that God helps

---

37. Otzen, "Neugefundenen hebräischen sektenschriften," 135-36. Otzen contended as well that both dualisms are ethical and thus influenced by Iranian religion, as opposed to the Hellenistic and gnostic dualism of body and soul.

38. Schweizer, "Gegenwart des Geistes."

39. Leaney, *Rule of Qumran*, 37. The entire discussion, including a survey of possible origins of this teaching and a valuable chart of relevant biblical, Jewish, and Christian texts, spans 37-56. On the interpretation of Osten-Sacken, *Gott und Belial*, see below.

40. Gammie, "Spatial and Ethical Dualism," 381.

the children of light in the present cosmic battle with the angel of darkness, and that God has set an eschatological limit to the existence of the spirit of deceit.[41]

A. E. Sekki characterized the teaching of the two spirits as a *reinterpretation of the community's traditional understanding of the spirit*. Because 1QS 3–4 is a reinterpretation, the traditional and revised views of the spirit coexist at three interpretative levels in 1QS 3.13—4.26. (1) The use of the feminine gender in the expression "two spirits" in 1QS 3.18–19 indicates that these two spirits, as well as "the spirits of light and of darkness" in 3.25, are human dispositions, for the word "spirit," in the feminine gender, tends to designate human dispositions in the Qumran scrolls. (2) The use of the masculine gender in the similar expression, "the spirits of truth and deceit" (1QS 4.23), indicates a reference to the good and evil spirits that fill the cosmos, for throughout the remainder of Qumran literature, references to angelic beings as "spirits" occur with relative consistency in the male gender. According to Sekki, the author of this essay on the two spirits allows these two interpretations to coexist in order to teach that "the pious must deal not only with their own sinful nature but also with the problem of demonic attack."[42] (3) Alongside references to two human dispositions and a multiplicity of angelic and demonic beings, the author of 1QS 3.13—4.26 refers as well to the singular spirit of God as the "spirit of holiness" and the "spirit of truth" (4.21) in an eschatological context replete with traditional allusions to Isa 44:3, Joel 3:1, and Ezek 36:25–27. 1QS 3–4, therefore, preserves various conceptions of the spirit as dispositions, angels, and an eschatological reality in order to reinterpret the traditional view of the sect for whom God, through the holy spirit, will deliver God's people from sin in the last days by describing the eschatological holy spirit as the spirit of truth (1QS 3.18–19). "In this way the author indicates that the 'holy Spirit' which will come from God in the future is really none other than the good spirituality given to the sectarian at his creation."[43]

Synthesis

This altogether too brief survey of scholarly positions on the two spirits suggests how little consensus there is even among scholars who agree that the cosmic and anthropological interpretations of the two spirits coexist in

---

41. Lichtenberger, *Studien zum Menschenbild*, 123–42.

42. Sekki, *Meaning of Ruaḥ*, 211. See also 4QShir[a] 1, 6, in which the demons attempt to destroy the heart of the faithful.

43. Sekki, *Meaning of Ruaḥ*, 217–18.

1QS 3–4. The solution to this conundrum, then, is one of the desiderata of Qumran scholarship.

Despite this lack of consensus, a return to the first decade of studies may suggest a complementarity in these studies that has led to the embrace of various interpretations of the spirit in 1QS 3–4. K. G. Kuhn and Dupont-Sommer provided, via external parallels, a credible explanation of the stark opposition between two cosmic spirits: the influence of Persian cultural hegemony, particularly Zoroastrian dualism, made inroads into early Jewish theology. What this hypothesis could not satisfactorily explain—the struggle within individuals—Wernberg-Møller, by approaching 1QS 3–4 on internal grounds, could: individuals within the community were ranked by the mixture or varieties of the spirits of truth and deceit within. Taken in tandem, with the caveat that neither adequately explains *every* reference to spirit in 1QS 3–4, these complementary approaches account quite satisfactorily for both the cosmic and anthropological aspects of this teaching.

The cogency of both sets of analyses, despite their one-sidedness, suggests why subsequent scholars preferred to interpret 1QS 3–4 as a combination of cosmic and anthropological elements. This does not mean that scholars agree over the fundamental issue at stake in 1QS 3–4; we have seen that they do not. Nor is there consensus about which particular references—of which there are sixteen—in 1QS 3–4 are to human spirits and which are to cosmic spirits. Sekki's survey of scholarly opinions on each reference to "spirit" in 1QS 3.13—4.26 catalogues the bewildering disagreement of scholars concerning which particular texts refer to angelic spirits and which to human spirits.[44] Despite this lack of consensus, scholars do affirm virtually unanimously that 1QS 3–4 is a teaching concerned *both* with the struggle within human beings *and* the cosmic struggle that has an impact upon their ability to live righteously.

The community at Qumran, however, was shaped not so much by systematic, abstract reflection upon the origin of evil or the nature of angels as by their Scriptures. It was the ability of the Teacher of Righteousness to interpret Torah and prophets that lent him status in the community. In this respect, Seitz's suggestion that the teaching of the two spirits is the product of the creative exegesis of 1 Sam 16:14 is essential to a holistic interpretation of 1QS 3–4. His interpretation, moreover, can be strengthened if it is juxtaposed with those of K. G. Kuhn, Dupont-Sommer, and Wernberg-Møller, for a weakness of Seitz's interpretation is its inability to address a disparity between 1 Sam 16:14 and 1QS 3–4. In 1 Sam 16:14, the evil and good spirits

---

44. Sekki, *Meaning of Ruaḥ*, 193–219.

do *not* coexist within Saul; the evil spirit enters after the departure of the good spirit. In 1QS 3.18, both spirits coexist within a human being. This conceptual shift can be explained by the influence of a Judaism that was shaped by Persian dualism; the mutually exclusive spirits of 1 Sam 16:14 may have been interpreted as two spirits that coexist within a human being in the context of the cosmic coexistence of the prince of light and the angel of darkness.

THE TWO SPIRITS: THEIR RELATION TO QUMRAN THOUGHT

Diversity within the Dead Sea Scrolls

A scant year before Wernberg-Møller attempted a frontal assault on the hypothesis of Zoroastrian influence, O. Betz drove a wedge into the assumption that Qumran conceptions of the spirit were relatively uniform. Betz discovered what he would designate the Spirit teaching (*Geistlehre*), which is located primarily in 1QH, and the Spirits teaching (*Geisterlehre*), which characterizes 1QS 3.13—4.26. These, contended Betz, "are so closely intertwined that Qumran research until now and probably also the sect itself did not discover their original independence."[45] For the division between a Spirit teaching and Spirits teaching, Betz offered several pieces of evidence.

Creation

The Spirit teaching is concerned primarily to describe the human spirit as an impure spirit, a "spirit of flesh," which is characterized by waywardness and sin. Thus, the Qumran psalmist thanks God for insight, even though a human being is

> a structure of dust fashioned with water,
> his counsel is the [iniquity] of sin,
> shame of dishonor and so[urce of] impurity
> and a depraved spirit rules over him. (1QH 5.21–22)

Strikingly different is the creation imagery in 1QS 3.18–19, where not one spirit, but two, are created and where these are not inbreathed but placed for humans to walk in them.

---

45. Betz, *Offenbarung und Schriftforschung*, 143.

This difference is explicable in part, according to Betz, because the Spirit teaching of 1QH is deeply influenced by Gen 2, with its images of breath and clay and its focus upon the creation of individual human beings. The Spirits teaching, in contrast, with its reference to "generations" and to the contrast between light and darkness, is spun from Gen 1 and therefore is directed toward generations of people, children of light and darkness.

Sin

According to the Spirit teaching, the spirit that God inbreathed into each individual can be tainted by sin. Based upon the conviction of Lev 11:43, that one's life or *nephesh* can be defiled by breach of the Levitical laws, the author of the Damascus Document similarly warns in CD 12.11 against the defilement of one's life or "spirit" and against the defilement of one's "holy spirit" in CD 5.11-12 and 7.3-4. Integral to this warning is the member's ability to choose, to resist defilement of one's spirit by stringent adherence to community rules. This emphasis upon individual choice and sin is absent from the Spirits teaching, according to which the ways of two groups of people are predetermined by their respective origins, either from a well of darkness or a spring of light (1QS 3.18-19). The decision concerning which group to join is not a human one but a divine one.

A further conviction divides the Spirit teaching from the Spirits teaching. The basic distinction between good and evil is depicted in the former by the contrast between spirit and flesh and in the latter by the contrast between two spirit worlds. We have seen above that the hymn writer describes himself as both "a creature of clay" and "a mistaken spirit." He has, according to 1QH 4.25, "a spirit of flesh." In 1QS 3-4, in contrast, the world is divided between spirits of deceit and truth, the prince of light and the angel of darkness, angels and demons, two ways with their respective effects and actions (4.2-16). There is here no conception of an individual spirit created good but gone bad, a spirit breathed from above but buried now under the impulse of the flesh. There is, in short, no need for purification in the here and now, although this is precisely the need that preoccupies the Qumran hymn writer.

Purification

We have seen that the proponents of the Spirit teaching could describe themselves as both creatures of clay and mistaken spirits. We have seen that the human spirit could, from this perspective, be defiled by disobedience. Of such human beings it must be said, "Born of a woman, how can he dwell before you, he whose kneading (is) from dust and whose corpse (is) food for maggots? He is (but) a discharge, (mere) pinched-off clay whose urge is for the dust. What can clay and that which is shaped (by) hand dispute; and what counsel does it comprehend?" (1QS 11.21-22). This is only part of the picture; it could also be said:

> I give you thanks, Lord,
> because you have sustained me with your strength,
> you have spread your holy spirit over me so that I will not stumble,
> you have fortified me against the wars of wickedness,
> and in all their calamities
> you have n[ot] discouraged (me) from your covenant. (1QH 15.6-8)

The difference between these assessments of human nature is striking, compelling Betz to suggest: "The difference between both pictures corresponds to the contrast between the natural and the newly created individual—between the person who lives according to the flesh, who possesses nothing other than an impure body and erring spirit, and the person who lives according to the spirit, who has received the power of God and the holy spirit."[46] In other words, "The spirit and power of God overcome human fleshly nature and straighten out his inclination, that is, spirit."[47]

This conception of new creation holds nothing in common with the conception of the two spirits in 1QS 3-4, in which one's predetermined lot among either the children of light or children of darkness is evident in whether one follows the way of the spirit of deceit (1QS 4.9-11) or the spirit of humility and patience (1QS 4.2-6). There is no individual new creation in the present age; there are rather two ways that coexist until the eschatological eradication of the spirit of deceit (1QS 4.20).

Betz's interpretation is not without its weaknesses. Because he wrote before the publication of Wernberg-Møller's study, he perhaps did not sufficiently consider the anthropological dimension of 1QS 3-4, which may have created a bridge between the Spirit teaching and the Spirits teaching. The notion of "a variety of spirits" and the conviction that the two spirits "struggle in the heart of humans" may have provided Betz with some

---

46. Betz, *Offenbarung und Schriftforschung*, 124. This realization can be traced to the important study of Sjöberg, "Neuschöpfung in den Toten-Meer-Rollen." Sjöberg drew attention to the function of the spirit, not only in creation, as in 1QS 3.18-19, nor exclusively in eschatology, as in 1QS 4.20-23, but in the new creation of the believer. Sekki regarded Sjöberg's study as paradigmatic (*Meaning of Ruaḥ*, 28-30).

47. Betz, *Offenbarung und Schriftforschung*, 125.

measure of concurrence between the Spirits teaching and the conviction of the Spirit teaching that the human spirit can err and be deceived. Such criticisms notwithstanding, Betz's clear definition of the dilemma, which previously had tended to go unrecognized, demonstrated that the spirit of truth in 1QS 3-4 cannot easily be identified with the holy spirit in the remainder of the Qumran documents, as had been done customarily in studies prior to Betz's.[48]

Diversity within the Qumran Hymns

A subsequent analysis by H.-W. Kuhn (a student of K. G. Kuhn) on Qumran eschatology served to buttress Betz's thesis. While Betz attempted to uncover a diversity of views on the spirit throughout the Qumran corpus, H.-W. Kuhn concentrated his attention upon the Qumran hymns in order to distinguish two conceptions of the spirit: the predestined spirit given to human beings at their creation, a conception whose fundamental formulation occurs in 1QS 3.13—4.26, and a subsequent gift bestowed upon entrance into the community.[49]

Kuhn's analysis of the first conception—the spirit as the predestined essence of a human being instilled at creation—consisted of two simultaneous tasks. One was to gather those texts in 1QH that exhibit a coalescence of vocabulary, including "spirit," "task," "to determine," and "to fashion." The other task was to demonstrate the association of these portions of 1QH with 1QS 3-4.

Kuhn located, for example, what he considered a substantial reference to the spirit as the predestined essence of humans granted at their creation in 1QH 7:

> I know that the impulse of every spirit is in your hand,
> [and all] its [task] you have established even before creating him. (7.16-17)

> You have fashioned the spirit

---

48. For a list of scholars who made this identification, see Sekki, *Meaning of Ruaḥ*, 56n218. Foerster attempted to rebut Betz by proffering numerous parallels between 1QS 3-4 and 1QH to demonstrate "the essential identification of the 'spirit of truth' with the 'holy spirit' of the hymns" ("Heilige Geist im Spätjudentum," 129-30). The parallels Foerster cited, however, tend to deal less with the spirit(s) than with other elements of 1QS 3-4 and 1QH, though Foerster contended (127) that the spirit's presence is presupposed in many contexts of 1QH where there is no explicit reference to the spirit.

49. Kuhn, *Enderwartung*, 120-39.

> and have organised its task [before the centuries.]
> From you comes the path of every living being. (7.25)[50]

Similar is 1QH 9.8–9:

> You have fashioned every spirit
> [...] and the judgment of all their deeds.[51]

Kuhn recognized an impressive agreement in vocabulary among these passages and contended that they are conceptually linked to 1QS 3–4. References to the fashioning of every spirit in conjunction with the word "task," for instance, recall the creation context of 1QS 3–4, particularly 1QS 3.16: "When they come into existence in their fixed times they carry through their task according to his glorious design."[52]

These observations led Kuhn to the conclusion that, while the spirit of a person in the Qumran hymns can represent a person's predestined essence, in most places in which "spirit" occurs in the anthropological sense, this "spirit" is simply, according to its usage in the Hebrew Bible, the natural spirit of a person as understanding, disposition, or mental constitution.[53] But this is, according to Kuhn, only part of the picture. Next to the characteristic conception of spirit as the predestined essence of a person that was apportioned to him, there occurs in the Qumran hymns also the other perception, that the spirit was given as a special divine gift to the pious upon entrance into the community."[54]

For evidence of this second strand of thought, Kuhn once again gathered texts on the basis of characteristic vocabulary. When God is said "to give the spirit to" a believer, this signals, according to Kuhn, entrance into the community. The Teacher, for example, writes:

> And I, the Instructor, have known you, my God,
> through the spirit which you gave in me,
> and I have listened loyally to your wonderful secret
> through your holy spirit. (1QH 20.11–12)

The verb "to draw near" also signals entry into the community. In 1QS 9.15–16, the prescription for entrance includes this term: "According to

---

50. Col. 7, line 25.

51. Kuhn followed the reconstruction: "By which you have determined their task" (*Enderwartung*, 124n4).

52. For further evidence Kuhn appealed to the similarities between 1QH 14.11–12 and 1QS 4.24–25 (*Enderwartung*, 125–26).

53. Kuhn, *Enderwartung*, 126.

54. Kuhn, *Enderwartung*, 130.

the cleanness of a man's hands he may approach, and upon the author of his insight he may draw near, and thus (establish) his love along with his hatred." Both expressions, the giving of the spirit and drawing near, occur in 1QH 8.19–20:

> I have appeased your face by the spirit which you have placed [in me,]
> to lavish your [kind]nesses on [your] serv[ant] for [ever,]
> to purify me with your holy spirit,
> to bring me near[55] by your will according to the extent of your kindnesses.

By isolating two clusters of characteristic terminology and demonstrating that only one of them exhibited affinities with 1QS 3–4, Kuhn strengthened the emerging *consensus communis* that the Dead Sea Scrolls contain a variety of conceptions of the spirit. Betz had demonstrated that the teaching on the two spirits in 1QS 3–4 was measurably different from conceptions of the spirit in the remainder of the Community Rule, in the Damascus Document, and in the Qumran hymns. Kuhn took this perspective a step farther by observing that diversity existed within the corpus of Qumran hymns. The next step would be taken by P. von der Osten-Sacken, who contended that there is diversity even within the teaching of the two spirits in 1QS 3.13—4.26.

Diversity within 1QS 3–4

Because Osten-Sacken intended to trace the history of dualism in the Qumran community, he naturally dealt extensively with the teaching of the two spirits. He regarded the War Scroll (1QM) as the earliest representative of dualism because of its intense eschatological expectation of a final battle and its clear opposition between Israel and the nations. This form of dualism, suggested Osten-Sacken, fits well the situation of the Maccabean Rebellion, when some of the Jews, incensed by the political and religious violations of Antiochus IV Epiphanes, fought for liberation from Seleucid Rule.

The fundamental structure of 1QS 3.20–25, contended Osten-Sacken, is the same as the beliefs in the War Scroll. The contrast between the sons of light and darkness, the enmity of the angel of darkness or Belial toward the children of light, the appointed time for the defeat of Belial and his angelic entourage, and God's help in the face of overwhelming opposition are elements that 1QM 1 and 1QS 3.20–25 have in common. Even the name

---

55. Literally, "to cause to draw near."

of God, "God of Israel," occurs eleven times in the War Scroll and otherwise only in 1QS 3.24.

Although 1QS 3.13—4.14, which contains 3.20-25, reflects this early form of dualism, the teaching of the two spirits actually belongs to a later stage in the development of Qumran dualism than the War Scroll. There is a lessening of eschatological and military dualism that would reflect a period of relative political stability; the cosmic battle now is seen from an ethical perspective as the ongoing opposition between good and evil. Dualism was instead associated with creation: "The editor of the teaching, 1QS 3.13—4.14, assimilated alongside the eschatological-dualistic tradition of 1QM an interpretation of an entirely different sort, the creation tradition, with a certain deterministic stamp, which it obtained in the Qumran community."[56] This emphasis upon creation is due to the influence of the Qumran hymns; Osten-Sacken, like H.-W. Kuhn, observed, for example, the similarity between 1QH 15.21-22—"You have fashioned the spirit and have organized its task"—and 1QS 3.16—"when they come into existence in their fixed times they carry through their task according to his glorious design."[57] In addition to the assimilation of an emphasis upon creation, the editor has also added a predestinarian thread in 1QS 3.17-19, probably, according to Osten-Sacken, due to Iranian (Zoroastrian) influence in a period subsequent to the writing of the War Scroll. Therefore, the original eschatological dualism of the War Scroll, which provides the ground structure of 1QS 3.13—4.14, diminished and was supplemented by a new emphasis upon creation, the ethical contrast of good and evil in the present, and predestination.

If 1QS 3.13—4.14 represents an intermediate stage in the development of Qumran dualism, then 1QS 4.15-26 comprises a still later phase. In this section, the anthropological struggle comes to the fore. The battle lines had shifted from the opposition between Israel and the nations (1QM) to the contrast between the sons of light and the sons of darkness, including Jews (1QS 3.13—4.14), to the individual's struggle between righteousness and evil (1QS 4.15-26).

According to Osten-Sacken, then, there are no less than three stages of Qumran thought reflected in 1QS 3.13—4.26. 1QS 3.20-25 reflects most clearly the dualistic origins of Qumran thought akin to the War Scroll. 1QS 3.13—4.14 adjusts that dualism for present experience by associating it with creation and predestination. The anthropological emphasis of 1QS 4.15-26 represents a further and subsequent ethicizing of this dualism.

56. Osten-Sacken, *Gott und Belial*, 130.
57. Osten-Sacken, *Gott und Belial*, 129.

Synthesis

The fissure created by Betz's study was developed in the studies of H.-W. Kuhn and Osten-Sacken into an irreparable fracture. All subsequent studies have been compelled to acknowledge that in the Qumran writings as a whole (Betz), the Qumran hymns (H.-W. Kuhn), and 1QS 3-4 (Osten-Sacken), multiple conceptions of God's spirit(s) were permitted to coexist. The burden of proof now rests upon scholars who identify the spirit of truth, from 1QS 3-4, with the holy spirit of the Qumran hymns.

CONCLUSION

An extravagant amount of attention has been paid during the first half-century of scholarship to the question of the two spirits in Qumran theology. This level of interest is hardly inappropriate in light of the importance of 1QS 3-4 for ascertaining conceptions of the spirit, perceptions of predestination, and descriptions of dualism in formative Judaism and nascent Christianity. Despite the erudition displayed in these studies, the first fifty years of research have yielded a bewildering lack of consensus concerning the two significant issues that have been the foci of this essay.

There exists still meager consensus concerning the fundamental questions that attend this pivotal passage in the scrolls. The question of Iranian influence continues to be debated, though with less intensity than in earlier years. Recently, M. Philonenko has resurrected the argument for Iranian influence in a study that argues not only for Iranian influence in general but for Zurvanite influence in particular. According to Philonenko, a Zurvanite origin of this teaching, as well as parallel conceptions in the Visions of Amram, is evident in the combination of dualism with a threefold schema of history—past, present, and eschatological future. Zurvanite conceptions are evident as well in the mélange of good and evil, light and darkness within human beings, that is, in the varying levels at which truth and perversity exist in humans. Belief in this mélange is discernible as well in the Horoscopes that have been preserved among the Dead Sea Scrolls. Although Philonenko does not, in my opinion, introduce new evidence into the debate, he does provide a characteristically competent and reliable discussion of the question of Iranian influence. More salutary about this study perhaps is the thoroughness with which he traces the alleged influence of Qumran dualism on other Jewish and Christian texts, including 2 Baruch (according to a citation of Cyprian), Philo Judaeus, the Fourth Gospel, Lactantius, and others.[58]

No more consensus is apparent with respect to the question of the cosmic or psychological dimensions of the two spirits. The present impasse concerning the nature of the two spirits reflects the more general question of how to negotiate the relationship between the environment of antiquity (K. G. Kuhn and Dupont-Sommer on Zoroastrianism), the texts themselves (Wernberg-Møller's internal grounds), and Qumran's biblical foreground (Seitz's analysis of the interpretation of 1 Sam 16:14). Our hurried passage, moreover, through the studies of Otzen, Schweizer, Leaney, Gammie, Lichtenberger, and Sekki revealed the dismaying variety of rationales that exist to support a putative correspondence between the cosmic and psychological dimensions.

Nor has a coherent theological exposé of unity and diversity vis-à-vis the spirit and the two spirits appeared as a worthy sequel to the pioneering study of O. Betz. This impressive half century of scholarship has, therefore, set the terms of the debate without ultimately resolving the issues to which it has so keenly and adeptly drawn attention.[59]

---

58. Philonenko, "Doctrine qoumrânienne."

59. Most recently, Jean Duhaime has employed the structuralist approach of Marc Girard to undertake an intricate analysis of this passage, with particular attention paid to the role of repetition and transitional phrases ("Voies des deux Esprits"). This detailed study, in which Duhaime delves into the most minute of literary details, provides an excellent exposé of each main section (1QS 3.15b—4.1; 4.2-14; 4.15-26) and subsection of this passage; it is not an attempt to address the questions that have tended to preoccupy students of this passage.

4

Inspiration and the Divine Spirit in the Writings of Philo Judaeus

I. INTRODUCTION

Many of Philo's references to πνεῦμα are ordered with remarkable consistency. Genesis 1:2, for example, is the anchor for Philo's description of the cosmic πνεῦμα.[1] The divine inbreathing of Gen 2:7 provides the basis for Philo's anthropology of the human spirit.[2] Philo's references to the inspiration of the divine spirit, on the other hand, are attached more tenuously to the Bible. Attempts to order these references have led scholars to widely divergent opinions, which attest to the confusing nature of Philo's view of the spirit's role in inspiration. During the first third of the twentieth century, H. Leisegang, H. Lewy, and E. R. Goodenough sought the genesis

---

1. E.g., Philo, *Gig.* 22-23; *Opif.* 22-35. On Philo's use and adaptation of Stoicism in his interpretation of Gen 1:2, see Laurentin, "Pneuma," 391-407; Verbeke, *Évolution*, 237-50; Weaver, "Πνεῦμα in Philo," 7-25, 55-72; Leisegang, *Heilige Geist*, 24-53; Isaacs, *Concept of Spirit*, 43-45. On Stoic views of πνεῦμα, see Sambursky, *Physics of the Stoics*, 1-48.

2. E.g., Philo, *QG* 1.4; 2.58-59; *Opif.* 134-48; *Spec.* 1.32-42; 4.123; *Her.* 55-57; *QE* 2.33. Numerous allusions and references to Gen 2:7 are cited in Centre d'analyse, *Philo d'Alexandrie*, 29. See Tobin, *Creation of Man*, 77-87; Levison, *Portraits of Adam*, 66-75.

of Philo's view of inspiration primarily in Hellenistic mystery religions.[3] In their view, the spirit mediates mystical vision—a sober intoxication—which surpasses rational knowledge.

This viewpoint elicited a negative response from G. Verbeke and H. A. Wolfson. Verbeke emphatically traced inspiration to the LXX alone, and not to "croyances populaires de la période hellénistique,"[4] while Wolfson discerned a combination of "the 'divine spirit,' which according to Scripture is the cause of prophecy, with the process of 'divine inspiration' or 'possession' which, according to Plato, is the cause of his various kinds of frenzy."[5]

Attempts to explain Philo's view of inspiration during the post-Wolfson era have been even more diverse. A. Laurentin and M. Weaver connected the spirit to the spiritual life. Laurentin discerned three stages of the spiritual life in which the spirit participates: faith, spiritual progress, and vision of God.[6] Weaver contended that Philo's "concern with the spiritual life gives the doctrine of πνεῦμα some internal cohesion."[7] The doctrine of the spirit belongs to a "theology of grace," that is, the spirit, and no human capacity, enables people to attain to mystical vision and to lead a life of virtue. In contrast to Laurentin and Weaver, M. Isaacs proffered another explanation of Philo's view of inspiration by tracing it to an apologetic motive. Philo recounts contemporary instances of inspiration, such as dream interpretation and prediction, but he limits possession by the spirit to the biblical prophets in order to assert implicitly "that the inspiration of the authors of scripture was qualitatively different from any subsequent insight."[8]

This lack of consensus is evident furthermore in two of the most recent studies of inspiration in the writings of Philo. R. Berchman portrayed Philo as an eclectic philosopher whose view was influenced by a wide range of Greco-Roman sources, from Plato to Plutarch.[9] H. Burkhardt situated Philo's understanding of inspiration within the wisdom tradition, according to which "Inspiration vollzieht sich entsprechend nicht unter Ausschaltung der menschlichen Vernunft, sondern als ihre Indienststellung

---

3. Leisegang, *Heilige Geist*, 53–69; Lewy, *Sobria Ebrietas*, 64–66; Goodenough, *By Light, Light*. Leisegang carefully argues that, according to Philo, the purpose of Hellenistic philosophies is to lead to mystical intuitive knowledge. When that knowledge is obtained, the secondary worth of these philosophies becomes evident (*Heilige Geist*, 62–64).

4. Verbeke, *Évolution*, 254.

5. Wolfson, *Philo*, 2:25.

6. Laurentin, "Pneuma," 424.

7. Weaver, "Πνεῦμα in Philo," 162; 142–63.

8. Isaacs, *Concept of Spirit*, 49.

9. Berchman, "Arcana Mundi: Magic"; Berchman, "Arcana Mundi: Prophecy."

und Begnadung mit über die Möglichkeiten empirischer und rationaler Erkenntniswege hinausführender Erkenntnis."[10]

There is, therefore, no consensus concerning the divine spirit in Philo's view of inspiration. On the contrary, nearly a century of Philonic studies has yielded a wide variety of interpretations, which portray Philo's view variously as the product of a mystic (Goodenough; Leisegang; Lewy), a biblical interpreter (Verbeke; Wolfson), a devotee of the spiritual life (Laurentin; Weaver), an apologist (Isaacs), an adherent of the wisdom tradition (Burkhardt), and an eclectic philosopher (Berchman). This lack of unanimity underscores the pressing need for a fresh approach to Philo's view of inspiration.

The purpose of this chapter is to pursue that fresh approach by situating Philo's references to the divine spirit within three of his dominant interests—exegesis; autobiographical experience; and apologetics—a task rendered rather more feasible due to the terrain which Philonic scholars have travelled recently. First, due to the work of scholars such as I. Christiansen, V. Nikiprowetsky, and T. M. Conley, Philo's role as exegete has become a dominant feature in the landscape of Philonic studies.[11] It should come as no surprise, then, that several references to the divine spirit in Philo's writings are substantial exercises in exegesis. Second, the authenticity of Philo's autobiographical accounts of inspiration have been brought to the fore by D. Winston, D. M. Hay, and S.-K Wan.[12] In light of their work on prophecy, mysticism, and inspiration, we may expect to discern a kinship between Philo's autobiographical accounts of inspiration and his descriptions of the divine spirit. The important role of the third interest, apology, is indisputable, particularly in those treatises, such as *De vita Mosis*, in which Philo self-consciously puts on the hat of apologist.[13] This motivation, we would suspect, influences at least some of Philo's references to the divine spirit.

These three motivations are, of course, inseparable. Still, the product of this analysis will be a typology of Philonic references to the inspiration of the divine spirit—a typology tempered by the reality that Philo, as often as not, defies categorization!

---

10. Burkhardt, *Inspiration heiliger Schriften*, 221.

11. Christiansen, *Technik der allegorischen Auslegungswissenschaft*; Nikiprowetsky, *Commentaire*; Conley, *Philo's Rhetoric*.

12. Winston, "Was Philo a Mystic?"; Hay, "Philo's View of Himself"; Wan, "Charismatic Exegesis," 63–71.

13. Philo can be considered an apologist despite our present inability to determine whether his primary audience was Jewish, non-Jewish, or both. On apology in general, see Tcherikover, "Jewish Apologetic Literature Reconsidered"; on *De vita Mosis*, see Tiede, *Charismatic Figure*, 105–8.

II. EXEGESIS AND THE DIVINE SPIRIT

The wide range of Philo's exegetical adaptations indicates the sizeable measure of freedom Philo permits himself to interpret the function and nature of the divine spirit. The simplest example of Philo's exegetical adaptations vis-à-vis the divine spirit is *Fug.* 186, an abbreviated version of Num 11:16, 17, 25, and 29 LXX. Philo prefers τὸ θεῖον . . . πνεῦμα,[14] substituting it for a variety of similar expressions, including τοῦ πνεύματος τοῦ ἐπὶ σοὶ (11:17), τοῦ πνεύματος τοῦ ἐπ' αὐτοῦ (11:25), and τὸ πνεῦμα αὐτοῦ [κύριος] (11:29).[15] His introduction of the adjective προφητικόν is a shorthand reference to the role of prophets (11:29) and prophesying (11:25) in the biblical narrative.

Philo's allegorical interpretation of Torah is apparent in *Mut.* 123, in which Philo preserves the words of Num 14:24 LXX, πνεῦμα ἕτερον ἐν αὐτῷ, but subjects them to his typical allegorical interpretation. The words "another spirit" in Numbers mean that Caleb was different from the rest of the unfaithful people in that he followed God; he would thus enter the promised land. Philo, however, proffers his own allegorical interpretation, in which the spirit that differentiated Caleb from the others signifies total transformation:

> But in Caleb we have a total change of the man himself. For we read "there was another spirit in him," as though the ruling mind in him was changed to supreme perfection. For Caleb is by interpretation "all heart."[16]

This exegetical transformation of the static conception, "another spirit," to a total change in Caleb is not surprising in light of the authority Philo attaches to the allegorical level of meaning.

Two further instances of Philo's interpretation of the divine spirit suggest how capably Philo merges the biblical text with conceptions from his own Greco-Roman era: *Mos.* 1.273–84 and *Gig.* 23–27. Philo as an exegete confronts a conundrum in the character of Balaam.[17] Philo himself consistently portrays Balaam as the worst of wizards, who is contrasted with

---

14. See also Philo, *Ios.* 116 (on Gen 41:38).

15. Citations, translations, and quotations from all classical writers are from LCL, unless otherwise stated.

16. Etymology probably based upon reading the Hebrew כלב as כל לב.

17. He is not alone in seeing the problem of an inspired non-Israelite seer who subsequently plots to ensnare Israel. On Josephus's interpretation of this difficult figure, see Feldman, "Prophets and Prophecy," 416–17; Levison, "Debut of Divine Spirit." On Pseudo-Philo's attempt to alleviate the difficulty of Balaam, see Levison, "Prophetic Inspiration."

true prophets,[18] just as he consistently contrasts true and false prophecy.[19] Balaam hardly fulfills the criteria of wisdom, justice, and goodness that, according to *Her.* 259, are necessary to receive divine inspiration.[20] According to Num 23:7 LXX, however, the spirit came upon Balaam (καὶ ἐγενήθη πνεῦμα θεοῦ ἐπ' αὐτῷ) after he received God's word to return to Balak and while he stood next to his whole burnt offerings in the presence of Balak and the princes of Moab. Philo deliberately alters this scenario when he writes in *Mos.* 1.277:

> He advanced outside, and straightway became possessed, and there fell upon him the truly prophetic spirit which banished utterly from his soul his art of wizardry. For the craft of the sorcerer and the inspiration of the Holiest might not live together.

In this Philonic text, the source and process by which Balaam the seer was inspired, though anchored in the biblical notion that God places a word in the prophet's mouth (Num 22:38; 23:5, 16; 25:13; Deut 18:18), is developed by means of conceptions of inspiration from Philo's Greco-Roman environment. As I have argued in detail elsewhere,[21] Philo recasts Num 22–24, with the result that Balaam's inspiration bears a significant resemblance to the explanation of Delphic inspiration proffered by Cleombrotus in Plutarch's *De defectu oraculorum*. Cleombrotus attributes the diminishing oracular activity at Delphi to "the total defection of the guardian spirits [δαιμονίοις]" (418C-D). Philo identifies the divine spirit as an angelic being, similar to the daemons in Cleombrotus's explanation, by drawing a close connection between the prediction of the angel in *Mos.* 1.274 and its fulfilment by the divine spirit in *Mos.* 1.277.[22] He cements the connection by repeating the verb θεσπίζειν in both texts to describe inspiration.

---

18. E.g., Philo, *Mut.* 202; *Deus* 181; *Conf.* 66, 159; *Migr.* 113; *Cher.* 32; *Det.* 71.

19. E.g., Philo, *Mut.* 202–3; *Conf.* 159; *Spec.* 1.59–65, 315; 4.48–52. Although the biblical source of this distinction is the contrast between Canaanite practices and the true Israelite prophet in Deut 18:10–11 and 15:18, Philo's polemic reflects as well the Greco-Roman distinction drawn, for example, by Cicero in *Div.* 1.11–12, between artificial (e.g., augury) and natural (e.g., dreams) forms of divination. For example, Philo's lists of false practices in *Spec.* 1.65 and 4.49 match the list of techniques of artificial divination in *Div.* 1.34 more closely than the longer list in Deut 18:10–11.

20. See Bockmuehl, *Revelation and Mystery*, 73.

21. Levison, "Prophetic Spirit as Angel."

22. Philo draws an explicit identification between what Moses calls angels and the Greeks daemons in *Gig.* 6; *Plant.* 14; *Somn.* 1.141; he alludes to Plato's important discussion in *Symp.* 202E (cf. Plutarch, *Is. Os.* 361C). On these texts, see Levison, "Prophetic Spirit as Angel."

The processes of inspiration are similar as well. Balaam's rational faculties are ousted (*Mos.* 1.274, 277) in a manner analogous to the Delphic pythia's loss of rationality. Moreover, the simile employed by both Philo and Plutarch's Cleombrotus to depict this sort of inspiration in general is a musical instrument. When the daemons return to a shrine, contends Cleombrotus, "the oracles, like musical instruments, become articulate, since those who can put them to use are present and in charge of them" (*Def. orac.* 418D). Commenting upon the word ἔκστασις in Gen 15:12, Philo describes "what regularly befalls the fellowship of the prophets. The mind is evicted at the arrival of the divine spirit." He continues (on Gen 15:13) by employing the metaphor of a musical instrument; the prophet's organs of speech "are wholly in the employ of Another... Unseen by us that Other beats on the chords with the skill of a master-hand and makes them instruments of sweet music, laden with every harmony" (*Her.* 264–66).

The apologetic benefits of transforming rather than discarding this difficult text, as I have observed elsewhere,[23] are enormous. The view of Cleombrotus has its roots in Plato's *Symp.* 202E–3A and thus claims unique authority in the Greco-Roman world. Equally important, Delphi was the most ancient and revered oracular shrine in the Greco-Roman world. Philo could not have been unaware of the appeal that a mode of inspiration associated with Delphi and traceable to Plato would have held for his readers.

Another interpretation of the divine spirit imbued with the hues of the Greco-Roman period occurs in Philo's explanation of Gen 6:3: "My spirit shall not abide for ever among men, because they are flesh" (*Gig.* 19). Philo illuminates the nature of the spirit in Gen 6:3 by means of another text, Exod 31:3. Philo's interpretation of Exod 31:3 in *Gig.* 23 contains four elements to capture the skill of Bezalel: πνεῦμα θεῖον, wisdom, understanding, and knowledge.[24]

This provisional definition of the divine spirit leads to an interpretation of "that spirit of perfect wisdom" (*Gig.* 24) that Philo discerns in Num 11:17: "I will take of the spirit that is on thee and lay it upon the seventy elders." This interpretation of Num 11:17 is somewhat startling, for here, where the leitmotiv of Num 11 is ecstatic prophecy, Philo discovers knowledge and wisdom, while from *Mos.* 1.273–84, on Balaam, where neither prophecy nor ecstasy is mentioned in Philo's *Vorlage*, Philo extrapolates the presence

---

23. See Levison, "Debut of Divine Spirit," 133–37.

24. See also *QG* 1.90, where Philo omits the reference to understanding. Philo does not paraphrase the parallel verse, Exod 35:31, which implies in the LXX omniscience (ἐπιστήμης πάντων), probably because he carefully distinguishes between Bezalel, who fashioned the shadows, and Moses, who fashioned the archetypes. Only Moses can possibly lay claim to knowledge of all things (e.g., Philo, *Plant.* 26–27; *Somn.* 1.206).

of ecstatic prophetic inspiration. In juxtaposition, therefore, *Mos.* 1.273–84 (Num 22–24) and *Gig.* 24 (Num 11:17) indicate unequivocally how freely and even—from our perspective—inconsistently Philo interprets biblical texts that focus upon the divine spirit.

Exodus 31:3 and Num 11:17, then, clarify the nature of the divine spirit of Gen 6:3, which does not remain permanently with humankind. This identification crescendos until *Gig.* 27, where Philo proffers a definitive identification of the divine spirit:

> But as it is, the spirit which is on him is the wise, the divine, the excellent spirit, susceptible of neither severance nor division, diffused in its fullness everywhere and through all things, the spirit which helps, but suffers no hurt, which though it be shared with others or added to others suffers no diminution in understanding and knowledge and wisdom.

In this fullest of definitions, Philo places wisdom in the first place and the spirit's divine character second, although Exod 31:3 LXX and Philo's own version of it in *Gig.* 23 refer to the "*divine* spirit of wisdom." This subtle exegetical alteration is attributable to the wisdom tradition (e.g., Isa 11:2, 9; Sir 39:6; Wis 7:7) and circles in Second Temple Judaism that were influenced by this tradition (e.g., T. Levi 2:3; 18:7; 1QH 12.11–12).

Moreover, another exegetical modification suggests that Philo shares with the author of the Wisdom of Solomon a view of the divine spirit deeply indebted to Stoicism. While Exod 31:3 states that the divine spirit *fills Bezalel*, Philo writes instead that the divine spirit *fills the entire cosmos*. The language of *Gig.* 27 indicates unequivocally that Philo is intent upon demonstrating the cosmic character of the divine spirit of wisdom. The language is similar to Wis 1:7: "Because the spirit of the Lord has filled the world, and that which holds all things together knows what is said . . ." Cicero's Balbus, in *Nat. d.* 2.19, claims that the world order is "maintained in unison by a single divine and all-pervading spirit." Alexander of Aphrodisias, an early third-century CE peripatetic philosopher, summarizes the theory of mixture held by Chrysippus, the leading third-century BCE Stoic thinker: "He assumes that the whole material world is unified by a spirit [πνεῦμα] which wholly pervades it [διήκοτος] and by which the universe is made coherent and kept together and is made intercommunicating [συμπαθές]."[25]

---

25. Alexander of Aphrodisias, *Mixt.* 216.14–17. See *Mixt.* 223.6–9, where he asks whether the Stoics are not wrong when they affirm "that the whole nature is united by a pneuma pervading all of it, and by which the universe is being held and kept together and is in sympathy with itself?" (quotations from Sambursky, *Physics of the Stoics*, 120–21). See also Cleomedes, *De motu circulari* 1.1 (Ziegler, *Cleomedis*, 8, lines 16–22); Stobaeus (*Eclogues* 153.34—154.5); Origen, *Cels.* 6.71.

If this modification demonstrates how far Philo is willing to walk the way of Stoicism, a third exegetical alteration of Exod 31:3 demonstrates the point at which he stops. His choice of the preposition "upon" to describe the divine spirit's relationship to Bezalel, in lieu of the conception of Bezalel's being filled with the divine spirit, is a subtle rebuttal of Stoic conceptions of the spirit, according to which the human spirit or soul was part and parcel of the cosmic spirit. Epictetus, for example, describes human souls as "parts and portions" of God's being (*Diatr.* 1.14.6). Cicero, quoting Chrysippus, describes the human being as "a small fragment of that which is perfect" (*Nat. d.* 2.37). In contrast to the perspective of Stoicism, namely that the human soul is inherently inspired by virtue of its character as πνεῦμα, Philo contends that the cosmic πνεῦμα is a supplement that temporarily imparts wisdom when it comes upon human beings. Wisdom is not innate but bestowed. Wisdom is not the permanent character of human life but a temporary experience. This limitation of the accessibility of the divine spirit is evident in the words that follow Philo's definition: "And so though the divine spirit may stay awhile in the soul it cannot abide there, as we have said" (*Gig.* 28).

From this discussion we can perceive, somewhat ironically—for Philo's indebtedness to Stoicism is here so apparent—Philo's persistent commitment to the literal meaning of the biblical text. In several other contexts, Philo freely adopts Stoic vocabulary to extol the nature of the human soul. In *Opif.* 135, for example, he interprets the inbreathing of Gen 2:7 as the impartation of a soul "which is a Divine breath that migrated hither from that blissful and happy existence for the benefit of our race." This description echoes Seneca's depiction of the human soul: "Just as the rays of the sun do indeed touch the earth, but still abide at the source from which they are sent; even so the great and hallowed soul, which has come down in order that we may have a nearer knowledge of divinity."[26] In *Leg.* 3.161, Philo again interprets the inbreathing of Gen 2:7 under the influence of Stoicism: the soul is "a portion of an ethereal nature." In contrast, when he interprets Gen 6:3, according to which the divine spirit does *not* remain permanently, Philo opts for a strikingly divergent interpretation of the divine spirit, which he buttresses with a literal reading of the text: "And Moses himself affirms this when he says that 'because they are flesh' the divine spirit cannot abide" (*Gig.* 29).

In summary, these few instances of Philo's exegesis reveal the freedom with which Philo interprets Torah. Some modifications affect merely phraseology (*Fug.* 186). Others serve as instances of Philo's characteristic

---

26. Seneca, *Ad Lucilium epistulae morales* 41.5.

allegorical interpretation (*Mut.* 123). Still others illustrate Philo's use of specific Greco-Roman conceptions, such as the view of Delphic inspiration represented by Cleombrotus or Stoic perspectives on πνεῦμα, to interpret the biblical text (*Mos.* 1.273-84; *Gig.* 23-29). The net result is that references to the divine spirit range in meaning, encompassing a shorthand reference to the prophetic spirit, human transformation interpreted allegorically, an angelic being that replaces reason, and a cosmic force akin to, yet also distinct from, the πνεῦμα of Stoicism.

III. AUTOBIOGRAPHY AND THE DIVINE SPIRIT

Philo himself recognizes the importance of autobiography when, as an aside, he notes, "For each one of us knows what he has himself experienced as no other can know it" (*Plant.* 21). Given its significance in his own estimation, Philo's autobiographical accounts of inspiration would appear to be a salutary point of departure for understanding his view of the divine spirit's functions in relation to inspiration. However, one of the few scholarly attempts to relate autobiography and inspiration was undertaken as long ago as 1926 by F. Büchsel, who addressed this issue only to drive a wedge between Philo's experience and his so-called theory of inspiration:

> Wer genau vergleicht, was nach Philons Theorie ein Prophet erlebt, und was Philon selbst erlebt hat, wird bemerken, daß beides nicht ganz zusammenstimmt. Nach der Theorie Philons ist der Zustand des Propheten völlige Ekstase ... Aber bei Philons Erleben ist das vernünftige Denken keineswegs gänzlich still gestellt ... Das Heftige, Derbe, das nach der Theorie dem Inspirationsvorgang wesentlich sein soll, fehlt im Erleben Philons augenscheinlich und muß in ihm fehlen.[27]

Although this rigid dichotomy between theory and experience is overdrawn, Büchsel's work marks an important attempt to determine the relationship between Philo's descriptive and autobiographical accounts of inspiration. Much more recently, D. Hay has indicated the potential benefits of resuming this task in a tantalizing but laconic comment upon Philo's view of himself as exegete. Hay conjectures that there "are many other places [than autobiography] in his works where he talks about inspiration or prophecy, and some of these probably reflect his personal experience without expressly saying so."[28] The resumption of this exploration in greater

---

27. Büchsel, *Geist Gottes*, 90.
28. Hay, "Philo's View of Himself," 47.

detail will prove essential for developing a typology of inspiration by the divine spirit in the treatises of Philo.

Such an exploration must begin, first of all, with Philo's autobiographical accounts, which present three distinct experiences of inspiration: (1) ecstatic inspiration (*Migr.* 34–35); (2) the ascent of the rational mind (*Spec.* 3.1–6); and (3) divine prompting of the rational mind (*Cher.* 27–28; *Somn.* 2.252). To develop a typology of the divine spirit's role in inspiration, this analysis must also cluster related texts around their closest autobiographical counterparts on the basis of shared words, themes, contexts, and purposes.

A. Ecstatic Inspiration (*Migr.* 34–35)

In *Migr.* 34–35, Philo illustrates, from his own experience, the thesis that "the offspring of the soul's own travail are for the most part poor abortions . . . but those which God waters with the snows of heaven come to the birth perfect, complete and peerless" (33). He recounts what has happened to him a thousand times:

> On some occasions, after making up my mind to follow the usual course of writing on philosophical tenets, and knowing definitely the substance of what I was to set down, I have found my understanding incapable of giving birth to a single idea, and have given it up without accomplishing anything, reviling my understanding for its self-conceit. (*Migr.* 34)

This is not the totality of Philo's experience, for, as he explains further,

> On other occasions, I have approached my work empty and suddenly become full, the ideas falling in a shower from above and being sown invisibly, so that under the influence of the Divine possession I have been filled with corybantic frenzy and been unconscious of anything, place, persons present, myself, words spoken, lines written. For I obtained language, ideas, an enjoyment of light, keenest vision, pellucid distinctiveness of objects, such as might be received through the eyes as the result of clearest shewing. (*Migr.* 35)

The affinities between this autobiographical account[29] and Philo's third-person explanations of prophetic ecstasy in *Mos.* 1.273–84; *Her.*

---

29. This experience appears to be authentic, for similar autobiographical descriptions exist in unrelated contexts, suggesting that Philo has learned about his own limitations in the crucible of actual experience. In *Leg.* 2.85–86, Philo discusses the source of insight when he recounts how preparation and isolation do not invariably heighten

264–66; *Spec.* 1.65; 4.49; and *QG* 3.9 are unmistakable. These accounts in general contain the elements of loss of consciousness, suddenness, and light.

The effect of inspiration which unites all of these texts is loss of consciousness, what Philo in *Migr.* 34–35 refers to summarily as corybantic frenzy.[30] Philo similarly identifies ἔκστασις in Gen 15:12 with a loss of consciousness: "So while the radiance of the mind is still all around us . . . we are self-contained, not possessed. But when it comes to its setting, naturally ecstasy and divine possession and madness fall upon us . . . Mortal and immortal may not share the same home. And therefore the setting of reason and the darkness which surrounds it produce ecstasy and inspired frenzy." This identification is even more evident in *QG* 3.9: "For ecstasy, as its very name clearly shows, is nothing else than the departing and going out of the understanding." The prophet has "no power of apprehension when he speaks" (*Spec.* 1.65); "the reason withdraws and surrenders the citadel of the soul" (4.49). Balaam is depicted as "understanding nothing, his reason as it were roaming" (*Mos.* 1.283).

Philo's conviction that this loss of rationality takes place suddenly is expressed by the word ἐξαίφνης in *Migr.* 35, implied by the word ἐξορκίζεται in *Her.* 265, and explicit in an interpretation of Gen 15:12, parallel to *Her.* 264–66, in *QG* 3.9: "For it does not come upon one gently and softly but makes a sudden attack." According to *Spec.* 1.65, the prophet appears suddenly. Balaam, too, was twice inspired suddenly (αὐτίκα in *Mos.* 1.277; ἐξαίφνης in 1.283).

The salient aspect of Philo's experience in *Migr.* 34–35 is "light, keenest vision." Similarly, in *Her.* 264–65, Philo depicts God's presence in prophetic ecstasy as light: "For when the light of God shines, the human light

---

his ability to interpret "some subject demanding contemplation;" on the contrary, amid a crowd, at times, distractions disappear and Philo is moved by God. The lesson, "that a favourable and unfavourable condition are not brought about by differences of place, but by God who moves and leads the car of the soul in whatever way He pleases," resembles the thesis of *Migr.* 33–35. In *Her.* 29–30, Philo confesses, "I have learnt to measure my own nothingness . . . And when I perceive that I am earth and cinders . . . it is just then that I have confidence to come before Thee, when I am humbled, cast down to the clay." This confession corresponds to his experience of "reviling my understanding for its self-conceit" (*Migr.* 34).

30. On the corybantic experience, see Linforth, "Corybantic Rites in Plato." Dionysius of Halicarnassus, Philo's earlier contemporary, proffers a parallel experience in the autobiographical account of his response to Demosthenes's speeches: "But when I pick up one of Demosthenes's speeches, I am transported: I am led hither and thither . . . I feel exactly the same as those who take part in the Corybantic dances . . . whether it is because these celebrants are inspired by the scents, [sights], or sound or by the influence of the deities themselves, that they experience many and various sensations" (*Dem.* 22).

sets; when the divine light sets, the human dawns and rises. This is what regularly befalls the fellowship of the prophets." In *QG* 3.9, Philo contrasts darkness and light. Although the element of light does not feature in *Spec.* 1.65 and 4.49 or *Mos.* 1.277 and 1.283, it remains central nonetheless to Philo's definition of his own and the prophetic experiences in *Migr.* 34–35 and *Her.* 264–66.

The recurrence of these elements—loss of consciousness, suddenness, and light—suggests a relationship between Philo's descriptions of both his experience and the experience of prophets. Moreover, these close connections suggest that the laconic words ὑπὸ κατοχῆς ἐνθέου in *Migr.* 35 are a shorthand reference to the inspiration of the divine spirit. According to Philo's descriptions of prophetic inspiration: "The mind is evicted at the arrival of the divine Spirit, but when that departs the mind returns to its tenancy" (*Her.* 264–66); "the reason withdraws and surrenders the citadel of the soul to a new visitor and tenant, the Divine Spirit" (*Spec.* 4.49); "there fell upon him [Balaam] the truly prophetic spirit" (*Mos.* 1.277). Similarly, recalls Philo, "I have approached my work and suddenly become full ... so that under the influence of the Divine possession [ὑπὸ κατοχῆς ἐνθέου] I have been filled with corybantic frenzy and been unconscious of anything" (*Migr.* 35).

Despite these similarities, subtle differences separate Philo's autobiographical account in *Migr.* 34–35 from his descriptions of prophetic inspiration. Absent from *Migr.* 34–35 is the conception of inspiration as the displacement of reason by the divine spirit or, put another way, the use of Philo's body as the vehicle of the divine spirit. In Philo's experience, the mind is not "evicted at the arrival of the divine Spirit" (*Her.* 265), nor does reason surrender the mind "to a new visitor and tenant" (*Spec.* 4.49). Philo does not become "an interpreter prompted by Another" (4.49) or "a channel for the insistent words of Another's prompting" (1.65). Of himself Philo does not say, as the angel does to Balaam, "I shall prompt the needful words without your mind's consent, and direct your organs of speech ... I shall guide the reins of speech, and, though you understand it not, employ your tongue for each prophetic utterance" (*Mos.* 1.274). Philo does not in *Migr.* 34–35 perceive himself to be a direct channel of God's words, written or oral.

In lieu of this model of inspiration, Philo colors his experience of inspiration, recounted in *Migr.* 34–35, with slightly different hues. First, inspiration is said to descend from above and impart, above all, wisdom. Soon after this autobiographical account, Philo describes "the Divine light, identical with knowledge, which opens wide the soul's eye, and leads it to apprehensions distinct and brilliant" (39). Philo's vision is a vision of divine wisdom, for "Wisdom is God's archetypal luminary and the sun is a copy and image of it" (40). Although Philo's language is more poetic and contains elements analogous to his descriptions of prophecy, *Migr.* 34–35 situates his experience within the Alexandrian wisdom tradition, for it parallels the conception of the descent of the divine spirit to impart wisdom in Wis 9:17: "Who has learned your counsel, unless you have given wisdom and sent your holy spirit from on high?"[31]

De migratione Abrahami 34–35 can be distinguished from Philo's descriptions of prophetic inspiration because of its emphasis upon the written word. At times, recalls Philo, he intends to write and cannot; on other occasions, he is possessed, although he is unconscious, among other things, of "words spoken, lines written [τὰ γραφόμενα]" (*Migr.* 35). This emphasis on literary creation must not be overlooked, for it provides a crucial clue to the particular form of inspiration Philo claims to have experienced. His instances of literary failure, with which he prefaces his recollection of inspiration, are distinctly reminiscent of Socrates's contention about the importance of poetic inspiration:

> But he who without the divine madness comes to the doors of the Muses, confident that he will be a good poet by art, meets with no success, and the poetry of the sane man vanishes into nothingness before that of the inspired madmen. (*Phaedr.* 245A)

Similarly, like the confident poet, Philo has many times come prepared to write but found himself unable to do so without divine inspiration. By means of this allusion, Philo interprets his own experience as an instance of poetic inspiration.[32] Plato's explanation of poetic inspiration in *Ion* 533D–36D provides the basis for understanding Philo's experience, for Plato asserts that "a poet is . . . unable to indite until he has been inspired [ἔνθεος] and put out of his senses, and his mind is no longer in him" (534B):

> And for this reason God takes away the mind of these men and uses them as his ministers, just as he does soothsayers and godly seers, in order that we who hear them may know that it is not they who utter these words of great price, when they are out of their wits, but that it is God himself who speaks and addresses us through them. (534C–D)[33]

31. See also Sir 39:6.
32. On the popularity of Plato during the Hellenistic period, see Hadas, "Plato in Hellenistic Fusion"; Hadas, *Hellenistic Culture*, 72–82.
33. See also Plato, *Apol.* 22C; *Meno* 99C. On Philo's use of Plato in general, the most important recent work is Runia's *Philo of Alexandria*.

Philo's reference to corybantic frenzy to depict his experience also echoes Plato's discussion of poetic inspiration, where Plato twice compares inspiration to corybantic possession: "Just as the Corybantian worshippers do not dance when in their senses, so the lyric poets do not indite those fine songs in their senses, but when ... they begin to be frantic, and it is under possession" (534A). In the second instance, Socrates attributes Ion's interpretation of Homer to divine possession (κατοκωχῇ), "just as the Corybantian worshippers are keenly sensible of that strain alone which belongs to the god whose possession is on them" (536C).

Plato's descriptions of poetic inspiration, although they provide a significant basis of Philo's thought, do not illuminate one element of the process of inspiration: the attribution of inspiration to an external impetus, such as the divine spirit. Nor can Philo's biblical source explain this element adequately. There is, of course, biblical precedent for attributing prophetic ecstasy to the divine spirit. J. Lindblom has demonstrated that the Bible affords glimpses of ecstatic forms of prophecy from throughout Israel's history.[34] In the eighth century BCE, Hosea criticizes Israel for saying, "The prophet is a fool, the man of the spirit is mad!" (9:7), while Micah contrasts the inability of false prophets, seers, and diviners with his own being filled with "the spirit of the LORD" (3:5-8). Later still, Deutero-Isaiah commands a hearing because "the LORD God has sent me and his spirit" (48:16), while Ezekiel claims that "the spirit lifted me up" (3:12, 14) in a vision and that "the spirit of the LORD fell upon me" (11:5). In texts such as these, the exact elements of ecstatic prophecy are left unclear, and the presence of ecstasy is rarely explicit.

For the level of detail that Philo reveals, he is indebted to his Greco-Roman milieu. Once again, as in the case of Balaam in *Mos.* 1.273-84, the writings of Plutarch illuminate the writings of Philo.[35] In particular, when Plutarch interprets Plato's four kinds of madness (μανία), he describes a second sort of madness, which he calls "enthusiasm" (ἐνθουσιαστικόν). Plutarch's discussion contains the element of an external afflatus that displaces reason:

> There is a second kind [of ecstasy], however, which does not exist without divine inspiration. It is not intrinsically generated but is, rather, an extrinsic afflatus that displaces the

---

34. Lindblom, *Prophecy in Ancient Israel*, 65-82, 122-37, 173-82.

35. It is difficult to assess Plutarch's popularity during the first century CE. L. H. Feldman observes, "The fact that not a single papyrus fragment has ever been found of any of his numerous works would indicate that he was not very popular, at least in Egypt, in the Roman period" (personal letter, Oct. 5, 1992). See Feldman, "Pro-Jewish Intimations," 231.

faculty of rational inference; it is created and set in motion by a higher power. This sort of madness bears the general name of "enthusiasm."[36]

Philo, in *Her.* 249–65, like Plutarch, bases his discussion upon Plato's four forms of madness. In *Her.* 265, he explains how the mind is evicted at the arrival of the divine spirit, with the result that ecstasy transpires. Both Philo and Plutarch, then, base their views of inspiration, at least in part, upon Plato, and both adhere to the conception of an external inspiring power.

The importance of Plutarch's discussion extends beyond this general illumination of Philo's perspective on inspiration because it permits us to glimpse both the similarities that unite and the distinctions that separate Philo's views on his own and prophetic inspiration. Under this second form of inspiration, Plutarch distinguishes between four sorts of enthusiasm: the prophetic, the bacchic, the poetic, and the military. Each is related to the other because all four are forms of enthusiasm. According to Plutarch, "The prophetic comes from the inspiration and possession of Apollo," while the "third kind comes from the Muses. It takes a pure and virgin soul,[37] strikes a spark in it and fans it into a blaze of poetic and musical creation."

Philo's and Plutarch's perspectives are rooted in Plato's descriptions of inspiration, for Plato too drew a close relationship between the inspiration of poets and prophets. Philo's description of the prophet whose "mind is evicted" and upon whom falls "ecstasy and divine possession and madness" (*Her.* 264–65) echoes Plato's description of the inspired poet as "put out of his senses," with "his mind no longer in him" (*Ion* 534B). Moreover, Plato himself drew a parallel between the inspiration of poets and seers: "And for this reason God takes away the mind of these [poets] . . . just as he does soothsayers and godly seers" (534C–D).

How then may we describe the relationship between Philo's autobiographical account of inspiration in *Migr.* 34–35 and his third-person accounts of prophetic inspiration in *Her.* 264–65, *Spec.* 1.65, 4.49, and *Mos.* 1.274–83? They represent, on the one hand, similar experiences of inspiration, according to which inspiration takes place suddenly by the presence of the divine spirit. There is a strong underlying unity between Philo's experience and that of ecstatic prophets. The shared perspectives of Plutarch and Philo on inspiration, both poetic and prophetic, suggest that Philo has shaped the experiences of inspiration along the lines of Greco-Roman perspectives rooted in Plato—with the significant difference that the external divine afflatus is the divine spirit of the Bible.

36. Plutarch, *Amat.* 16 (II.758E).
37. An allusion to Plato, *Phaedr.* 245A.

On the other hand, Philo's autobiographical and third-person accounts of ecstatic inspiration differ. In *Migr.* 34–35, with echoes of Plato's views of poetic inspiration, Philo describes his inspired ability to write. When he turns to describe prophecy, he has recourse to popular Greco-Roman views of oracular prophecy, such as Cleombrotus's explanation of Delphic inspiration in *De defectu oraculorum*. Therefore, while Philo recognizes the underlying unity between his own experience and that of the prophets, he shapes them differently in his accounts. His is the ecstasy of the inspired poet, theirs of oracular prophets.

B. Rational Ascent (*Spec.* 3.1–6)

The autobiographical reflections Philo proffers in *Spec.* 3.1-6 differ markedly from *Migr.* 34–35. In *Migr.* 34–35, Philo is stationary, and inspiration descends upon him like a snow shower. In *Spec.* 3.1-6, Philo either ascends or descends, depending upon his own disposition. He recounts: an upward ascent, in which he travels around with the sun, moon, and other heavenly bodies; a downward plunge into civil cares; and another ascent, in which he rides on the waves of the lower air.

Philo does not attribute this ascent to the divine spirit in *Spec.* 3.1-6; he refers rather to divine possession with the word ἐπιθειασμόν. Several other closely related passages in Philo's treatises indicate that this word is intended to suggest the presence of the divine spirit in Philo's experience. These texts coalesce around the two central foci of *Spec.* 3.1-6: (1) the ascent of the mind that is separated from earthly cares; (2) the correspondence that Philo draws between the ascent of the mind and allegorical interpretation.

1. The Ascent of the Mind and Earthly Cares

The first words in *Spec.* 3.1-6, "There was a time when I had leisure for philosophy," provide the context of inspiration. Philo intends to recount his experiences of inspiration as a philosopher. He garnishes this self-portrait by peppering it with allusions to Plato's description of philosophical inspiration. Philo's definition of philosophy as "the contemplation of the universe and its contents" and his subsequent description of becoming a "fellow-traveller with the sun and moon and the whole heaven and universe" recall the words of Pindar cited in Plato's *Theaet.* 173C-74A, which Socrates quotes:

> His mind . . . is borne in all directions, as Pindar says, "both below the earth," and measuring the surface of the earth, and

"above the sky," studying the stars, and investigating the universal nature of every thing that is, each in its entirety, never lowering itself to anything close at hand.[38]

Philo establishes the philosophical nature of the ascent of his mind with several allusions to Plato's well-known description of the ascent of the soul in *Phaedr.* 246A–53C. The opening reference to philosophy (φιλοσοφίᾳ) comprises an initial allusion to Socrates's contention that "it is just that the mind of the philosopher only has wings" (249C). The direction of the ascent in *Spec.* 3.1 (ἄνω . . . φέρεσθαι), the circling of the mind (συμπεριπολεῖν) to describe his experience as a fellow traveller with heavenly bodies (3.1), and the reference to wings (ὑπόπερος in 3.5) sharpen the allusions to Plato's *Phaedrus*, in which the soul "traverses [περιπολεῖ] the whole heaven" (246B) and "is carried round [συμπεριηνέχθη] in the revolution" (248A). Even the puzzling introduction of envy (φθόνος in *Spec.* 3.3) as the enemy of ascent which plunges one into civil cares echoes the vision of the heavenly world in *Phaedr.* 247A, where "jealousy [φθόνος] is excluded from the celestial band."[39] These allusions to Plato's *Phaedrus* underscore the impression that Philo's own ascent is that of the philosopher.[40]

The philosophical context of inspiration that characterizes *Spec.* 3.1–6 appears also in *Plant.* 18–26, which constitutes Philo's commentary on Lev 1:1,[41] where Philo writes, "Above all is it strange if this [ascent] is not so with the mind of the genuine philosopher" (24). Like *Spec.* 3.1–6, this text also contains a significant number of allusions to Plato's *Phaedrus*.[42] Philo writes

---

38. On this allusion, see Méasson, *Char ailé de Zeus*, 231. Socrates's attempt in this dialogue to contrast the philosopher, whose mind considers life in the city "petty and of no account," with the lawyer, who is enslaved to civil cares, finds its counterpart in the concern of Philo, which permeates *Spec.* 3.1–6, to disentangle himself from "the ocean of civil cares" and "civil turmoils."

39. See also Plato, *Tim.* 29E, and the discussion of Méasson, *Char ailé de Zeus*, 234.

40. See also 248D, according to which "the soul that has seen the most [of the heavenly region] shall enter into the birth of a man who is to be a philosopher or lover of beauty, or one of a musical or loving nature"; 249A: "For each soul returns to the place whence it came in ten thousand years . . . except the soul of him who has been a guileless philosopher or a philosophical lover; these, when for three successive periods of a thousand years . . . become winged in the three thousandth year." On Philo's allusions to *Phaedrus* in *Spec.* 3.1–6, see Méasson, *Char ailé de Zeus*, 231–41.

41. This passage contains four elements that suggest a connection to *Spec.* 3.1–6. First, it describes the ascent of the mind (*Plant.* 22; *Spec.* 3.1–2). Second, the mind is that of the philosopher (*Plant.* 24–25; *Spec.* 3.1–2). Third, the goal of the ascent is wisdom and knowledge (*Plant.* 23; *Spec.* 3.3). Fourth, the vehicles of sight are the eyes of the soul (*Plant.* 22; *Spec.* 3.5–6).

42. Philo, *Plant.* 17, contains as well an unmistakable allusion to Plato, *Tim.* 90A, according to which the soul is "not an earthly but a heavenly plant."

that "The strong yearning to perceive the Existent One gives them [the eyes of the soul] wings" (*Plant.* 22). The integral association that Philo draws between yearning and wings is reminiscent of *Phaedr.* 251B–C. Moreover, Socrates contends that beauty comes through the eyes, bringing with it a yearning that causes the hardened parts, which will eventually become wings, to be moistened and warmed and to fill the soul with joy. Philo in shorthand recalls this description by contending that "strong yearning" gives the "eyes" of the soul "wings." The end result, as in *Spec.* 3.1–6, echoes *Phaedr.* 247B–C: the winged soul passes beyond the heavenly region.

This passage is significant because in it Philo departs from Plato by explicitly attributing the ascent of the philosopher's mind to the divine spirit:[43] "It is strange if a light substance like the mind is not rendered buoyant and raised to the utmost height by the native force of the Divine spirit, overcoming as it does in its boundless might all powers that are here below" (24). In *Plant.* 18–26, Philo establishes the affinity of the mind with the divine logos. In particular, the divine spirit causes the mind of the philosopher to ascend:

> Above all is it strange if this is not so with the mind of the genuine philosopher. Such an one suffers from no weight of downward pressure towards the objects dear to the body and to earth. From these he has ever made an earnest effort to sever and estrange himself. So he is borne upward insatiably enamoured of all holy happy natures that dwell on high. (24–25)

This description of the mind's ascent, following immediately upon the reference to the divine spirit, is similar to *Spec.* 3.1, where Philo describes his former life as a philosopher: "I had no base or abject thoughts nor grovelled in search of reputation or of wealth or bodily comforts, but seemed always to be borne aloft into the heights with a soul possessed by some God-sent inspiration." The significance of this correspondence between Philo's description of the philosopher and his self-portrait as a philosopher is that it permits us to define more accurately the otherwise inchoate word ἐπιθειασμόν in *Spec.* 3.1. Based upon this correspondence between *Plant.* 24–25 and *Spec.* 3.1, ἐπιθειασμόν should be understood as a shorthand reference to the divine spirit as that which lifts the mind of Philo, the philosopher, into the heavenly world.

Another text in which Philo attributes the ascent of the mind to the divine spirit is *Gig.* 29–31, part of Philo's lengthy commentary on Gen 6:3 (*Gig.* 19–57), where he focusses upon the words "because they are flesh" to explain why the divine spirit does not abide permanently with people.

---

43. Other passages describe the ascent of the mind without reference to the spirit, e.g., Philo, *Opif.* 69–71; *Mut.* 179–80; *Praem.* 26, 121–22; *Conf.* 95–97.

He asserts that those who sever their ties with the flesh and persist in their quest for wisdom can ascend:

> For souls that are free from flesh and body spend their days in the theatre of the universe and with a joy that none can hinder see and hear things divine, which they have desired with love insatiable. (*Gig.* 31)

This experience mirrors Philo's in *Spec.* 3.1–2 and the philosopher's in *Plant.* 24–26. In all three, the mind is lifted to the heavens by means of the divine spirit, which, according to *Gig.* 31, must abide in order for the mind to ascend. These minds, like Philo's, are inspired and traverse the upper air; the divine spirit raises them to the utmost heights (*Plant.* 24) and abides with them so that they spend their days in the theater of the universe (*Gig.* 29–31).

This description of the ascent of the mind is one side of a coin. On the other side is the reality that human cares and concerns impede the ascent of the mind. The introduction to *De legatione ad Gaium* suggests that Philo feels personally the tension between earthly cares and the heavenly ascent.[44] It is this tension that provides the rationale for the presence of the divine spirit in the ascent of the mind: without the divine spirit, the mind is drawn down into the realm of earthly cares. This side of the coin surfaces in *Spec.* 3.1–6; *Plant.* 18–26; and *Gig.* 29–31.

In his autobiographical account of philosophical inspiration, Philo leaves no doubt that possession by the divine spirit takes place only for the person who is prepared. Philo's ascent occurs when he is in the company of divine truths and when he has no base ambitions. Only then does possession (ἐπιθειασμόν) overtake him and cause him to be borne aloft into the heights (*Spec.* 3.1–2). Likewise, envy causes Philo to descend, plunging him "in the ocean of civil cares, in which I am swept away, unable even to raise my head above the water" (3.3). When he is subsequently lifted again by the invitation of knowledge through the medium of culture, his soul's eyes see only "dimly indeed because of the mist of extraneous affairs" (3.4). When he does obtain "a calm from civil turmoils," his ride on the winds of knowledge is the exception rather than the rule of his life, and he is "a truant as it were from merciless masters in the shape not only of men but of affairs" (3.5).

Such a tension explains also why, according to *Plant.* 18–26, the mind, despite its affinity with the logos, cannot naturally ascend. The "powers that are here below" and the "weight of downward pressure towards the objects dear to the body and to earth" impede its ascent (24, 25). The forceful power of the divine spirit, like a tornado, is necessary to overcome "in its boundless

---

44. See also his portrait of the sage in *Somn.* 2.225–34, as well as *Migr.* 191; *Fug.* 23–47.

might all powers that are here below" (24).⁴⁵ With this description of the spirit, Philo returns to his preoccupation with the tension between worldly cares and the ascent of the mind. Just as in his own experience, culture and knowledge must woo him upwards, so in general the divine spirit is necessary to lift even the lightest of substances, the human mind.

Such a tension surfaces as well in *Gig.* 29–31, where Philo explains that the divine spirit cannot abide permanently because "they [humans] are flesh" (Gen 6:3). Essentially he means here what he says also in *Spec.* 3.1–6 and *Plant.* 18–26, when he writes in *Gig.* 29 that "marriage, and the rearing of children, and provision of necessities, and disrepute following in the wake of poverty, and the business of private and public life, and a multitude of other things wither the flower of wisdom before it blooms."⁴⁶

In conclusion, Philo's attribution of the mind's ascent to the divine spirit, explicitly in *Plant.* 24 and *Gig.* 31, and implicitly in *Spec.* 3.1, has significant implications for his understanding of inspiration. First, despite the mind's affinity with the logos, external aid is necessary for the ascent of the mind; it does not occur naturally. The divine spirit is necessary to conquer the enemy of divine ascent, earthly cares. Philo describes these variously as extraneous affairs and civil turmoils (*Spec.* 3.4–5), powers that are here below and objects dear to the body and the earth (*Plant.* 24–25), and obligations such as earning a living, marriage, the raising of children, poverty, private and public life (*Gig.* 29).

Second, human preparation and inspiration are not mutually exclusive. According to *Plant.* 23–25, philosophers first must sever themselves from earthly cares. They must "crave for wisdom and knowledge with insatiable persistence" to be called upwards. The divine spirit overcomes earthly cares in conjunction with the philosopher's having severed ties with earthly cares. In *Gig.* 30, Philo asserts that wisdom is thwarted by ignorance and lack of learning, implying the need for knowledge and education. Similarly, according to *Spec.* 3.1–6, Philo recalls that inspiration overtook him when his constant companions were divine words and truths, when he had no interest in status or wealth or bodily comforts. This observation is important in part because it differs so markedly from *Migr.* 34–35, where Philo receives inspiration despite all preparation.

---

45. Philo employs a forceful verb and noun, νικάω and δυνατός, to emphasize the powerful function of the divine spirit.

46. Another specific parallel occurs between the role of culture and learning in *Spec.* 3.4 ("planted in my soul from my earliest days I keep the yearning for culture which ever has pity and compassion for me") and in *Gig.* 30 ("our fleshly nature ... For on it ignorance and scorn of learning rest").

Third, despite numerous allusions to Plato, Philo is not satisfied by the Platonic conception of inspiration. His own view of inspiration requires the presence of the divine spirit. The sources, then, of Philo's view of inspiration are twofold; Philo has combined a Platonic conception—the ascent of the mind—with a Jewish one—the divine spirit.[47] The close relationship between his third-person descriptions in *Plant.* 18–26 and *Gig.* 29–31 and his autobiographical account in *Spec.* 3.1–6 indicates that he combines them because he has experienced the ascent of his mind as an inspiration whose source is the divine spirit.

2. The Ascent of the Mind and Allegorical Interpretation

In his autobiographical account of philosophical inspiration, Philo draws a significant correspondence between the ascent of his mind and his ability to interpret Torah. He accomplishes this primarily by the way he structures the passage, which begins with the heavenly ascent and sojourn (3.1–2), is interrupted by a plunge into the ocean of civil cares (3.3–4), and concludes with an ascent on the winds of knowledge, which leads to Philo's concluding words: "So behold me daring, not only to read the sacred pages of Moses, but also in my love of knowledge to peer into each of them and unfold and reveal what is not known to the multitude" (3.5–6). Within this structure, the initial ascent to contemplate the upper air corresponds to the final ascent to interpret the Bible. Philo reinforces this correlation by employing the same verb, διακύπτειν, to describe the experiences of ascent and interpretation. The words "Ah then I gazed down [διακύπτων] from the upper air" (3.2) correspond to "Behold me daring . . . to peer into [διακύπτειν] each of them [the sacred messages of Moses] and unfold . . ."

This correspondence is extremely important for Philo's self-identity if we recall that Plato, in *Phaedr.* 249E, to which Philo alludes, regards the philosophical form of inspiration as "the best and of the highest origin to him who has it or who shares in it." The correlation between ascent and interpretation, then, reveals that Philo places his role as interpreter on a

---

47. The closest biblical antecedent to the ascent of the mind is the frequent elevation of Ezekiel by the spirit (e.g., 3:12, 14). The purpose of Ezekiel's elevations, however, is substantially different from the elevation of Philo's mind. The purpose of Ezekiel's visions is conveniently to transport Ezekiel horizontally between Babylon and Judea. In contrast, Philo's mind, and the mind alone apart from the flesh, is drawn heavenward. Indeed, Ezekiel's experiences are depicted vividly as physical transport, even though they are not; he is taken in toto "by a lock of my head . . . between earth and heaven . . . to Jerusalem" (8:3; see 12:24). The parallels between the experiences of Philo and Ezekiel are, to say the least, attenuated.

plateau parallel to his experience as a philosopher whose mind ascends to the upper regions of the cosmos. Two other passages, one from the commentary on Gen 6:3 and the other from the commentary on the Decalogue, illuminate the divine spirit's role in this correlation between ascent and interpretation.

Toward the end of his commentary on Gen 6:3, in *Gig.* 53–54, Philo discusses Moses's ascent. The focus is Moses, who "pitched his tent outside the camp and the whole array of bodily things... and entering the darkness, the invisible region, abides there while he learns the secrets of the most holy mysteries." This description of Moses's ascent is strikingly similar in three respects to Philo's autobiographical description of his role as allegorical interpreter in *Spec.* 3.5–6. First, the objects of contemplation are both "holy." Moses is initiated into τὰς ἱερωτάτας τελετάς, and Philo peers into τοῖς ἱεροῖς Μωυσέως. Second, Philo contrasts the one and the many. Just as the spirit abides in Moses and not ἐν . . . τοῖς πολλοῖς, so also what Philo learns is not γνώριμα τοῖς πολλοῖς. Third, Moses and Philo are leaders of a band of initiates. Moses is the hierophant,[48] "the teacher of the divine rites, which he will impart to those whose ears are purified." The conclusion of *Spec.* 3.6, in which Philo's role is to "unfold and reveal what is not known to the multitude," implies the presence of a group of people whom Philo teaches, which can be distinguished from the many.[49]

The relationship of *Gig.* 53–54 to *Spec.* 3.1–6 and *Plant.* 18–26 is apparent also in the allusions to Plato's *Phaedrus* that it exhibits, the first two of which are characteristic also of *Spec.* 3.5–6. First, Philo's description of the divine mysteries in *Gig.* 54, τελούμενος τὰς ἱερωτάτας τελετάς, is particularly reminiscent of *Phaedr.* 249C, τελέους ἀεὶ τελετὰς τελούμενος, even more so than his reference to τοῖς ἱεροῖς Μωυσέως in *Spec.* 3.5–6. Second, the experiences of Plato's philosopher and Philo's Moses, and Philo himself in *Spec.* 3.5–6, are contrasted with "the many." The philosopher is misunderstood

---

48. On Moses as hierophant, see Meeks, *Prophet-King*, 120–22.

49. This correlation between Philo as interpreter and Moses as hierophant is evident also in *Cher.* 48, which makes explicit what is implicit in *Spec.* 3.6. Philo directly addresses the initiates, that is, those who have listened to Philo's allegorical interpretation of the writings of Moses (*Cher.* 43–47), under whom Philo was initiated (*Cher.* 49): "These thoughts, ye initiated, whose ears are purified, receive into your souls as holy mysteries indeed and babble not of them to any of the profane. Rather as stewards guard the treasure in your keeping... But, if ye meet with anyone of the initiated, press him closely, cling to him, lest knowing of some still newer secret he hide it from you; stay not till you have learnt its full lesson." The words ἱερὰ . . . μυστήρια correspond to τὰς ἱερωτάτας τελετάς in *Gig.* 54 and to τοῖς ἱεροῖς μυωσέως in *Spec.* 3.6, while reference to the initiates as those with "purified ears" is made in both *Gig.* 54 and *Cher.* 48. Therefore, the distinction between one and "many" uninitiated/profane, which is implicit in *Spec.* 3.6, is explicit in *Cher.* 48 and *Gig.* 54.

by "the many"(τῶν πολλῶν) who do not know that he is inspired (*Phaedr.* 249D). For Philo, the experience of "the many" is the opposite of Moses's: "Thus it is that in the many [τοῖς πολλοῖς], those, that is, who have set before them many ends in life, the divine spirit does not abide, even though it sojourn there for a while." The third echo of *Phaedr.* 249C is of Socrates's explanation that the many rebuke the philosopher because he separates from human interests and turns instead toward the divine. Philo, in an allegorical interpretation of Exod 18:14, portrays Jethro as scolding Moses for finding tranquility amid the storms of life:

> Worldly-wise vanity called Jethro, struck with amazement before the wise man's rule of life, which never swerves from its absolute consistency, never changes its tenor or its character, begins to scold and ply him with questions thus. "Why dost thou sit alone?" For indeed one who sees the perpetual war-in-peace of men . . . can well wonder that another should find fair weather in the storm, or calm amid the surges of the tempestuous sea. (*Gig.* 50–51)

Jethro here represents the many who are wrapped in earthly concerns; like the many of Plato's *Phaedrus*, he scolds the person whose mind is absorbed in a higher realm.

These numerous points of contact and allusions to the *Phaedrus* myth in Philo's autobiographical reflection (*Spec.* 3.1–6) and his allegorical interpretations of Lev 1:1 (*Plant.* 18–26) and Exod 33:7 (*Gig.* 54) forcefully suggest the presence of a consistent model of inspiration, in which the divine spirit is the source of the ascent of the philosophical mind. Moreover, the correlation between Moses's ascent and Philo's ability to interpret is significant in three respects. First, it provides clues, few of which Philo gives us, about the status he accords to his ability to interpret Torah allegorically: it is a function parallel to Moses's reception of the divine laws. Second, the importance of this function demands the inspiration of the divine spirit. Philo concludes Moses's ascent in *Gig.* 53–54 with the generalization about Moses that "he then has ever the divine spirit at his side" (55). Philo does not say this of himself in *Spec.* 3.5–6, but the parallel portrayals of Moses's and his own roles as interpreter imply that Philo too must possess the divine spirit whenever he interprets Torah. Third, this implication dovetails with *Spec.* 3.1–6, according to which the ascent of Philo's mind under the possession of the divine spirit (3.1–2) corresponds to Philo's ability to interpret Torah allegorically (3.5–6). By paralleling his interpretative abilities (*Spec.* 3.5–6) with Moses's ascent by the divine spirit (*Gig.* 53–54) and the ascent of his own mind by the divine spirit (3.1-2), Philo implies forcefully that the divine spirit must be active in the process of allegorical interpretation.

A similar collocation of references to the divine spirit, the ascent of the mind, and interpretation characterizes *Decal.* 175.[50] In this paragraph, Philo distinguishes the Decalogue, which God delivers in God's own person without Moses, from the particular laws, which God delivers "by the mouth of the most perfect of the prophets whom He selected for his merits and having filled him with the divine spirit, chose him to be the interpreter of His sacred utterances."[51]

De decalogo 175 contains two elements in common with *Gig.* 53-54 and *Spec.* 3.1-6, interpretation and the divine spirit, with the third element, the ascent of Moses, readily supplied from the biblical text.[52] That Philo would interpret Moses's ascent allegorically as the ascent of the mind is evident in *Gig.* 53-54 and other passages in which he allegorizes Moses's ascent.[53] Therefore, on the basis of explicit references to the divine spirit and interpretation and an implicit reference to Moses's ascent, what Philo assumes but does not say can be inferred: the divine spirit inspired Moses to obtain the particular laws by means of Moses's ascent—literally up the mountain and allegorically as the ascent of the mind.

In *Decal.* 175, *Gig.* 53-54, and *Spec.* 3.1-6, then, Philo draws a correspondence between interpretation and the ascent of the mind and traces both to the inspiration of the spirit. Within *Spec.* 3.1-6, Philo parallels his own ascent under divine possession by the spirit (3.1-2) with his ability

---

50. Philo, *Decal.* 175, contains three elements with which it is related to *Spec.* 3.1-6. First, the contexts of both *Spec.* 3.1-6 and *Decal.* 175 are discussions of the Decalogue. *Spec.* 3.1-6 occurs at the juncture between the first and second halves of the Decalogue, and *Decal.* 175 occurs after the discussion of the Decalogue is complete. Second, the topic of both passages is the so-called particular laws rather than the Decalogue. And third, both deal specifically with interpretation.

51. On this distinction, see also Philo, *Praem.* 2: "The legislative part has two divisions, one in which the subject matter is more general, the other consisting of the ordinances of specific laws. On the one hand there are the ten heads or summaries which we are told were not delivered through a spokesman but were shaped high above in the air into the form of articulate speech: on the other the specific ordinances of the oracles given through the lips of a prophet." Also Philo, *Decal.* 18-19: "that some of them God judged fit to deliver in His own person alone without employing any other, and some through His prophet Moses whom He chose as of all men the best suited to be the revealer of verities. Now we find that those which He gave in His own person and by His own mouth alone include both laws and heads summarizing the particular laws, but those in which He spoke through the prophet all belong to the former class." Philo distinguishes them with the categories of genus and species in *Spec.* 4.132; see also 2.189. On the divine voice, see Wolfson, *Philo*, 2:33-42; Winston, "Two Types."

52. E.g., Exod 19:20; 20:21; 24:1-2, 13-18; 32:1—34:35.

53. E.g., Philo, *QE* 2.29, 43, 44; *Post.* 13-16.

to interpret Torah allegorically (3.5–6). In *Gig.* 53–54, the description of Moses's ascent, which takes place because the spirit abides in him, parallels the description of Philo's allegorical interpretation of Torah in *Spec.* 3.5–6. In *Decal.* 175, Moses's role as interpreter, which, according to Torah, takes place by means of ascent, is possible because Moses is filled with the divine spirit.

The coalescence of references to the divine spirit, ascent, and interpretation is especially significant, for it demonstrates the importance of autobiography for understanding Philo's view of inspiration. The correspondence between the ascent of the mind and allegorical interpretation appears to be original to Philo. The autobiographical focus of *Spec.* 3.1–6 suggests that the genesis of this correspondence lies not so much in an external source as in Philo's own experience of inspiration. The recurrence of this viewpoint mutatis mutandis in *Gig.* 53–54 and *Decal.* 175 suggests as well that Philo has allowed his own experience to shape his third-person portrait of the inspiration of Moses as interpreter.

These three are not the only texts that relate inspiration to interpretation. Philo draws a similar correspondence in his autobiographical accounts of inspiration in *Cher.* 27–29 and *Somn.* 2.252, to which we now may turn.

C. Divine Prompting and the Rational Mind (*Cher.* 27–29 and *Somn.* 2.252)

In *Cher.* 27–29, Philo introduces a "higher word," viz. the allegorical meaning of the two Cherubim, with an autobiographical explanation: "But there is a higher thought than these. It comes from a voice in my own soul, which oftentimes is god-possessed and divines where it does not know. This thought I will record in words if I can. The voice told me." In *Somn.* 2.252, Philo interrupts his praise of the vision-seeking mind in order to speak autobiographically: "I hear once more the voice of the invisible spirit, the familiar secret tenant, saying, 'Friend.'"

An impressive array of parallels between *Cher.* 21–29 and *Somn.* 2.252 suggest that Philo is describing two closely related experiences of inspiration. First, both accounts contain similar formal features: (1) an introduction that identifies the source (soul; spirit) and means (prompting; divining) of inspiration; (2) a description of the content of teaching; (3) a concluding self-directed exhortation ("Receive the image unalloyed" and "Let it then be"). Second, both passages provide a solution to an exegetical conundrum (the Cherubim; two different names given for Jerusalem). Third, the content of the teaching that solves both conundrums is the two potencies of God. Fourth, the solution comes from within (the soul; the vision-seeking mind). Fifth, both introduce teaching of something otherwise unknown by Philo with the same verb, ἀναδιδάσκειν. These similarities of form, purpose, content, and language indicate that Philo is describing a similar experience in two different passages.

Two preliminary questions about this experience require answers. First, is the spirit in *Somn.* 2.252 the divine or the human spirit? Second, is the experience in *Cher.* 27–29 ecstatic or rational?

First, although Philo normally distinguishes the divine spirit by the adjective θεῖον, he does not do so here, when he writes, "I hear once more the voice of the invisible spirit, the familiar secret tenant, saying..."[54] He may not, then, have the divine spirit in mind. However, two observations suggest a reference to the divine spirit. First, Philo employs the word πνεῦμα to refer to the nature or essence of the rational part of the soul, or the mind (νοῦς), but he does not identify the mind itself as πνεῦμα.[55] Therefore, it would be unusual for Philo in *Somn.* 2.252 to refer to the "human spirit" because he refers to the human component usually as the human mind or rational soul. He would more typically write that the human soul prompts from within.[56]

Moreover, although prompting does, according to Philo, occasionally arise from within a person without divine aid,[57] far more often the source is divine. For example, four times God is said to prompt Balaam to prophesy (*Migr.* 114; *Her.* 259; *Mos.* 1.274, 281). In *Praem.* 55, the prophet is prompted inwardly by God. God prompts the interpreter of dreams (*Somn.* 1.164). Joseph, after giving the basic interpretation of Pharaoh's dream, hears "promptings of the divine voice," which bring advice about how to deal with the upcoming famine (*Ios.* 110). The brilliance of the mind is described, not as the result of its own prompting, but the prompting of another: "as though dictated by an inward prompter" (*Praem.* 50). God even prompts, not only prophetic utterances, but also good decisions (*Legat.* 245).

For two reasons, then, it seems that Philo in *Somn.* 2.252 refers to the divine spirit. First, if he intended human prompting, he would probably refer to the soul or the mind. Second, Philo may regard the customary adjective θεῖον as superfluous because the notion of prompting, particularly in a context about inspiration, presupposes the presence of an external source.

54. Greek ὑπηχεῖ δέ μοι πάλιν τὸ εἰωθὸς ἀφανῶς ἐνομιλεῖν πνεῦμα ἀόρατον καί φησιν.

55. E.g., in *Spec.* 4.123, Philo contends that "the essence or substance of that other [intelligent and rational] soul is divine spirit."

56. In Philo, *Abr.* 73, the mind prompts the senses.

57. E.g., in *Prob.* 123, Philo explains, without recourse to a divine source, that Diogenes's reply was prompted or echoed from within.

The second preliminary question concerns whether Philo's experience in *Cher.* 27–29 is ecstatic or rational.[58] On first reading, the verbs μαντεύεσθαι and θεοληπτεῖσθαι conjure the image of an ecstatic experience, when Philo writes, "But there is a higher thought than these. It comes from a voice in my own soul, which oftentimes is god-possessed and divines where it does not know" (*Cher.* 27). On closer scrutiny, however, neither verb can bear the weight of this interpretation.

The phrase περὶ ὧν οὐκ οἶδε μαντεύεσθαι is too general to define Philo's experience as either ecstatic or rational, for elsewhere Philo uses similar language to describe Moses's prophetic gift *in general*, a gift that encompasses both the guidance of Moses's mind and his prophetic utterances. In *Mos.* 2.187, Philo discusses Moses's prophetic gift:

> He must have kingship, the faculty of legislation, priesthood and prophecy, so that in his capacity of legislator he may command what should be done and forbid what should not be done, as priest dispose not only things human but things divine, *as prophet declare by inspiration what cannot be apprehended by reason.*[59]

In the ensuing statements, Moses's gift of prophecy encompasses his interpretation of the laws which takes place through the guidance of his mind rather than ecstasy: "Of the divine utterances, some are spoken by God in His own Person with His prophet for interpreter" (*Mos.* 2.188). That prophecy extends beyond ecstasy becomes evident when Philo distinguishes Moses's role as prophet *in general* from a particular form of prophecy "in the strict sense" (2.191), which ought to be construed as ecstatic prophecy. Thus, Moses the prophet functions as an interpreter, both through the ascent of his mind and through prophecy in the strict sense under divine possession.[60]

Two other Philonic texts suggest that Philo's experience in *Cher.* 27–29 is rational rather than ecstatic. First, in *Aet.* 76–77, Philo employs the cognate adjective of θεοληπτεῖσθαι to depict an experience defined by rational

---

58. For a defense of the view that *Cher.* 27–28 presupposes an ecstatic experience, see Wan, "Charismatic Exegesis," 63–71.

59. Emphasis added. Greek διὰ δὲ τῆς προφητείας ὅσα μὴ λογισμῷ καταλαμβάνεται θεσπίζῃ.

60. Similarly, in *Mos.* 2.6, Philo introduces prophecy as the fourth gift of Moses, in addition to his roles as king, lawgiver, and high priest: "Moses necessarily obtained prophecy also, in order that through the providence of God he might discover what by reasoning he could not grasp. For prophecy finds its way to what the mind fails to reach." Moses's prophetic gift is a general category that cannot be limited to ecstatic prophecy.

judgment. Two Stoics, Boethus of Sidon and Panaetius, observes Philo, "did under divine inspiration [ἅτε θεόληπτοι] abandon the conflagrations and regenerations and deserted to the more religious doctrine that the whole world was indestructible" (*Aet.* 76). This discussion is introduced with reference to rational judgment; Boethus and Panaetius are illustrations of the thesis that "some conquered by truth and the arguments of their opponents have changed their views" (*Aet.* 76). Philo supplements the examples of Boethus and Panaetius with that of Diogenes, who later in life began to suspend judgment about the Stoic doctrine of conflagration, not through unreliable sense perception, "but by mind when absolutely pure and unalloyed" (*Aet.* 77). Rather than implying ecstasy and loss of reason, then, the verb θεοληπτεῖσθαι denotes the activation of the reasoning process.

The second Philonic text that tips the balance in favor of a rational experience is Philo's autobiographical account in *Fug.* 53–58. Like its counterparts, *Somn.* 2.252 and *Cher.* 27–29, this experience arises from the conundrum of an apparent biblical redundancy that requires explanation. In this instance, Philo listens to the voice of another: "So I attended the lectures of a wise woman, whose name is 'Consideration,' and was rid of my questioning" (*Fug.* 55). The experience is clearly a rational exegetical process, for Consideration, notes Philo, "confirmed what she said [about Exod. 21:12–14] by holy oracles," including Deut. 4:4; 30:15, 20.[61]

De somniis 2.252, *Cher.* 27–29, and *Fug.* 53–58, taken together, contain other details that point to a rational experience of inspiration. First, Philo's experience is preeminently one of being taught. The occurrence of the verb ἀναδιδάσκειν in these contexts suggests that the divine spirit or voice is a teacher. The spirit introduces the explanation in *Somn.* 2.252, while Philo concludes the explanation in *Cher.* 29 by observing that he has "learnt its [the image of the two Cherubim's] clear lesson of the sovereignty and beneficence of the Cause." Philo's account of his experience with Consideration in *Fug.* 53–58 confirms the preeminence of rational instruction in these experiences. He begins by observing an exegetical difficulty. This observation leads first to an internal debate and subsequently to the lectures of Consideration. She "taught" (ἐδίδαξε) him the exegetical solution, confirmed in characteristic midrashic fashion by appeal to other related biblical texts.

Second, Philo's experience is addressed to his mind (διάνοια). A reference to the "vision-seeking mind, the mind which is eager to see all things and never even in its dreams has a wish for faction or turmoil" leads directly to Philo's autobiographical account in *Somn.* 2.252, implying that the spirit is about to instruct Philo's own open, peaceful mind. In *Cher.* 29, Philo

---

61. See Hay, "Philo's View of Himself," 49.

explicitly directs the solution to his mind: "O then, my mind, admit the image unalloyed of the two Cherubim, that having learnt its clear lesson . . . thou mayest reap the fruits of a happy lot." The prominence of the mind is evident also in *Fug.* 54–55, both in Philo's own internal debate and the name "Consideration."

Finally, the location of divine aid within the soul that characterizes *Cher.* 27–29 and *Somn.* 2.252 is evident as well in a prayer that Philo records in *Somn.* 1.164–65a:

> But even if we do close the eye of our soul and either will not take the trouble or have not the power to regain our sight, do thou thyself, O Sacred Guide, be our prompter and preside over our steps and never tire of anointing our eyes, until conducting us to the hidden light of hallowed words thou display to us the fast-locked lovelinesses invisible to the uninitiate. Thee it beseems to do this.

This prayer constitutes Philo's request that God lead people to the allegorical level of interpretation, for it is preceded by praise of "the sacred oracles," which give "the gift of eyesight, enabling them to judge of the real nature of things, and not merely rely on the literal sense." That concern and the request for prompting draw this prayer into the circle of texts on interpretation, which includes *Cher.* 27–29, *Somn.* 2.252, and *Fug.* 53–58.[62] God's prompting in this prayer, then, corresponds to the prompting of the spirit in *Somn.* 2.252, the higher thought from within Philo's own soul in *Cher.* 27–29, and Consideration's teaching in *Fug.* 53–58.

In this wide array of Philonic texts, one model of interpretation predominates: the spirit prompts the mind to embrace a higher level of meaning. Philo's experience, which underlies this model of inspiration, consists of being led by an external divine aid to solve exegetical conundrums. The *source* of inspiration is an external divine aid, which Philo describes variously as the spirit (*Somn.* 2.252), a higher word that Philo hears from within his own soul (*Cher.* 27), Consideration (*Fug.* 54), or hierophant (*Spec.* 1.164). The *means* of inspiration is rational instruction addressed to the mind (*Somn.* 2.252; *Cher.* 27–29), accompanied at times by exegetical

---

62. The importance of interpretation is evident also in the distinction between initiates and the uninitiate, which we saw already vis-à-vis Philo's parallel between the ascent of the mind and allegorical interpretation (e.g., *Spec.* 3.1–6; *Gig.* 53–54; *Cher.* 48–49). For Philo on the rational process, see also *Praem.* 50: "For good abilities and natural gifts are a matter of rejoicing. The mind exults in the facility of its apprehension and the felicity for the process by which it discovers what it seeks without labour, as though dictated by an inward prompter. For to find the solution of difficulties quickly must bring joy."

confirmation (*Fug.* 53–58). The *goal* of inspiration is a higher level of meaning, which, for Philo, consists of the allegorical meaning of the Bible. Philo applies this model of inspiration as well to his description of two prominent biblical characters, Joseph and Moses, who undergo similar experiences of inspiration.

In his retelling of Joseph's ability to interpret Pharaoh's dream, Philo does not explain how Joseph is able to interpret the bare facts of Pharaoh's dream (*Ios.* 107–9). In contrast, Philo introduces the next level of insight by referring to the source of interpretative insight:

> Such are the facts which appear from the interpretation, but I also hear the promptings of the divine voice, devising safeguards for the disease, as we may call it. (*Ios.* 110)[63]

This is the level of interpretation that attracts Philo's attention, for this level arises from "the promptings of the divine voice."[64] Joseph's ability to ascertain the meaning of the dream is left unexplained, but his ability to move beyond the facts of the dream requires external aid.

The correspondence between Joseph and Philo continues even beyond this point. Pharaoh, impressed by Joseph's interpretation and advice, says to his companions, "Sirs, shall we find another man such as this, *who has in him the spirit of God?*" (*Ios.* 116).[65] In the same way, Philo attributes his ability to ascertain the higher level of meaning in the Bible to the divine spirit, "the familiar secret tenant" (*Somn.* 2.252), who speaks from within his soul (*Cher.* 27), granting insight beyond the literal meaning of the Bible.

This model shapes also Philo's explanation of how Moses predicted the Sabbath:

> Moses, when he heard of this and also actually saw it, was awestruck and, guided by what was not so much surmise as God-sent inspiration, made announcement of the sabbath. I need hardly say that conjectures of this kind are closely akin to prophecies. For the mind could not have made so straight an aim if there was not also the divine spirit guiding it to the truth itself. (*Mos.* 2.264–65)

Two aspects of this description of Moses's abilities indicate that the mind of Moses, according to Philo, was sharpened by the divine spirit. First, the two most significant words Philo employs in *Mos.* 2.265 to explain Moses's

---

63. Five provisions required to prepare for the upcoming famine without alarming the people follow (*Ios.* 110–15).

64. Greek ὑπηχεῖ δέ μοι καὶ ἐκλαλεῖ τὸ θεῖον ὑποβάλλον.

65. Emphasis added. Greek ὃς ἔχει πνεῦμα θεῖον ἐν ἑαυτῷ.

rational prophetic ability, εἰκασία and ποδηγετέω, Philo employs elsewhere in association with the rational processes of the human mind.⁶⁶

The context of *Mos.* 2.265 also indicates that inspiration here entails the incorporation rather than vitiation of the rational capacity. Philo gives four examples of pronouncements of Moses spoken: at the crossing of the Red Sea (2.246-57); to predict the Sabbath (2.258-69); following the golden calf (2.270-74); and after the rebellion of Korah (2.275-87). In each instance, Philo adheres to a strict pattern to describe Moses's prophetic ability, in which he draws an integral connection between Moses's emotional state, his experience of inspiration, and his utterance before the people of Israel.⁶⁷ In this pattern, there is no displacement of reason but rather a direct line drawn, via inspiration, from Moses's human response to his oracle, and there is no indication of wild, frenzied transformation, such as so often characterizes the pythia or prophets of antiquity. In the case of the Sabbath, Moses, awestruck by what was proclaimed and seen in the doubling of food, did not so much guess at but was possessed to speak of the Sabbath (2.264). Here, the adverbial participle, καταπλαγείς, together with a second parallel participle, θεοφορηθείς, provides the context of Moses's utterance: ἐφ᾽ οἷς ἀγγελλομένοις ἅμα καὶ ὁρωμένοις καταπλαγεὶς Μωυσῆς οὐκ ἐστοχάσατο μᾶλλον ἢ θεοφορηθεὶς ἐθέσπισε. The inspiration Moses experienced is, according to the syntax of this account, continuous with his human response and perception.

Both the vocabulary Philo employs to explain Moses's inspired ability to predict the Sabbath and the context into which he sets this explanation, then, are indications of how consistently Philo portrays this model of inspiration, which he similarly describes in *Somn.* 2.252, *Cher.* 27-29, *Fug.* 53-58, and *Ios.* 110-16. In each case, the mind is enabled by the divine spirit to perceive something otherwise inscrutable.

Because I have discussed the antecedent of this model of inspiration in detail elsewhere,⁶⁸ it would be superfluous to dwell unduly upon it here. Nonetheless, I should point out that Philo is, in my opinion, indebted to discussions of Socrates's daemon, such as can be found particularly in

---

66. For a thorough analysis, see Levison, "Prophetic Spirit as Angel." On εἰκασία, see Philo, *Legat.* 21; *Conf.* 159; *Cher.* 69; *Somn.* 1.23; *Mos.* 1.294; *Spec.* 1.38; 1.63; 4.50; *Post.* 80; *Her.* 98; *Mos.* 1.68. For the adjective, εἰκαστικός, see Philo, *Cher.* 116; *Sacr.* 13. The verb ποδηγετέω occurs without exception in Philo's writings in association with the path toward virtue, which requires reason: *Opif.* 70; *Praem.* 84; *Post.* 31; *Spec.* 1.269; *Deus* 182; *Migr.* 23; *Fug.* 21; *Virt.* 215.

67. For a detailed analysis of this pattern, see Levison, "Two Types."

68. Levison, "Prophetic Spirit as Angel."

Plutarch's *De genio Socratis*, for the contours of this model. For instance, Socrates's ability to hear the divine voice or sign is attributed to his possession of

> an understanding which, being pure and free from passion, and commingling with the body but little, for necessary ends, was so sensitive and delicate as to respond at once to what reached him. What reached him, one would conjecture, was not spoken language, but the unuttered words of a daemon, making voiceless contact with his intelligence by their sense alone. (*Gen. Socr.* 588D–E)

M. Pohlenz's suggestion that Philo alludes to the figure of Socrates in *Somn.* 2.252[69] is borne out by his use of the word εἰωθός to describe the recurrent presence of the divine spirit, for Socrates's daemon (δαιμόνιον) is often depicted as a "customary" presence in Socrates's life.[70] This allusion in *Somn.* 2.252 and the many points of contact between this model in Philo's writings and discussions of Socrates's inspiration indicate that both Philo's own expectations and his biblical interpretations took shape under the long shadow of Socrates and the mode of inspiration often attributed to him.

D. Summary

Many of Philo's references to the divine spirit coalesce around three foci of Philo's experience, glimpses of which he proffers as *autobiography*. In these rare and precious windows of personal reflection, Philo delineates three relatively distinct modes of inspiration: (1) poetic ecstasy, (2) philosophical ascent, and (3) the inner voice.

In *Migr.* 34–35, Philo describes his inspiration as poetic ecstasy. Despite the presence of vivid detail, which recounts suddenness, light, and loss of reason, the elliptical phrase ὑπὸ κατοχῆς ἐνθέου hardly constitutes a direct reference to the divine spirit. Nonetheless, close parallels between *Migr.* 34–35 and Philo's explicit references to the divine spirit in *Her.* 264–65, *QG* 3.9, *Spec.* 1.65, 4.49, and *Mos.* 1.277 suggest that Philo has the divine spirit in view in *Migr.* 34–35. Philo also distinguishes his experience from prophetic inspiration. His autobiography in *Migr.* 34–35 is replete with allusions to Plato's view of poetic inspiration, while his

---

69. Pohlenz, "Philon von Alexandreia," 473. See also Hay, "Philo's View of Himself," 44–45nn9–10; Tiede, *Charismatic Figure*, 30–42.

70. See Plato, *Phaedr.* 242B; *Euthyd.* 272E; *Apol.* 31D; 40A; Pseudo-Plato, *Theages* 128D; Plutarch, *Gen. Socr.* 580C; 589E–F.

descriptions of prophets, who function as channels of divine prompting, have a closer kinship with the Greco-Roman explanations of prophetic inspiration such as transpired at Delphi.

In *Spec.* 3.1–6, Philo describes his inspiration as philosophical ascent. Philo's wistful reminiscence of philosophical leisure is passionate, yet his reference to the source of inspiration, intimated in one word, ἐπιθειασμόν, is oblique. Nevertheless, close parallels between *Spec.* 3.1–6 and Philo's explicit reference to the divine spirit in *Plant.* 18–26, *Gig.* 29–31, 53–54, and *Decal.* 175 suggest that Philo has the divine spirit in view in *Spec.* 3.1–6. Such a comparison of texts indicates also that two aspects of his view of inspiration have their origin in Philo's personal experience. First, Philo's unique contribution with respect to the philosophical ascent of the mind is that he attributes it explicitly to the divine spirit in *Plant.* 18–26 and *Gig.* 29–31. The implicit attribution of this ascent to the divine spirit in *Spec.* 3.1–6 locates the genesis of this view in his own experience. Philo knows from personal experience that the divine spirit is necessary to lift the mind above because earthly worries and civil cares inexorably draw the mind downward. Second, in *Spec.* 3.1–6, Philo draws a correspondence between the inspired ascent of his mind and his ability to interpret Torah allegorically. In other treatises, Philo attributes the ascent of Moses as the interpreter of God's (particular) laws to the divine spirit (*Gig.* 53–54; *Decal.* 175). This association of ascent, interpretation, and divine spirit is unique to Philo; its presence in an autobiographical account pinpoints its origin in his own experience of the divine spirit as the source of philosophical ascent for the purpose of biblical interpretation.

In *Cher.* 27–29, *Somn.* 2.252, *Fug.* 53–58, and the prayer of *Somn.* 1.164–65, Philo proffers a third type of experience according to which the divine spirit prompts and leads the rational mind to truth otherwise unobtainable. The prompter Philo describes variously as the spirit (*Somn.* 2.252), a voice from within his soul (*Cher.* 27–29), Consideration (*Fug.* 54), or the hierophant (*Spec.* 1.164). This type of inspiration takes the form of instruction directed toward the rational mind for the sake of solving exegetical conundrums. Analogies to this model of inspiration can be found in Joseph's ability to interpret Pharaoh's dream and Moses's prediction of the Sabbath.

The divine spirit, therefore, functions in three complementary ways in Philo's experience. The divine spirit generates his ecstasy as a poet, elevates his reason as a philosopher cum biblical interpreter, and leads him to insight as an exegete.

IV. APOLOGY AND THE DIVINE SPIRIT

At other places, Philo's discussions of inspiration stretch the seams of consistency, particularly in texts with an explicit apologetic intent, when Philo engages in a wholehearted effort to extol the ancestors of Israel. One occurs in *De vita Mosis*, the purpose of which is overtly apologetic: "I hope to bring the story of this greatest and most perfect of men to the knowledge of such as deserve not to remain in ignorance of it" (*Mos.* 1.1). The other, in which the divine spirit is the source of Abraham's ecstasy, occurs in *Virt.* 211–19, which is also apologetic, for in it Philo discusses a "better class, whose ancestors were men of guilt, but their own lives were worthy of emulation and full of good report" (211). These two references to the divine spirit, then, are situated within texts that are intended to extol the virtues of Moses and Abraham.

A. Moses and the Gift of Prophecy

We have seen already two instances in which a form of inspiration Philo claims for himself characterizes also the inspiration he attributes to Moses. The divine spirit as the source of the philosophical ascent of the mind characterizes both *Spec.* 3.1–6 and *Gig.* 53–54. The divine spirit, which prompts higher rational insight, is the primary element of Philo's experience in *Somn.* 2.252 and *Cher.* 27–29 and Moses's in *Mos.* 2.265. What we have not yet observed, however, is that even here, where Philo presupposes similar experiences of inspiration, Moses's is unique.

The uniqueness of Moses is patently obvious in *Gig.* 53–55. Although Philo devotes much of his lengthy interpretation of Gen 6:3 (*Gig.* 19–57) to demonstrating that "though the divine spirit may stay awhile in the soul it cannot abide there" (28)—an interpretative point, we may note, that is consistent with Gen 6:3—Philo says of Moses, "He then has ever the divine spirit at his side, taking the lead in every journey of righteousness, but from those others, as I have said, it quickly separates itself, from these to whose span of life he has also set a term of a hundred and twenty years" (55). In what follows, Philo faces this inconsistency, admitting that Moses too died at 120 years—without forfeiting the permanent presence of the divine spirit. He offers the casual explanation that "things which bear the same name are not in all cases alike" (56) and evasively postpones a "closer discussion of this matter . . . till we inquire into the prophet's life as a whole, when we have become fit to learn its mystery" (57). Moses clearly does not fit into conventional human categories.

The uniqueness of Moses, according to Philo, is evident also in Moses's prophetic gift. Philo dedicates the first three quarters of his *De vita Mosis* to demonstrating that "Moses was the best of kings, of lawgivers and of high priests" (2.187). He then turns to demonstrate that Moses was also "a prophet of the highest quality." To accomplish this, Philo distinguishes three types of oracles in the production of which Moses the prophet takes part.

The first group are given by God through Moses as an interpreter. These are the laws that expand the Decalogue. The second sort of oracles that Philo introduces is the kind that Moses receives through question and answer with God: "The prophet asks questions of God about matters on which he has been seeking knowledge, and God replies and instructs him" (*Mos.* 2.190), particularly when Moses does not feel himself entirely capable of deciding.[71]

Of a very different character, and most important for understanding the divine spirit in Philo's writings, is the third sort of oracles, which "are spoken by Moses in his own person, when possessed by God and carried away out of himself' (2.188). This description of Moses contains two incompatible parts. One is Moses's speaking in his own person, and the other is Moses's being carried out of himself by inspired possession. What exactly these two descriptions entail is explained in the following two descriptions of Moses as prophet par excellence.

On the one hand, these oracles arise when "the speaker appears under that divine possession in virtue of which he is chiefly and in the strict sense considered a prophet" (2.191). This statement clarifies the meaning of the second part of Philo's statement: "Moses . . . when possessed by God and carried away out of himself" (2.188). This is the language of ecstasy of the most extraordinary sort. Moses, who is of course always a prophet, or better, *the* prophet, experiences also a form of possession that transforms him into a prophet "in the strict sense."

This emphasis begins with Philo's transition statement from illustrations of oracles of the second mixed sort to those of the third sort, in which Moses is a prophet "in the strict sense," where Philo writes, "I will proceed next to describe those delivered [θεσπισθέντα] by the prophet himself under divine inspiration [κατ' ἐνθουσιασμόν] . . . The examples of his possession [τῆς θεοφορήτου κατοκωχῆς]" (2.246). In these examples, which occupy the remainder of *De vita Mosis*, Philo replaces the simple word εἶπεν with an extraordinarily high concentration of words related to inspiration: crossing the Red Sea (*Mos.* 2.246–57), the appearance of manna and announcement

---

71. E.g., two addressing incidents that provide the grounds for stoning (2.192–220); one that deals with ritual observances at unusual times (2.221–33a); and another that results in the promulgation of inheritance laws (2.233b–35).

of the Sabbath (2.258-69), the golden calf (2.270-74), and Korah's rebellion (2.275-87).

(1) Moses, according to Exod 14:13-14, "said [εἶπεν] to the people" that they should be courageous and watch God's salvation at the Red Sea. Philo instead writes: "The prophet . . . was taken out of himself by divine possession and uttered these inspired words" (2.250). The first phrase in particular, οὐκέτ' ὤν ἐν ἑαυτῷ, signifies ecstasy.[72]

(2) Philo interprets three utterances related to the Sabbath. According to Exod 16:15, "Moses said [εἶπεν] to" the Israelites that the manna was the bread of God. Philo adds that Moses spoke *under inspiration* (ἐπιθειάσας) (*Mos.* 2.259). Second, according to Exod 16:23, Moses "said [εἶπεν] to them" that they should rest on the Sabbath. Philo instead writes that Moses "under God-sent inspiration, made announcement of the sabbath" (2.264). Third, according to Exod 16:25-26, Moses said (εἶπεν) that the people should eat what was preserved from the prior day rather than searching in the field on the Sabbath. Philo transforms this statement into pure prediction (2.268-69) by emphasizing that it occurred, not on the Sabbath, but on the day prior to the Sabbath (τῇ . . . προτεραίᾳ); by extolling the character of the oracle (χρησμὸν τερατωδέστατον); and by replacing "said" with "prophesied" (θεσπίζει). The result of these predictions, Philo observes in fine apologetic fashion, is Israel's acknowledgement of Moses "the prophet as a true seer, an interpreter of God, and alone gifted with foreknowledge of the hidden future" (2.269). Finally, Philo summarizes yet again that Moses's explanation of manna was "his pronouncement under divine inspiration [κατεχόμενος ἐθέσπισεν]" (2.270). Thus Moses's utterances concerning the manna and the Sabbath, described consistently in Exod 16 with the simple verb "said," are transformed by Philo into instances of prophetic inspiration.

(3) According to Exod 32:26, following the creation of the golden calf, Moses said (εἶπεν), "Who is on the LORD's side?" According to Philo, this was spoken by Moses only after he "became another man, changed both in outward appearance and mind; and inspired [ἐπιθειάσας]" (*Mos.* 2.272).[73]

(4) According to Num 16:28, Moses said (εἶπεν) that the people would know if he was God's emissary if Korah, Dathan, Abiram, and their families should die an unnatural death. Philo introduces the story by remarking that this proposal "came from his [Moses's] own mouth when again under possession [πάλιν κατασχεθεὶς ἀνεφθέγξατο]" (*Mos.* 2.275). Not to leave the point understated, Philo recounts of Moses that

---

72. See, for example, Plato, *Ion* 534B; Lucan, *De bello civili* 5.163-67; Josephus, *Ant.* 4.118, 119, 121 (on Balaam); 6.223 (on Saul); Philo, *QG* 3.9.

73. Translation mine, in preference to "filled with the spirit."

"inspiration came upon him, and, transformed into a prophet, he pronounced these words" (*Mos.* 2.280).

In these examples, Philo leaves no doubt in the minds of his readers that Moses is the greatest of the prophets. The occurrence of the word "said" in the Bible is employed by Philo as a window of opportunity through which he introduces countless references to inspiration. Moses experiences inspiration, possession, and transformation, and, therefore, when he is "possessed by God and carried away out of himself," Moses speaks "under that divine possession in virtue of which he is chiefly and in the strict sense considered a prophet" (2.188, 191).

This is, however, only one aspect of Moses's inspiration. We have seen already, both in our analysis of *Mos.* 2.265 and the pattern by which Moses's own emotional state leads to an oracular utterance in these same examples, that Moses's mind is simultaneously sharpened by the divine spirit. In other words, Moses also receives God's own knowledge: "God has given to him of his own power of foreknowledge and by this he will reveal future events" (2.190). This statement clarifies the meaning of Philo's statement "in his own person." Despite the pervasive vocabulary of inspiration in *Mos.* 2.191–92, Moses is not, like Balaam and the race of prophets, a mindless, ecstatic channel for God's words; on the contrary, his inspiration is characterized predominantly by the possession of God's own foreknowledge. The third sort of oracles, therefore, result from the highest level of rational experience, which encompasses God's own knowledge.

This uneasy alliance between ecstatic and rational forms of inspiration, occasioned by Philo's apologetic motives, is apparent also in *Praem.* 53–55, in which Philo summarizes the offices which Philo illustrates at length in *De vita Mosis*:

> ... piety, which Moses, the teacher of divine lore, in a special degree had for his own, and through it gained among a multitude of other gifts, which have been described in the treatises dealing with his life, four special rewards, the offices of king, legislator, prophet and high priest. (*Praem.* 53)

Philo explains further the nature of Moses's prophecy: "For the prophet is the interpreter of God who prompts from within what he should say" (*Praem.* 55). This explanation is significant because of the exceptional points of contact and contrast it provides between Moses's form of prophetic inspiration and the inspiration experienced by other prophets, which Philo describes in *Spec.* 1.65. Both descriptions begin with exactly the same words, apart from the necessary difference between plural and singular:

> For prophets are the interpreters of God (*Spec.* 1.65)
> For the prophet is the interpreter of God (*Praem.* 55)

Despite this similarity, Philo's descriptions of the processes by which prophetic utterances are produced differ markedly:

> who makes full use of their organs of speech to set forth what He wills (*Spec.* 1.65)
> who prompts from within what he should say (*Praem.* 55)

Although the race of prophets and Moses alike are interpreters of God, the processes God employs with them differs. God employs the vocal chords of prophets without their ability to apprehend, but God prompts Moses's words from within.

These two streams reflect Philo's apologetic strategy. He wants to demonstrate, at one and the same time, that Moses embodies both the highest level of rational thought ("in his own person") and the most intense form of prophetic inspiration ("carried away out of himself"). Because the Bible is put to such unabashedly apologetic use, these two streams vie for prominence and converge wildly in the course of Philo's biblical interpretation, producing at times confusing whirlpools.

B. Abraham and Transformation by the Divine Spirit[74]

In his praise of Abraham, Philo attributes to the divine spirit a cluster of noteworthy attributes:

> Thus whenever he was possessed, everything in him changed to something better, eyes, complexion, stature, carriage, movements, voice. For the divine spirit which was breathed upon him from on high made its lodging in his soul, and invested his body with singular beauty, his voice with persuasiveness, and his hearers with understanding. Would you not say that this lone wanderer without relatives or friends was of the highest nobility, he who craved for kinship with God and strove by every means to live in familiarity with Him, he who while ranked among the prophets, a post of such high excellence, put his trust in nothing created rather than in the Uncreated and Father of all, he who as I have said was regarded as a king by those in whose midst he settled. (*Virt.* 217–18)

---

74. On Philo's treatment of Abraham, particularly in *De Abrahamo*, see Sandmel, *Philo's Place in Judaism*, 96–211.

Here Philo regards Abraham as the ideal orator, the ideal king, the ideal sage, and the ideal prophet. There is a measure of overlap between these attributes of Abraham, so that he is at once the sage king, his beauty is that of the ideal ruler, etc. Still, each can be discussed in brief.

The divine spirit inspires Abraham's skill of persuasion as a public orator. The transformation of his body—eyes, complexion, stature, carriage, movements, voice—comprises a description of the orator's delivery. Cicero, for instance, describes the components of delivery: "That needs to be controlled by bodily carriage, gesture, play of features and changing intonation of voice."[75] The author of the first-century handbook Rhetorica ad Herennium defines delivery as "the graceful regulation of voice, countenance, and gesture."[76] The unique aspect of *Virt.* 217–19 that distinguishes it is that Abraham receives superior delivery by divine inspiration, while the rhetorical handbooks list guidelines and examples so that students may refine their delivery through practice.[77]

Philo appropriately includes this description within a treatise on virtue and, more specifically, within a discussion of Abraham's virtue and "greatness of soul" (217), for the ideal orator must be a good person. In the introduction to his *Institutio oratoria*, Quintilian writes, "My aim, then, is the education of the perfect orator. The first essential for such an one is that he should be a good man, and consequently we demand of him not merely the possession of exceptional gifts of speech, but of all the excellence of character as well."[78]

The goal of rhetorical skill during the Greco-Roman period was the ability to rule properly, and to this end rhetoric was a central component in the education of Rome's leading citizens.[79] It is not surprising, then, that Philo's description of Abraham's rhetorical skill follows a description of him as an ideal king:

> By those among whom he settled he was regarded as a king, not because of the outward state which surrounded him, mere commoner that he was, but because of his greatness of soul, for his spirit was the spirit of a king. Indeed, they continued to treat him with a respect which subjects pay to a ruler, being

---

75. Cicero, *De or.* 1.18.
76. Rhet. Her. 1.3; see also 3.19–27.
77. Rhet. Her. 3.20; Cicero, *De or.* 3.213–27.
78. Quintilian, *Inst.* 1.9; see also the entirety of *Inst.* 12.
79. On the role of rhetoric in Roman education, see Kennedy, *Art of Rhetoric*, 318–21.

awe-struck at the all-embracing greatness of his nature and its more than human perfection. (216–17)[80]

This portrayal of Abraham as ideal ruler explains why Philo says that "the divine spirit which was breathed upon him from on high made its lodging in his soul, and invested his body with singular beauty" (217). The combination of inward and external beauty expresses the Greco-Roman ideal of beauty, such as we find described by Plato in *Resp.* 3.402D:

> Then . . . when there is a coincidence of a beautiful disposition in the soul and corresponding and harmonious beauties of the same type in the bodily form—is not this the fairest spectacle for one who is capable of its contemplation?

More important is Plato's application of this definition to the ideal ruler in *Resp.* 7.535A: "The most stable, the most brave and enterprising are to be preferred, and, so far as practicable, the most comely." According to Philo, Abraham fulfils this ideal combination of inward virtue and external beauty when he is possessed by the spirit.

The unique characteristic of Philo's description of Abraham, then, is the attribution of his virtues to the divine spirit. His beauty is not natural, his rhetorical skill not learned through practice, and his kingship not his by birth or social class. It is rather the divine spirit that causes Abraham to become the ideal Greco-Roman ruler.

Philo portrays Abraham, not only as ideal orator and ruler, but also as the ideal sage, who is a sojourner on the earth and who yearns for kinship with the divine.[81] So too is he a prophet, "a post of such high excellence" (*Virt.* 218). Philo does not directly attribute Abraham's roles as sage and prophet to his possession by the divine spirit; rather, they provide the basis upon which Abraham can embody, by means of the divine spirit, the ideals of oratory and beauty.

Now we must turn to the question of what motivates Philo to attribute this transformation of Abraham to the divine spirit. It is not exegetical interests, for the exegetical foundation for Philo's viewpoint in *Virt.* 217–19 is nil, and this treatise is on the whole more topical than exegetical. Nor is it autobiographical, for Philo does not discuss physical transformation and persuasiveness with respect to his own inspiration. Nonetheless, in addition to the observation that this portion of *De virtutibus* is intended to extol the

---

80. See also Goodenough, *Politics of Philo Judaeus*, 83–84, 91–92, esp. Philonic passages in notes. Tiede, *Charismatic Figure*, 53n80.

81. Philo subtitles *De Abrahamo* "The Life of the Wise Man Made Perfect through Teaching." On the sage as sojourner and king, see Goodenough, *By Light, Light*, 83–84 and 91–92, respectively.

virtue of Abraham, there is another reason for supposing that Philo is motivated by apologetic interests. The collocation of the divine spirit, physical transformation, and leadership is not entirely unique. It occurs also with respect to Adam and Moses in contexts that are highly apologetic, that is, where Philo's main purpose is to extol the surpassing character of these biblical figures.

The purpose of *Opif.* 136–50 is to praise the first human. Philo begins by praising Adam's body and soul. Adam, contends Philo, excelled all others with his ideal beauty:

> That first man, earth-born, ancestor of our whole race, was made, as it appears to me, most excellent in each part of his being, in both soul and body, and greatly excelling those who came after him in the transcendent qualities of both alike; for this man really was the one truly "beautiful and good." (136)

Adam's body was excellent for three reasons: it was composed of newly formed matter; God chose the best clay to become a shrine for the rational soul; and God used consummate skill to make the first man as beautiful as possible (136–38). Adam's soul was also excellent. The basis for this contention is the familiar combination of Gen 1:27 and 2:7: Adam's soul, which was breathed into Adam's face, was patterned according to divine reason. The inspiration of the divine spirit into a perfect body rendered the first man perfectly beautiful. Having demonstrated Adam's beauty, Philo turns to describe him along the lines of the Stoic sage. Adam was "the only citizen of the world." He exhibited two key functions of the sage, wisdom and dominion, when he named the animals:

> Quite excellently does Moses ascribe the bestowal of names also to the first man: for this is the business of wisdom and royalty, and the first man was wise with a wisdom learned from and taught by Wisdom's own lips, for he was made by divine hands; he was, moreover, a king, and it befits a ruler to bestow titles on his several subordinates. (148)

The purpose of this description is to demonstrate the superiority of the first human about which Moses wrote: "So greatly did he excel in all noble traits, thus attaining the very limit of human happiness" (150). In this respect, this lengthy description reveals the apologetic motivation that causes Philo to discuss the divine spirit and the divine artistry, which combined to create the body and soul of the first human, who exercised two prerogatives of the sage: wisdom and dominion.[82]

---

82. See Levison, *Portraits of Adam*, 69–75.

Philo's apologetic motivation is evident also in similar descriptions of Moses. We saw in *De vita Mosis* two instances that combine allusions to the divine spirit with the inward and external beauty of Moses in contexts where Moses functions as king (*Mos.* 1.57–59) and prophet (2.272)—precisely the two explicit categories that Philo employs to describe Abraham in *Virt.* 217–19. Philo extols Moses's role as ideal king in book 1 of *De vita Mosis*. In this context, he narrates Moses's encounter with the seven daughters of the priest, including his future spouse in *Mos.* 1.57–59; Moses's prophetic ability ("he grew inspired and was transfigured into a prophet") intimidated the Arabs who had usurped their well. Subsequently, their father the priest "was at once struck with admiration of his face, and soon afterwards of his disposition, for great natures are transparent and need no length of time to be recognized" (1.59). A similar coalescence occurs in a section of book 2 of *De vita Mosis*, in which Philo extols Moses's role as ideal prophet. In the narrative of the golden calf, Philo recounts the transformation of Moses by means of divine possession: "He therefore became another man, changed both in outward appearance and mind" (2.272).

These descriptions of Adam, Moses, and Abraham combine references or allusions to the divine spirit with the attributes of ideal beauty and the ideal king. In each, the explicit motivation is apologetic. Philo describes Adam's ideal beauty and his sagacious kingship in a passage dedicated to demonstrating the superiority of the first human. Philo illustrates Moses's exercise of kingship through his dealings with Arabs and Israelites alike; in both narratives he comments upon the inward and outward aspects of Moses. Philo depicts in detail the transformation of the king-sage-prophet Abraham into the ideal orator in a passage devoted explicitly to demonstrating the nobility of Abraham despite his being the son of idolatrous parents.

C. Summary

Philo is an apologist, and his desire to extol the virtues of Israel's ancestors motivates him to go beyond the usual boundaries of his own view of inspiration by the divine spirit. In the overtly apologetic treatise *De vita Mosis*, Philo distinguishes the inspiration of Moses from all others' (2.265). Moses's inspiration is perennial, not transitory, and of him alone can it be said that the spirit is always at his side (*Gig.* 53–55). His inspiration is different from the prophets, for he is not a channel but speaks from himself. Philo also distinguishes the inspiration of Abraham, in an apologetic portion of *De virtutibus*, by attributing to the divine spirit his transformation into an ideal ruler who surpasses Greco-Roman standards of supreme rhetorical skill and ideal beauty.

The unique effects that Philo attributes to the divine spirit with respect to Moses and Abraham, therefore, can be explained by his desire to extol the virtues of the ancestors of Israel. Because they arise less from an attempt to develop a consistent view of inspiration or prophecy than from a desire to heighten the superiority of Israel's ancestors, these descriptions fit maladroitly alongside Philo's more usual references to the divine spirit. Philo pays this price in order to portray the ancestors of Israel as ideal Greco-Roman rulers.

V. CONCLUSION

An initial typology of the divine spirit's role in inspiration has emerged from this study, despite the complexity and prolixity of Philo's discussions. The process itself has, admittedly, been complex, but three foci for this typology have surfaced, around which references to inspiration by the divine spirit can be clustered: exegesis, autobiography, and apology.

In addition to developing a typology, this chapter contributes to our comprehension of Philo Judaeus by bringing to the fore three key issues: the relationship between inspiration and exegesis, the diversity of Philo's experiences, and the uniqueness of Philo's views.

A. The Divine Spirit and Allegorical Interpretation

What is the relationship between inspiration by the divine spirit and Philo's view of himself as allegorical interpreter? D. Hay has contributed substantially to this issue by clarifying the methods required to ascertain Philo's self-assessment. Nevertheless, he concludes with a question, "Did he place himself on a level with Jeremiah or the psalmists," which elicits merely a tentative solution: "The reverence with which he cites their statements *suggests a sense* of their canonical rank which *implies* they have an authority which Philo does not claim for himself."[83] The provisional tone of Hay's answer is appropriate because it is extremely difficult to discern the self-consciousness of ancient writers.

This chapter contains the seeds of further clarification by highlighting the role that the divine spirit plays in allegorical interpretation. (1) In *Spec.* 3.1–2 and 3.5–6, Philo draws a correspondence between the ascent

---

83. Hay, "Philo's View of Himself," 50; emphasis added.

of his mind under possession of the spirit and his ability to interpret Torah allegorically. (2) Philo's description of Moses's ascent, which takes place because he always possesses the spirit, in *Gig.* 53–54, contains vocabulary similar to the autobiographical account of Philo's ability to interpret Torah allegorically in *Spec.* 3.5–6. These correspondences between Philo's or Moses' ascents and Philo's ability to interpret Torah suggest that allegorical interpretation is a process that requires the inspiration of the divine spirit because it is on a par with the inspired philosophical ascent of the mind. (3) This suggestion is borne out by *Somn.* 2.252, in which the spirit is the source of the solution to a biblical conundrum. *De somniis* 2.252 and related passages, including *Cher.* 21–29, *Somn.* 1.164–65, and *Fug.* 53–58, attribute the higher, allegorical level of meaning to divine aid. According to the scenario evident in these passages, Philo ponders a difficulty in the text and then receives instruction from a divine source, which directs his rational mind to a solution.

B. The Divine Spirit and Varieties of Inspiration

What forms of inspiration does the divine spirit take? Burkhardt's *Forschungsbericht* demonstrates the gulf that separates those scholars who emphasize the ecstatic from those who emphasize the more rational form of inspiration.[84] Some scholars have detected both strains in Philo's writings. For example, Büchsel noted the putative difference between Philo's so-called theory of ecstatic prophecy, in which the mind is violently displaced, and Philo's experience of inspiration, which preserves rational thought.[85] More recently, Winston has championed the view that Philo distinguishes a radical form of ecstatic prophecy, characteristic of the prophets, from a milder form of prophecy, characteristic of Moses.[86]

This chapter complements these important attempts to ascertain varieties of inspiration by organizing Philo's references to the divine spirit around the diverse forms of inspiration that he embraces. (1) In *Migr.* 34–35, the divine spirit inspires a sort of poetic ecstasy that enables writing. (2) In *Spec.* 1.65, 4.49, and *Her.* 259–66, the divine spirit employs prophets as channels akin to musical instruments. (3) Similarly, in *Mos.* 1.273–84, the divine spirit is an angel who ousts Balaam's skill in artificial divination

---

84. Burkhardt, *Inspiration heiliger Schriften*, 6–72.

85. Büchsel, *Geist Gottes*, 89–90. This distinction is probably incorrect, for Philo himself claims to experience ecstasy in *Migr.* 34–35, and Philo offers several examples of the inspiration of others that do not include ecstasy (e.g., *Plant.* 18–26; *Virt.* 217–19).

86. Winston, "Two Types."

and employs his vocal organs as channels. (4) In *Spec.* 3.1–6, *Plant.* 18–26, *Gig.* 29–31, and 53–54, the divine spirit inspires the philosophical ascent of the mind. (5) In *Somn.* 2.252 and *Cher.* 27–29, the divine spirit inspires the exegete through instruction directed toward the rational mind. Joseph interprets dreams, in *Ios.* 110–16, in an analogous manner. (6) In *De vita Mosis*, the divine spirit directs Moses's mind to the truth while he is simultaneously inspired to become an ecstatic prophet. (7) In *Virt.* 217–19, the divine spirit transforms Abraham so that he can become the ideal ruler who displays both inward and outward beauty and who masters rhetorical skill. (8) In *Gig.* 23–27, the divine spirit is knowledge and wisdom, which, though it permeates the cosmos, must nonetheless still be placed upon the sage.

This analysis, then, demonstrates that Philo regards the divine spirit as the source of many forms of inspiration. Also significant is the realization that Philo distinguishes between these forms of inspiration. His poetic inspiration and the prophetic inspiration of Moses, for instance, have much in common with ecstatic prophetic inspiration. Nonetheless, Philo distinguishes his experience as a poet and Moses's as a prophet who is prompted from the experience of prophets who function as mouthpieces for spoken divine words.

C. The Divine Spirit and the Uniqueness of Philo

What is uniquely Philonic in these views of inspiration?[87] Few studies have ventured strong responses to this question. A notable exception is Verbeke, who contended that Philo was the first to develop a conception of the prophetic spirit and to spiritualize the conception of πνεῦμα.[88] The present chapter contains several more instances of Philo's unique imprint upon the conception of inspiration by the divine spirit.

(1) Philo's conviction that virtue is the necessary basis for true prophecy motivates him to portray the inspiration of Balaam as an ousting of false wizardry, i.e., artificial divination. Such an exegetical solution to this dubious character is Philo's own; Josephus and Pseudo-Philo, for example, present different solutions.

---

87. The attempt to ascertain unique Philonic contributions was undertaken by Wolfson, who titled the final chapter of his *Philo*, "What Is New in Philo?" (2:429–60). Radice provides a helpful methodology when he undertakes to demonstrate that Philo's theory of the ideas as the thoughts of God is uniquely his own ("Observations").

88. Verbeke, *Évolution*, 259–60. According to Verbeke, Philo develops the former on the basis of the Bible alone and the latter under the influence of the Bible and Platonic-Aristotelianism.

(2) Philo's descriptions of prophetic inspiration in *Spec.* 1.65, 4.49, and *Mos.* 1.263-99 are influenced by Greco-Roman views of inspiration, such as can be found in Plutarch's writings. Philo identifies "an external afflatus that displaces the faculty of rational inference" with the divine spirit of early Judaism and, with respect to Balaam, identifies the divine spirit of Num 24:2 with the angel of Num 22:35, with the result that the mode of inspiration exhibits a striking resemblance to Cleombrotus's view in Plutarch's *De defectu oraculorum*. Wolfson intimates that this fusion is for Philo an intellectual process which follows a "general method."[89] I have suggested as well that Philo's experience, which he recounts in *Migr.* 34-35, is the crucible in which this fusion of Greco-Roman and biblical elements takes place.

(3) Philo attributes the philosophical ascent of the mind to the divine spirit implicitly in *Spec.* 3.1-6 and explicitly in *Plant.* 18-26 and *Gig.* 29-31. This too is a fusion of Platonic and biblical elements, and it also stems, not from an intellectual process alone, but from Philo's experience. His autobiographical account in *Spec.* 3.1-2 reveals that Philo attributes his own rational ascent to the divine spirit. Once again, then, the distinct influences of Plato (and his Greco-Roman interpreters) and the Bible fuse in the experience of Philo.

(4) The correspondence Philo draws between rational ascent and allegorical interpretation in *Spec.* 3.1-2 and 3.5-6, as well as *Spec.* 3.5-6 and *Gig.* 53-54, is Philo's own. Once again, this unique element in Philo's thought is traceable to autobiography, particularly where Philo ponders his own experience of obtaining allegorical insight (e.g., *Spec.* 3.5-6; *Somn.* 2.252; *Cher.* 27-29; 48-52; *Fug.* 53-58).

(5) Philo's apologetic interest leads to unique portraits of the inspiration of Moses and Abraham by the divine spirit. In his attempt to extol Moses and Abraham, Philo portrays them as excelling all prophets and rulers. Their greatness lies in their *exceptional* attainments; therefore, the portraits of Moses in *Mos.* 2 and Abraham in *Virt.* 217-19 are exceptions to Philo's more general view of inspiration, which emerges from his own experience of inspiration by the divine spirit.

In conclusion, this analysis reveals the profundity of Philo's unique contributions to first-century conceptions of inspiration. He neither merely reiterates the Bible nor accepts unquestioningly the views of Plato and his

---

89. Wolfson writes, "Following his general method, Philo will combine the 'divine spirit,' which according to Scripture is the cause of prophecy, with the process of 'divine inspiration' or 'possession' which, according to Plato, is the cause of his various kinds of frenzy, and especially the frenzy of divination. Thus the process of prophesying through the divine spirit will become with him identical with the process of divine inspiration or divine possession in Greek philosophy" (*Philo*, 2:25).

commentators on inspiration. His unique conceptions of inspiration by the divine spirit arise from his commitment to Torah, from his own experiences of the divine spirit, and from his endeavor to extol the virtues of Israel's ancestors.

5

Ascent and Inspiration in the Writings of Philo Judaeus

In his masterful study of ascent in antiquity, Alan Segal writes, "Philo is a logical place to begin tracing the history of the Jewish traditions, not because he is the earliest Jew to deal with these ideas but because, in giving the ideas philosophical clarity, he achieved a brilliant synthesis of Greek thought and native Hebrew tradition."[1] Whether or not the writings of Philo are a more logical place to start than, for example, the Enoch cycle of literature, need hardly be debated.[2] Nor can it be said with certainty that Philo's synthesis of putatively Greek and Hebrew elements is brilliant. What Segal points out, without a doubt, is that ascent is an essential ingredient of Philo's thought.[3] The conception of ascent, however, is not uniform in

---

1. Segal, "Heavenly Ascent," 2:1354.

2. This study expands my published work on the spirit, esp. *Spirit in First-Century Judaism* and "Inspiration and Divine Spirit."

3. In Collins et al., *Apocalypticism and Mysticism*, the title of Gregory E. Sterling's article, "Dancing with the Stars: The Ascent of the Mind in Philo of Alexandria" (155–66), offers colorful entrée to the notion of the ascent of the mind—with the stars—in the writings of Philo Judaeus. The occurrence of the word "journeys," alongside a reference to the book of Revelation, with its heavenly visions, in the title of Paul B. Decock's article, "Journeys toward Fullness of Life: A Comparison between Philo and the Apocalypse of John" (167–87), in the same volume offers another signal of the centrality of ascent for Philo.

Philo's writings.[4] Little is. The purpose of this study, therefore, is to establish central elements of ascent through an analysis of *On the Creation of the World* (*Opif.*) 69–71—Philo's first reference to ascent in his oeuvre—as well as *Concerning Noah's Work as a Planter* (*Plant.*) 18–26, *On the Giants* (*Gig.*) 29–31 and 53–55, and *On the Special Laws* (*Spec.*) 3.1–6.[5]

THE COMPOSITE HUMAN AND THE ASCENT OF THE MIND IN *OPIF.* 69–71

The possibility of ascent preoccupies Philo almost from the start of his exegetical work. A reference to God's image and likeness as early as Gen 1:26–27 becomes the jumping-off point for describing in relative detail the ascent of the mind. "After all these other creatures, as has been stated, he [Moses] says that the human being has come into existence after God's image and after his likeness." Philo continues:

> This is most excellently said, for nothing earthborn bears a closer resemblance to God than the human being. But no one should infer this likeness from the characteristics of the body, for God does not have a human shape and the human body is not God-like. The term image has been used here with regard to the director of the soul, the intellect.
>
> On that single intellect of the universe, as on an archetype, the intellect in each individual human being was modelled. In a sense it is a god of the person who carries it and bears it around as a divine image. For it would seem that the same position that the Great Director holds in the entire cosmos is held by the human intellect in the human being. It is itself invisible, yet it sees all things. Its own nature is unclear, yet it comprehends the natures of other things. By means of the arts and sciences it opens up a vast network of paths, all of them highways, and passes through land and sea, investigating what is present in both realms. Next it is lifted on high and, after exploring the air and the phenomena that occur in it, it is borne further upwards towards the ether and the revolutions of heaven. Then, after

---

4. For a sketch of the variety of ascents in Philo, see Borgen, "Heavenly Ascent in Philo." For studies of ascent in antiquity more generally, see (in chronological order): Bousset, "Himmelsreise der Seele"; Segal, "Heavenly Ascent"; Dean-Otting, *Heavenly Journeys*; Tabor, *Things Unutterable*; Himmelfarb, *Ascent to Heaven*; Collins, "A Throne in the Heavens."

5. First references to a Philonic text contain the entire title in English, according to the LCL edition. Subsequent references, with numbered paragraphs, contain abbreviations. Unless otherwise indicated, translations of Philo's writings are from LCL.

being carried around in the dances of the planets and fixed stars in accordance with the laws of perfect music, and following the guidance of its love of wisdom, it peers beyond the whole of sense-perceptible reality and desires to attain the intelligible realm. And when the intellect has observed in that realm the models and forms of the sense-perceptive reality things which it had seen here, objects of overwhelming beauty, it then, possessed by a sober drunkenness, becomes enthused like the Corybants. Filled with another longing and a higher form of desire, which has propelled it to the utmost vault of the intelligibles, it thinks it is heading towards the Great King himself. But as it strains to see, pure and unmixed beams of concentrated light pour forth like a torrent, so that the eye of the mind, overwhelmed by the brightness, suffers from vertigo.[6]

Several dimensions of Philo's thought emerge from this interpretation of *imago Dei*. First, Philo's thought is grounded in exegesis of the Septuagint. Philo's paraphrase of Gen 1:26, if not slavish, is certainly faithful to the text itself, particularly the tandem elements of image and likeness. His adherence to the text notwithstanding, Philo is expansive in his interpretation of the image of God. The sheer amount of lines he devotes to it indicates this. Yet he does not fail to interpret the likeness, as well, though it plays a subordinate role in his thought. The element of likeness, though not as vaunted a term as image, still communicates for Philo the accuracy of the impression made upon humankind by God: "Since, however, not every single image resembles its archetypal model, but many are dissimilar, he added to the words after the image as an extra indication the words 'after his likeness,' in order to emphasize that it is an accurate and clearly marked casting" (*Opif.* 71).

A second central characteristic of *Opif.* 69–71 is the composite character of human beings: the mind, not the body, comprises the *imago Dei*, and only the mind is able to ascend.[7] The composite nature of human beings comes to the fore in the paragraphs that follow *Opif.* 69–71, where Philo solves the conundrum of why God required helpers—let *us* make—to create humankind. With the help of Plato's *Timaeus* (*Tim.*) 41–42, in which the demiurge creates the immortal part of a human being and the subordinates create the mortal parts, Philo argues that God created the portion of human beings that possesses virtue, while God's helpers created the portion that produces vice. Anthropologically and ethically, human beings are divided

---

6. Translation from Runia, *On the Creation*, 64.

7. This is Philo's predominant view of the *imago Dei*. See Jervell, *Imago Dei*, 56–58; Eltester, *Eikon im Neuen Testament*, 50–51; Jobling, "'And Have Dominion...'" 52–55.

between immortal and mortal, between virtue and vice, between *imago Dei* and physical body. Only the immortal, virtuous *imago Dei* is able to ascend.

Third, the ability to ascend is fundamental to Philo's interpretation of the human mind. David Runia documents five stages of "the human quest for knowledge and wisdom," in which ascent plays a pivotal role: (1) exploration of the earthly region by land and sea; (2) turning upward, the mind explores the air and meteorological phenomena; (3) farther along, the mind reaches heaven, where it joins heavenly bodies in celestial motion; (4) guided by wisdom, the mind contemplates the world of ideas; (5) with further yearning, the mind longs to see the great king, although it cannot, overwhelmed as it is by radiating beams of light that cause it to experience vertigo.[8]

Fourth, integral to Philo's exegesis is his Greco-Roman literary milieu. It is difficult to sift through this, so that an interpreter is left to ask whether Philo taps into Plato or later Middle-Platonic interpretations of Plato, often with a heavy dose of Stoicism. Nevertheless, the impact of Plato's *Phaedrus* is apparent through Philo's exegesis of Gen 1:26-27.[9] Without the impetus of Plato's *Phaedrus*, certainly without the substance of *Phaedr.* 246A-53C, Philo could not derive the ascent of the mind from Gen 1:26-27. For example, though the conception of wings is widespread, Philo's description of the mind's upward flight is reminiscent of Plato's "pair of winged horses and a charioteer" (*Phaedr.* 246A), the "natural function of the wing . . . to soar upwards" (246D), and the person who "feels his wings growing" (249D). The concluding reference in *Opif.* 69-71, to love as what directs the soul in its upward journey, crystallizes another dominant theme in Plato's *Phaedrus*:

> All my [Socrates's] discourse so far has been about the fourth kind of madness, which causes him to be regarded as mad, who, when he sees the beauty on earth, remembering the true beauty, feels his wings growing and longs to stretch them for an upward flight, but cannot do so, and, like a bird, gazes upward and neglects the things below. My discourse has shown that this is, of all inspirations, the best and of the highest origin to him who has it or who shares in it, and that he who loves the beautiful, partaking in this madness is called a lover. (*Phaedr.* 249D-E)

De opificio mundi 69-71 also evinces some striking similarities of vocabulary with Plato's *Phaedr.* 246-53. Philo's description of God as ὁ μέγας ἡγεμών, the great ruler, matches Plato's description of Zeus in *Phaedr.* 246E. The notion of peering beyond, over the edge (ὑπερκύψας), mirrors ἀνακύψας in

---

8. Runia, *On the Creation*, 222-23.

9. See the detailed analysis on Philo's writings in Méasson, *Char ailé de Zeus*, 377-402.

Phaedr. 249C. As Runia notes, the difference between these verbs is a matter of perspective: "Philo replaces it with the other verb because he is primarily interested in the view 'outwards,' i.e. of the intelligible realm."[10] The highest arc of realities perceptible to the mind, which mirrors *Phaedr.* 247B, Philo describes as ἀψίς.[11]

De opificio mundi 69-71 is a studied amalgamation—perhaps concoction is a better way of phrasing it—of several elements: exegesis; Greco-Roman conceptions, particularly from the *Phaedrus* and its interpreters; a clear anthropology, in which body and soul, mind and matter, are readily distinguishable; and a view of human learning that has as its goal an ascent toward God. This is a good bit more than a casual ancient reader might have been prone to discover in Gen 1:26-27, but Philo Judaeus was far from a casual ancient reader. Therefore, in *Opif.* 69-71, he ably sets up a template for the ascent of the human mind.

EPHEMERAL AND ENDURING ASCENT IN *ON THE GIANTS*

In *Opif.* 69-71, Philo's depiction of the grandeur of the human mind renders external aid superfluous. What separates *Opif.* 69-71 from some other descriptions of the mind's ascent, such as *Plant.* 18-26 and *Gig.* 19-55, is the ingredient of an external impulse, which prompts an ascent to the heavenly world of sun and stars[12] or beyond this heavenly world to the outer arc of heaven and the world of ideas.[13] In *Plant.* 18-26 and *Gig.* 19-55, that impulse is the divine spirit, which functions as part of a sophisticated polemical strategy by which Philo adopts Greco-Roman conceptions of ascent while simultaneously calling them into question. The inclusion of the spirit into the process of ascent even calls into question the ability of the human mind to ascend unaided.

In *Gig.* 29-31, after asserting that the chief cause of ignorance, even beyond the preoccupation of worldly responsibilities, is the flesh, Philo claims:

---

10. Runia, *On the Creation*, 231. For other allusions to Plato's *Phaedrus*, along with other texts in Philo (e.g., *Det.* 79-90; *Praem.* 37; *Mut.* 179-80), see Runia, *On the Creation*, 222-35.

11. Borgen identifies a variety of early Jewish texts in order to counter a tendency to what he perceives to be an overemphasis upon the Greco-Roman character of Philo in studies by Bousset, Dean-Otting, and Tabor (Borgen, "Heavenly Ascent in Philo"). See n4 on p. 101 above.

12. See also Philo, *Spec.* 1.37, 207; *Praem.* 121-22.

13. Philo, *Opif.* 69-71; *Mut.* 179-80; *Praem.* 30; *Legat.* 5.

Souls that are free from flesh and body spend their days in the theatre of the universe and with a joy that none can hinder see and hear things divine, which they have desired with love insatiable. But those which bear the burden of the flesh, oppressed by the grievous load, cannot look up to the heavens as they revolve, but with necks bowed downwards are constrained to stand rooted to the ground like four-footed beasts. (*Gig.* 31)

Philo arrives at this point through a series of exegetical moves, each one leading farther from the literal meaning of Gen 6:3, which reads, "My spirit shall not abide forever among men, because they are flesh." The obvious literal meaning of Gen 6:3 is that the spirit is what men and women possess from birth to death; in Philo's parlance, this may be the soul. Yet Philo does not opt for this interpretation. Instead, he moves away from a literal interpretation of the text, beginning first with the contention "that souls and demons and angels are but different names for the same one underlying object" (*Gig.* 16).

A patently Greco-Roman identification of daemons with souls proves essential to Philo's interpretation of Gen 6:2-3. He identifies angels with what "other philosophers call demons (or spirits)" (*Gig.* 6). He assumes that these daemons are "souls that is which fly and hover in the air" (*Gig.* 6), and he further identifies these souls with stars, for "the stars are souls divine and without blemish throughout" (*Gig.* 8).

No longer in the orbit of the literal meaning of Gen 6:3, Philo delineates three sorts of souls: those that are pure and free from the flesh, which "have never deigned to be brought into union with any of the parts of the earth"; those that escape and become free from the flesh, that is, "the souls of those who have given themselves to genuine philosophy"; and those that remain entangled in the flesh, "souls which have sunk beneath the stream" (*Gig.* 13-15).[14]

---

14. Philo's distinction between stars, daemons, and souls may be indebted to the myth of Timarchus, who entered into a crypt and received a vision of the cosmos (*Gen. Socr.* 589F-92F). In the course of this vision, Timarchus observes the movement of the universe, including sun, moon, and stars. Timarchus's daemon explains what Timarchus sees: some souls ascend to the moon and are rescued from the cycle of rebirth; other souls are forbidden by the moon to approach and so must descend into the cycle of rebirth. After identifying these as daemons (*Gen. Socr.* 591D), Timarchus's daemon describes three classes of daemons: (1) stars that are extinguished are souls that have sunk entirely into their body and become distracted by their passions; (2) stars that are lit again, reappearing from below, are souls that free themselves from the body and participate with understanding, like a buoy that keeps the soul from being entirely submerged in the body; (3) stars that move about "on high" are daemons.

This division of souls allows Philo another opportunity to loop farther away from the literal interpretation of Gen 6:3. The angels of Gen 6:1–4, understood from the perspective of this threefold classification of souls, represent the incorrigible class of people among whom the spirit cannot dwell: "Among such as these then it is impossible that the spirit of God should dwell and make for ever its habitation, as also the Lawgiver himself shows clearly. For (so it runs) 'the Lord God said, My spirit shall not abide for ever among men, because they are flesh'" (*Gig.* 19).

According to Philo, then, the effect of this spirit is not life itself, which is apportioned equally to the entirety of humankind for only 120 years, as in Gen 6:1–4. Philo interprets the spirit in quite another way to mean, not the breath that all possess, but the spirit that infrequently grants a vision of God to the mass of humankind:

> The spirit sometimes stays awhile, but it does not abide for ever among us, the mass of men. Who indeed is so lacking in reason or soul that he never either with or without his will receives a conception of the best? Nay, even over the reprobate hovers often of a sudden the vision of the excellent, but to grasp it and keep it for their own they have not the strength. In a moment it is gone. (*Gig.* 20)

Having made this point, Philo then turns to Exod 31:3, in which God called up Bezalel and "filled him with the divine spirit, with wisdom, understanding, and knowledge to devise in every work."[15] Philo is satisfied that "in these words we have suggested to us a definition of what the spirit of God is" (*Gig.* 23). What is it? The knowledge that sages possess.

This definition is apparently inadequate, so Philo shifts from Exod 31:3 to Num 11:17: "I will take of the spirit that is on thee and lay it upon the seventy elders." God must do this because the seventy elders "cannot be in real truth even elders, if they have not received a portion of that spirit of perfect wisdom" (*Gig.* 24). With these shifts from Gen 6:3 to Exod 31:3 to Num 11:17, Philo clarifies that the divine spirit consists essentially of wisdom.

Philo draws from Num 11 the lesson that this spirit matures when imparted to disciples, bringing about "the perfect consummation of knowledge" (*Gig.* 26).[16] On the basis of Num 11, interpreted in association with Gen 6:3 and Exod 31:3, Philo claims:

---

15. Philo mentions but dismisses Gen 1:2 in *Gig.* 22 because πνεῦμα, he suggests, means only "air."

16. In citations of Num 11 in this context, Philo deletes references to prophesying, which he elsewhere regards as an ecstatic activity (e.g., Philo, *Her.* 264–66; *Spec.* 1.65; 4.49).

> If, then, it were Moses' own spirit, or the spirit of some other created being, which was according to God's purpose to be distributed to that great number of disciples, it would indeed be shredded into so many pieces and thus lessened. But as it is, the spirit which is on him is the wise, the divine, the excellent spirit, susceptible of neither severance nor division, diffused in its fullness everywhere and through all things, the spirit which helps, but suffers no hurt, which though it be shared with others or added to others suffers no diminution in understanding and knowledge and wisdom. And so though the divine spirit may stay awhile in the soul it cannot abide there, as we have said. (*Gig.* 26–28)

With this definition, Philo treads the path of Alexandrian Jewish exegesis, if the Wisdom of Solomon is an exemplar of such exegesis. The first reference to the spirit in the Wisdom of Solomon attributes similar cosmic qualities to the spirit: "Because the spirit of the Lord has filled the world, and that which holds all things together knows what is said" (1:7). Such an affirmation is similar to Philo's belief that the spirit is "diffused in its fullness everywhere and through all things" (*Gig.* 27).

The Stoic underpinning of this point of view is unmistakable. Chrysippus, for example, espoused the view that "the whole material world is unified by a spirit [πνεῦμα] which wholly pervades it and by which the universe is made coherent and kept together and is made intercommunicating."[17]

Despite embracing these Stoic qualities of πνεῦμα, Philo is clear on one point: the divine spirit of Gen 6:3 is not the human soul. In this way, he takes the very text he interprets, in which God's spirit remains 120 years, to the breaking point. "And so though the divine spirit may stay awhile in the soul," he concludes, "it cannot abide there, as we have said" (*Gig.* 28). The spirit and the soul are not one and the same. The spirit is not the locus of human life or virtue.

This interpretation has much in common with *Opif.* 69–71, not least the belief that humans are composite beings. "But nothing thwarts its growth so much as our fleshly nature," observes Philo, "for on it ignorance and scorn of learning rest" (*Gig.* 30). It is, in fact, the flesh that keeps the spirit from staying awhile in the soul. "The chief cause of ignorance is the flesh, and the tie which binds us so closely to the flesh." This observation leads Philo to quote again Gen 6:3: "And Moses himself affirms this when he says that 'because they are flesh' the divine spirit cannot abide" (*Gig.* 29).

---

17. Alexander of Aphrodisias, *Mixt.* 216.14–17.

What stalls inspiration, beyond worldly responsibilities such as marriage and child-rearing, is the flesh, the source of ignorance.

If the flesh breeds ignorance, what happens to souls that are able to rise above the flesh? Naturally, they ascend. "For souls that are free from flesh and body spend their days in the theatre of the universe and with a joy that none can hinder see and hear things divine, which they have desired with love insatiable." In contrast, "those which bear the burden of the flesh, oppressed by the grievous load," Philo contends, "cannot look up to the heavens as they revolve, but with necks bowed downwards are constrained to stand rooted to the ground like four-footed beasts" (*Gig.* 30–31).

Ascent is not physical, of course, a corporeal rapture to paradise and parts unknown; those burdened by the flesh cannot even look upward. Nor is ascent mystical in the sense that it takes a person out of body into a world of ecstatic rapture. Ascent here may mean little more than the respite that learning and knowledge bring, looking around and up at matters of wisdom that elude the average human being. This, of course, is no small feat. The ability to deflect human obligations and to live free of the weight of flesh, so as to float joyfully in the theater of the universe, is a keen reward for a love of the divine. If ascent does not lead to a mystical encounter with fiery chariots or a vision of postmortem realities, this is no matter; for Philo, freedom to bask in the theater of the universe is joy enough.

Ascent does not take place, however, because the mind is well suited to it or because the human spirit is a fragment of aether or the cosmic spirit and, as a consequence, is naturally drawn above to the theater of the universe. In *Gig.* 19–31, the human soul is not in itself capable of producing an uninterrupted life of virtue, beset as it is by daily cares and, in the case of most, mired in the flesh. The soul needs the aid of the spirit and the wisdom the spirit imparts. Even the reprobate can experience the abiding of the spirit, however fleetingly. Still, the unfortunate reality is that "though the divine spirit may stay awhile in the soul it cannot abide there."

With one exception: Moses. Toward the end of his commentary on Gen 6:3, in *Gig.* 53–54, Philo returns to the familiar theme that with those "who have set before them many ends in life, the divine spirit does not abide, even though it sojourn there for a while." By way of exception, Moses, and others like him, "who, having disrobed themselves of all created things and of the innermost veil and wrapping of mere opinion, with mind unhampered and naked will come to God." Moses "pitched his own tent outside the camp and the whole array of bodily things . . . and entering the darkness, the invisible region, abides there while he learns the secrets of the most holy mysteries." The biblical text, Exod 33:7, in which Moses enters the tent outside the camp, prompts Philo to talk less of ascent than of entry;

Moses, "entering the darkness, the invisible region, abides there while he learns the secrets of the most holy mysteries."

Entry borders ascent. This is apparent in two ways. First, earlier in *On the Giants*, the occasional presence of the spirit, though it cannot remain permanently, led those free of the flesh to a flight in the theater of the universe. If Philo's discussion of Moses is of a piece with that discussion earlier in *On the Giants*—as it seems to be, since both are part of the same interpretative trajectory rooted in Gen 6:3—then Moses becomes exhibit A for the possibility, and reality, of ascent. Only the language of Exodus—Moses's entry into the tent—keeps Philo from making the connection explicit. The second reason for seeing entry as an alternative depiction of ascent lies in the close parallels between *Gig.* 53-55 and *Spec.* 3.1-6, which we shall interpret later in more detail. In that bit of autobiographical reflection, Philo adopts vocabulary similar to *Gig.* 53-55 to describe his own ascent. First, the objects of contemplation are "holy" in both texts. Second, in both, Philo distinguishes the one—himself or Moses—from the many. Third, Moses and Philo are both teachers of mysteries and revelations. Moses is "the teacher of the divine rites, which he will impart to those whose ears are purified." Philo is able to "unfold and reveal what is not known to the multitude." Fourth, as we will see, *Phaedr.* 246-53 underlies the conception of ascent in Philo's depiction of Moses's experience, as well as his own.

In *On the Giants*, this characterization of a mystical Moses leads, through many exegetical twists and turns, straight—and surprisingly, perhaps—back to Gen 6:3: "He then has ever the divine spirit at his side, taking the lead in every journey of righteousness, but from those others, as I have said, it quickly separates itself, from these to whose span of life he has also set a term of a hundred and twenty years, for he says, 'their days shall be a hundred and twenty years'" (*Gig.* 55).

THE PHILOSOPHER AND ASCENT IN *ON THE PLANTING OF NOAH*

In *Plant.* 18-26, Philo interprets Gen 9:20: "Noah began to be a husbandman tilling the ground, and he planted a vineyard." His interpretation begins with an exegetical leap from the earth to the universe: "It is incumbent on one, who is going to discourse on the work of planters and husbandmen as carried on in this or that place, to begin by marking well the plants set in the universe, those most perfect of all plants, and their great Planter and Overseer" (*Plant.* 2).

The exegetical leap from the ground to the universe requires that Philo identify God as planter par excellence and the world as a plant (*Plant.* 2). Such an interpretation of this simple text is hardly due to straightforward inference. It arises rather from introducing "an old saying" into his discussion of Gen 9:20, that a human being is "a plant not earthly but heavenly" (*Plant.* 17). This "old saying" is a reference to Plato's *Tim.* 90A.

It is, then, Plato's *Timaeus*, rather than Gen 9:20, that permits Philo to transfer the discussion from Noah as tiller in his garden to humankind as stargazers in the "field of the universe" (*Plant.* 28). Philo observes that plants and irrational animals are fashioned analogously with their roots and heads downward. Humans alone gaze upward: "But the build allotted to man was distinguished above that of other living creatures. For by turning the eyes of the others downwards He made them incline to the earth beneath them. The eyes of man, on the contrary, He set high up that he might gaze on heaven, for man, as the old saying says, is a plant not earthly but heavenly" (17). It is not so much the uncomplicated text of Gen 9:20 as the Platonic depiction of human beings as a heavenly plant, therefore, that sets up Philo's discussion of the mind's ascent in *Plant.* 18–26. This text is essential to understanding ascent in Philo's writings and, consequently, worthy of full citation:

> Now while others, by asserting that our human mind is a particle of the ethereal substance have claimed for man a kinship with the upper air; our great Moses likened the fashion of the reasonable soul to no created thing, but averred it to be a genuine coinage of that dread Spirit, the Divine and Invisible One, signed and impressed by the seal of God, the stamp of which is the Eternal Word. His words are "God in-breathed into his face a breath of Life"; so that it cannot but be that he that receives is made in the likeness of Him Who sends forth the breath. Accordingly we also read that man has been made after the Image of God (Gen i.27), not however after the image of anything created. It followed then, as a natural consequence of man's soul having been made after the image of the Archetype, the Word of the First Cause, that his body also was made erect, and could lift up its eyes to heaven, the purest portion of our universe, that by means of that which he could see man might clearly apprehend that which he could not see. Since, then, it was impossible for any to discern how the understanding tends towards the Existent One, save those only who had been drawn by Him—for each one of us knows what he has himself experienced as no other can know it—He endows the bodily eyes with the power of taking the direction of the upper air, and so makes them a

distinct representation of the invisible eye. For, seeing that the eyes formed out of perishable matter obtained so great reach as to travel from the earthly region to heaven, that is so far away, and to touch its bounds, how vast must we deem the flight in all directions of the eyes of the soul? The strong yearning to perceive the Existent One gives them wings to attain not only to the furthest region of the upper air, but to overpass the very bounds of the entire universe and speed away toward the Uncreated. This is why those who crave for wisdom and knowledge with insatiable persistence are said in the Sacred Oracles to have been called upwards; for it accords with God's ways that those who have received His down-breathing should be called up to Him. For when trees are whirled up, roots and all, into the air by hurricanes and tornadoes, and heavily laden ships of large tonnage are snatched up out of mid-oceans, as though objects of very little weight, and lakes and river are borne aloft, and earth's hollows are left empty by the water as it is drawn up by a tangle of violently eddying winds, it is strange if a light substance like the mind is not rendered buoyant and raised to the utmost height by the native force of the Divine spirit, overcoming as it does in its boundless might all powers that are here below. Above all is it strange if this is not so with the mind of the genuine philosopher. Such a one suffers from no weight of downward pressure toward the objects dear to the body and to earth. From these he has ever made an earnest effort to sever and estrange himself. So he is borne upward insatiably enamoured of all holy happy natures that dwell on high. Accordingly Moses, the keeper and guardian of the mysteries of the Existent One, will be one called above; for it is said in the Book of Leviticus, "He called Moses up above" (Lev. i.1). One called up above will Bezalel also be, held worthy of a place in the second rank. For him also does God call up above for the construction and overseeing of the sacred works.

In *Gig.* 19-55, Philo's relationship to Stoicism appeared to be ambivalent. In *Plant.* 18-26, it is more adversarial: "Now while others, by asserting that our human mind is a particle of the ethereal substance, have claimed for man a kinship with the upper air; our great Moses likened the fashion of the reasonable soul to no created thing."[18] Humankind is made after God's im-

18. Philo, *Plant.* 18. Greek ἀλλ' οἱ μὲν ἄλλοι τῆς αἰθερίου φύσεως τὸν ἡμέτερον νοῦν μοῖραν εἰπόντες εἶναι συγγένειαν ἀνθρώπῳ πρὸς αἰθέρα συνῆψαν. Diogenes Laertius, in the context of a summary of Stoics, including Chrysippus, Zeno, Apollodorus, and Posidonius, attributes to Stoicism the view that the world is "a living being, rational, animate and intelligent," which is "endowed with soul, as is clear from our several souls being each a fragment of it" (*Lives* 7.143). Cicero, quoting Chrysippus, describes the

age, "not however after the image of anything created." Philo interprets the breath of life from Gen 2:7 in similar terms as an uncreated element: "The body, then, has been formed out of earth, but the soul is of the upper air, a particle detached from the Deity: 'for God breathed into his face a breath of life, and the human became a living soul.' ... The soul being a portion of an ethereal nature has on the contrary ethereal and divine food" (*Legat.* 3.161).

Elsewhere in his writings, in *Spec.* 4.123, Philo supplements this interpretation of Gen 2:7 with his own suggestion that the rational portion of the soul is composed of something better than aether:

> For the essence or substance of that other soul is divine spirit, a truth vouched for by Moses especially, who in his story of the creation says that God breathed a breath of life upon the first human, the founder of our race, into the lordliest part of his body, the face ... And clearly what was then thus breathed was ethereal spirit, or something if such there be better than ethereal spirit, even an effulgence of the blessed, thrice blessed nature of the Godhead.

In *Plant.* 18–19, where the polemical edge is sharper, Philo's conception of the spirit neither affirms a Stoic point of view, as in *Opif.* 135, nor qualifies Stoicism, as in *Spec.* 4.123; here he tends to refute Stoicism:

> Now while others, by asserting that our human mind is a particle of the ethereal substance, have claimed for man a kinship with the upper air; our great Moses likened the fashion of the reasonable soul to no created thing, but averred it to be a genuine coinage of that dread [unseen] Spirit, the Divine and Invisible One, signed and impressed by the seal of God, the stamp of which is the Eternal Word. (*Plant.* 18)

The human spirit is not a particle of aether but a part of the unseen, divine spirit. Otherwise prone to eclecticism, Philo stakes his own claim over against the Stoics.

The dominant influence upon Philo's view of the ascent of the mind in *Plant.* 18–26 lies, not surprisingly, elsewhere—in Plato's *Phaedr.* 246–53, as it does for his conception of creation (*Opif.* 69–71); his allegorical interpretation of the ascent of Moses (*Gig.* 50–55); and, as we shall soon see, his own experience (*Spec.* 3.1–6).

On the Planting of Noah 22, for example, is rife with Platonic vocabulary: "The strong yearning to perceive the Existent One gives them [the eyes

---

human being as "a small fragment of that which is perfect" (*Nat. d.* 2.38). Epictetus views human souls as "parts and portions" of God's being (*Diatr.* 1.14.6).

of the soul] wings to attain not only to the furthest region of the upper air, but to overpass the very bounds of the entire universe and speed away toward the Uncreated."[19] This description recalls Socrates's description of the fourth sort of madness, philosophical love of beauty, which drives the philosopher's soul to sprout wings and to ascend beyond the heavenly regions.

There is more than a general reflection of the *Phaedrus* myth in *Plant.* 18–26. The association of the growth of wings with the soul's "yearning" mirrors Socrates's reference to yearning after beauty, which provides the impulse toward a growth of wings (*Phaedr.* 251C, E). The image of wings, moreover, is fundamental to the *Phaedrus* myth, which begins by comparing the soul to "a pair of winged horses and a charioteer" (246A), continues with the observation that the "natural function of the wing is to soar upwards" (246D), and is summarized with a description of the person who "feels his wings growing" (249D). Philo's contention that "strong yearning" gives the "eyes" of the soul "wings" is, therefore, a shorthand way of recollecting Socrates's contention that beauty comes through the eyes, bringing with it a yearning that causes the hardened parts, which will eventually become wings, to be moistened and warmed and to fill the soul with joy.

The winged soul's ability to pass beyond the heavenly region corresponds to Socrates's contention that immortal souls, "when they reach the top, pass outside and take their place on the outer surface of the heaven, and when they have taken their stand, the revolution carries them round and they behold the things outside of the heaven" (*Phaedr.* 247B–C).

Finally, this description applies exclusively to the philosopher. Philo writes, "Above all it is strange if this [ascent] is not so with the mind of the genuine philosopher. Such a one . . . has ever made an earnest effort to sever and estrange himself from objects dear to the body" (*Plant.* 24–25). Similarly, Socrates explains, "And therefore it is just that the mind of the philosopher only has wings . . . he separates himself from human interests and turns his attention toward the divine" (*Phaedr.* 249C).

Philo, of course, is in good company in his dependence upon the *Phaedrus* for his understanding of the ascent of the mind. Plutarch, in *Quaest. plat.* 6, asks why the soul is closely akin to the divine. He responds: "While there are a good many faculties of the soul concerned with the body, the faculty of reason or thought, whose objects he has said are things divine and celestial, is most closely akin to the divine. This faculty he not inappropriately called a pinion because it bears the soul up and away from the things that are base and mortal."

19. Greek: ἅπερ ὑπὸ πολλοῦ τοῦ τὸ ὂν κατιδεῖν τηλαυγῶς ἱμέρου πτερωθέντα οὐ μόνον πρὸς τὸν ἔσχατον αἰθέρα τείνεται, παραμειψάμενα δὲ καὶ παντὸς τοῦ κόσμου τοὺς ὅρους ἐπείγεται πρὸς τὸν ἀγένητον.

Although other philosophers were influenced by Plato's *Phaedrus*, Maximus of Tyre's discussion of the topic "the mind sees and the mind hears" provides a clear example of the sort of philosophical milieu that indelibly shaped Philo's *Plant.* 18–26. Maximus of Tyre writes:

> And the soul maintains its sovereignty by means of true reason and healthy yearning ... And to the one who puts away things below, always the distinct and the brightest things and the preliminary nature of God are before him. And as it proceeds further, it hears the nature of God, and mounting higher it sees. The end of the journey is not heaven, nor the bodies which are in heaven. These are indeed beautiful and marvelous, as they are the genuine descendants and the offspring of that one and suited to what is most beautiful. But it is necessary to go beyond these, and to look over [the border of] heaven at the true place and the calm [sea] which is there.[20]

The mind intact, the overcoming of things below, ascent, yearning, the need to peer over the boundaries of the created world—these characterize Philo's description of the ascent of the mind in *Plant.* 18–26.[21]

Philo then infers: "This is why those who crave for wisdom and knowledge with insatiable persistence are said in the Sacred Oracles to have been called upwards; for it accords with God's ways that those who have received His down-breathing should be called up to Him" (*Plant.* 23). Although all people presumably receive God's down-breathing (Gen 2:7), only philosophers, who crave for wisdom and knowledge, are those most likely to be called up (based upon Lev 1:1) to God. A philosopher's mind is one which

---

20. My translation, based upon Hobein, *Maximi Tyrii*, 140–41. Prior to this passage come the question and initial answer "How therefore does the mind see? And how does it hear? With a healthy and true soul, looking straight toward that pure light, and not dizzied, nor descending to the earth. But it stops the ears and turns the eyes and the other senses toward the self. And the things below—mourning, sighing, pleasure, opinion, honor and dishonor—it utterly forgets."

21. Third-century CE Neo-Platonic philosopher Plotinus, in his *Enneades*, begins by describing the preparation that is requisite to ascent, which elsewhere he identifies as mathematics and dialectics, for "gaining footholds in the intelligible and settling ourselves firmly there and feasting on its contents" (*Enn.* 6.7.36). This preparation, however, is only a precursor to the vision of the intelligible world, where "one lets all study go; up to a point one has been led along and settled firmly in beauty and as far as this one thinks that in which one is, but is carried out of it by the surge of the wave of Intellect itself and lifted on high by a kind of swell and sees suddenly, not seeing how, but the vision fills his eyes with light and does not make him see something else by it, but the light itself is what he sees" (*Enn.* 6.7.36). This description is similar to Philo's writings, with preparation through knowledge (*Opif.* 69; *Spec.* 3.1–6) and a final vision of light (*Opif.* 69; *Spec.* 3.6).

"suffers from no weight of downward pressure towards the objects dear to the body and to earth" (*Gig.* 25).[22]

To follow the *Phaedrus* fully, Philo need only refer to recollection. By recollecting the true nature of beauty, which he knew prior to being embodied (*Phaedr.* 254B), the philosopher's mind takes wings in heavenward flight. But Philo does not take this tack, as natural as it may have seemed to him. Instead of introducing the notion of recollection, Philo reintroduces the spirit (*Plant.* 24).

According to Plato, Plutarch, and Maximus of Tyre, the philosophical mind ascends to a vision of the ideal world. Philo appears to opt wholeheartedly for this view, not only with Platonic allusions and elements, but also by describing the mind as a copy of the breath and logos and locating its origin in the down-breathing of God. Although the character of the mind should be sufficient to raise it to the heights, as in *Opif.* 69–71, in *Plant.* 18–26, Philo introduces the spirit as the sole power that is able to lift the mind upwards. The mind is raised, rendered buoyant, not by recollection but by the spirit.

Philo's references to the spirit in *Plant.* 18–26 and *Gig.* 19–55 are altogether different from one another, though neither is rooted in any obvious way to the biblical text. In *Plant.* 18–26, the spirit is introduced into a discussion of the "field of the universe," which is tied tenuously to a description of Noah's farming in Gen 9:20. In *Gig.* 19–55, in contrast, a single biblical text, Gen 6:3, is the topic of interpretation. Nevertheless, Philo departs from the literal meaning of the biblical text, with the result that the spirit becomes the source of the vision of God, which comes infrequently to the majority of humankind, rather than the source of physical life for 120 years. In neither case, therefore, does the literal meaning of the biblical text tether Philo's exegetical imagination.

Though attached tenuously to biblical texts, this spirit, according to Philo, exhibits enormous power. Like a hurricane or tornado, it is capable of lifting heavy substances into the air. The scope of its power includes all things below; no human concern can resist its uplifting force. How much more can the spirit lift the featherweight philosophical mind, which is already poised to ascend?

The extent to which the spirit lifts a philosopher may vary. Some it lifts only to a place within the created world; this sort of philosopher is represented by Bezalel, whose name means, according to Philo, "making in shadows." Moses, in contrast, is lifted up into the intelligible world, a world

22. Plotinus would later write, "But the philosopher—he is the one who is by nature ready to respond and 'winged,' we may say, and in no need of separation like the others" (*Enn.* 1.3.3).

of archetypes and not copies, a world that yields "a clearer, more radiant vision, as though in unclouded sunshine" (*Plant.* 27).

This accent upon the uniqueness of Moses's ascent brings us again to Philo's discussion in *On the Giants*. In *Gig.* 55, Philo describes the ascent of Moses with direct reference to Gen 6:3: "He then has ever the divine spirit at his side, taking the lead in every journey of righteousness, but from those others, as I have said, it quickly separates itself, from these to whose span of life he has also set a term of a hundred and twenty years, for he says 'their days shall be a hundred and twenty years.'" As in *Plant.* 18–26, in which the spirit is the source of the mind's ascent, the spirit cannot be identified with the soul. The image of accompaniment in *Gig.* 55 excludes that possibility. Once again, then, ascent requires a finely tuned philosophical mind, but that mind cannot ascend by its own means, by recollection, by a yearning for beauty. On the contrary, the philosophical mind may be prepared by such attributes but is lifted only by the divine spirit, which takes the lead in every journey of righteousness and overcomes in its boundless might all powers that are below.

ASCENT AND THE INTERPRETATION OF TORAH IN *ON THE SPECIAL LAWS*

Philo regards himself first and foremost as an interpreter of Scripture. His enthusiasm about the interpretation of Torah preoccupies him in *Spec.* 3.1–6, where he puts the famed language of the ascent of the soul from Plato's *Phaedrus* to another use: to describe his exceptional ability to interpret Scripture. When on occasion Philo is able to "obtain a spell of fine weather and a calm from civil turmoils," he is able to "open the soul's eyes," to be wafted on the winds of knowledge, and to become "irradiated by the light of wisdom." During these rare moments of respite, Philo finds himself "daring, not only to read the sacred pages of Moses, but also in my love of knowledge to peer into each of them and unfold and reveal what is not known to the multitude."

This sort of experience is the exception rather than the rule for Philo. In *Spec.* 3.1–6, Philo recalls wistfully:

> There was a time when I had leisure for philosophy and for the contemplation of the universe and its contents, when I made its spirit my own in all its beauty and loveliness and true blessedness, when my constant companions were divine themes and verities, wherein I rejoiced with a joy that never cloyed or sated. I had no base or abject thoughts nor grovelled in search of

reputation or of wealth or bodily comforts, but seemed always to be borne aloft into the heights with a soul possessed by some God-sent inspiration, a fellow-traveller with the sun and moon and the whole heaven and universe. Ah then I gazed down from the upper air . . . But, as it proved, my steps were dogged by the deadliest of mischiefs, the hater of the good, envy, which suddenly set upon me and ceased not to pull me down with violence till it had plunged me in the ocean of civil cares . . . Yet amid my groans I hold my own, for, planted in my soul from my earliest days I keep the yearning for culture which ever has pity and compassion for me, lifts me up and relieves my pain. To this I owe it that sometimes I raise my head and with soul's eyes— dimly indeed because the mist of extraneous affairs has clouded their clear vision . . . And if unexpectedly I obtain a spell of fine weather and a calm from civil turmoils, I get me wings and ride the waves and almost tread the lower air, wafted by the breezes of knowledge which often urges me to come to spend my days with her, a truant as it were from merciless masters in the shape not only of men but of affairs, which pour in upon me like a torrent from different sides. Yet it is well for me to give thanks to God even for this, that though submerged I am not sucked down into the depths, but can also open the soul's eyes, which in my despair of comforting hope I thought had now lost their sight, and am irradiated by the light of wisdom, and am not given over to lifelong darkness. So behold me daring, not only to read the sacred pages of Moses, but also in my love of knowledge to peer into each of them and unfold and reveal what is not known to the multitude.

Philo in this autobiographical reflection characterizes himself as a philosopher. The first words in *Spec.* 3.1–6, "There was a time when I had leisure for philosophy," provide the context of inspiration. Philo intends to recount his experiences of inspiration as a philosopher. He peppers this description of his occasional experience with allusions to Plato's description of philosophical inspiration. His definition of philosophy as "the contemplation of the universe and its contents" and his subsequent description of becoming a "fellow-traveller with the sun and moon and the whole heaven and universe" recall the words of Pindar in Plato's *Theaet.* 173C–74A, which Socrates quotes: "His mind . . . is borne in all directions." These include below the earth, the surface of the earth, and "above the sky," where the philosopher studies the stars and investigates the nature of everything that is.

Philo supports his depiction of himself as a philosopher through allusions to Plato's *Phaedr.* 246A–53C. These allusions reinforce that his own ascent is that of the philosopher, for Socrates contends that "it is just that the mind of the philosopher only has wings" (249C). More specifically, Philo's description of his experience as a fellow traveller with heavenly bodies sharpens the allusions to *Phaedr.* 246B, in which the soul "traverses the whole heaven," and 248A, in which the soul "is carried round in the revolution." Finally, Philo's slightly odd mention of jealousy, which plunges him again into civil cares, may recall *Phaedr.* 247A, in which "jealousy is excluded from the celestial band."[23]

Philo's self-depiction as a philosopher is only one side of the coin in *Spec.* 3.1–6. His reflection contains a striking correspondence between the ascent of the philosopher's mind and the discernment of an interpreter's mind. The passage begins with philosophical ascent and possession (3.1–2), is interrupted by a plunge into the ocean of civil cares (3.3–4), and concludes with an ascent on the winds of knowledge to interpret Torah (3.5–6). Within this structure, the initial ascent to contemplate the upper air corresponds to the final ascent to interpret Torah. Philo reinforces this correlation between philosopher and interpreter by employing the same verb, "to stoop," to describe the experiences of ascent and interpretation. The words "Ah then I stooped [gazed down] from the upper air" (3.2) correspond to "Behold me daring . . . to stoop [peer] into each of them [the sacred messages of Moses] and unfold" (3.6).[24]

In those rare moments, Philo experiences what he calls possession or enthusiasm. The nuances of this word are not entirely clear. Elsewhere, Philo uses this term to describe prophetic inspiration, though only vaguely so. In *Who Is the Heir*, it has the suggestion of ecstatic rapture:

> Therefore, my soul, if thou feelest any yearning to inherit the good things of God, leave not only thy land, that is the body, thy kinsfolk, that is the senses, thy father's house (Gen. xii.1), that is speech, but be a fugitive from thyself also and issue forth from thyself. Like persons possessed and corybants, be filled with inspired frenzy, even as the prophets are inspired. (*Her.* 69)

---

23. See also Plato, *Tim.* 29E, and the analysis of Méasson, *Char ailé de Zeus*, 234. On Philo's use of Plato's *Phaedrus* in general in *Spec.* 3.1–6, see Méasson, *Char ailé de Zeus*, 231–41.

24. My translation, based upon the LCL edition. The correlation between Philo as an inspired interpreter and Moses as an inspired teacher is evident in *Cher.* 48, which includes what is implicit in *Spec.* 3.6. For further analysis, see Levison, *Filled with the Spirit*, 194n29.

This description continues with ascent:

> For it is the mind which is under the divine afflatus, and no longer in its own keeping, but is stirred to its depths and maddened by heavenward yearning, drawn by the truly existent and pulled upward thereto, with truth to lead the way and remove all obstacles before its feet, that its path may be smooth to tread—such is the mind, which has this inheritance. (*Her.* 70)

In this description, then, Philo is able to combine ecstatic rapture with the ascent of the mind.

Even if the precise nature of inspiration is elusive, Philo is certain that the experience of being a philosopher cum interpreter arises from intense learning. While prophets speak when they fall under the power of ecstasy and divine possession, when "the mind is evicted at the arrival of the divine Spirit,"[25] philosophers like Philo prepare through learning. As a result, they are able, even momentarily, to wrest themselves from civil responsibilities. The result is that the philosopher-interpreter's mind becomes more alert, not less, as his ability to interpret Torah intensifies rather than diminishes.

The correspondence between philosophical ascent and the interpretation of Scripture gives *Spec.* 3.1–6 a distinctive ring in the writings of Philo. In reality, ascent may at times prove to be little more than an escape from worldly cares that gives him time to pore over the writings of Moses. In short, the mind of a philosopher, like Philo, takes wing—to adopt the language of *Phaedrus*—when he drops his or her nose into the depths of Torah. The ascent of the mind, in other words, is simultaneously a plunge into the depths of an inspired literary corpus.

CONCLUSION

If, as Alan Segal proposes, Philo is the starting point for the study of ascent in the Jewish tradition, then it is important, if not indispensable, to outline the central elements in Philo's conception of ascent. These can be encapsulated in five questions. First, what ascends? Second, who ascends? Third, what precedes ascent? Fourth, to where does ascent lead? Fifth, what propels ascent?

---

25. Philo, *Her.* 265.

What Ascends?

For Philo, there can be no question that only the mind ascends.[26] The mind alone is suited to ascent. The mind alone is the image and likeness of God, "a god to him who carries and enshrines it as an object of reverence" (*Opif.* 69). The mind is a particle of something even purer than aether—"a genuine coinage of that dread Spirit, the Divine and Invisible One, signed and impressed by the seal of God, the stamp of which is the Eternal Word" (*Plant.* 18); this Philo can say on the basis of his interpretation of both the inbreathing of Gen 2:7 and the image of Gen 1:27. The deftness of the human mind is evident in Philo's interpretation of Gen 15:4, 6, in which Abraham "said in his mind." This prompts Philo to praise the mind, "which none of the creatures whose swiftness of foot we admire can outrun" (*Mut.* 178).

The confidence with which Philo states his belief that the mind alone, apart from—or perhaps despite—the body, ascends separates his conception of ascent from others', such as the apostle Paul's, who claims, "I know a person in Christ who fourteen years ago was caught up to the third heaven—whether in the body or out of the body I do not know; God knows. And I know that such a person—whether in the body or out of the body I do not know; God knows—was caught up into Paradise and heard things that are not to be told, that no mortal is permitted to repeat" (2 Cor 12:2-4). Paul cannot say whether this experience took place in his body or out of body; Philo evinces no such ambivalence. The mind ascends despite the pull of the body downward. Those who ascend, in fact, suffer "no weight of downward pressure towards the objects dear to the body and to earth" (*Plant.* 25).

Who Ascends?

The philosopher. Time and again, Philo claims that only people of philosophical bent, immersed in the pursuit of knowledge and wisdom, have minds capable of ascent. Philo praises the impossible but not fruitless pursuit of God's ineffable essence:

> As for the divine essence, though in fact it is hard to track and to apprehend, it still calls for all the inquiry possible. For nothing is better than to search for the true God, even if the discovery of Him eludes human capacity, since the very wish

---

26. Philo can also say the soul ascends, by which he means the upper or rational portion of the soul, that is, the mind.

> to learn, if earnestly entertained, produces untold joys and pleasures. (*Spec.* 1.36)

Who bears testimony to the benefit of this pursuit? Philosophers, whose ascent leads them as far upward as is humanly possible.

> We have the testimony of those who have not taken a mere sip of philosophy but have feasted more abundantly on its reasonings and conclusions. For with them the reason soars away from the earth into the heights, travels through the upper air and accompanies the revolutions of the sun and moon and the whole heaven and in its desire to see all that is there finds its powers of sight blurred, for so pure and vast is the radiance that pours therefrom that the soul's eye is dizzied by the flashing of the rays. (*Spec.* 1.37)

In *Gig.* 13–14, we may recall, Philo delineates three types of souls. Those in the middle, in the body but striving to be detached from it, "are the souls of those who have given themselves to genuine philosophy, who from first to last study to die to the life in the body, that a higher existence immortal and incorporeal, in the presence of Him who is Himself immortal and uncreated, may be their portion" (*Gig.* 14). These souls have alternately descended into the body—philosophers are mortal, after all—and "at other times have been able to stem the current, have risen to the surface and then soared upwards back to the place from whence they came" (*Gig.* 13). Elsewhere, in a discussion of the perils of pleasure, Philo returns to this theme: "But the roads of sound-sense and self-mastery and of the other virtues, if not untrodden, are at all events unworn; for scanty is the number of those that tread them, that have genuinely devoted themselves to the pursuit of wisdom" (*Agr.* 104). In an effort to encourage his readers to pursue knowledge of God, however unattainable it is, Philo attributes the work of asking two essential questions—whether the Deity exists and what the Deity consists of—to the genuine philosopher. There is an intensity to this adverb, "genuinely" (ἀνόθως), which Philo often associates with the philosophical task.[27] When, then, Philo adopts this word in *Plant.* 24 to describe the one who is called up, he invests the task of the philosopher with a stirring impulse.

It is not just the professional philosopher whose mind can ascend. Philo's love of learning encompasses the world of practiced virtue, as well, so that he can write, "For the soul of the lover of God does in truth leap from earth to heaven and wing its way on high, eager to take its place in

---

27. On this adverb, see also Philo, *Migr.* 86; *Virt.* 185; *Prob.* 99.

the ranks and share the ordered march of sun and moon and the all-holy, all-harmonious host of the other stars" (*Spec.* 1.207).

What Precedes Ascent?

Though ascent may involve rapture or ecstasy, it begins with learning and a yearning for knowledge. Repeatedly, including in his autobiographical narrative of ascent, Philo understands the bedrock of ascent to be the relentless pursuit of knowledge, wisdom, and the presence of God. The mind, made in God's image, "opens by arts and sciences roads branching in many directions" (*Opif.* 69). In *Plant.* 23–25, philosophers must sever themselves from earthly cares. They must "crave for wisdom and knowledge with insatiable persistence" to be called upwards. In *Gig.* 30, Philo claims that wisdom is thwarted by ignorance and lack of learning, implying the need for knowledge and education. Similarly, according to *Spec.* 3.1–6, Philo recalls that inspiration overtook him when his constant companions were divine words and truths, when he had no interest in status or wealth or bodily comforts.

In his treatise on rewards and punishments, Philo comments on a trinity consisting of Abraham, Isaac, and Jacob, who together reject vanity. In *On Rewards and Punishments* (*Praem.*) 25–26, the person who rejects vanity "cannot be contained by the whole compass of the earth but reaches to Heaven, possessed with an intense longing to contemplate and for ever be in the company of things divine." This trinity consists of: Abraham, who is taught to believe in God and is rewarded with faith (*Praem.* 28–30); Isaac, self-taught, who comes by nature to God and is rewarded with joy (31–35); and Jacob, who practices and is rewarded with a vision, in which he is named Israel (36–46). Jacob's vision is borne of the effort to see beyond the material world. "In his former years the eyes of his soul had been closed, but by means of continuous striving he began though slowly to open them and to break up and throw off the mist which overshadowed him" (37).

In a moment of magnanimity, Philo even concedes that those outside his tradition are able to ascend in visionary rapture. These must be people of peculiar virtue:

> All who practice wisdom, either in Grecian or barbarian lands, and live a blameless and irreproachable life, choosing neither to inflict nor retaliate injustice, avoid the gathering of busybodies and abjure the scenes which they haunt, such as law-courts, council-chambers, markets, congregations and in general any gathering or assemblage of careless men. Their own aspirations are for a life of peace, free from warring. They are the closest

> observers of nature and all that it contains; earth, sea, air and heaven and the various forms of being which inhabit them are food for their research, as in mind and thought they share the ranging of the moon and sun and the ordered march of the other stars fixed and planetary. While their bodies are firmly planted on the land they provide their souls with wings, so that they may traverse the upper air and gain full contemplation of the powers which dwell there, as behooves true "cosmopolitans" who have recognized the world to be a city having for its citizens the associates of wisdom, registered as such by virtue to whom is entrusted the headship of the universal commonwealth. (*Spec.* 2.44–45)

Even parents are charged with inculcating the sort of learning that leads, at least for the few, to a vision beyond the perceptible world. The building blocks of education—music and math, literature and philosophy—become the stepping stones to ascent:

> Further, who could be more truly called benefactors than parents in relation to their children? First, they have brought them out of non-existence; then, again, they have held them entitled to nurture and later to education of body and soul, so that they may have not only life, but a good life. They have benefited the body by means of the gymnasium and the training there given, through which it gains muscular vigor and good condition and the power to bear itself and move with an ease marked by gracefulness and elegance. They have done the same for the soul by means of letters and arithmetic and geometry and music and philosophy as a whole which lifts on high the mind lodged within the mortal body and escorts it to the very heaven and shews it the blessed and happy beings that dwell therein, and creates in it an eager longing for the unswerving ever-harmonious order which they never forsake because they obey their captain and marshal. (*Spec.* 2.229–30)

To Where Does Ascent Lead?

At the most basic level, ascent offers an escape from worldly cares. This is the gist of Philo's autobiographical narrative, in which he recalls, from the standpoint of a civic leader, that time in life when he "seemed always to be borne aloft into the heights with a soul possessed by some God-sent inspiration, a fellow-traveller with the sun and moon and the whole heaven and universe. Ah then I gazed down from the upper air" (*Spec.* 3.1–2). Occasionally, he ascends in the midst of civil cares. Where does he find this respite? In the study of Torah, as he interprets for others "the sacred messages of Moses" (*Spec.* 3.6).

Philo seems to have something similar in mind in *Praem.* 121–22, where he describes "the mind, the initiate of the holy mysteries, the fellow traveler of the heavenly bodies as they revolve in ordered march." Such a mind lives in quiet contemplation, provided it exists in a healthy body, which allows it to pursue wisdom and to feast "on holy thoughts and doctrines."

This autobiographical narrative does not encompass the geography of ascent. Early in his oeuvre, in his commentary on Gen 1:26, Philo lays out the various layers of ascent. First, the mind explores, through the arts and sciences, "a vast network of paths, all of them highways, and passes through land and sea, investigating what is present in both realms" (*Opif.* 69). Second, the mind probes the atmosphere (70). Third, higher still are the planets and stars (70). Fourth and farther in ascent, the mind contemplates the Platonic world of ideas, "the intelligible world," with its "sights of surpassing loveliness," which fill the mind with inspiration and corybantic frenzy (71). Now, at "the topmost arch of the things perceptible to the mind," it is "on its way to the Great King," whom the mind cannot see (71). This is the fifth and final stage of ascent.

Philo puts this more succinctly in *QE* 2.40. To explain the meaning of the words "Come up to Me to the mountain and be there" in Exod 24:12, Philo writes, "This signifies that a holy soul is divinized by ascending not to the air or to the ether or to heaven (which is) higher than all but to (a region) above the heavens. And beyond the world there is no place but God." There is no place for the world of ideas in this response, but the geography of ascent is nonetheless clear. Unfortunately, notes Philo, most people will not experience such an ascent, "for those who have a quickly satiated passion for reflexion fly upward for only a short distance under divine inspiration and then they immediately return. They do not fly so much as they are drawn downward, I mean, to the depths of Tartarus. But those who do not return from the holy and divine city, to which they have migrated, have God as their chief leader in the migration."

A similar, if truncated, geography of ascent is apparent in Philo's depiction of the speed with which the mind travels: "For the mind moves at the same moment to many things material and immaterial with indescribable rapidity and reaches at once the boundaries of land and sea... At the same time it leaps so high from the earth that it passes through the lower to the upper air and scarcely comes to a stop even when it reaches the furthermost sphere of the fixed stars." Still, the mind travels swiftly farther, "across wide spaces outside the limits of all this world of sense to the world framed from the ideas to which it feels itself akin" (*Mut.* 180). The mind, in short, travels from the earth to the stars to the world of ideas: the first, second, third, and fourth regions delineated in *Opif.* 69–71—but not the fifth.

The philosopher's mind travels similarly, according to *Spec.* 1.37: "For with them the reason soars away from the earth into the heights, travels through the upper air and accompanies the revolutions of the sun and moon and the whole heaven and in its desire to see all that is there finds its powers of sight blurred, for so pure and vast is the radiance that pours therefrom that the soul's eye is dizzied by the flashing of the rays." These minds cannot pass, it seems, from the heavenly realm to the world of ideas, at least in this passage. The lover of God, too, reaches "the ordered march of sun and moon and the all-holy, all-harmonious host of the other stars" (*Spec.* 1.207).

In *Concerning Noah's Work as a Planter*, Philo speaks more generally of the upward call, though the limits of ascent seem to lie among the stars. He conjectures that, if "the eyes formed out of perishable matter obtained so great reach as to travel from the earthly region to heaven," then "the strong yearning to perceive the Existent One gives them wings to attain not only to the furthest region of the upper air, but to overpass the very bounds of the entire universe and speed away toward the Uncreated" (*Plant.* 22–23). "This is why," explains Philo, "those who crave for wisdom and knowledge with insatiable persistence are said in the Sacred Oracles to have been called upwards." Though the mind speeds toward God, where does it stop? Philo says little specifically about the geography of ascent except perhaps when he says that someone can be "borne upward insatiably enamoured of all holy happy natures that dwell on high" (*Plant.* 25). These happy natures are probably souls that now dwell as stars in the heavenly realm.

Those Greeks and barbarians whom Philo praises experience similar limits, according to *Spec.* 2.46. They observe nature (level 1 in *Opif.* 69–71); beings in the atmosphere (level 2); and the moon, stars, and planets (level 3). Philo does not say that their ascent reaches to the world of ideas or to God. Similarly, parents educate their children so that their minds can be lifted to heaven, where they see "the blessed and happy beings that dwell therein" (*Spec.* 2.230). As in *Plant.* 25, these are probably souls whom God now marshals as stars, moon, and planets.

It is possible to ascend farther, though barely so. Jacob, symbol of the person of practice, is led by a charioteer to the world of ideas, where he is blinded by "beams of undiluted light" (level 4 in *Opif.* 69–71, though in *Opif.* 69–71, light occurs at the fifth and final level). God pities the person of practice and grants a vision of God—not what God is but only that God is. Still, this vision leads higher than most others, which tend to end at the planetary sphere (*Praem.* 39).

Philo is circumspect even about Moses's experience of God.[28] In *On the Giants*, Philo suggests that souls free from flesh and body "spend their days in the theatre of the universe," that is, in the company of the stars, moon, and planets (*Gig.* 31). This accords with many other of Philo's depictions of ascent. Moses, however, free of conjecture and the physicality of the flesh, enters the darkness—in the tent outside the camp, according to Exod 33:7—the "invisible region," where "he learns the secrets of the most holy mysteries. There he becomes not only one of the congregation of the initiated, but also the hierophant and teacher of divine rites, which he will impart to those whose ears are purified" (*Gig.* 53–54).

Others travel in the theater of the universe, among the sun, the planets, the moon, and the stars, but Moses enters beyond the blinding light into the darkness. This is unique, a realm reserved for Moses alone. Except, perhaps, for Philo, who, like Moses, contemplates holy matters. Yet even Philo, claims and confidence notwithstanding, sees the difference. Moses learns and teaches what he has completed—the *holiest* rituals—while Philo studies and teaches only the holy matters of Moses (*Spec.* 3.6).

What Propels Ascent?

Why is Moses able to ascend to where others cannot? There are, of course, countless reasons, to which Philo can appeal. In *Gig.* 55, he selects but one: "He then has ever the divine spirit at his side, taking the lead in every journey of righteousness." This is not typical for Philo. More often than not, the character of the mind is the cause for ascent. This is an understandable state of affairs, given how dependent Philo is on Plato's *Phaedrus* for his accounts of ascent. In the course of this study, we have carefully plotted ample allusions to the *Phaedrus* in Philo's writings, which set him in a trajectory of interpreters for whom the *Phaedrus* is the impetus for portrayals of ascent, including Plutarch's *Platonic Questions*, Maximus of Tyre's *Philosophumena*, and Plotinus's *Enneades*.

Given the inexorable impact of the *Phaedrus* on Philo's thought, it is striking that he does not choose to attribute the mind's ascent to recollection. Given the impact of Platonism and Stoicism more generally, it is also arresting to note that he deviates from the belief that the mind is naturally drawn to the upper realms, since the mind is, in Stoic terms, a particle of

---

28. For further analysis of Moses in Philo, see the classic study by Meeks, *Prophet-King*, 102–31, esp. 122–25.

the divine realm, understood as aether. Philo, in short, has no need even to nod to the divine spirit in his depictions of ascent; he has enough fodder for the ascent of the mind in the *imago Dei* of Gen 1:26–27 and the divine inbreathing of Gen 2:7.

Yet he does, at least occasionally, attribute the ascent of the mind to the divine spirit—implicitly in *Spec.* 3.1–6 and explicitly in *Plant.* 18–26 and *Gig.* 29–31. This is a fusion of Platonic and biblical elements, and it stems, not from an intellectual process alone, but from Philo's experience, if his claims may be trusted. His autobiographical account in *Spec.* 3.1–6 reveals that Philo attributes the occasional and ephemeral ascent of his mind to the divine spirit, with its powerful surge, which draws the mind upward. The spirit is a hurricane's gale, a tornado's gust, with the power to draw well-tended philosophical minds in its train. Ultimately, it is not recollection, and it may not be a pure intellect, that propels the mind upward but the violent impulse of the spirit, which severs the mind from its earthly home, its corporeal shell, and leads it to its true home. For Philo, at least, that home is Scripture, the sacred oracles of Moses. The mind travels so far only to alight on the inspired page.

6

The Prophetic Spirit as an Angel According to Philo[1]

Nearly a century ago, Paul Volz, who is known primarily for his research on early Jewish eschatology, wrote a provocative analysis of the divine spirit in Jewish antiquity; one quarter of this study is devoted to "the spirit hypostasis" (*Geisthypostase*), that is, spirit (πνεῦμα) interpreted as an independent being rather than a natural element, such as wind, or the spiritual element of humankind, such as the soul.[2] In the context of this intriguing discussion, Volz observed that "Philo unequivocally describes the spirit as an hypostasis,"[3] for it mediates God's own power (*Mittelwesen*), accomplishes concrete actions, such as visiting[4] and leading to truth,[5] and possesses particular characteristics, such as invisibility[6] and complete wisdom.[7] According

---

1. This chapter was written with the generous support of the Alexander von Humboldt Foundation at the Institut für antikes Judentum und hellenistische Religionsgeschichte of the Eberhard-Karls-Universität in Tübingen.

2. Volz, *Geist Gottes*, 145-94.

3. "Philo beschreibt den Geist unzweideutig als Hypostase, namentlich wo er der A.T.lichen Vorstellungswelt freier gegenübersteht" (Volz, *Geist Gottes*, 159).

4. Philo, *Somn.* 2.252.

5. Philo, *Mos.* 2.265.

6. Philo, *Somn.* 2.252.

7. Philo, *Gig.* 24.

to Volz, however, Philo understood this spirit hypostasis less as a personal being than a cosmic principle:

> The personal character of the Philonic *pneuma* normally retreats into the background, despite its hypostatic character. The reason for this lies probably in Stoic influence, from which Philo took over the pan-psychic *pneuma*, and moreover in the Philonic conception of the Logos, alongside which the *pneuma* could never fully be developed.[8]

The personal nature of the divine spirit in Philo's thought aroused meager subsequent interest, with a notable exception. Nearly half a century later, Harry A. Wolfson reopened the inquiry. His discussion is punctuated, however, by uncertainty. The divine spirit is reputed to be "like the angels," and, as a result, "a sort of" angelic being and "a sort of intermediary."[9]

Volz's difficult effort to distinguish the divine spirit as a hypostasis and yet to establish its impersonal nature, as well as Wolfson's indecisive response to the question of the angelic nature of the divine spirit, suggest that the question of the personal nature of the divine spirit in Philo's writings should be reexamined. Concerning this question, in fact, two extraordinarily important repositories of evidence exist within the Philonic corpus which require detailed analysis. The first consists of Philo's version of Balaam in *De vita Mosis* (1.273-84) and his definition of ecstasy in *Quis rerum divinarum heres sit* (264-66). The second, which Volz already recognized as an indication of the hypostatic nature of the divine spirit, consists of Philo's explanation of Moses's prediction of the Sabbath in *Mos.* 2.265 and his autobiographical reflections on inspiration in *Somn.* 2.252. Both repositories, understood within their Philonic and Greco-Roman contexts, provide significant data, demonstrating that Philo understood the divine spirit, in these contexts, as an angelic being.

PHILO'S ANGELIC SPIRIT AND CLEOMBROTUS'S DAEMONES

In the biblical tale of Balaam, Balak, king of Midian, sent for Balaam to receive from him an oracle that would ensure military victory. While travelling

---

8. "Der personhafte Charakter tritt übrigens beim philonischen Pneuma trotz des Hypostatischen zurück. Das hat seinen Grund wohl in dem stoischen Einfluß, von dem Philo das pan-psychische Pneuma übernahm, und außerdem in der philonischen Logosidee, neben der das Pneuma sich nicht voll entfalten konnte" (Volz, *Geist Gottes*, 160).

9. Wolfson, *Philo*, 2:30-31.

to meet Balak, an angel confronted Balaam, the seer, who ironically did not at first see the angel, while his ass did. Although the angel then commanded Balaam to say only that which the angel would command (Num 22:35), Balaam's oracles are also attributed to God (Num 22:20, 38; 23:4-5, 12, 16, 26; 24:13) and the spirit of God (Num 24:2 [Num 23:7 LXX]).

The predominant interpretation of Num 22-24 is that God was the source of Balaam's oracles. It is difficult to assess precisely what roles the angel and the divine spirit play in the production of Balaam's oracles.

Philo eliminated this ambiguity by attributing inspiration to the angel and the prophetic spirit—but not God. In an expanded version of Num 22:35, the angel predicted:

> I shall prompt the needful words without your mind's consent, and direct your organs of speech as justice and convenience require. I shall guide the reins of speech, and, though you understand it not, employ your tongue for each prophetic utterance.[10]

This prediction was fulfilled when Balaam "advanced outside, and straightway became possessed, and there fell upon him the truly prophetic spirit which banished utterly from his soul his art of wizardry."[11] Philo created this integral relationship between the prediction of the angel and its fulfillment by the divine spirit by omitting the intervening references 22:38 and 23:5. Such an alteration results in the interpretation of the divine spirit as an angel. While according to Num 22-23, God placed words in Balaam's mouth, in Philo's version the angel who promised to prompt Balaam's words, direct his vocal organs, guide the reins of speech, and employ his tongue actually accomplished this when it reappeared, identified as the prophetic spirit.[12] The prediction of the angel in *Mos.* 1.274 and the prophetic spirit's accomplishing of this prediction in *Mos.* 1.277 describe the same event, the former prospectively and the latter retrospectively.

In particular, the prediction that Balaam would prophesy without understanding was fulfilled in the ousting of his abilities of artificial divination.[13] Balaam was a mantic especially skilled in augury. He represented the very best of what Cicero called "artificial divination," that is, the ability rationally to predict the future by the discernment of such signs as astrological

---

10. Philo, *Mos.* 1.274. All biblical references are to the Septuagint; I assume that Philo used the Septuagint.

11. Philo, *Mos.* 1.277 (Colson, LCL).

12. On the ease with which ἄγγελος and πνεῦμα were identified by early Jewish authors, see Levison, "Debut of Divine Spirit"; Schoemaker, "Use of רוח," 37-38, 40-41; Sekki, *Meaning of Ruaḥ*, 145-71. See also Job 4:15-16 LXX.

13. Philo, *Mos.* 1.274, 277.

and meteorological omens.[14] In contrast, in this tale Balaam predicted the future correctly, not because he employed his mind and senses rationally to observe the movements of birds, but because the angelic spirit, as it had predicted, rendered his mental capacities inoperative.

Philo confirmed this identification of the angel with the prophetic spirit by means of a crucial exegetical modification. According to Num 23:5, God was the source of Balaam's oracle. Instead of this direct reference to God, Philo, however, substituted an oblique reference to "another" (ἑτέρου). That this "other" is the angel is evident in the repetition of the verb θεσπίζειν (to prophesy) in *Mos.* 1.274 and 1.277. The angel had claimed that it would prophesy (θεσπίζων) by using Balaam's tongue without his understanding; now Balaam prophesied (θεσπίζει) by means of "another" who "cast into" (ὑποβάλλοντος ἑτέρου) him what he should say.

According to Philo's version of Balaam's inspiration, then, an inspiring angelic spirit displaced Balaam's rational faculties and utilized his vocal organs to produce a prophetic utterance. The presence of these elements cannot be attributed to Philo's biblical foreground.[15] They can rather readily be understood in light of the view of inspiration that Cleombrotus represented in Plutarch's *De defectu oraculorum*. Cleombrotus attributed the obsolescence of oracles at Delphi to the departure of the mediating daemones, the divine messengers:

> Let this statement be ventured by us, following the lead of many others before us, that coincidently with the total defection of the guardian spirits [δαιμονίοις] assigned to the oracles and prophetic shrines, occurs the defection of the oracles themselves; and when the spirits flee or go to another place, the oracles themselves lose their power.[16]

The method of inspiration that these guardian spirits or daemones utilized is explained by the simile of musical instruments. According to Cleombrotus, when the daemones return, "the oracles, like musical instruments, become articulate, since those who can put them to use are present and in charge of them."[17] The unique coalescence of possession by a daemonic being, the total passivity of the speaker, and the production of prophetic utterances in Plutarch's *De defectu oraculorum* and Philo's *De vita Mosis* reveals the level to which Philo shared the view of inspiration that Cleombrotus represented.

14. Cicero, *Div.* 1.11–12.
15. See the discussion in Levison, "Debut of Divine Spirit," 128–29.
16. Plutarch, *Def. orac.* 418C–D (Babbitt, LCL). See also 431B.
17. Plutarch, *Def. orac.* 418D (Babbitt, LCL).

Philo was particularly prepared to embrace this interpretation. He frequently attempted to identify biblical angels with Greco-Roman daemones because the mediatorial function of these daemones corresponds to the function of angels and to what the divine spirit accomplished in the tale of Balaam. Of special interest in this regard are the explicit references Philo made to Plato in his discussion of angelic beings. Plato had identified love as "a great daemonic being" (δαίμων μέγας), that is, one of these daemones who mediate between the divine and human worlds (καὶ γὰρ πᾶν τὸ δαιμόνιον μεταξύ ἐστι θεοῦ τε καὶ θνητοῦ), "interpreting and transporting human things to the gods and divine things to men; entreaties and sacrifices from below, and ordinances and requitals from above: being midway between."[18] Plutarch interpreted Plato's *Symposium*: "Plato calls this class of beings an interpretative and ministering class, midway between gods and men, in that they convey thither the prayers and petitions of men, and thence they bring hither the oracles and the gifts of good things."[19]

On several occasions, the nature of Philo's descriptions of angels indicates the influence of Plato's *Symposium* and Greco-Roman interpretations of this text, such as Plutarch's *De Iside et Osiride*. In Philo's *De gigantibus*,[20] his most important description of angels, Philo introduced a comparison: "It is Moses' custom to give the name of angels to those whom other philosophers call demons (δαίμονας) . . . souls that is which fly and hover in the air."[21] The subsequent description of the purer angels as mediating beings indicates that Philo was indebted to the aforementioned passage in Plato's *Symposium*. These angels, wrote Philo, are "consecrated and devoted to the service of the Father and Creator whose wont it is to employ them as ministers and helpers, to have charge and care of mortal man."[22] In *De plantatione*, Philo referred to "Greek philosophers" and proceeded to describe angels in terms that are once again reminiscent of Plato's *Symposium*:

> These are the purest spirits of all, whom Greek philosophers call heroes, but whom Moses, employing a well-chosen name, entitles "angels," for they go on embassies bearing tidings from the great Ruler to His subjects of the boons which He sends them, and reporting to the Monarch what His subjects are in need of.[23]

---

18. Plato, *Symp.* 202E (Lamb, LCL).
19. Plutarch, *Is. Os.* 361C (Babbitt, LCL).
20. Philo, *Gig.* 6–18 (on Gen 6:2).
21. Philo, *Gig.* 6 (Colson and Whitaker, LCL).
22. Philo, *Gig.* 12 (Colson and Whitaker, LCL).
23. Philo, *Plant.* 14.

It is not surprising that the discussion of angels reappears in Philo's commentary on Jacob's dream; moreover, the same two elements—reference to philosophers and the description of angels as mediators—are employed. Here, however, Philo argued that Moses's word "angel" is superior to "demon":

> These are called "demons" [δαίμονας] by the other philosophers [rather than Moses], but the sacred record is wont to call them "angels" or messengers, employing an apter title, for they both convey the biddings of the Father to His children and report the children's need to their Father.[24]

These texts demonstrate how deeply concerned Philo was to draw a connection between biblical angels and Greco-Roman daemones.[25] Cleombrotus's attribution of inspiration to daemones dovetails with this concern and explains why Philo attributed Balaam's inspiration to an angel playing upon Balaam's vocal organs. Moreover, the apologetic advantage of incorporating Cleombrotus's view is enormous. By incorporating his view, Philo located within the biblical tradition a form of mediation that Plato had espoused and associated with Delphi.[26]

Philo's interpretation of ecstasy in Gen 15:12 confirms that Philo did indeed incorporate Cleombrotus's view as expressed in Plutarch's *De defectu oraculorum*. Philo equated the presence of ecstasy with the arrival of the divine spirit: "This is what regularly befalls the fellowship of the prophets. The mind is evicted at the arrival of the divine spirit."[27] He then connected this interpretation of Gen 15:12 with the words "it was said to Abraham" (Gen 15:13):

> For indeed the prophet, even when he seems to be speaking, really holds his peace, and his organs of speech, mouth and tongue, are wholly in the employ of Another, to shew forth what He wills. Unseen by us that Other beats on the chords with the skill of a master-hand and makes them instruments of sweet music, laden with every harmony.[28]

---

24. Philo, *Somn.* 1.141 (on Gen 28:12) (Colson and Whitaker, LCL).

25. See the discussion of Winston, *Two Treatises of Philo*, 197–200, in which he places Philo's discussion into the context of Middle Platonism; see bibliography on 371. See also Runia, *Philo of Alexandria*, 228–29.

26. On the apologetic benefits that would result from a Jewish adoption of Cleombrotus's point of view, see Levison, "Debut of Divine Spirit," 133–37.

27. Philo, *Her.* 265 (Colson and Whitaker, LCL).

28. Philo, *Her.* 266 (Colson and Whitaker, LCL).

The elements of prophetic inspiration familiar from Philo's tale of Balaam—loss of rationality, prompting of the vocal organs, passivity of the prophet—coalesce in this text. The antecedent of the "other" is the divine spirit that evicts the mind. As in the tale of Balaam, then, it was the divine spirit and not God who manipulated the vocal chords of the prophet.

There is, moreover, something new here—the metaphor of the musician. This metaphor even more closely connects Philo's definition of prophetic inspiration with the view that Cleombrotus—who described the return of daemonic beings to oracular shrines—represented.

> When the spirits [δαιμονίοις] flee or go to another place, the oracles themselves lose their power, but when the spirits return many years later, the oracles, like musical instruments, become articulate, since those who can put them to use are present and in charge of them.[29]

The divine spirit that plays upon the vocal chords of the prophet as upon musical instruments, as Philo described, is akin to the daemonic beings that play upon the oracles as upon musical instruments, as Plutarch's Cleombrotus described. This divine spirit is nothing other than the angelic being or prophetic spirit that inspired Balaam.

Philo was not idiosyncratic in this transformation of the Bible. In a related article, I provided evidence to demonstrate that Josephus similarly identified the angel of Num 22:35 with the divine spirit of Num 24:2 (and Num 23:7 LXX), and that this exegetical modification is due in good measure to the importance that Josephus placed upon the view represented by Cleombrotus in Plutarch's *De defectu oraculorum*.[30] Therefore, not one but two first-century Jewish authors, both of whom devoted serious attention to prophecy, were in accord when they identified the divine spirit as an angelic being who inspired Balaam's oracular utterance.

These texts are not the sole instances in which Philo understood the divine spirit as an angelic being. Philo's discussion of Moses's prophetic abilities and Joseph's ability to interpret dreams, as well as Philo's ability to interpret the Torah allegorically, exhibit a similar interpretation of inspiration. This interpretation reveals the influence of Greco-Roman interpretations of Socrates's daemon.

---

29. Plutarch, *Def. orac.* 418D (Babbitt, LCL).

30. Levison, "Debut of Divine Spirit" (included as chapter 8 on pp. 177–92 in this volume).

PHILO'S ANGELIC SPIRIT AND SOCRATES'S DAEMON

Philo expended a great deal of energy to demonstrate that Moses was the greatest of the prophets "in the strict sense," by which he meant that Moses prophesied, at one and the same time, by being "carried out of himself" and "in his own person."[31] In other words, Moses both became extraordinarily inspired and remained wholly rational.[32] In the context of four illustrations of this remarkable prophetic ability, Philo introduced the divine spirit as the source of Moses's ability to predict the Sabbath:

> Moses, when he heard of this and also actually saw it, was awestruck and, guided by what was not so much surmise as God-sent inspiration, made announcement of the sabbath. I need hardly say that conjectures of this kind are closely akin to prophecies. For the mind could not have made so straight an aim if there was not also the divine spirit guiding it to the truth itself.[33]

This explanation is an exegetical expansion of Exod 16:22–23, in which Philo repeatedly underscored the inspiration that Moses experienced. First, according to Exod 16:15, Moses responded to the Israelites' question about the manna with a straightforward description of it as bread, prefaced by the words, "Moses said (εἶπεν) to them." Philo added that Moses spoke "under inspiration" (ἐπιθειάσας).[34] Second, in Exod 16:23, Moses "said [εἶπεν] to them" that they should rest on the Sabbath, preparing what they need the day before. Philo instead wrote that Moses, "under God-sent inspiration, made announcement of the sabbath."[35] Third, in Exod 16:25–26, Moses said (εἶπεν) that the people should eat what was preserved from the prior day rather than searching in the field on the Sabbath. Philo transformed this statement (εἶπεν) into pure prediction by emphasizing that Moses's perception and proclamation of the Sabbath transpired not on the Sabbath but on the day prior to the Sabbath (τῇ ... προτεραίᾳ), by extolling the character of the oracle (χρησμὸν τερατωδέστατον), and by replacing "said" with "prophesied" (θεσπίζει).[36] Philo observed in apologetic fashion that the result of these predictions was Israel's acknowledgement of Moses "the prophet as a

---

31. Philo, *Mos.* 2.188–91 (Colson, LCL).

32. For analysis of Philo's *Mos.* 2.187–91, see Burkhardt, *Inspiration heiliger Schriften*, 166–67.

33. Philo, *Mos.* 2.264–65 (Colson, LCL).

34. Philo, *Mos.* 2.259 (Colson, LCL).

35. Philo, *Mos.* 2.264 (Colson, LCL).

36. Philo, *Mos.* 2.268–69 (Colson, LCL).

true seer, an interpreter of God, and alone gifted with foreknowledge of the hidden future."³⁷ This is not, however, the end of Philo's description, for in his transition to another illustration of Moses's predictive ability, Philo reiterated that Moses's explanation of manna was "his pronouncement under divine inspiration [κατεχόμενος ἐθέσπισεν]."³⁸ Philo therefore transformed Moses's utterances concerning the manna and the Sabbath—described consistently in Exod 16 LXX with the simple verb εἶπεν—into instances of prophetic inspiration. Moses was a prophet who spoke "when possessed by God and carried away out of himself."³⁹

Philo was careful, however, to deny that Moses's possession entailed the vitiation of his rational capacities.⁴⁰ On the contrary, the "God-sent inspiration" that Moses experienced led his mind to the truth. The two most significant words that Philo employed to explain Moses's *rational* prophetic ability, εἰκασία (conjecture) and ποδηγετέω (to guide),⁴¹ occur elsewhere exclusively in association with the processes of the human mind.

Philo typically associated conjecture with negative elements, such as false or artificial divination⁴² and false opinions.⁴³ The rational element of conjecture is also evident in contrasts that Philo drew. For instance, Philo observed, "The human mind in its blindness does not perceive its real interest and all it can do is to take conjecture and guesswork for its guide instead of knowledge."⁴⁴ Human knowledge of heaven, noted Philo, is "based on guess-work and conjecture, not on the solid reasoning of truth."⁴⁵ Balaam had compared his own inspired "oracles from above" with his own plan to seduce Israel, which was merely "suggestions [conjectures] of my own designing."⁴⁶ Philo also contrasted artificial divination and conjecture with "undoubted, naked truth"⁴⁷ because "everyone who pursues the spurious scurvy trade of divination ranks his surmises and conjectures with truth,

37. Philo, *Mos.* 2.269 (Colson, LCL).
38. Philo, *Mos.* 2.270 (Colson, LCL).
39. Philo, *Mos.* 2.188 (Colson, LCL).
40. On the importance of the rational element in these illustrations, see Levison, "Two Types."
41. Philo, *Mos.* 2.265. These terms are foreign to the Hellenistic Jewish tradition. Neither word occurs in the Septuagint, the Greek pseudepigrapha, or the writings of Josephus. Josephus does employ the cognate noun εἰκαστής in *Ant.* 18.321.
42. Philo, *Conf.* 159.
43. Philo, *Cher.* 69.
44. Philo, *Legat.* 21 (Colson, LCL).
45. Philo, *Somn.* 1.23 (Colson and Whitaker, LCL).
46. Philo, *Mos.* 1.294 (Colson, LCL).
47. Philo, *Spec.* 1.63 (Colson, LCL).

a position ill-suited to them."[48] Less often, Philo regarded "conjecture" as a neutral term, and even in this case the term implies rational processes: he included it among human ideas, purposes, and aims[49] and described it as "second to the true vision . . . conjecture and theorizing and all that can be brought into the category of reasonable probability."[50]

When Philo, therefore, described Moses's prediction of the Sabbath by defining his seeing the manna as a conjecture, he indicated unequivocally that the process Moses used to predict was rational. The association of the divine spirit with this rational process becomes explicit in Philo's explanation that the divine spirit guides the mind to the truth. In Philo's writings, the verb ποδηγετέω occurs without exception in association with the path toward virtue. Four times this path is an ascent. Guides in this ascent include a love of wisdom;[51] a love of heaven,[52] which leads the mind toward a vision of heaven; God, who guides the person in the trek from the lower world of passions to the upper world of virtue;[53] and wisdom itself.[54] In this last text, where wisdom is the guide, the rational element is presented with exceptional clarity:

> The mind is cleansed by wisdom and the truths of wisdom's teaching which guide its steps to the contemplation of the universe and all that is therein, and by the sacred company of the other virtues and by the practice of them shewn in noble and highly praiseworthy actions.[55]

The road to virtue is therefore concomitant with the purification of the mind.

A similar emphasis upon the rational is apparent in the description of the guide as reason or logos. Philo identified the angel who confronted Balaam as "Conviction, the divine reason, the angel who guides our feet."[56] Joseph's desire to have his bones removed from Egypt to Palestine represents allegorically the movement from what is mortal by following "the guiding

---

48. Philo, *Spec.* 4.50 (Colson, LCL).

49. Philo, *Post.* 80.

50. Philo, *Spec.* 1.38 (Colson, LCL); see Philo, *Her.* 98. In Philo's *Mos.* 1.68, εἰκασία simply denotes a comparison. For the adjective εἰκαστικός, see Philo, *Cher.* 116; *Sacr.* 13; *Det.* 38, where the adjective is used of specious rhetoric.

51. Philo, *Opif.* 70.

52. Philo, *Praem.* 84.

53. Philo, *Post.* 31.

54. Philo, *Spec.* 1.269.

55. Philo, *Spec.* 1.269 (Colson, LCL).

56. Philo, *Deus* 182 (Colson and Whitaker, LCL).

steps of Moses, the Law-giving Word."[57] Twice divine oracles are the guides toward virtue and a vision of God. Jacob's flight from Esau is interpreted allegorically as the flight of the mind toward virtue: "I, however," says Jacob, "took no man to help me to find the way that leads to virtue, but paid heed to Divine oracles bidding me depart hence, and to this moment they guide my steps."[58] Abraham's yearning for God "was fanned by the divine warnings" that "guide his steps."[59]

Philo's use of two nonbiblical words, εἰκασία and ποδηγετέω, to explain Moses's prediction unambiguously attributes the highest achievement of rational thought to the divine spirit. The divine spirit is an exceptional element of a rational form of inspiration that leads the mind intact to truth otherwise unknown.

Philo also applied this model of inspiration to Joseph's success in interpreting Pharaoh's dream. Philo attributed to a divine voice the advice that Joseph tendered as he interpreted the dream—for example, the storing of a fifth of the grain during the seven good years: "Such are the facts which appear from the interpretation, but I also hear the promptings of the divine voice, devising safeguards for the disease, as we may call it."[60] This description occurs immediately prior to the account of Joseph's advice. Immediately following this advice, Philo quoted Gen 41:38:

> The king having heard both his interpretation of the dreams, so exactly and skillfully divining the truth, and his advice to all appearance most profitable in its foresight for the uncertainties of the future, bade his companions come closer to him so that Joseph might not hear, and said: "Sirs, shall we find another man such as this, who has in him the spirit of God?"[61]

Philo's introduction and conclusion to Joseph's advice produces a remarkable identification between the promptings of the divine voice and spirit in Joseph. The rational character of the process is evident in Pharaoh's remark, following his acknowledgement of the divine spirit, that Joseph is a "man of prudence and sense."[62]

Repetition of vocabulary demonstrates the extent to which Philo adhered to this model of inspiration.[63] Moses made a "keen-sighted aim"

57. Philo, *Migr.* 23 (Colson and Whitaker, LCL).
58. Philo, *Fug.* 21 (Colson and Whitaker, LCL).
59. Philo, *Virt.* 215 (Colson, LCL); see also wisdom's teaching in Philo, *Spec.* 1.269.
60. Philo, *Ios.* 110 (Colson, LCL).
61. Philo, *Ios.* 116 (Colson, LCL).
62. Philo, *Ios.* 117 (Colson, LCL).
63. Philo, *Mos.* 2.265; *Ios.* 116.

(εὐσκόπως εὐθυβόλησεν), as did Joseph (εὐθυβόλως καὶ εὐσκόπως). Both were led to the truth (ἀλήθεια) by means of the divine spirit (πνεῦμα). Even the process of rational inference is described similarly. Both Moses and Joseph made conjectures. The words Philo used to describe these conjectures—εἰκασίαι of Moses and στοχαζομένην of Joseph—are synonyms and therefore interchangeable. As nouns they occur in tandem (στοχασμοῖς καὶ εἰκασίαις).[64] In *Mos.* 2.265 and *Ios.* 116, then, Philo used strikingly similar vocabulary to describe the various elements in the process of inspiration: the level of accuracy, goal, source of inspiration, and means of rational inference.

This view of inspiration also informed Philo's autobiographical reflections on his ability to interpret Torah allegorically. In *De Somniis*, Philo interrupted his praise of the vision-seeking mind with a reference to the invisible voice that he has heard:

> I hear once more the voice of the invisible spirit, the familiar secret tenant, saying, "Friend, it would seem that there is a matter great and precious of which thou knowest nothing, and this I will ungrudgingly shew thee, for many other well-timed lessons have I given thee."[65]

These autobiographical reflections contain the two elements that characterize Moses's prophetic experience "in the strict sense." As in *Mos.* 2.265, the divine spirit is the essential factor in leading to knowledge that is not readily apparent; for Moses this was the discernment of the Sabbath and for Philo this was the solution to an exegetical difficulty. As in *Mos.* 2.265, the process that leads to this knowledge is rational. The verb ἀναδιδάσκω indicates that Philo's experience was primarily one of being taught. The instruction of the divine spirit is directed toward the human mind (διάνοια), which Philo had already depicted as the "vision-seeking mind, the mind which is eager to see all things and never even in its dreams has a wish for faction and turmoil."[66]

These common elements of the divine spirit and rational instruction or guidance bring *Mos.* 2.265, *Ios.* 110–16, and *Somn.* 2.252 into close association with one another. These three texts preserve a common model

---

64. For example, in Philo, *Somn.* 1.23; *Spec.* 1.38, 4.50; *Legat.* 21.

65. Philo, *Somn.* 2.252 (Colson and Whitaker, LCL). For a fuller discussion of this text and an explanation of why the spirit of *Somn.* 2.252 is divine rather than human, see Levison, "Inspiration and Divine Spirit" (included as chapter 4 on pp. 53–99 in this volume). That chapter also contains a detailed analysis of *Cher.* 27–29 and *Fug.* 53–58, in which Philo reflected similarly upon the process of allegorical interpretation, which is at once both inspired and rational.

66. Philo, *Somn.* 2.251 (Colson and Whitaker, LCL).

of rational inspiration, according to which the receptive mind confronts something which it cannot fully comprehend, receives guidance by the divine spirit, and is led to truth that was formerly inaccessible.

Although it may now be clear that the divine spirit, in addition to ousting the mind of the prophet, is also capable of leading the rational mind intact to the truth, the nature of that spirit remains elusive. Once again, the writings of Plutarch—in this instance not his *De defectu oraculorum* but his *De genio Socratis*—prove indispensable for ascertaining this element of Philo's thought. The introduction to the first discussion (580B–82C) and the entirety of the second discussion (588B–89F) of the nature of Socrates's daemon contain in orderly fashion what appears in Philo only in snatches—in his apologetic demonstration of Moses's prophetic gift, his brief but significant clarification of Joseph's ability to interpret dreams, and his autobiographical reflections upon exegesis.

Plutarch's discussions are not isolated cases of curiosity about the nature of Socrates's daemon. The significance of this daemon is evident in the contention, held by both Plato and Xenophon, that this divine daemon constituted the primary ground upon which Socrates was sentenced to death.[67] Neither Plato nor Xenophon, however, clarified the nature of this daemon, and this lack of explanation led to a growing interest in its nature. The author of the *Theages* concluded with a lengthy discussion between Socrates and Theages on the nature of this daemonic sign. In the century prior to Plutarch, Cicero discussed Socrates's daemon.[68] Less than a century after Plutarch, Maximus of Tyre devoted the eighth of forty-one exhortations to the question "What is the daemon of Socrates?"[69] In light of this interest, the absence of allusions to Socrates's daemon in the writings of Philo would perhaps be more surprising than their presence.

In Plutarch's *De genio Socratis*, Theocritus introduced the discussion of Socrates's daemon:

> Very well... but what, my dear sir, do we call Socrates' *daemon*? For my part, nothing reported of Pythagoras' skill in divination has struck me as so great or so divine; for exactly as Homer has represented Athena as "standing at" Odysseus' "side in all his labours," so heaven seems to have attached to Socrates from his earliest years as his guide in life a vision of this kind, which alone "Showed him the way, illumining his path" in matters

---

67. See, for example, Plato, *Euthyphr.* 3B; Xenophon, *Mem.* 1.1–2.
68. Cicero, *Div.* 1.122–24.
69. Hobein, *Maximi Tyrii*.

dark and inscrutable to human wisdom, *through the frequent concordance of the inspiring daemon with his own decisions.*[70]

This introduction contains several elements in common with Philo's Moses. First, Plutarch's initial explicit description of the daemon is as a guide (προποδηγόν); Philo used the cognate verb, ποδηγετέω, to describe the guidance of the divine spirit in *Mos.* 2.265. Second, the primary function of Socrates's daemon in this introduction corresponds to the primary function of inspiration in the introduction to Philo's treatment of Moses's prophetic gift in *Mos.* 2.187, of which *Mos.* 2.265 is an illustration. The daemon illumined matters inscrutable to human wisdom; Moses as prophet was to "declare by inspiration what cannot be apprehended by reason."[71] Third, the contention that Socrates's daemon confirmed his decisions—it did not initiate them or overcome him to produce them—is similar to Philo's assertion that Moses spoke "in his own person,"[72] an assertion Philo established through four illustrations.[73] According to these illustrations, Moses's inspiration emerged from his own psychological condition.[74] This extraordinarily important component of Moses's inspiration finds a striking counterpart in Plutarch's insistence upon Socrates's initiative. Fourth, inspiration is described by the same verb. The "inspiring daemon" (δαιμόνιον ἐπιθειάζον) confirmed Socrates's decisions; the Sabbath prediction was a product of Moses's inspiration (ἐπιθειάσας).[75] The recurrence of this fairly common verb becomes significant alongside these other shared conceptions between Plutarch's description of Socrates's inspiration and Philo's portrayal of Moses's inspiration. Fifth, the attribution of these concepts to Plutarch's Theocritus is important, for he represents the view that the process of inspiration is entirely rational. Philo also included these concepts in his attempt to demonstrate the highly rational nature of Moses's form of prophetic inspiration.

The second discussion of Socrates's daemon in Plutarch's *De genio Socratis* is also indispensable for understanding Philo's conception of the inspiration of the mind by the divine spirit. Simmias explained that only certain people—those whose souls are not commingled with their bodies—are

---

70. Plutarch, *Gen. Socr.* 580C–D (Lacy and Einarson, LCL); translation in italics is mine.
71. Philo, *Mos.* 2.187 (Colson, LCL).
72. Philo, *Mos.* 2.188.
73. Philo, *Mos.* 2.246–87.
74. On this pattern, see Levison, "Two Types."
75. Philo, *Mos.* 2.263.

capable of hearing this language of the daemones. These are the most rational of all people:

> The messages of daemons pass through all other men, but find an echo in those only whose character is untroubled and soul unruffled, the very men in fact we call holy and daemonic. In popular belief, on the other hand, it is only in sleep that men receive inspiration from on high; and the notion that they are so influenced when awake and in full possession of their faculties is accounted strange and incredible. This is like supposing that a musician uses his lyre when the strings are slack, but does not touch or play it when it has been adjusted to a scale and attuned.[76]

Simmias's explanation illuminates the laconic language of Philo's *Somn.* 2.251–52. First, Philo described the preparedness of his mind as free from faction and turmoil. Plutarch contended similarly that, in contrast to the ignorant masses whose souls are in turmoil,[77] only those untroubled and unruffled can hear daemonic language. Second, Philo laconically described the process by which the divine spirit speaks as an echo (ὑπηχεῖ δέ μοι). This reflects the predominant image employed by Plutarch to explain how the language of daemones is communicated: the "messages of daemons pass through all other men, but find an echo [ἐνηχοῦσι] in those only whose character is untroubled and soul unruffled." These connections produce a striking parallel between Socrates and Philo. Even as the ultimate source of Socrates's voice was a daemonic communication to him because its unspoken language echoed within his untroubled soul, so the ultimate source of Philo's exegetical insight was the divine spirit that communicated to him by echoing within his untroubled soul.

These corresponding elements between Philo's divine spirit and Socrates's daemon can be anchored by what Max Pohlenz already recognized as an intentional allusion to Socrates's daemon: "With regard to his own person, he [Philo] speaks with distinct allusion to Socrates' Daimonion of the unseen Pneuma, whose voice he perceives in his inner being."[78] Philo's use of the word εἰωθός to describe the recurrent presence of the divine

---

76. Plutarch, *Gen. Socr.* 589D (Lacy and Einarson, LCL).

77. Philo was free of turmoil (ταραχῆς) (*Somn.* 2.251). Simmias accused the ignorant of being in turmoil (ταραχῆς) for believing that one hears only in sleep (Plutarch, *Gen. Socr.* 589E).

78. "Im Hinblick auf seine eigene Person spricht er *Somn.* II 252 mit deutlicher Anspielung auf Sokrates' Daimonion von dem unsichtbaren Pneuma, dessen Stimme er in seinem Innern vernimmt" (Pohlenz, "Philon von Alexandreia," 473). Hay accepts Pohlenz's interpretation ("Philo's View of Himself," 44–45nn9–10).

spirit[79] constitutes an important allusion to this key word in Plato's description of Socrates's daemon. Socrates referred to "the customary prophetic inspiration of the daemon,"[80] "the daemonic and customary sign,"[81] and "my customary daemonic sign."[82] Socrates claimed to have heard this voice from his childhood,[83] a contention that both the author of *Theages*[84] and Plutarch[85] confirmed. The implication of this allusion is evident: as Socrates customarily heard the voice of a daemon, so Philo customarily heard the voice of the divine spirit.

That Plutarch understood Socrates's δαιμόνιον not as an unspecified reference to deity but as a daemonic being is evident throughout Simmias's discussion.[86] Simmias inferred from Socrates's resistance to visions of heaven that Socrates's daemon was "the perception of a voice or else the

---

79. See also the autobiographical reflections of Philo in *Cher.* 27.
80. Plato, *Apol.* 40A: ἡ γὰρ εἰωθυῖά μοι μαρτικὴ ἡ τοῦ δαιμονίου (my translation).
81. Plato, *Phaedr.* 242B: τὸ δαιμόνιόν τε καὶ τὸ εἰωθὸς σημεῖόν μοι (my translation).
82. Plato, *Euthyd.* 272E: τὸ εἰωθὸς σημεῖον τὸ δαιμόνιον (my translation).
83. Plato, *Apol.* 31D.
84. Pseudo-Plato, *Theages* 128D.
85. Plutarch, *Gen. Socr.* 580C, 589E-F.

86. The precise nature of this daemon was not always clear. The basic conviction concerning Socrates is that he possessed an extraordinary gift. Plato consistently designated this gift as (a) daemon (*Euthyphr.* 3B; *Apol.* 40A: δαιμόνιον) or, using an adjective, as "something divine and daemonic" (*Apol.* 31D: θεῖόν τι καὶ δαιμόνιον). In Plato, *Phaedr.* 242B-C (Fowler, LCL), Socrates associates it with a sign, "the daemon and the customary sign" (see also *Euthyd.* 272E), and attributes to it a voice, "and I thought I heard a voice from it" (*Phaedr.* 242C). Despite these ample references, it remains unclear whether the daemon is to be understood more generally as "the divine" or more specifically as "a daemonic being." Nor does Xenophon clarify this question. Because he began his *Memorabilia Socratis* with a refutation of the charge that Socrates rejected the gods of the state, he defended Socrates by demonstrating his conformity to the state religion. Therefore, he referred to this daemon in terms that conform to rather than differ from the state religion. Xenophon went so far as to include Socrates's daemon alongside commonplace forms of divination such as augury (*Mem.* 1.1.4) and twice stated in general terms that it pointed the way (σημαίνειν) for Socrates (*Mem.* 1.1.2-3). The process of conforming Socrates's daemon to the state gods extends so far that Xenophon referred to it as a god (*Mem.* 1.1.5). Neither Plato nor Xenophon, therefore, offered a satisfactory definition of the precise nature of the daemon that accompanied Socrates. The author of *Theages* also entered the quest for clarity, giving a straightforward answer: what accompanied Socrates from his youth up was a voice (ἔστι δὲ τοῦτο φωνή), which functioned as a sign to Socrates to prohibit an action (128D-29D). Despite this attempt at clarity, this author's answer retains a certain ambiguity about the source of this voice. He can write, "The voice of the daemon" (128E). Although the voice is the central focus in the *Theages*, then, the ultimate source of that voice remains shrouded in obscurity.

mental apprehension of language that reached him in some strange way." He continued with a fuller explanation:

> Socrates . . . had an understanding which, being pure and free from passion, and commingling with the body but little, for necessary ends, was so sensitive and delicate as to respond at once to what reached him. What reached him, one would conjecture, was not spoken language, but the unuttered words of a daemon, making voiceless contact with his intelligence by their sense alone.[87]

The thoughts of these "daemons are luminous and shed their light on the daemonic man."[88]

Following this rational explanation, Simmias related the myth of Timarchus of Chaeroneia who, desiring to ascertain the nature of Socrates's sign, descended into a crypt and had a vision in which he saw a variety of stars, some trembling above the great abyss, others sinking, and others shooting up from the abyss. A voice explained to Timarchus, "You see the daemons themselves."[89] The orderly daemones are connected to "souls which good nurture and training had made submissive to the rein."[90] From these souls, "which from their very beginning and birth are docile to the rein and obedient to their daemon, comes the race of diviners and of men inspired."[91]

It is to this race that Moses, Joseph, and Philo himself belonged. These are the ones whose minds the divine spirit guides, who hear the voice of the familiar spirit, who are inspired people. Philo's claim to this form of inspiration for his race suits his apologetic purposes admirably, for Philo held Socrates in high esteem, praising him as the embodiment of a central tenet in Philo's own thought:

> They say that in olden time one who was enraptured by the beauty of wisdom . . . after watching the array of a procession pass by on which vast sums had been lavished, fastened his eyes on a group of his associates and said, "See, my friends, of how many things I have no need." And yet he was wearing absolutely

---

87. Plutarch, *Gen. Socr.* 588D–E (Lacy and Einarson, LCL).
88. Plutarch, *Gen. Socr.* 589B (Lacy and Einarson, LCL).
89. Plutarch, *Gen. Socr.* 591D (Lacy and Einarson, LCL).
90. Plutarch, *Gen. Socr.* 592A (Lacy and Einarson, LCL).
91. Plutarch, *Gen. Socr.* 592C (Lacy and Einarson, LCL). This interpretation of Socrates's daemon as a daemonic being reappears in Maximus of Tyre's *Orationes*. His discussion of Socrates's daemon (τὸ δαιμόνιον) mentions a variety of daemonic beings (9.7). The inspiration of the daemon is entirely rational (3.3).

nothing beyond necessary clothing... This is the mind which, as the lawgiver [Moses] insists, should be that of those who provide themselves with no property that has its place among things created, but renounce all these on the ground of that intimate association with the Uncreate, to possess Whom, they are convinced, is the only wealth, the only gauge of consummate happiness.[92]

Philo used the figure of Socrates by locating the form of inspiration associated with him in the experience of key figures of the biblical period. Philo devoted entire apologetic treatises to Joseph and Moses, and he regarded Moses as the greatest of prophets. Thus the most prominent biblical figures experienced a form of inspiration that also characterized the most respected of all Greek philosophers. More surprisingly, Philo claimed that he himself was an inspired exegete. From antiquity to the present, the divine spirit has guided the minds of Jewish interpreters and prophets—minds prepared to hear the echo of this daemon to which others are not attuned.

CONCLUSION

The primary purpose of this chapter has been to demonstrate that in several contexts Philo Judaeus conceived of the divine spirit as an angelic being. Retreat from the details of this analysis, and one can discern three aspects of this thesis that underline its reliability.

First, the discovery that the divine spirit is an angelic being is immune from the charge that this interpretation exists in isolation from other aspects of Philo's thought, for the view spans several disparate Philonic contexts. This angelic being is believed to act in two entirely different contexts: the overpowering of the prophet (Balaam), which produces irrationality, and the instruction of exemplary Jews (Moses, Joseph, and Philo himself), which produces the sharpening of the mind. This interpretation, moreover, does not hinge upon a single, isolated Greco-Roman model of inspiration—either Cleombrotus's daemonic beings or Socrates's daemon, for

---

92. Philo, *Plant.* 65–66 (Colson and Whitaker, LCL). See Philo, *Deus* 146–47. Philo is dependent upon a tradition found also in Cicero, *Tusc.* 5.91, in which Socrates is explicitly mentioned. The story is also recounted in Diogenes Laertius (*Lives* 2.25). In another reference to Socrates, Philo included Socrates's physiological observations in support of his allegorical interpretation of why the door of Noah's ark is at the side: "[This is] very excellent, for, as Socrates used to say, whether taught by Moses or moved by the things themselves" (*QG* 2.6 [Marcus, LCL]). In *Contempl.* 57 (Colson, LCL), Philo considered the "two celebrated and highly notable examples" of banquets held in Greece to be those in which Socrates took part.

example—but upon views from both contexts, in which divergent forms of inspiration are discussed.

Second, Philo's interpretation of the divine spirit as an angelic being has remarkably close parallels in the writings of Josephus. I have contended that Josephus incorporated into his tale of Balaam the view of inspiration that Cleombrotus represented in Plutarch's *De defectu oraculorum*.[93] I did not mention that Josephus also referred explicitly to the daemon of Socrates when discussing the Athenians's unwillingness to tolerate "a single word about the gods contrary to their laws":

> On what other ground was Socrates put to death? He never sought to betray his city to the enemy, he robbed no temple. No; because he used to swear strange oaths and give out ... that he received communications from *a certain daemon*, he was therefore condemned to die by drinking hemlock.[94]

The significance of this statement is extraordinary. Josephus here indicated his awareness of Plato's and Xenophon's view—that the fundamental charge against Socrates involved his daemon. Moreover, his use of the indefinite Greek pronoun τι, "a certain," signals that he, like Plutarch and Philo, understood the words τι δαιμόνιον to refer to a specific, daemonic being.[95] The word δαιμόνιον does not refer generically to "deity" when accompanied by τι, but to a "particular" (τι) daemon, to some identifiable daemonic being.

Third, the Greco-Roman data required of this thesis can be pinpointed with relative accuracy and traced to a single author, Plutarch, who was born in approximately 46 CE, probably before Philo died. Plutarch, moreover, was a popularizer, a relatively unoriginal Platonist who was satisfied to present a variety of opinions in an interesting format. Whether he refuted, championed, or merely reported them, Plutarch proffered the points of view that circulated widely during Philo's lifetime.[96]

Equally important, the support set forth cannot be construed as esoteric. Delphic inspiration was embellished and ridiculed over a span of centuries during the Greco-Roman era.[97] The shadow of Socrates also cast

---

93. Levison, "Debut of Divine Spirit."

94. Josephus, *Ag. Ap.* 2.262–63 (Thackeray, LCL; italicized text is my translation): τίνος γὰρ ἑτέρου χάριν Σωκράτης ἀπέθανεν; οὐ γὰρ δὴ προεδίδου τὴν πόλιν τοῖς πολεμίοις οὐδὲ τῶν ἱερῶν ἐσύλησεν οὐδέν, ἀλλ' ὅτι καινοὺς ὅρκους ὤμνυεν καί τι δαιμόνιον αὐτῷ σημαίνειν ἔφασκεν ... διὰ ταῦτα κατεγνώσθη κώνειον πιὼν ἀποθανεῖν.

95. This view of Socrates's daemon may also have influenced Josephus's descriptions of John Hyrcanus in *J.W.* 1.69–70.

96. On this characteristic of Plutarch, see Flacelière, *Plutarque*, 50–52.

97. In addition to the texts analyzed here, see also Lucan, *De bello civili* 5.163–67;

itself widely during this time.[98] The thesis that Philo interpreted the divine spirit as an angelic being, therefore, is based upon an ability to pinpoint the Greco-Roman data to a single author, Plutarch, and popular points of view during the first century.

The significance of the views Plutarch summarized for interpreting Philo's writings does not imply that Philo was more Greco-Roman philosopher than biblical exegete.[99] Rather, Greco-Roman points of view served as tools to sharpen inchoate elements of the Bible. By exploiting potential points of contact between biblical text and Greco-Roman context, Philo ably clarified biblical and personal experiences of inspiration in ways that his Roman audience—both Jewish and Greek—would have appreciated and perhaps themselves embraced.

Origen, *Cels.* 3.25; Chrysostom, *Hom. 1 Cor.* 29.1 (PG 61:242); Pseudo-Longinus, *Subl.* 13.2.

98. See Tiede, *Charismatic Figure*, 30–42.

99. On this issue, see Amir, "Authority and Interpretation," 421–22.

7

Prophetic Inspiration in Pseudo-Philo's Liber Antiquitatum Biblicarum[1]

I. INTRODUCTION

Despite the fact that Pseudo-Philo's Liber antiquitatum biblicarum (LAB; first century CE) contains more explicit references to the divine spirit than does the entire corpus of Josephus's writings, the topic of prophetic inspiration in LAB has been virtually ignored. D. Hill ignores it; D. Aune very briefly analyzes its formal characteristics; R. P. Menzies's analysis treats LAB only cursorily by including it in a pastiche of early Jewish texts under the heading "The Spirit and Prophetic Inspiration: Various

---

1. This chapter was written for an NEH summer seminar for college teachers on the topic "The Greek Encounter with Judaism in the Hellenistic Period," directed by Louis H. Feldman, professor of classics at Yeshiva University. I am deeply in Professor Feldman's debt for meeting weekly to discuss this research and for his invaluable critique, attentive advice, extensive bibliographical data, and then, two months after the completion of the seminar, very extensive comments on this manuscript.

Texts."[2] The best critical edition of LAB devotes only one page to the topic of "L'esprit et la prophétie."[3] Even the commentary of F. J. Murphy, devoted exclusively to LAB, treats the role of the divine spirit in prophetic inspiration only in passing.[4]

A notable exception to this tendency is A. Piñero, who, in an analysis of inspiration in LAB, contends that

> this Jewish writer, who probably composed his work in Hebrew, although explaining texts of the Bible which deal with the activities of the prophetic spirit, attributes to this spirit one central function, the elimination of the human mind while prophesying. This is also equally central to the concepts on prophecy of Philo and ultimately, [to] his source, Plato the Athenian. In other words: notwithstanding his deep Jewish feeling, the author of *Biblical Antiquities*, at least in his ideas about the process of inspiration, adopts more of the Greco-Roman than of the biblical mentality.[5]

The present chapter will explore this same issue of Greco-Roman influence on LAB's concept of inspiration but will differ from it in two important respects.

First, Piñero devotes less than two pages to the analysis of inspiration in LAB and concludes that two elements characterize Pseudo-Philo's

---

Note on dates: In the course of this study, several classical and Christian authors will be mentioned. Of fundamental importance are Cicero (106–43 BCE) and Plutarch (ca. 46–120 CE), whose lives and writings bracket the era in which LAB was probably written. The treatises of Cicero and Plutarch comprise an important quarry for our knowledge about religion in the Greco-Roman era. Cicero wrote *De divinatione* to explore the nature of divination, which Cicero had passed over in an even more comprehensive treatment of religion, *De natura deorum* (*Div.* 1.8–9; 2.3). Plutarch devoted *De defectu oraculorum*, *De E apud Delphos*, and *De Pythiae oraculis* to the Delphic oracle, of which he was appointed a priest for life in 95 CE; large segments of *De genio Socratis* to Socrates's daemonion; and *De Iside et Osiride* to Egyptian religion. Other classical authors include: Euripides (ca. 485–ca. 406 BCE); Plato (429–347 BCE); Virgil (70–19 BCE); Aelius Aristides (ca. 117 or 129–81 CE or later); Lucan (39–65 CE); Tacitus (born ca. 56 CE); Iamblichus (ca. 250–325 CE). Christian literature includes: *Cohortatio ad Graecos*, a third-century CE work falsely attributed to Justin Martyr, and the *Collationes* of John Cassian (ca. 360–ca. 435 CE).

2. Hill, *New Testament Prophecy*; Aune, *Prophecy in Early Christianity*; Menzies, *Early Christian Pneumatology*, 74–76. See also the neglect of LAB in recent monographs on the divine spirit that contain studies of late antique Judaism: Chevallier, *Ancien Testament*; Manns, *Symbole eau-esprit*, 122–25.

3. Pseudo-Philon, *Antiquités Bibliques*, 2:63–64.

4. Murphy, *Pseudo-Philo*, 88–89, 132, 149.

5. Piñero, "Mediterranean View," 24.

concept of inspiration: the "inhabitation of the spirit" and the "elimination of the mental capacities of the prophet."[6] I intend to demonstrate that there is a good deal more complexity to Pseudo-Philo's understanding than Piñero's description indicates. Therefore, the bulk of the present chapter will consist of detailed analyses of the four primary passages of LAB in which prophetic inspiration occurs.

Second, the reason why Piñero spends so little time on LAB itself is that he wants to demonstrate that

> this double conception [inhabitation of the spirit and elimination of mental capacities] as represented in *LAB* finds its most natural explanation not in the classical prophetic world of the Hebrew Bible, not in a return to previous concepts [of prophecy] of the *nevi 'im*, not in an internal Jewish theological evolution, but in the reception of foreign ideas about the prophetic trance from the milieu of the Hellenized Jewish circles.[7]

In an attempt to drive this wedge firmly between Hellenism and the Bible, Piñero devotes the remainder of his article to a survey of inspiration in the Hebrew Bible, the ancient Near East, Philo, Plato, Greco-Roman writers, and the rabbis. In contrast, the assumption of the present chapter is that Pseudo-Philo's primary commitment was to the Bible, for LAB is in fact rewritten Bible. Only when the Bible is demonstrably not the source of Pseudo-Philo's view shall I turn to analyze the literary sources that were produced within his Greco-Roman milieu.

This approach will allow us to avoid any unnecessary either/or alternatives and to explore, instead, resources of both the Bible and the Greco-Roman world. Both comprise Pseudo-Philo's world, and it is their intermingling that results in an interpretative fusion that scholars cannot afford any longer to ignore if they are to appreciate the panoply of creativity that characterized Judaism of late antiquity.

II. FOUR INSPIRED FIGURES IN LIBER ANTIQUITATUM BIBLICARUM

In LAB, four figures experience prophetic inspiration: Balaam, Joshua, Kenaz, and Saul. Because Saul's experience is the simplest, our analysis will begin with him.

---

6. Piñero, "Mediterranean View," 29.
7. Piñero, "Mediterranean View," 29.

A. Saul

LAB 62.2 is an abbreviated retelling of Saul's prophetic frenzy among the band of Samuel's prophets (1 Sam 19:20-24). Pseudo-Philo writes:

> And a spirit abided in Saul, and he prophesied, saying, "Why are you led astray, Saul, and whom are you pursuing in vain? The time allotted to your kingdom has been completed. Go to your place. For you will die, and David will reign. Will not you and your son die together? And then the kingdom of David will appear." And Saul went away and did not know what he had prophesied.[8]

The most important aspects of this account for understanding LAB's view of prophetic inspiration are present in the introduction and conclusion to the prophecy. The account begins with the juxtaposition of the spirit and prophesying: *Et mansit spiritus in Saul et prophetavit dicens*. It concludes with the detail, foreign to 1 Sam 19:24, that Saul could not recollect what he had prophesied: *Et abiit Saul et non scivit que prophetavit*.

The juxtaposition of spirit and prophesying in the introduction of LAB 62.2 is traceable to 1 Sam 19:20-24, which is the source for Pseudo-Philo's description of Saul's activity as *prophesying*. Five times, the verb נבא occurs in 1 Sam 19:20-24. In the parallel biblical account of Saul's frenzy, 1 Sam 10:5-6, 10-13, the verb also occurs five times. The Septuagint translates all ten occurrences consistently with προφητεύειν. Similarly, the Vulgate translates all ten occurrences with *prophetare*. These parallel translations leave little room to doubt that the Hebrew verb underlying the Latin, *prophetavit*, in LAB likewise was נבא.

First Samuel 19:20-24 is also a unique instance in the so-called Deuteronomistic History of ecstatic prophecy that is inspired by the spirit of God. Three times, Saul's messengers fall under the sway of a company of prophets, led by Samuel, who are themselves in a state of prophetic frenzy. Finally, Saul too falls into a prophetic frenzy. In Samuel's presence, Saul succumbs to prophetic frenzy, marked by stripping his clothes, prophesying, and lying naked all day and night. The story concludes, "Therefore it is said, 'Is Saul also among the prophets?'" (1 Sam 19:24; see 10:12).[9]

The Bible elsewhere affords only rare glimpses of prophetic ecstasy, but J. Lindblom has demonstrated that ecstatic prophecy persisted well

---

8. Quotations of LAB are from Harrington, "Pseudo-Philo." Latin quotations are from the *Sources chrétiennes* edition (Harrington et al.).

9. First Samuel 10:6, 10-13 is probably a doublet of 1 Sam 19:18-24, in which the "spirit of the Lord" and "spirit of God" evoke prophetic frenzy.

beyond this earliest stage in Israel's development."[10] In the eighth century BCE, Hosea criticizes Israel for saying, "The prophet is a fool, the man of the spirit is mad!" (9:7),[11] while Micah contrasts the inability of false prophets to obtain visions and revelations, the disgrace of the seers, and the shame of the diviners, with himself being filled with power and "the spirit of the Lord," i.e., the ability to obtain visions and revelations. The latter claim of exilic prophets to inspiration suggests experiences of ecstasy. Deutero-Isaiah commands a hearing because "the Lord God has sent me and his spirit" (48:16), while Ezekiel claims that "the spirit lifted me up" in a vision (3:12, 14) and "the spirit of the Lord fell upon me" (11:5).[12]

When Pseudo-Philo paraphrases 1 Sam 19:18–24, therefore, he appears to situate Saul in a long, albeit submerged, line of interpretation that views the spirit as the source of ecstatic prophesying. This is not, however, the case, for Pseudo-Philo has omitted from his paraphrase of 1 Sam 19:18–24 the two ingredients that would indicate ecstatic prophesying. First, he omits the communal contagion that is central to 1 Sam 19. Lindblom observes, "This ecstasy was of the collective kind and contagious. It was through contact with the ecstatic band that Saul himself fell into ecstasy."[13] In contrast, it is not through contact with the ecstatics that Saul and his messengers prophesy in LAB. Pseudo-Philo omits entirely the messengers' threefold falling into ecstasy and presents Saul as alone in pursuit of David when he prophesies. Second, Pseudo-Philo omits the activities that indicate ecstasy in 1 Sam 19: Saul's stripping, falling, and lying naked for the duration of the day and night. We may add, third, that Pseudo-Philo, although he is familiar with 1 Sam 10:6,[14] and although he frequently combines biblical passages kaleidoscopically,[15] does not embellish his account of Saul's prophesying with any of the accoutrements of 1 Sam 10 that suggest ecstasy, such as the use of harp, tambourine, flute, and lyre (1 Sam 10:5). It is evident,

---

10. Lindblom, *Prophecy in Ancient Israel*, 173–78.

11. See also b. B. Bat. 12b: "From the day the Temple was destroyed, prophecy was taken away from the prophets and given to fools and children."

12. Lindblom, *Prophecy in Ancient Israel*, 65–82, 122–37, 173–82.

13. Lindblom, *Prophecy in Ancient Israel*, 48. He continues: "How effective the ancient narrator imagined the contagious power of the ecstasy to be, we can see from what he tells us about the messengers whom Saul sent to David. Three times messengers were sent; but all three groups fell into ecstasy at the mere sight of a company of ecstatic prophets."

14. See LAB 20.2; 27.10.

15. This tendency to gather together a variety of biblical texts, or to utilize key phrases in contexts different from the Bible, becomes apparent by perusing ch. 15, "Index of Biblical Citations and Parallels in LAB," of Feldman's prolegomenon to James, *Biblical Antiquities of Philo*.

then, that, although he paraphrases the biblical account of Saul's prophesying, Pseudo-Philo omits all indicators of ecstasy in the biblical account that would otherwise identify Saul as an ecstatic prophet.

Despite this severe alteration of 1 Sam 19, there is no reason to look farther afield than Pseudo-Philo's biblical source to understand the introductory words, "And [a] spirit abided in Saul, and he prophesied."[16] The spirit is already central in 1 Sam 19:20-24, and references to prophecy and prophesying, as noun and verb, occur no less than twelve times in 1 Sam 10 and 19.

The source of Pseudo-Philo's conclusion, however, is altogether different. The addition of the words "[Saul] did not know what he had prophesied" cannot be explained by adducing biblical antecedents. On the contrary, the Hebrew Bible is replete with instances, from all periods of its composition, demonstrating that prophets were to recollect rather than to forget the divine words communicated during revelation. The enigmatic man of Judah in 1 Kgs 13:9 refuses to go home with another "man of God" because he remembers God's warning: "Thus I was commanded by the word of the Lord." Isaiah recalls what he heard during an ecstatic experience: "For the Lord spoke thus to me while his hand was strong upon me, and warned me not to walk in the way of this people, saying..." (8:11).[17] Ezekiel, following his remarkable and extended visions of chs. 8–11, has perfect recollection: "The spirit lifted me up and brought me in a vision by the spirit of God into Chaldea, to the exiles. Then the vision that I had seen left me. And I told the exiles all the things that the Lord had shown me." The biblical paradigm, in which God speaks to the prophet in order that the prophet may convey

---

16. Harrington translates *spiritus* with the indefinite article, "a" ("Pseudo-Philo," 2:374); James (*Biblical Antiquities of Philo*, 235) translates "the spirit"; Harrington et al. translate "l'esprit" (Pseudo-Philon, *Antiquités Bibliques*, 1:373); and Dietzfelbinger (*Pseudo-Philo*, 257) translates "der heilige Geist." Whether or not *spiritus* should be translated "a spirit" or "the spirit," for two reasons it should probably be regarded as benign rather than malevolent (i.e., demonic). First, references to the spirit in other instances of prophetic inspiration in LAB can be traced to biblical references to the spirit of God (LAB 18.10 to Num 24:2 or 23:7 LXX; LAB 20.2 to Deut 34:9 and possibly Isa 11:2; LAB 27.9-10 to Judg 3:9 and 6:34; LAB 28.6 to Ezek 8:1 and 20:1). Second, Pseudo-Philo has already established that the spirit that inspires is God's spirit: Balaam is inspired by the "spirit of God" (18.10) or "holy spirit" (18.11); Kenaz is empowered for battle by "the spirit of the Lord" (27.9); Barak attributes Deborah's prophetic ability to God's spirit, for upon discovering Sisera dead, he says, "Blessed be the Lord, who sent his spirit and said, 'Into the hand of a woman Sisera will be handed over'" (32.9); Gideon puts on "the spirit of the Lord" to defeat the Midianites (36.2). By this point in the narrative, therefore, the reader can probably assume that the spirit that inspires Saul is God's spirit.

17. Lindblom argues cogently that the language of this passage indicates an ecstatic experience (*Prophecy in Ancient Israel*, 121, 135-36, 174-75).

those words to the people of God, is exemplified by Ezek 3:10–11: "Mortal, all my words that I shall speak to you receive in your heart and hear with your ears; then go to the exiles, to your people, and speak to them."[18]

Although Pseudo-Philo is indebted elsewhere to Ezekiel[19] in particular and to the prophetic tradition in general, his conclusion to Saul's inspiration, in which he contends that Saul "did not know what he had prophesied," can hardly lie in sharper contrast to the biblical prophetic model of remembering God's words. However, the inability to recall one's inspired experience became a popular hallmark of oracular ecstasy during the Greco-Roman era. Pseudo-Philo may have chosen to omit all biblical references to prophetic ecstasy in LAB 62.2, but his addition of the concluding words "did not know what he had prophesied" reintroduces the element of ecstasy in a manner that recalls not Moses et al. but Plato, whose view of mantic inspiration was reinterpreted during the Greco-Roman era.

In *Apol.* 22C and *Meno* 99C, Plato contends that inspired poets (οἱ θεομάντεις and οἱ χρησμῳδοί) do not know what they are saying (ἴσασιν δὲ οὐδὲν ὧν λέγουσι[ν]).[20] This view was [mis]interpreted in the Greco-Roman era by diverse figures to mean that those who experience ecstasy cannot remember what they saw or heard. The second-century CE public speaker and man of letters Aelius Aristides, following his defense of the Delphic priestesses of Apollo, discusses the inspiration of the priestesses of Zeus in Dodona, "who know as much as the god approves, and for as long as he approves." These inspired priestesses have no knowledge of Zeus's oracles prior to inspiration, "nor afterwards do they know anything which they have said, but all inquirers understand it better than they."[21]

The second- or third-century Christian author Pseudo-Justinus, in his *Cohortatio ad Graecos*, discusses Plato's admiration for the Sibyl because her prophecies came to pass. To support his case, Ps-Justin paraphrases Plato's *Meno*, in which prophetic persons are said to be divine. Twice in this paraphrase, Ps-Justin expresses the opinion that the Sibyl cannot recall what she said while inspired:

---

18. According to 10:20–22, Ezekiel can recollect elements of a prior ecstatic vision: "These were the living creatures that I saw underneath the God of Israel by the river Chebar; and I knew that they were cherubim."

19. E.g., LAB 9.10 and Ezek 10:2; LAB 28.6 and Ezek 8:1 and 20:1 (see the discussion of Kenaz below); LAB 37.2 and Ezek 3:18.

20. All texts and translations of classical literature are from LCL unless otherwise indicated.

21. Aelius Aristides, *In Defense of Oratory* 43. Greek οὔθ' ὕστερον οὐδὲν ὧν εἶπον ἴσασιν ἀλλὰ πάντες μᾶλλον ἢ ἐκεῖναι.

For, unlike the poets who, after their poems are penned, have power to correct and polish . . . she was filled indeed with prophecy at the time of the inspiration, *but as soon as the inspiration ceased, there ceased also the remembrance of all she had said.* (37.2) . . .

They said also that they who then took down her prophecies, being illiterate persons, often went quite astray from the accuracy of the metres; and this, they said, was the cause of the want of metre in some of the verses, *the prophetess having no remembrance of what she had said*, after the possession and inspiration ceased, and the reporters having, through their lack of education, failed to record the metres with accuracy. (37.3)[22]

John Cassian, who lived during the late fourth and early fifth centuries, includes in his *Collationes*, or institutes for monastic orders, a discussion of demon possession. He contrasts two types of possessed people, those who "are affected by them [demons] in such a way as to have not the slightest conception of what they do and say, while others know and afterwards recollect it."[23]

Although Plato himself did not contend that inspiration entailed an inability to remember, these interpreters did. This interpretation spanned several centuries, claiming adherents from a variety of perspectives: an affluent second-century Greco-Roman rhetorician, a second-century Christian apologist, and a fourth-century Christian monastic leader. The diversity of these witnesses to a shared view of inspiration or possession with respect to recollection suggests that this was a popular, widely held view during the Greco-Roman era, during which LAB was composed. The breadth and longevity of its popularity suggests that Pseudo-Philo could easily have known this tradition without a literary dependence upon these or other Greco-Roman authors.

B. Kenaz

M. R. James describes Pseudo-Philo's tale of Kenaz as a "sudden burst of inventiveness," which "draws freely on his own imagination."[24] This imagi-

---

22. Translation from *ANF* 1:289; emphasis added. Greek of emphases: παυσαμένης δὲ τῆς ἐπιπνοίας ἐπέπαυτο καὶ ἡ τῶν εἰρημένων μνήνη (37.2); and καὶ τῆς ἐπιπνοίας μὴ μεμνημένης τῶν εἰρημένων (37.3). Greek text is from Marcovich, *Pseudo-Iustinus*, 76.

23. Cassian, *Collationes* 12. Translation from *NPNF*[2] 11:366. Latin *Quidam enim sic adflantur, ut nequaquam ea quae gerunt uel loquuntur intellegant, quidam uero norunt et postea recordantur.* Latin text is from Pichery, *Jean Cassien*, 256.

24. James, *Biblical Antiquities of Philo*, 146.

native tale is the centerpiece of Pseudo-Philo's understanding of the divine spirit. Its biblical underpinning is Judg 3:9–11:

> But when the Israelites cried out to the Lord, the Lord raised up a deliverer for the Israelites, who delivered them, Othniel son of Kenaz, Caleb's younger brother. The spirit of the Lord came upon him, and he judged Israel; he went out to war . . . So the land had rest forty years. Then Othniel the son of Kenaz died.

Pseudo-Philo states far more elaborately that the spirit clothed Kenaz in order to grant him military success: "And Kenaz arose, and the spirit of the Lord clothed him, and he drew his sword" (LAB 27.9); "And when Kenaz heard their words, he was clothed with the spirit of power and was changed into another man, and he went down to the Amorite camp and began to strike them down" (LAB 27.10).[25] This recasting of the Bible contains two biblical allusions. First, Pseudo-Philo eschews the more passive Hebrew vocabulary of Judg 3:9, ותהי עליו, and replaces it with the metaphor of clothing, which he extracts from the story of Gideon in Judg 6:34: "But the spirit of the Lord took possession of [i.e., לבשה, clothed] Gideon."[26]

---

25. James contends that Pseudo-Philo "may be following a current fashion" when he presents Kenaz rather than Othniel as the first judge (*Biblical Antiquities of Philo*, 146–147). Josephus takes this tack as well (*Ant.* 5.182), and the first-century Palestinian Lives of the Prophets 10.9 contains the detail that Jonah "was buried in the cave of Kenaz, who became judge of one tribe in the days of the anarchy" (dated by Hare, "Prophets, Lives of the," *ABD* 5:502). Hare follows the explanation of J. Jeremias, who suggests "that the change reflects local Idumean tradition, which glorified Kenaz as the ancestor of an important Edomite tribe. The cave of Kenaz thus constituted the Idumean response to the cave of Machpelah, the grave of the patriarchs near Hebron" (Hare, "Lives of the Prophets," 2:393).

26. Judg 6:34 also inspires, not surprisingly, Pseudo-Philo's description of Gideon's success in LAB 36.2: "And as soon as Gideon heard these words ['And now let us rise up and take care for our own lives and flee'], he put on the spirit of the Lord and was strengthened and said to the three hundred men, 'Rise up, let each one of you gird on his sword.'" We should note that the occurrence of Judg 6:34 with respect both to Gideon and to Kenaz is consistent with Pseudo-Philo's portrayal of these figures. He draws significant parallels between the victories of Kenaz and Gideon: the same number of soldiers, three hundred (LAB 27.5; 36.1); the prominence of the sword (27.7–12; 36.2); the request for a sign (27.7; 35.6–7); and the ambush of the enemies' camp (27.10; 36.1–2). See also Dietzfelbinger, *Pseudo-Philo*, 34–35.

One difference does distinguish the role of the spirit in LAB 27.9–10 and 36.2: Kenaz is clothed by the spirit, but Gideon puts on the spirit as clothing. In other words, in the case of Gideon, Pseudo-Philo alters his biblical source from "the spirit of the Lord took possession [i.e., clothed] of Gideon" to "Gideon . . . put on the spirit of the Lord." To alleviate this difficulty, Harrington suggests that LAB's *induit spiritum* be emended to *induit spiritus* in order to restore the original biblical meaning ("Pseudo-Philo," 2:349). This emendation is not necessary for three reasons. First, as we shall see in the discussion of Joshua, there is precedent in LAB for the metaphor of putting on the

Second, by depicting Kenaz as "changed into another man," Pseudo-Philo alludes to 1 Sam 10:6, in which Samuel addresses Saul: "Then the spirit of the Lord will come mightily upon you, and you shall prophesy with them and be turned into another man." Pseudo-Philo obscures the original biblical context, in which transformation is related to prophecy, and relates the transformation to military prowess.

Pseudo-Philo also transforms Judg 3:9–11 into a description of the prophetic ability of Kenaz. The introduction and conclusion, as in the description of Saul's inspiration, are particularly important for understanding prophetic inspiration in LAB. It begins, "And when they had sat down, a holy spirit came upon Kenaz and dwelled in him and put him in ecstasy, and he began to prophesy, saying . . ." (28.6).[27] It concludes, "And when Kenaz had spoken these words, he was awakened, and his senses came back to him. But he did not know what he had said or what he had seen" (28.10a).[28] Four elements of this introduction and conclusion provide insight into the sources and nature of prophetic inspiration in LAB.

1. Kenaz's vision takes place within a community: "And when they had sat down." The communal character of Kenaz's vision is reminiscent of two of Ezekiel's ecstatic experiences. Ezekiel's vision of temple abominations takes place among the elders: "As I sat in my house, with the elders of Judah sitting before me, the hand of the Lord God fell upon me there" (8:1). Ezekiel later receives a word from God when "certain elders of Israel came to consult the Lord, and sat down before me" (20:1). Moreover, in both cases the elevation is attributed to the divine spirit, and the result is a vision.

2. The spirit elevated (*extulit*) Kenaz's mind (*sensum*) (28.6). Although the verb *effero*, in the phrase *extulit sensum eius*, is used transitively and therefore probably should be understood as the carrying up or elevation of Kenaz's *sensus*, these words could possibly indicate the carrying away or loss of mental or physical sense.[29] The allusion to Ezek 8:1, however, suggests that this exegetical addition to Judg 3:9–11 was prompted by the

---

spirit as clothing (LAB 20.1–2). Second, Pseudo-Philo modifies Judg 6–8 substantially, and we should hardly expect him to reproduce each idiom slavishly. Third, it may be that Pseudo-Philo intentionally stresses Gideon's initiative. For Gideon he emphasizes Gideon's initiative, while for Kenaz he underscores the spirit's ability to overpower.

27. *Et dum sederent, insiluit spiritus sanctus habitans in Cenez, et extulit sensum eius, et cepit prophetare dicens.*

28. *Et factum est cum locutus fuisset Cenez verba hec, expergefactus est et reversus est sensus eius in eum. Ipse autem nesciebat que locutus fuerat, neque que viderat.*

29. The noun *sensus* may be translated in a variety of ways, including: sense perception, the senses themselves, mental faculties of perception, self-awareness or self-consciousness, the faculty of judgment or understanding, an emotion, thought, etc.

elevation of Ezekiel in 8:3 (cf. 3:12, 14) and should, therefore, be interpreted as a description of the elevation of Kenaz's mind.

The purpose of Ezekiel's elevations, however, is substantially different from the elevation of Kenaz's mind. The purpose of Ezekiel's visions is to transport Ezekiel conveniently between Babylon and Judea. In contrast, Kenaz stays put. Indeed, Ezekiel's experiences are depicted as physical transport, even though they are not; he is taken "by a lock of my head ... between earth and heaven ... to Jerusalem" (8:3; see 12:24). Pseudo-Philo, in contrast, specifically refers only to the elevation of Kenaz's mind (*sensum*).

Despite the allusion to Ezek 8:1-3, then, Pseudo-Philo interprets that elevation with quintessentially Greco-Roman conceptions, most of which are developments of Plato. In particular, Cicero, in *De divinatione*, sheds significant light on Pseudo-Philo's portrait of Kenaz's prophetic inspiration. *De divinatione*, which was composed during the mid-first century BCE, is significant because it contains a variety of viewpoints from the Greco-Roman period and earlier. A. S. Pease, following Heeringa, suggests that book 1, which concerns us, was based upon Posidonius's work on divination, which itself "contained a collection of the *placita* of earlier philosophers."[30] Therefore, Cicero offers a panoramic view of inspiration in the Greco-Roman period, including even those positions he refutes.

In *Div.* 1.114, Cicero, in a discussion of inspiration, develops Plato's poignant description of the soul as a chariot led by two winged horses (*Phaedr.* 246A–47E).[31] Of those inspired, Cicero writes:

> Those then, whose souls, spurning their bodies, take wings abroad—inflamed and aroused by a sort of passion—these men, I say, certainly see the things which they foretell in their prophecies. Such souls do not cling to the body and are kindled by many different influences ... In all these cases the frenzied soul sees the future long in advance.

In this text, the soul, by rising from the body, is able to foretell the future long in advance. Similarly, Kenaz's *sensus* is lifted to see the future seven thousand years in advance.[32] Pseudo-Philo is indebted to his Greco-Roman milieu for this interpretation of Platonic inspiration, which

---

30. Pease, *M. Tulli Ciceronis*, 1:22, 24.

31. See also Plato's description of the ascent of the philosopher's mind in *Theaet.* 173C–74A: such a "mind ... is borne in all directions, as Pindar says, 'both below the earth' ... and 'above the sky.'"

32. Or four thousand. See Feldman, "Prolegomenon," in James, *Biblical Antiquities of Philo*, cxv.

provides one of the central ingredients in his portrayal of Kenaz's prophetic inspiration.

3. Kenaz experienced a loss and restoration of mind, which required awakening: "He was awakened, and his senses came back to him." Biblical texts occasionally refer vaguely to prophets as "madmen" (Hos 9:7), and their actions are often bizarre, but otherwise the view that the mind of the prophet is elevated or lost and subsequently restored or awakened has only weak biblical precedent.

The closest biblical antecedent to this experience is not one of the prophets but, oddly enough, Nebuchadnezzar, when he returns to normalcy following his illness. Nebuchadnezzar recounts, "At that time my reason returned to me" (Dan 4:36).[33] The Vulgate translation (Dan 4:33), *sensus meus reversus est ad me*, is strikingly similar to LAB 28.10: *et reversus est sensus eius in eum*. However, despite the parallel between the Latin of LAB and the Vulgate, four observations seriously call into question the likelihood that Dan 4 is the antecedent of LAB 28.10. First, the return of Kenaz's mind cannot be taken in isolation, for in LAB 28.6–10 it is integrally related to the ability to prophesy: *et extulit sensum eius, et cepit prophetare dicens . . . expergefactus est et reversus est sensus eius in eum*. This is certainly not Nebuchadnezzar's experience in Dan 4. Second, the restoration follows entirely different experiences. Nebuchadnezzar is ill, while Kenaz is in a trance from which he must be awakened. Third, Kenaz is the quintessential military and prophetic leader in LAB; the elevation and restoration of his mind present him, in his final hours, as a visionary who foretells the future. Nebuchadnezzar is a misled, proud foreign ruler who "ate grass like oxen." Fourth, Pseudo-Philo emphasizes the role of the divine spirit in Kenaz's experience, while in Dan 4 Nebuchadnezzar simply returns to health. It is unlikely, in light of these differences, that Pseudo-Philo intends a parallel between Kenaz and Nebuchadnezzar.

Even if Pseudo-Philo does extract this expression from Dan 4, the new meaning he gives to it by placing it within the context of Kenaz's vision—with its components of elevation, prophesying, awakening, and the inability to remember—is not derived from its context in the Bible. However, the loss of rationality, which the expression in LAB 28.10 implies, is precisely the central ingredient in the Platonic view of inspiration. In *Ion* 533D–34E, Plato asserts that poets indite only when they are not in their own minds,

---

33. See also Dan 4:34.

when they are "out of their minds,"[34] when their mind is no longer in them.[35] It is through this condition—being out of one's mind—that God speaks:

> And for this reason God takes away the mind of these men and uses them as his ministers, just as he does soothsayers and godly seers, in order that we who hear them may know that it is not they who utter these words of great price, when they are out of their wits, but that it is God himself who speaks and addresses us through them. (534C–D)

Authentic divination, then, cannot occur when the mind is rational: "No man achieves true and inspired divination when in his rational mind, but only when the power of his intelligence is fettered in sleep or when it is distraught by disease or by reason of some divine inspiration" (*Tim.* 71E). Equally significant, Plato employs similar language in his discussion of μανία, where he contends that prophetesses confer benefits only when they are mad or manic (*Phaedr.* 244A–B).[36]

This Platonic emphasis on the displacement of rationality was developed during the Greco-Roman era. Plutarch, for example,[37] who held a priesthood for life at Delphi from the year 95 CE, devoted several dialogues to the topic of oracles.[38] In a discussion of the four kinds of friendship in *Amatorius* (758D–E), Plutarch refers to the four kinds of inspiration which Plato categorized as ecstasy (*Phaedr.* 265B). The second, observes Plutarch, entails the displacement of the rational mind:

> There is a second kind, however, which does not exist without divine inspiration. It is not intrinsically generated but is, rather, an extrinsic afflatus that displaces the faculty of rational inference; it is created and set in motion by a higher power. This sort of madness bears the general name of "enthusiasm" [ἐνθουσιαστικόν].

---

34. ἔνθεος ... ἔκφρων (534B).

35. ὁ νοῦς μηκέτι ἐν αὐτῷ ἐνῇ (534B).

36. See 245C on inspired philosophers who are thought by the vulgar to be mad; also Cicero, *Div.* 1.80.

37. On the popularity of Plato in the Greco-Roman period, see Hadas, "Plato in Hellenistic Fusion"; Hadas, *Hellenistic Culture*, 72–82.

38. It is difficult to assess Plutarch's popularity during the first century CE. L. H. Feldman observes: "The fact that not a single papyrus fragment has ever been found of any of his numerous works would indicate that he was not very popular, at least in Egypt, in the Roman period" (personal letter, Oct. 5, 1992). See Feldman, "Pro-Jewish Intimations," 231.

A similar description of inspiration occurs in Plutarch's *Def. orac.* 432D. In this instance, he discusses the ability to foretell the future.

> But that which foretells the future, like a tablet without writing, is both irrational [ἄλογον] and indeterminate in itself, but receptive of impressions and presentiments through what may be done to it, and inconsequently grasps at the future when it is farthest withdrawn [ὅταν ἐκστῇ μάλιστα] from the present. Its withdrawal [ἐξίσταται δέ] is brought about by a temperament and disposition of the body as it is subjected to a change which we call inspiration [ἐνθουσιασμόν].

Plutarch is dependent in both of these discussions on Plato's view of inspiration, according to which the rational capacity is displaced by an outside or higher power. This is precisely what transpires for Kenaz in LAB, whose mind must be restored to him (*reversus est*) once it is elevated.[39]

It is important to observe, in addition, that Pseudo-Philo describes the return of Kenaz's lost mind as an awakening (*expergefactus*). The search for a clear biblical antecedent to the restoration of the mind as awakening leads only to distant parallels. The clearest biblical reference to awakening, Zech 4:1, actually says the opposite of LAB 28.10, for there Zechariah is awakened, not after the vision, but before it; in other words, he has a vision in an awakened state. Other examples include Daniel, who frequently falls into trances; but this takes place after rather than before visions, while the angel talks with him.[40] In contrast to Zechariah and Daniel, Kenaz has a vision while his mind is asleep, and he is subsequently awakened, having been the whole time in the presence of a gathered community.[41]

In contrast, the association of the elevation of the mind, the loss of rationality, and awakening are conceptions entirely at home in Pseudo-Philo's Greco-Roman milieu. This association is evident in texts closely related to the passages already discussed vis-à-vis Greco-Roman inspiration and the

---

39. Also in the first century, Tacitus discusses the oracle of the Clarian Apollo: the priest responds to inquirers with set verses, although he himself is "ignorant generally of writing of metre" (*Annals* 2.54). The length of Plato's shadow is apparent in the *De Mysteriis* of Iamblichus, the late third-century (ca. 250–325) Neo-Platonist: enthusiasm "exterminates entirely our own proper consciousness and motion" (Taylor, *Iamblichus*, 129). For the Greek and a more recent French translation, see Places, *Jamblique*, 108. On Plutarch's and Iamblichus's interpretations of Delphic inspiration, as well as Pollux's in *Onomasticon* 1.15, see the discussion of Reiling, *Hermas and Christian Prophecy*, 114–21.

40. Dan 7:13–15; 8:15–18, 27; 10:8–9, 16–17.

41. The presence of this community suggests that the dreams and night visions of Daniel (7:2) are not the antecedent of the depiction of Kenaz's vision.

elevation or loss of mind. I have quoted the *Tim.* 71E, according to which "no man achieves true and inspired divination when in his rational mind, but only when the power of his intelligence is fettered in sleep or ... by reason of some divine inspiration." Among Plato's interpreters, Cicero preserves this association: dreams and ecstasy are the two states in which natural divination takes place:[42]

> Moreover, divination finds another and a positive support in nature, which teaches us how great is the power of the soul when it is divorced from the bodily senses, as it is especially in sleep, and in times of frenzy or inspiration. For, as the souls of the gods, without the intervention of eyes or ears or tongue, understand each other and what each one thinks ... so the souls of men, when released by sleep from bodily chains, or when stirred by inspiration and delivered up to their own impulses, see things that they cannot see when they are mingled with the body. (*Div.* 1.129)

Plutarch is no less aware of this association. Just prior to his discussion of foretelling in *Def. orac.* 432D, quoted above with respect to the displacement of the mind, Plutarch interprets Plato's *Tim.* 71E when he too associates dreams and the loss of reason:

> Souls therefore, all possessed of this power [memory], which is innate but dim and hardly manifest, nevertheless oftentimes disclose its flower and radiance in dreams ... when the body becomes cleansed of all impurities and attains a temperament adapted to this end, a temperament through which the reasoning and thinking faculty of the souls is relaxed[43] and released from their present state as they range amid the irrational and imaginative realms of the future. (432C)

The popularity of the view that sleep is the condition of inspiration is apparent in the words of Simmias, in Plutarch's *Gen. Socr.* 589C–D, in which he summarizes a view he himself rejects: "In popular belief, on the other hand, it is only in sleep that men receive inspiration from on high."

Like Plato and his Greco-Roman interpreters, Pseudo-Philo draws an integral connection between the loss of the rational mind and sleep when he writes that Kenaz was awakened and his mind restored to him. When we add to this that Pseudo-Philo, like Plato and his Greco-Roman

---

42. Cicero defines divination as "the foresight and knowledge of future events" (*Div.* 1.1).

43. ἢ τὸ λογιστικὸν καὶ φροντιστικὸν ἀνίεται.

interpreters, portrayed inspiration as an elevation of the soul or *sensum*, we discern a web of related concepts—elevation of mind, loss of rationality, and sleep—which points unmistakably to a Greco-Roman milieu as the source of Pseudo-Philo's portrait of Kenaz's prophetic inspiration. None of these individual elements, with the sole exception of dreams, plays a role in the Bible. Consequently, there is no biblical precedent for their association. In contrast, all of them, individually and in relation to each other, are part and parcel of Greco-Roman views on inspiration, which were so popular as to be included by Plutarch and Cicero in their collections of views on inspiration and divination.

4. Kenaz could recall neither what he had said nor seen: "But he did not know what he had said or what he had seen." The addition of this element further demonstrates the depth to which Pseudo-Philo is indebted to Greco-Roman views of inspiration. We saw in our discussion of Saul's inspiration that the biblical prophets cannot be regarded as prototypes for this element of inspiration because they were mandated to recall what they heard and saw in order to warn Israel. In contrast, a diverse cross-section of authors concur in their interpretation of Plato by contending that possession and inspiration can result in an inability to recall what was experienced.

Although the setting of Kenaz's prophetic inspiration is reminiscent of Ezekiel's own prophetic visions, its ingredients are Greco-Roman: the elevation of the mind, the loss of the mind, awakening from inspiration, and the inability to recall what was said or seen. Pseudo-Philo's "sudden burst of inventiveness" is, therefore, a creative transformation of biblical precedents by means of Greco-Roman conceptions of inspiration.

C. Joshua

Although LAB 20.2–3 contains no explicit reference to the divine spirit, the confluence of biblical and Greco-Roman vocabulary, when taken together, suggests that Pseudo-Philo is here depicting another instance of spirit-inspired prophetic ecstasy. Very little of LAB's description of the commissioning of Joshua is taken from Joshua 1; rather, in his characteristic manner, Pseudo-Philo gathers a cornucopia of biblical allusions and merges them creatively with Greco-Roman concepts. The result is a creative and extremely independent rewriting of the Bible:

> Then God said to Joshua the son of Nun, "Why do you mourn and why do you hope in vain that Moses yet lives? And now you wait to no purpose, because Moses is dead. Take his garments of wisdom and clothe yourself, and with his belt of knowledge

gird your loins, and you will be changed and become another man . . ." And Joshua took the garments of wisdom and clothed himself and girded his loins with the belt of understanding. And when he clothed himself with it, his mind was afire and his spirit was moved, and he said to the people . . .

The most likely immediate biblical source for this commissioning, with its emphasis upon wisdom and understanding, is Deut 34:9a, which provides the rationale for the commissioning that takes place just a few lines later in Josh 1: "Joshua son of Nun was full of the spirit of wisdom, because Moses had laid his hands on him." Although the images of LAB 20.2-3 and Deut 34:9, both of which are succession scenes, differ—the laying on of hands versus clothing—the common element that unites both succession scenes is wisdom. Joshua will succeed because he receives the wisdom of Moses.

Unlike the story of Kenaz, which contains explicit references to the divine spirit, the story of Joshua's commissioning does not. At first glance, Pseudo-Philo seems unexpectedly to have struck the reference to the spirit (of wisdom) from his source, Deut 34:9a: "Joshua son of Nun was full of the spirit of wisdom, because Moses had laid his hands on him." However, the image of clothing, which derives from Judg 6:34, and the description of transformation into another person, which derives from 1 Sam 10:6, indicate that Pseudo-Philo regards the divine spirit as the source of Joshua's inspiration.

First, the dominant metaphor of LAB 20.2-3 is clothing. In two other significant scenes of LAB, Pseudo-Philo employs the metaphor of clothing to depict the powerful presence of the spirit. We saw that in LAB 27.9-10 Pseudo-Philo twice employs the metaphor of clothing to emphasize the role of the spirit as the source of Kenaz's military strength: "And Kenaz arose, and the spirit of the Lord clothed him, and he drew his sword" (27.9);[44] "And when Kenaz heard their words, he was clothed with the spirit of power and was changed into another man, and he went down to the Amorite camp and began to strike them down" (27.10).[45] Although the verb used most frequently in the Bible to depict the spirit's overpowering force is "to come mightily upon" (צלח), Pseudo-Philo prefers the metaphor of clothing, which he derives from Judg 6:34: "But the spirit of the Lord took possession of [לבשה, clothed] Gideon."

---

44. *Et induit eum spiritus Domini.* The verb *induere* is used frequently for putting on arms and going to war (e.g., *arma induere*). See *Oxford Latin Dictionary*, s.v. "induō."

45. *Indutus est spiritu virtutis.*

Judges 6:34 is rewritten in LAB 36.2, in which Gideon is strengthened by the spirit to defeat the Midianites. As in the case of Kenaz, the metaphor employed to depict the spirit's possession of Gideon is clothing: Gideon heard the enemies say, "'And now let us rise up and take care for our own lives.' And as soon as Gideon heard these words, he put on the spirit of the Lord [*induit spiritum Domini*] and was strengthened and said to the three hundred men, 'Rise up.'" Twice, then, in LAB, Pseudo-Philo adopts the metaphor of clothing from Judg 6:34 in contexts with explicit references to the divine spirit. In LAB 20.2-3, his repeated references to clothing comprise an allusion to the power of the spirit.

A second biblical allusion further demonstrates that Pseudo-Philo depicts Joshua as the successor to the spirit that empowered Moses. Joshua, according to LAB 20.2, will "become another person" (*eris in virum alium*) when he puts on Moses's garments. Again, we saw that, in the tale of Kenaz, Pseudo-Philo employs similar words and attributes this transformation to the spirit: "He [Kenaz] was clothed with the spirit of power and was changed into another man [*transmutatus in virum alium*]" (27.10). He has culled this expression from 1 Sam 10:6, which depicts the transformation of Saul by the power of the spirit into a prophet through his experience of prophetic ecstasy: "Then the spirit of the Lord will possess you, and you will be in a prophetic frenzy along with them [the band of prophets] and be turned into a different person." In both his biblical source and the story of Kenaz, the spirit is said explicitly to transform a person "into another person." This expression in LAB 20.2-3, therefore, is no uncertain allusion to the transforming power of the spirit.[46]

Pseudo-Philo's version of Joshua's commissioning contains, then, precisely the same two biblical allusions as does his version of Kenaz's reception of the divine spirit: Judg 6:34 and 1 Sam 10:6. The presence of the same allusions in these two stories suggests that Pseudo-Philo has not excluded the biblical reference to the spirit; on the contrary, he has reshaped it to correspond to his portrayals of the reception of the divine spirit by Gideon and Kenaz.

---

46. A third possible allusion is evoked by the juxtaposition of wisdom and knowledge in LAB 20.2-3. This is not an uncommon collocation in the Bible, particularly in Job and Proverbs, but in LAB it seems to be yet another allusion to the spirit. We have already observed that the immediate source of LAB 20.2-3 is Deut 34:9, according to which the "spirit of wisdom" was passed from Moses to Joshua. The notion of the "spirit of wisdom" occurs elsewhere, in Isa 11:2, where it is juxtaposed with understanding: "And the spirit of the Lord shall rest upon him, the spirit of wisdom and understanding." It is possible that the expression in Deut 34:9, alongside the clothing metaphor and the expression "into another person," both of which depict the spirit's power, led to an association with the spirit of wisdom and understanding in Isa 11.

The spirit in LAB has a twofold effect on Joshua: "His mind was afire and his spirit was moved" (*incensa est mens eius et spiritus eius commotus est*). There are no biblical antecedents that explain sufficiently this description of the spirit's effect upon Joshua. A few descriptions of the psychological agitation of prophets may parallel the words "his spirit was moved" in LAB 20.3: Jeremiah's heart beats wildly (Jer 4:19); he has an incurable wound (15:18); Isaiah experiences what seem like birth pangs, accompanied by a reeling mind and trembling (Isa 21:3); Habakkuk trembles within, and his lips quiver while his steps tremble (Hab 3:16); Daniel's spirit is troubled and terrified (Dan 7:15); he enters a trance, prostrate on the ground (8:17–18), lies down sick (8:27), lacks strength (10:8–9), and is speechless and prostrate (10:15–17). However, these descriptions differ from LAB because they occur after a vision or revelation which portends horrible calamity; the prophets' pain, trembling, and enervated states are the result of, rather than the prelude to, their vision. They are images of horror at the future destruction which has just been revealed to them.[47] In contrast, Joshua's spirit is agitated in preparation for what he has to say and not as a response of fear to imminent horrors. These ecstatic experiences, therefore, cannot be considered antecedents to LAB 20.2–3.

Two prophetic texts may correspond to the other effect on Joshua: "His mind was afire." In Jer 20:9, the prophet cries out, "If I say, 'I will not mention him [God], or speak any more in his name,' then within me there is something like a burning fire shut up in my bones; I am weary with holding it in, and I cannot." This is probably not, however, an antecedent because Jeremiah is talking, not about an ecstatic experience, but about a compulsion to prophesy judgment (20:10). In the context of Jer 20, fire is an effective simile for Jeremiah's inexorable need to speak terror even at the expense of his closest friendships. The second text, Ezek 3:14, depicts Ezekiel's transport to Babylon: "The spirit lifted me up and bore me away; I went in bitterness in the heat of my spirit [ואלך מר בחמת רוחי], the hand of the Lord being strong upon me." In this depiction of an ecstatic state,[48] a reference to heat may suggest agitation. But heat is by no means fire, and the reference to the human spirit in both Ezek 3:14 and LAB 20.3 is hardly noteworthy. Apart from the loose parallel between heat and fire, therefore, there is little to commend Ezek 3:14 as the antecedent of LAB 20.3.

---

47. In Ezek 21:15, similar words are employed by the prophet to describe what the people feel when they see the swords about to slaughter them: "Therefore hearts melt and many stumble." These words describe fear, not ecstatic experiences.

48. On ecstasy and the hand of the Lord, see Lindblom, *Prophecy in Ancient Israel*, 134–35, 174–75.

The Bible, therefore, does not provide a sufficient antecedent to explain either the inflammation of Joshua's mind or the agitation of his spirit, let alone both together. In marked contrast, Greco-Roman texts provide not only parallels to each of the elements but also to both elements in tandem. From among Greco-Roman authors, Cicero's *De divinatione*, Lucan's *De bello civili*, and two books of Plutarch's *Moralia* contain vivid descriptions of inspiration that correspond closely to Pseudo-Philo's description of Joshua's inspiration as inflammation and agitation.

Inflammation and agitation occur in sharp juxtaposition in Cicero's description of dreams and ecstasy. I have already noted the significance of *Div.* 1.114 and 1.129 for understanding Kenaz's inspiration. *De divinatione* 1.114 also sheds invaluable light upon Joshua's inspiration. Cicero writes:

> Those then, whose souls, spurning their bodies, take wings and fly abroad—inflamed and aroused [*inflammati atque incitati*] by a sort of passion—these men, I say, certainly see the things which they foretell in their prophecies.

Inflammation and agitation here are the effects of inspiration, the purpose of which is prediction.[49] Similarly, LAB 20.3 contains the juxtaposition of inflammation and agitation in a context where Joshua is inspired by the spirit to predict the dire consequences that will occur if the Israelites prove unfaithful.

Lucan, who was born in Spain, 39 CE, and died in Rome, 65 CE, provides a startling description of the Delphic priestess as she is inspired by Apollo. The effect of Apollo's invasive inspiration of the priestess is depicted by Lucan chiefly as inflammation and severe agitation:

> Frantic she careers about the cave . . . she scatters the tripods . . . she boils over with fierce fire, while enduring the wrath of Phoebus. Nor does he ply the whip and goad alone, and dart flame into her vitals: she has to bear the curb as well, and is not permitted to reveal as much as she is suffered to know. (*De bello civili* 5.169–77)[50]

---

49. See also Plutarch, *Def. orac.* 432E–F.
50. *Bacchatur demens aliena per antrum . . .*
Obstantes tripodas magnoque exaestuat igne
Iratum te, Phoebe, ferens. Nec verbere solo
Uteris et stimulos flammasque in viscera mergis:
Accipit et frenos, nec tantum prodere vati
Quantum scire licet.

In this vivid account, inspiration is a fire, and the metaphor of plying the whip probably represents agitation, for, in the Sibylline Oracles, the Sibyl cries, "And why is my spirit lashed like a whip?" (3.4–5).

Similarly, in *Amat.* 758D–E, which I had cited to clarify Kenaz's loss of rationality, Plutarch depicts inspiration or enthusiasm as agitation of the soul (σάλος ψυχῆς). In *De defectu oraculorum* 432D, he discusses at length the effect of the "prophetic current and breath" (μαντικὸν ῥεῦμα καὶ πνεῦμα θειότατόν) on body and soul. He quotes Euripides approvingly, "For Bacchic rout / And frenzied mind contain much prophecy," interpreting this to refer to the moment "when the soul becomes hot and fiery (ὅταν ἔνθερμος ἡ ψυχὴ γενομένη καὶ πυρώδης), and throws aside the caution that human intelligence lays upon it, and thus often diverts and extinguishes the inspiration."[51] Once again, inflammation and agitation accompany the inspired loss of reason.

These Greco-Roman descriptions of inspiration are far closer to LAB 20.2–3 in content and wording than are the ecstatic experiences of the prophets as they are recounted in the Bible. They provide the source for Pseudo-Philo's depiction of Joshua's inspiration as inflammation and agitation. Once again, I should mention that these descriptions are popular rather than esoteric, so that Pseudo-Philo could easily adopt, consciously or unconsciously, these conceptions of inspiration without any literary dependence upon specific texts. The subject of Lucan's account, the Delphic oracle, was well known,[52] and Lucan himself was dependent for his account upon Virgil's *Aeneid* 6.42–102. Plutarch was a leading figure at Delphi whose works, particularly *De defectu oraculorum*, reflect more widely held opinions, in this instance of Euripides and Plato. And Cicero's *De divinatione* is a compendium of many views of divination.

D. Balaam

Pseudo-Philo's portrait of Balaam is hardly less a "burst of imagination" than his portrait of Kenaz. Although he follows the bare outline of Num 22–24, he modifies his source in several ways. He abbreviates the text, such as when he reduces the tale of the talking ass to "And his she-ass came by way of the wilderness and saw an angel and lay down beneath him" (LAB 18.9). Pseudo-Philo omits elements, such as the greed of Balaam, implied in Num 22 by the increasing gifts offered him and the growing prestige

---

51. On the popularity of Euripides in the first century CE, see Lucas, *Euripides and His Influence*.

52. For example, Josephus refers to it in *Ant.* 3.139; *Ag. Ap.* 2.131, 162.

of the servants sent to him. In LAB, Balaam is not tempted in the least by money (18.11). Although he truncates the biblical version, Pseudo-Philo freely supplements the Bible with his own material, such as the contents of God's message to Balaam in his first night vision, in which God recalls the election of Abraham (18.4–6). Pseudo-Philo also liberally transforms material, especially the oracles of Balaam, virtually creating his own in lieu of the four biblical oracles. The first speech of Num 23:7–10, although it retains a similar emphasis on the inability to curse whomever God has blessed, contains images and vocabulary that are nowhere to be found in the biblical oracle. Similarly, the reference to the planting by God in the second oracle, in LAB 18.10, may constitute a distant allusion to the "planting" of Num 24:6, but otherwise the oracle in LAB is altogether different. In light of this burst of creativity, Pseudo-Philo's radical transformation of Balaam's prophetic inspiration is hardly surprising.

Three references to the divine spirit punctuate LAB 18, of which only 18.10 is traceable directly to the Bible: "And when he saw part of the people, the spirit of God did not abide in him" (*Et cum vidisset partem populi, non permansit in eo spiritus Dei*). The first part of this sentence, "And when he saw part of the people" is from Num 22:41b, "And from there he could see part of the people." These words are combined with either Num 24:2 or the version represented by Num 23:7 LXX.[53]

Whatever the source, Pseudo-Philo's alteration is noteworthy, for his version flatly contradicts the biblical version. According to LAB 18.10, Balaam loses rather than receives the spirit. Unlike Saul, Joshua, and Kenaz in LAB, or Balaam in the biblical version, Balaam's oracle arises from the absence rather than the presence of the spirit. This reality is borne out by two of Balaam's own statements about the spirit, which Pseudo-Philo adds, without precedent, in the text of Numbers. When Balak's messengers first approach him, Balaam retorts, "Now he does not realize that the spirit that is given to us is given for a time" (18.3). Later, in the midst of his prophetic oracle, he proclaims: "I am restrained in my speech and cannot say what I see with my eyes, because there is little left of the holy spirit that abides in me. For I know that, because I have been persuaded by Balak, I have lessened the time of my life. And behold my remaining hour" (18.11d–12a).

53. Numbers 24:2 reads, "Balaam looked up and saw Israel camping tribe by tribe. Then the spirit of God came upon him." Numbers 23:7 LXX reads, "And the spirit of God came upon him" (καὶ ἐγενήθη πνεῦμα θεοῦ ἐπ' αὐτῷ). Because of the similarity between these statements, it is not possible finally to determine which is the source of Pseudo-Philo's reference to the spirit. More generally, Pseudo-Philo did not, in all probability, use the LXX but, more likely, a Hebrew text on which the LXX depended. On that text, see Harrington, "Biblical Text"; Harrington, "Original Language," 503–14; Feldman, "Prolegomenon," in James, *Biblical Antiquities of Philo*, li–lii.

In his three statements about the spirit, then, Pseudo-Philo distinguishes between the fullness of inspiration experienced by Kenaz and Joshua, which he depicts as clothing, or even the inspiration of Saul at the close of his troubled life, and Balaam who, in contrast, delivers his prophetic oracle with a "little left" of the spirit—which is tantamount to none ("the spirit of God did not abide in him"). Consequently, he is unable to say whatever he sees. How different an assessment this is from the Bible's, according to which Balaam is "the man whose eye is clear . . . one who hears the words of God, who sees the vision of the Almighty, who falls down, but with eyes uncovered" (Num 24:3-4).

The reason for this alteration of Num 24:2 or 23:7 LXX is probably the ambivalence Pseudo-Philo feels about attributing the oracle of a non-Jewish "interpreter of dreams" (18.2) to the spirit of God. He is not alone in this for, as Feldman has demonstrated, Josephus also confronts the dilemma of Balaam, a figure whom the rabbis regard as a prophet but who is also a foreigner who leads the people of Israel astray by means of Midianite women.[54]

Pseudo-Philo feels this same tension, apparently, and solves it by stressing that this is the final, diminishing prophetic oracle of Balaam. The spirit remains in Balaam only to permit him to utter one remaining oracle. While Pseudo-Philo is dependent upon the Bible for his attribution of Balaam's oracle to the spirit, therefore, he contradicts it by introducing the simple negating particle "not" into either Num 24:2 or 23:7 LXX.

Determining the effect of inspiration on Balaam is difficult because the central sentence that may depict that effect is obscure. The subject may be either Balaam or Balak: *Et ipse nescivit quoniam ideo elatus est sensus eius, ut festinet perditio eius.* M. R. James and the editors of Sources chrétiennes interpret Balak as the subject of this sentence and the verb *elatus est* as a description of his hubris or elevated self-esteem.[55] According to these translations, Balaam indicts Balak for thinking that he can purchase a blessing but failing to realize that he has actually incurred God's condemnation. In contrast, Harrington, in his own translation, regards Balaam as the subject of this sentence by interpreting it, not as part of Balaam's oracle, but as a narrative aside that explains the oracle: "And he [Balaam] did not know that his consciousness was expanded so as to hasten his own destruction." One piece of evidence is determinative for a decision between these alternatives.

54. On this tension, see Feldman, "Josephus' Portrait of Balaam."
55. James translates, "And *Balac* himself hath not known it, because his mind is puffed up, to the intent his destruction may come swiftly" (*Biblical Antiquities of Philo*, 125; emphasis original). Harrington et al. translate: "Mais (Balac) ne s'est pas aperçu lui-même que son intelligence s'était exaltée au point de précipiter sa perte" (Pseudo-Philon, *Antiquités Bibliques*, 2:155).

The expression *elatus est sensus eius* employs the same verb (*effero*), noun (*sensus*), and pronoun (*eius*) as the expression that depicts the raising of Kenaz's mind prior to his prophetic vision: *extulit sensum eius*. Both contexts have in common references to the spirit and prophecy (18.12) or prophesying (28.6). In a context with references to the spirit and prophecy, and in light of the tight verbal parallel between Balaam and Kenaz at this point, the effect of inspiration should be identified as the elevation of the mind.

As a reference to Balaam's inspiration rather than to Balak's pride, the phrase *elatus est sensus eius* has the full Greco-Roman flavor that it possesses in LAB's tale of Kenaz. It is reminiscent of the flight of the soul in Plato's *Phaedrus* and parallel to the inspired soul that takes wings, flies abroad, and foretells the future in Cicero's *De divinatione*.

Once again, however, it is apparent that Pseudo-Philo does not allow this Greco-Roman conception of inspiration to float freely in his rewritten Bible; on the contrary, in his view, the level of inspiration is determined by the presence of God's spirit. It is not the Stoic notion of the soul's kinship with the gods, or the air's being full of immortal souls, or gods who converse through dreams, that ultimately inspire, as in Cicero's *De divinatione* (e.g., 1.64), but the spirit of God. Pseudo-Philo may indeed understand the effects of inspiration in Greco-Roman categories, but he insistently attributes such inspiration to the spirit which he finds in the Bible. To the extent that Kenaz, Joshua, and Saul receive this spirit, they are able to prophesy. To the extent that Balaam lacks this spirit, he is unable fully to prophesy. As surely as Pseudo-Philo understands and describes inspiration as a Greco-Roman phenomenon that looks much more like Cicero's diviners or Plutarch's mantics than the ecstatic prophets of the Bible, so he regards the spirit that he identifies from his own tradition as the source of that inspiration.

III. CONCLUSION

These four analyses, although presented separately, converge to reveal Pseudo-Philo's conceptions of prophetic inspiration.[56] Several features of his

---

56. Two other references to prophetic inspiration should be mentioned, although they are far less developed than the four we analyzed. First, a unique reference to the spirit and dreams occurs in the story of Miriam (9.10). This is one dream among many in LAB (e.g., 9.15; 18.4, 8, 11; 23.3; 28.4; 32.16; 53.3-4; 56.3), but the only dream that is attributed to the divine spirit. Unfortunately, Pseudo-Philo gives us little clue to the dream's significance, and there are insufficient data to determine whether this dream, which Pseudo-Philo creates without biblical precedent, is due to the Greco-Roman (e.g., Cicero) or biblical emphasis upon the importance of dreams. See Feldman, "Prolegomenon," in James, *Biblical Antiquities of Philo*, xcii, on LAB 9.10.

portrait deserve consideration, particularly since they require a modification of A. Piñero's groundbreaking analysis of prophetic inspiration in LAB.

1. *Complexity.* A. Piñero isolates LAB's most distinctive features of divine inspiration: inhabitation of the spirit and elimination of mental capacities.[57] Both of these elements are important, but there are many more that Pseudo-Philo incorporates into his presentations of prophetic inspiration.

Inspiration does not always transpire, as Piñero contends, as "an *invasion* from the outside."[58] Kenaz and Saul were overcome without warning, but Joshua took up the garments of wisdom, viz. the spirit, and clothed himself, just as Gideon clothed himself with the spirit in preparation for battle. As for Balaam, the spirit did not invade him; rather it retreated from him, although he sought inspiration through sacrifice.

The effect of inspiration is depicted in a variety of ways: inflammation of mind and agitation of spirit (Joshua); transformation into another person (Joshua; also Gideon); the attainment of wisdom and understanding (Joshua); the elevation of the mind, *sensus* (Kenaz and Balaam); the loss of the mind, which requires restoration (Kenaz); a sleeplike state, which requires awakening (Kenaz); the inability to recollect what was seen or said (Kenaz and Saul).

It is important to note here that Pseudo-Philo is not systematic in his portrayal of inspiration. He does not, for example, distinguish between what D. Aune calls a possession trance (possession by spirits) and a vision trance (visions and adventures during the soul's absence from the body),[59] or what E. R. Dodds analogously calls shamanistic ("prophetic madness due to an innate faculty of the soul itself . . . when liberated by sleep, trance, or religious ritual both from bodily interference and from rational control") and the doctrine of possession.[60] Rather, Kenaz and Balaam experience both possession (spirit's presence) and visionary/shamanistic (elevated minds) inspiration, while Saul and Joshua, it seems, experience only possession.

Second, a laconic reference to the spirit and prophecy occurs in the story of Deborah. Following their victory, Barak recalls that God predicted the fall of Sisera through a woman (Judg 5:29-30; LAB 31.1). He attributes this predictive prophecy to the "Lord, who sent his spirit and said, 'Into the hand of a woman Sisera will be handed over.'"

These instances are significant because they demonstrate that Pseudo-Philo views women as the recipients of the spirit. The spirit inspires Miriam's dream and Deborah's predictive ability.

57. Piñero, "Mediterranean View," 29.
58. Piñero, "Mediterranean View," 7; emphasis original.
59. Aune, *Prophecy in Early Christianity*, 19-21.
60. Dodds, *Greeks and the Irrational*, 71.

Pseudo-Philo, therefore, tends not to systematize but to cluster a variety of descriptions from Greco-Roman culture and the Bible around key inspired figures. The criterion of how many elements are collected at one time seems to be the importance of the character rather than a clear doctrine of inspiration. Balaam and Saul, both ambiguous figures, exhibit only one experience each: the elevation of the mind and the inability to recollect, respectively. Joshua, Moses's successor, experiences inflammation and agitation, obtains wisdom and understanding, and is transformed into another person. Kenaz, the paradigmatic judge and central character of LAB, is inspired for military success and, at the end of his life, is inspired to foresee the future, an experience that entails an elevated mind, requires the restoration of sense and awakening, and results in the inability to recollect what he said and saw.

2. *Biblical characteristics*. Piñero contends that the "inhabitation by the spirit . . . finds its most natural explanation not in the classical prophetic world of the Hebrew Bible . . . but [in] the *milieu* of the Hellenized Jewish circles."[61] On the contrary, each reference to the spirit in the context of inspiration can be traced to the Bible: Balaam's to Num 24:2 or 23:7 LXX; Joshua's to Deut 34:9; Kenaz's to Judg 3:9, 6:34, Ezek 8:1, and 20:1; Saul's to 1 Sam 19:23–24. Therefore, it may be an overstatement to say that Pseudo-Philo and Plutarch were "in complete agreement" about the spirit's role in inspiration.[62] The most basic difference is that the spirit in Pseudo-Philo's source is granted by the particular God of that source, the Bible.

The association of the spirit with prophecy is another biblical element of LAB. This association does occur, of course, in Greco-Roman authors (e.g., Plutarch), but it is present in the Bible generally throughout much of the prophetic tradition and, more important, in the biblical accounts of Balaam and Saul upon which Pseudo-Philo depends. It would be incautious to attribute this association to a Greco-Roman milieu when it is present already in Pseudo-Philo's primary source.

3. *Greco-Roman characteristics*. Piñero correctly attributes the loss of the rational faculty to Pseudo-Philo's Greco-Roman milieu.[63] Several other characteristics of prophetic inspiration cannot be traced to the Bible and must, therefore, be due to Pseudo-Philo's adoption of Greco-Roman conceptions: the inability to remember what was said or done, the elevation of the mind, inflammation of mind and agitation of spirit, the need to be awakened.

---

61. Piñero, "Mediterranean View," 29; e.g., Philo.
62. Piñero, "Mediterranean View," 25.
63. Piñero, "Mediterranean View," 24, 29.

4. *Rewritten Bible in a Greco-Roman milieu.* The creative artistry of LAB is evident in its fusion of the biblical and Greco-Roman horizons. This fusion takes place in two ways.

First, Pseudo-Philo may (I am not certain) extract biblical phrases and hellenize them by placing them in an entirely new context. The best example of this tendency is the expression *reversus est sensus eius in eum*, the biblical antecedent of which may be Dan 4:34 and 36. But there it denotes Nebuchadnezzar's return to health, while in LAB 28.9–10 it denotes the end of Kenaz's vision. Even if he extracts it from Dan 4, Pseudo-Philo hellenizes this expression by integrally connecting it with (other) Greco-Roman concepts: the elevation of Kenaz's sense, awakening from his prophetic vision, and Kenaz's inability to remember what he said or saw. The same sort of transformation may be true of the image of inflammation in LAB 20.2. Even if its origin is Jeremiah's fiery compulsion to speak the word of God (Jer 20:9) or the heat of Ezekiel's spirit (Ezek 3:14), by connecting inflammation integrally with agitation, Pseudo-Philo portrays Joshua's experience in a manner that has much more in common with the Greco-Roman views of inspiration held by Cicero, Lucan, and Plutarch than with biblical conceptions of prophecy.

Second, Pseudo-Philo also rewrites the Bible by intermingling disparate elements from both milieux in his depiction of prophetic inspiration. He achieves this fusion in two instances merely by adding a single detail to the biblical story. In LAB 62.2, he adds to 1 Sam 19:18–24, with its conception of the spirit and prophesying, the concluding detail that Saul could not remember what he had said. This conception reflects the popular Greco-Roman interpretations found in Aelius Aristides, Pseudo-Justinus, and John Cassian. An equally clear fusion marks Pseudo-Philo's version of Balaam; by adding the detail *elatus est sensus eius* to a biblical story, he transforms Balaam's visionary experience into an instance of inspiration that conforms to the flight of the soul, depicted eloquently by Plato and popularized by Cicero.

The fusion is slightly more complex in the case of Joshua. LAB 20.1–3 is replete with biblical features, including the context of Josh 1, allusions to Deut 34:9 (spirit of wisdom), Judg 6:34 (the spirit's clothing), and 1 Sam 10:6 (transformation into another person), and characteristic biblical vocabulary, such as "Moses, my servant," "gird your loins," and "wisdom and understanding." Into this mix of biblical conceptions and vocabulary he interjects the association of inflammation and agitation that is present, not in the Bible, but in first-century Greco-Roman descriptions of inspiration written by Cicero, Lucan, and Plutarch.

Not surprisingly, the most complex fusion of Greco-Roman and biblical elements occurs in Pseudo-Philo's dual descriptions of Kenaz's inspiration for the purposes of military victory and divination. In the first instance, Pseudo-Philo does not incorporate any Greco-Roman notions of inspiration. Instead, he combines Judg 3:9 (the spirit and Othniel), Judg 6:34 (the spirit's clothing), and 1 Sam 10:6 (transformation into another person). Kenaz's military prowess is depicted entirely in biblical categories. However, as we have been led to suspect, Pseudo-Philo's depiction of Kenaz's prophetic inspiration is another fusion of biblical and Greco-Roman conceptions. The onslaught of the spirit is traceable ultimately to Judg 3:9. The setting of the prophecy is reminiscent of Ezekiel, with the elders gathered around him. The presence of the spirit and the reference to prophecy confirm the allusion to Ezek 8:1 and 20:1. But the effects of the spirit resonate much more with Greco-Roman conceptions of inspiration: the elevation of the soul espoused by Plato and Cicero; the loss of rationality described by Plato, Plutarch, and Cicero; the image of awakening, which parallels the role of sleep and dreams in notions of inspiration championed by Plato, Plutarch, and Cicero; and the inability to recall what he saw or said—a feature of inspiration included in the writings of Aelius Aristides, Pseudo-Justinus, and John Cassian.

5. *Unconscious adoption of Greco-Roman conceptions.* Piñero concludes his article by asserting, "The Palestinian theologian, the author of *LAB*, is not to be blamed for his surrender to foreign ideas. This fits in with the general intention of Jewish writers in Hellenistic times to present the Jewish religion with as many contact points as possible with the religious ideas of the region."[64] In this respect, the closest parallel to Pseudo-Philo that Piñero finds is Philo of Alexandria. I would caution against this comparison between Pseudo-Philo and Philo precisely over the issue of their "intention." Philo, according to Wolfson, consciously models prophetic inspiration (ecstatic, rational, and prognostic) along the lines of Plato's fourfold view of inspiration.[65] Three brief observations suggest that this sort of conscious adoption is not the case with Pseudo-Philo, whose adoption of Greco-Roman conceptions was probably unconscious. First, the views he holds were sufficiently popular and widespread to have influenced him unconsciously. Second, his conceptions were sufficiently eclectic and unsystematic to have been adopted without a great deal of reflection. Third, and most important, if his adoption is intentional, why does he omit much characteristic Greco-Roman vocabulary? Typical Greco-Roman vocabulary for

---

64. Piñero, "Mediterranean View," 30.
65. Wolfson, *Philo*, 2:11–14. See also Berchman, "Arcana Mundi: Prophecy," 406–7.

inspiration finds no correspondence in the Liber antiquitatum biblicarum, such as ἔνθεος, ἐκ τοῦ θεοῦ κάτοχος, ἐνθουσιασμός, or ἔκστασις.

Piñero may have overlooked the complexity of prophetic inspiration in LAB, understated the Jewish character of prophetic inspiration in LAB, and overemphasized the conscious adoption of Greco-Roman conceptions of prophetic inspiration in LAB. Nonetheless, his observation of extensive Greco-Roman influence on Pseudo-Philo's interpretation of prophetic inspiration by the divine spirit suggests that Pseudo-Philo, although he writes in Palestine and opposes Roman domination, does not, *at least in this one respect*, resist Greco-Roman influence.[66]

---

[66]. On the Palestinian context of LAB, see Murphy, *Pseudo-Philo*, 6; Mendels, "Pseudo-Philo's *Biblical Antiquities*." The view I propose stands in opposition to the regnant view on the level of hellenization in first-century Palestine. See Feldman, "Josephus' Portrait of Saul," 56–57; Feldman, "Josephus' Version of Samson," 172; Feldman, "Josephus' Portrait of Noah," 56; Feldman, "Josephus' *Jewish Antiquities*." Although writing in Hebrew may suggest resistance to Greco-Roman influence, Feldman has cited as a parallel to indirect Greco-Roman influence on LAB the third- or fourth-century work in Hebrew on magic, *Sefer ha-Razim* (personal letter, Oct. 5, 1992). This document includes references to divination and even contains Greek names, terms, and formulae. See Goldin, "Magic of Magic," 132–38. On this issue, see also Sevenster, *Do You Know Greek*; Feldman, "How Much Hellenism," esp. 91–93. In contrast to Feldman, Hengel contends, "Astrology, manticism and magic played just as great a role in Judaism at the beginning of our era as they did in the pagan environment" (Hengel with Markschies,"*Hellenization*" *of Judaea*, 48). I cannot fully answer the question of whether the Greco-Roman elements in LAB are the product of the first-century author or a later translator, but the observation that the most influential authors who provide the raw material for Greco-Roman influence are first century BCE (Cicero) and first century CE (Plutarch) suggests that these elements belong to the original composition rather than to a subsequent free translation.

8

The Debut of the Divine Spirit in Josephus's *Antiquities*[1]

INTRODUCTION

Josephus's version of Num 22–24 is a significant source for ascertaining his understanding of the divine spirit. On the one hand, this story contains the highest concentration of references to the divine spirit in the *Antiquities*. Josephus regularly omitted references to the divine spirit, leaving, apart from this passage, a mere five.[2] In marked contrast to this tendency, his version of Num 22–24 has three references to the divine spirit (*Ant.* 4.108, 118, 119), while the biblical version has but one (Num 24:2).[3] The result is

---

1. This chapter was written with the generous support of the Alexander von Humboldt Foundation at the Institut für antikes Judentum und hellenistische Religionsgeschichte of the Eberhard-Karls-Universität in Tübingen. I am especially indebted to Professors Otto Betz, Louis H. Feldman, and Ronald E. Heine for their insightful comments.

2. Josephus, *Ant.* 6.166, 222 and possibly 223; 8.408; 10.239. He added a reference in 8.114.

3. The Septuagint adds, although without the addition of much meaning, a reference in Num 23:7. It is not possible to determine conclusively which of these passages is the basis for Josephus's paraphrase. Josephus probably did not use the Septuagint itself in his paraphrase of the Torah, but this does not exclude the possibility that he utilized a version with similarities to the Septuagint. On Josephus's sources, see Feldman, "Use, Authority and Exegesis," 1:455–66.

that one third of Josephus's references to the divine spirit are concentrated in the tale of Balaam and the ass.

On the other hand, this tale contains the debut of the divine spirit in the *Antiquities* and the only references to the divine spirit in Josephus's version of the books of Moses. This singular appearance is no accident; Josephus needed to eliminate all other references in the Torah in order for the divine spirit to appear first to the ass. He replaced the reference to the divine spirit in the story of the king's amazement at Joseph, using instead the phrase "intelligence and wisdom" (τὴν φρόνησιν καὶ τὴν σοφίαν) (*Ant.* 2.87 = Gen 41:38). In describing Bezalel and Oholiab, the architects of the tabernacle, he replaced the words, "divine spirit of wisdom and intelligence" (πνεῦμα θεῖον σοφίας καὶ συνέσεως) with the statement that they were appointed by the command of God (*Ant.* 3.105 = Exod 31:3) and with the description of them as "noble" (ἄριστοι) (*Ant.* 3.200 = Exod 35:31).[4] Josephus omitted entirely the story of the seventy elders in Num 11, which contains five references to the divine spirit.[5] Finally, although he added to the biblical text the statement that Joshua prophesied (προεφήτευσε) (*Ant.* 4.311 = Num 28:1) in the presence of Moses and took on the prophetic role of Moses (ἐπί τε ταῖς προφητείαις) (*Ant.* 4.165 = Num 27:18), Josephus did not say, as does Num 27:18, that Joshua has the spirit in him (ὅς ἔχει πνεῦμα ἐν ἑαυτῷ). He also omitted Deut 34:9, in which Joshua is filled with a spirit of understanding (ἐνεπλήσθη πνεύματος συνέσεως) because Moses laid hands upon him.[6]

The deliberate elimination of all other references to the divine spirit in the books of Moses and the conscious addition of two of his own in this story demonstrate that the interpretation of the divine spirit in this story is not due to the passive reception and unthinking reiteration of biblical elements. On the contrary, the care with which Josephus constructed the debut of the divine spirit in *Ant.* 4.102–130 indicates that it is a focal point for Josephus's understanding of inspiration.

---

4. He also omitted Exod 28:3, in which the craftpersons are filled with a spirit of discernment.

5. That this omission is intentional is evident in Josephus's preservation of several other elements of Num 11 in *Ant.* 3.295–299: the reference to Esermoth (Num 11:35); the revolt (Num 11:4); quails (Num 11:18–19); and "graves of lust" (Num 11:34). Thackeray detected an allusion to prophesying: "There was yet one who admonished them not to be unmindful of Moses" (Thackeray, in Josephus, *Ant.* 3.297nc).

6. Josephus also reinterpreted Gen 1:1 and 6:3 without reference to the divine spirit. He drastically abbreviated the context of Exod 15:8, 10, merely stating that "they passed the whole night in melody and mirth." This abbreviation entails the omission of references to the blast from God's nostrils and the wind (πνεῦμα) that God blew over the sea.

THE DIVINE SPIRIT

In the biblical story of Balaam and the ass, the Midianite king Balak sent for Balaam, a seer, in order to receive from him an oracle predicting the defeat of Balak's enemy, Israel. After some equivocation, Balaam set off on his ass. On the way, this ass was confronted by an angel, which Balaam, the seer, ironically failed to perceive. After the ass startled Balaam by explaining its vision, Balaam continued on, having resolved to speak on behalf of Israel, rather than for Balak. In the biblical tale, the sources of Balaam's oracles are threefold: in Num 22:35, the angel commanded Balaam to say only what the angel told him; in Num 24:2 (and 23:7 LXX), the spirit of God inspired Balaam; throughout most of the tale, God alone placed the word in Balaam's mouth (Num 22:20, 38; 23:4–5, 12, 16, 26; 24:13). Although the ass perceived the angel, nowhere in the biblical tale is it associated with the divine spirit.

In the *Antiquities*, in contrast, the ass is the first to become conscious of the divine spirit: "The ass whereon Balaam rode, conscious of the divine spirit approaching her, turning aside thrust Balaam against one of these fences."[7] The introduction of the divine spirit at precisely this point results in the identification of the divine spirit with the angel. Josephus carefully drew a parallel between the approach of the divine angel and the ass's perception of the divine spirit:

> But on the road an angel of God confronted him [ἀγγέλου θείου προσβαλόντος αὐτῷ] in a narrow place ... and the ass whereon Balaam rode, conscious of the divine spirit approaching her [συνεῖσα τοῦ θείου πνεύματος ὑπαντῶντος], turning aside thrust Balaam against one of these fences.[8]

Adolf Schlatter, Ernest Best, and Morton Smith have recognized this identification of divine angel with divine spirit, which can be explained by Josephus's Jewish heritage.[9] In the nonbiblical Hebrew scrolls at Qumran, רוח is often understood as an angel or demon.[10] Ps 104:4 identifies מלאביו (his angels) with רוחות (spirits), and the quotation of this Psalm in Heb 1:7 ("he makes his angels spirits" [ὁ ποιῶν τοὺς ἀγγέλους αὐτοῦ πνεύματα]) reveals the presence of this identification during the first century CE.

---

7. Josephus, *Ant.* 4.108 (Thackeray and Marcus, LCL).

8. Josephus, *Ant.* 4.108 (Thackeray and Marcus, LCL).

9. Schlatter, *Wie sprach Josephus*, 32; Best, "Use and Non-Use," 222 (he writes tentatively, "This may imply identification of the two and the divine spirit is here to be thought of as 'a spirit'"); Smith, "Occult in Josephus," 240.

10. See Sekki, *Meaning of Ruaḥ*, 145–71. He contends that this identification occurs fifty-eight times. For a thorough bibliography of the identification of "angel" and "spirit" at Qumran, see 148n11.

Three elements of Josephus's version, however, suggest that *Ant.* 4.102–130 reflects not only his Jewish legacy but also the Greco-Roman culture in which he wrote the *Antiquities*. These three elements, which I shall discuss in turn, are the interpretation of Balaam's sacrifices, the method of inspiration, and the verb used to describe inspiration in *Ant.* 4.118.

In Josephus's version of the interpretation of sacrifices, the first reflection of Greco-Roman culture is revealed. Josephus interpreted the sacrifices that preceded Balaam's oracle as instances of pyromantism. According to Num 22–24, although sacrifices preceded Balaam's reception of a word of God (Num 23:1–6, 14–17) or the spirit (Num 23:27—24:2), there is a dichotomy between sacrifice and oracular inspiration. Balaam's usual practice is to turn aside to a place away from the sacrifices to seek omens (Num 24:1–2). In contrast, Josephus drew an integral relationship between revelation, sacrifice, and utterance in order to portray Balaam as a diviner who employed the methods of pyromancy. On the journey, God had instructed Balaam "to announce whatsoever He himself should indicate [σημαίνειν]" (*Ant.* 4.111).[11] In burning the sacrificial victims, Balaam perceived what was indicated.

> The king having promptly ministered to his wishes, he burnt the slaughtered victims whole; and when he saw the indications of inflexible Fate [εἶδε σημαινομένην], "Happy," said he, "is this people."[12]

This repetition of the verb σημαίνειν indicates that Balaam discovered God's revelation in the color, smoke, disfigurations, or flames of the sacrificial victims.

This interpretation of sacrifice as pyromantism cannot be attributed to Num 22–24. On the contrary, the narrator minimized the role of artificial divination in the production of Balaam's oracle: "Balaam saw that it pleased the Lord to bless Israel, so he did not go, as at other times, to look for omens, but set his face toward the wilderness" (Num 24:1). In his oracle, moreover, Balaam proclaimed, "Surely there is no enchantment against Jacob, no divination against Israel" (Num 23:23). Neither Philo Judaeus nor Pseudo-Philo, whose writings Josephus knew or with whom he shared common traditions, introduced pyromantism into the story. In LAB, a first-century CE Palestinian paraphrase of biblical history from Adam to David, falsely

---

11. I have changed Thackeray's translation "put into his heart" because it does not take into account the repetition of the verb σημαίνειν in *Ant.* 4.111, 113. This verb indicates that God signified what should be said by means of the sacrifice rather than by direct inspiration, as Thackeray's translation implies.

12. Josephus, *Ant.* 4.113–114 (Thackeray and Marcus, LCL).

attributed to Philo, Pseudo-Philo altered the biblical text substantially.[13] According to LAB 18.7–10, sacrifices are simply offerings to God. Josephus's interpretation stands in direct contrast to Philo's interpretation in *Mos.* 1.277, according to which the sacrifice has nothing whatsoever to do with oracles: Balaam "advanced outside . . . became possessed . . . returned, and, seeing the sacrifices and the altars flaming, he spake these oracles."[14]

For the interpretation of sacrifice as pyromantism Josephus tapped the multifarious source of Greco-Roman conceptions of artificial divination. Along with augury, astrology, and a vast variety of other means, the future could be predicted on the basis of observations of sacrifices, which "have for their object the color, the shrivelling, the changes of form, the oozing of the flesh placed on the grill, and, additionally, the brightness of the flame or the hue and direction of the smoke."[15] In the hands of Josephus, the focus of the biblical tale becomes a pyromantic who utilized techniques of artificial divination that have no place in Israelite prophecy but rather are part of the stock-in-trade of Greco-Roman diviners.[16]

In addition to the interpretation of sacrifices, the method of inspiration found in Josephus's version of the story is additional evidence of the influence of Greco-Roman culture. Josephus placed a speech in Balaam's mouth, which, when interpreted in light of the ass's experience of the divine spirit, illuminates the precise mode of Balaam's inspiration. Balaam responded to Balak's accusation and anger:

> Thinkest thou that it rests with us at all to be silent or to speak on such themes as these, when we are possessed by the spirit of

---

13. On Josephus's relationship to Pseudo-Philo, see Feldman, "Prolegomenon," in James, *Biblical Antiquities of Philo*, lviii–lxvi. He notes thirty parallels that occur only in Josephus and Pseudo-Philo and fifteen where both share with other authors a common tradition. On the possibility of Josephus's dependence upon Philo's writings, see Feldman, "Use, Authority and Exegesis," 1:474–75. For a bibliography, see Feldman, *Josephus and Modern Scholarship*, 410–19.

14. Philo, *Mos.* 1.277 (Colson and Whitaker, LCL).

15. "[Ils] ont eu pour objet la couleur, le grésillement, les changements de forme, les exsudations des chairs posées sur le brasier, et, accessoirement, l'éclat de la flamme ou la nuance et la direction de la fumée" (Bouché-Leclercq, *Histoire de la divination*, 1.179). For an example of the political role of pyromantism, see Euripides: "And the priests slew the sheep: flame-tongue they marked, / And flame-cleft, steamy reek that bodeth ill, / The pointed flame, which hath decisions twain, / Betokening victory or overthrow" (*Phoen.* 1255–58 [Way, LCL]). In the same play, the pyromantic Teiresias's words to Creon reflect a predicament not dissimilar to Balaam's: "Who useth the diviner's art / Is foolish. If he heraldeth ill things, / He is loathed of those to whom he prophesies. / If, pitying them that seek to him, he lie, / He wrongs the Gods" (lines 954–58 [Way, LCL]). See also Euripides, *Iph. taur.* 16; Josephus, *Ant.* 8.108; 17.121.

16. For further analysis, see Feldman, "Prophets and Prophecy," 416–17.

God? For that spirit gives utterance to such language and words as it will, whereof we are all unconscious.[17]

Josephus drew a significant parallel between the experience of the ass and the experience of Balaam; despite the complication of a textual variant, this parallel illuminates the method of inspiration that Balaam describes. The ass speaks with a human voice (φωνὴν ἀνθρωπίνην ἀφεῖσα or λαβοῦσα).[18] Balaam explains with similar vocabulary that the divine spirit takes hold (λάβῃ) and lets loose sounds and words (φωνὰς ... λόγους ... ἀφίησιν). Just as the divine spirit utilizes (ἀφεῖσα or λαβοῦσα) the body of the ass to produce a human sound, so does the divine spirit utilize (λάβῃ ... ἀφίησιν) the seer's mouth to produce the sounds and words it wills. For Balaam, this experience entails the loss of rationality. He is not himself (οὐκ ὢν ἐν ἑαυτῷ) (Ant. 4.118); he becomes unconscious (οὐδὲν ἡμῶν εἰδότων) (4.119); and he no longer possesses his faculties (οὐδὲν γὰρ ἐν ἡμῖν ἔτι φθάσαντος εἰσελθεῖν ἐκείνου ἡμέτερον) (4.122).

With this story in mind, we can pinpoint with relative accuracy Josephus's understanding of the nature of inspiration. The divine spirit is an angelic being that can enter an ass or take bodily form. This divine being utilizes the mouths of ass and seer alike to produce the words and sounds of its choosing. Neither can resist speaking as the being directs. The ass, of course, cannot, and Balaam's rational faculties are rendered inactive by the invading presence of the divine spirit.

The antecedents of this description of inspiration cannot be discerned in the Bible. References to inspiration in Num 22–24 are laconic and formulaic: "the Lord opened the mouth of the donkey" (Num 22:28); "the Lord put a word in [Balaam's] mouth" (Num 23:5, 16); "the spirit of God came upon him" (Num 24:2; see 23:6 LXX). Prophetic inspiration in the Bible, moreover, is not understood as the utilization of a mouth by an invading angelic being. Prophetic ecstasy is described as madness (as in Hos 9:7), elevation of the prophet (as in Ezek 3:12, 14), or a general descent of the spirit no more specific than Num 24:2 (as in Ezek 11:5). None of these descriptions of prophetic ecstasy characterizes Balaam's experience in the *Antiquities*.[19] Jeremiah 20:9 expresses the predicament of speaking words

---

17. δοκεῖς ἐφ' ἡμῖν εἶναί τι περὶ τῶν τοιούτων σιγᾶν ἢ λέγειν, ὅταν ἡμᾶς τὸ τοῦ θεοῦ λάβῃ πνεῦμα; φωνὰς γὰρ ἃς βούλεται τοῦτο καὶ λόγους οὐδὲν ἡμῶν εἰδότων ἀφίησιν (Josephus, *Ant*. 4.119 [Thackeray and Marcus, LCL]); see also 4.121.

18. The reading λαβοῦσα is supported by Codex Regius Parisinus and Codex Oxoniensis (Bodleianus), and the reading ἀφεῖσα by all other manuscripts quoted by Niese, whose Greek text (*Flavii Iosephi opera*) is the basis of Thackeray's translation. For this variant, see Josephus, *Ant*. 4.109 (Thackeray and Marcus, LCL).

19. See Lindblom, *Prophecy in Ancient Israel*, 65–82, 122–37, 173–82.

of condemnation: "If I say, 'I will not mention [God], or speak any more in his name,' then within me there is something like a burning fire shut up in my bones; I am weary of holding it in and I cannot." Balaam, however, reveals none of the tortured compulsion of Jeremiah; he would gladly have spoken a falsehood if the divine spirit had not rendered him unconscious and spoken through him. Nebuchadnezzar could provide a model for Balaam's experience, for Nebuchadnezzar had lost his reason ("At that time my reason returned to me" [Dan 4:36]); but this followed an illness and not an invasion by the divine spirit.

In addition, the writings of other important first-century Jewish authors, such as Pseudo-Philo and Philo, cannot be credited as the source of Josephus's interpretation. In Pseudo-Philo's *Liber antiquitatum biblicarum* (18.3, 10–12), Balaam already possesses the spirit and is on the verge of losing it because of his willingness to compromise with Balak and be persuaded by him; this oracle is his last oracular gasp, so to speak, and not the result of a divine invasion.[20] Philo Judaeus's explanation, in contrast, has two important elements in common with Josephus's version: the loss of reason and the utilization of the voice. The angel says to Balaam,

> I shall prompt the needful words without your mind's consent, and direct your organs of speech as justice and convenience require. I shall guide the reins of speech, and, though you understand it not, employ your tongue for each prophetic utterance.[21]

Nonetheless, in Philo's version, the divine spirit does not appear to the ass; in the *Antiquities* this encounter is the key ingredient in the identification of the angel with the divine spirit. Moreover, for Philo, Balaam's experience was an instance of prophetic inspiration (*Mos.* 1.283); for Josephus, it was not. Josephus never referred to Balaam as a prophet, nor to his inspiration as prophetic. Even the shape of the versions differs. Philo followed the Bible closely, altering details throughout (*Mos.* 1.263–91); Josephus abbreviated the account yet inserted a speech in Balaam's mouth to explain inspiration (*Ant.* 4.119–121). These differences suggest that Philo was not Josephus's primary source.

Plutarch's *De defectu oraculorum*, written perhaps while Josephus was composing his *Bellum Judaicum*, provides in summary form the source of Josephus's interpretation. In this dialogue, Plutarch sought to explain the decrease of oracular activity at Delphi in comparison with past ages. From the standpoint of Josephan studies, the importance of *De defectu oraculorum*

---

20. For detailed analysis, see Levison, "Prophetic Inspiration."
21. Philo, *Mos.* 1.274 (Colson and Whitaker, LCL).

is paramount, for it contains a précis of several views on inspiration current during the first century CE.[22] One of these, the view propounded by the character of Cleombrotus, represents Plutarch's own view, according to Robert Flacelière[23] and Eugène de Faye,[24] and is of particular importance in explaining Josephus's interpretation. Cleombrotus attributed the obsolescence of oracles at Delphi to the departure of the mediating daemons, the divine messengers. This was, he observed, a long-standing view:

> Let this statement be ventured for us, following the lead of many others before us, that coincidently with the total defection of the guardian spirits [δαιμονίοις] assigned to the oracles and prophetic shrines, occurs the defection of the oracles themselves; and when the spirits flee or go to another place, the oracles themselves lose their power.[25]

Moreover, the method of inspiration utilized by these demigods is explained by the simile of musical instruments. According to Cleombrotus, when the daemons return, "the oracles, like musical instruments, become articulate, since those who can put them to use are present and in charge of them."[26]

The similarities between Cleombrotus's view of inspiration and Josephus's illuminate the way in which Josephus adapted the Bible in light of this popular viewpoint. First, Josephus omitted all prior references to the divine spirit and then added his first reference in a context where it is identified with an angel who mediates divine oracles to Balaam.[27] In the Balaam episode, then, Josephus seized the opportunity to present the divine spirit as a figure who mediates between the divine and human worlds and who inspires oracular utterances. Second, Josephus presented the ass and Balaam as the passive instruments of the divine spirit, vehicles for the sounds it

---

22. Robert Flacelière noted that Plutarch claimed adherence to the New Academy which, based upon the ideas of Socrates and Plato, namely, that every opinion has two faces, suspended judgment on issues that could not be solved with certainty (see, for example, Plutarch, *Def. orac.* 431A) (*Plutarque*, 50–52). The question of the obsolescence of the Delphic oracles is just such a question, as is apparent in Lamprias's closing speech, which does not opt for one interpretation or the other but instead attempts a synthesis (Plutarch, *Def. orac.* 436D–438E). Unlike his later work, *De Pythiae oraculis*, then, the *De defectu oraculorum* represents a stage in Plutarch's thought when Plutarch was satisfied to present a variety of viewpoints.

23. Flacelière, *Plutarque*, 48.

24. Faye, *Ambiance philosophique*, 110.

25. Plutarch, *Def. orac.* 418C–D (Babbitt, LCL). See also 431B.

26. Plutarch, *Def. orac.* 418D (Babbitt, LCL).

27. Josephus referred to Balaam's words as "his oracles" (αὐτοῦ τὰς μαντείας) (*Ant.* 4.157–158).

wishes to produce. They are like unconscious musical instruments under the control of a daemonic being.

The third sort of evidence for the influence of Greco-Roman culture on this passage is found in Josephus's use of the word ἐπιθειάζειν. In a narrative aside following Balaam's oracle, Josephus explained:

> Such was the inspired utterance of one who was no longer his own master but was overruled by the divine spirit to deliver it [καὶ ὁ μὲν τοιαῦτα ἐπεθείαζεν οὐκ ὢν ἐν ἑαυτῷ τῷ δὲ θείῳ πνεύματι πρὸς αὐτὰ νενικημένος].[28]

The verb ἐπιθειάζειν, which Josephus employed to describe Balaam's inspiration, does not appear in the Septuagint or the Greek pseudepigrapha. It does occur, however, in Greek literature, where it denotes either divine inspiration or an appeal, for example, to the gods. Josephus used this verb in both senses,[29] and in *Ant.* 4.118 it clearly refers to inspiration. What particular sort of inspiration, is the question at hand?[30]

For this question, Plutarch's *De genio Socratis* rather than his *De defectu oraculorum* illuminates Josephus's use of the verb ἐπιθειάζειν.[31] In *De genio Socratis*, Plutarch devoted two lengthy discussions (580B–82C and 588B–89F) to the nature of Socrates's inspiration. One of the characters in the dialogue, Theocritus, introduced the first discussion with the question, "Very well . . . but what, my dear sir, do we call Socrates' daemon?" He answered by attributing Socrates's inspiration to a δαιμόνιον ἐπιθείαζον. With

---

28. Josephus, *Ant.* 4.118 (Thackeray and Marcus, LCL).

29. In Josephus, *Ant.* 19.141, people in the theater "appeal to soldiers" to spare them. In *Ant.* 2.338 and 8.109, ἐπιθειάζειν refers to the prayers of Moses and Solomon to God. In Josephus, *J.W.* 1.656, which depicts Herod's illnesses, the word presumably refers to diviners of some sort who "pronounce his maladies a judgement on him for his treatment of the professors" (Thackeray, LCL).

30. Unfortunately, Philo's writings are not altogether useful in this endeavor. His penchant for Greek terminology led him to employ this verb and its cognate noun ἐπιθειασμός for nearly every form of inspiration included in his writings. He employed it in association with Abraham's perception of truth (*Virt.* 214; see also *Deus* 4) and his transformation by the divine spirit (*Virt.* 217); the inspiration of Moses that takes place "in his own person" (*Mos.* 2.188, 259, 263, 272) and prior to death (*Mos.* 2.291); Joshua's reception of oracles (*Virt.* 55); prophetic ecstasy that is akin to corybantic or bacchic ecstasy (*Her.* 69); ancient prophets in general (*Deus* 139); biblical prophetic inspiration (*Somn.* 2.172); the soul that passes to death (*Post.* 10); his own soul when it was lifted into the upper spheres by philosophical reflection (*Spec.* 3.1); the mind that loves virtue (*Mut.* 113) and the inspired mind (*Migr.* 84); and the rapt communal enthusiasm of the Therapeutae (*Contempl.* 84).

31. See Arnim, *Plutarch über Dämonen*, 3–17.

this description, Theocritus brings together the concepts of a divine being and inspiration.[32]

Because the word δαιμόνιον has a wide range of meanings, however, encompassing "the divine," "the satanic," the "daemonic," or a divine sign such as an earthquake, it does not necessarily denote a daemonic being. Plato employed this ambiguous word for Socrates's inspiration and Plutarch followed him, referring to that which inspired Socrates as τὸ δαιμόνιον (*Gen. Socr.* 589F). Plutarch further clarified the nature of Socrates's inspiration through the words of Simmias, who leads the discussion on this topic (589D). Simmias interprets τὸ δαιμόνιον unequivocally as a daemonic, divine being that inspires human beings. Socrates, he says, belonged to that race of holy people who heard the unuttered words of the daemons (οἱ τῶν δαιμόνων λόγοι).

This interpretation of τὸ δαιμόνιον as a daemonic being is confirmed by a myth that Simmias subsequently relates about Timarchus of Chaeroneia who, "in his desire to learn the nature of Socrates's sign," descended into a crypt and had a vision in which he saw a variety of stars, some trembling above the great abyss, others sinking, and others shooting up from the abyss. A voice explains to Timarchus, "You see the daemons themselves." The orderly daemons are connected to "souls which good nurture and training had made submissive to the rein," from whom comes "the race of diviners and of men inspired," including, of course, Socrates.[33]

The words τὸ δαιμόνιον and ἐπιθειάζειν recur together in this context, in which τὸ δαιμόνιον is understood as a daemonic being. Significantly, these words describe a nonrational form of inspiration akin to Balaam's inspiration in the *Antiquities*, which Simmias repudiates. Simmias contends that only exceptional people, such as Socrates, receive inspiration. He contrasts his own view with the incorrect popular opinion that inspiration occurs when people are not conscious:

> In popular belief, on the other hand, it is only in sleep that men receive inspiration from on high [τὸ δαιμόνιον ἀνθρώποις ἐπιθειάζειν] and the notion that they are so influenced when awake and in full possession of their faculties is accounted strange and incredible.[34]

---

32. Plutarch, *Gen. Socr.* 580C–D (Lacy and Einarson, LCL).

33. Plutarch, *Gen. Socr.* 591D–92C (Lacy and Einarson, LCL); Josephus adopts this point of view in *Ag. Ap.* 2.263–64.

34. Inspiration should not here be limited to sleep, which represents loss of consciousness in general. Cicero, for instance, associated frenzy with sleep (*Div.* 1.34–35). He later discussed in close succession the soul that foresees because it is withdrawn by sleep from sensual ties (*Div.* 1.63), the soul that foresees because it is separated from the body by the nearness of death (*Div.* 1.64–65), and the soul that presages because it

Once again, Plutarch presented an opinion widely held in the first century CE,[35] and it is this popular belief that illuminates Josephus's description of Balaam. Three elements—inspiration (ἐπιθειάζειν), the absence of rational faculties, and daemonic beings—coalesce in this attempt to explain the extraordinary guidance Socrates received. These same three elements define Balaam's experience, according to Josephus's summary: Balaam is inspired (τοιαῦτα ἐπεθείαζεν), is no longer his own master (οὐκ ὢν ἐν ἑαυτῷ), and is conquered by a divine spirit that Josephus has identified with the divine angel (τῷ δὲ θείῳ πνεύματι πρὸς αὐτὰ νενικημένος).

In summary, Josephus's description of the divine spirit reflects the juncture of the Jewish and Greco-Roman worlds at which he himself stood. The easy identification of the divine spirit with an angel reflects his Jewish legacy, but its association with divination by pyromancy, the attribution of oracles to daemonic beings who play upon the Delphic priestesses, and the verb ἐπιθειάζειν reveal the influence of Greco-Roman views of inspiration, particularly the view espoused by Cleombrotus in Plutarch's *De defectu oraculorum*.

THE APOLOGETIC BENEFITS OF THIS INTERPRETATION

Josephus's motivation for interpreting Num 22–24 in this way can be understood readily in light of the ways in which this interpretation bolstered his apologetic intent. In his version of particularly thorny biblical passages, Josephus tended to diminish God's role in the human drama.[36] The story of Num 22–24 is clearly one such instance, as its concluding counsel to the reader reveals: "On this narrative readers are free to think what they please."[37] This polite conclusion often accompanies accounts that might have been difficult for Josephus's readers to swallow. Yet Josephus could not merely jettison the tale; the detailed recounting of this story in Pseudo-Philo's Liber antiquitatum biblicarum and Philo's writings, as well as the considerable discussion of it in rabbinic literature, attests to its significance for early Judaism.[38] Therefore, Josephus here encountered a story that was

---

is frenzied or inspired (*abstractus divino instinctu concitatur*) (*Div.* 1.66–67).

35. See Plutarch, *Def. orac.* 418D above.

36. Most recently, see Feldman, "Josephus' Portrait of Moses," 301–2, esp. n161.

37. Josephus, *Ant.* 4.157–158 (Thackeray and Marcus, LCL). See also *Ant.* 1.108; 2.347–248; 3.81; 10.281; 17.354.

38. See Betz, "Bileamtradition"; Feldman, "Josephus' Portrait of Balaam"; Baskin, "Attitudes towards the Gentiles," 113–71, 198–210.

impossible to avoid and in which he was compelled to portray God as influential but not directly involved.

Furthermore, other views of inspiration were liable to crude misinterpretations, and were Josephus to have adopted them to explain Num 22–24, his work could have ended in embarrassment. In particular, the viewpoints of Ammonius and Lamprias in Plutarch's *De defectu oraculorum*, in and of themselves quite understandable, could lead to vulgar misinterpretations. Ammonius and Lamprias explain in very different ways the paucity of prophetic activity at Delphi.

Ammonius contends that the god Apollo is directly responsible for the lack of prophetic activity at Delphi, for "prophecy is something created by a god, and certainly no greater or more potent force exists to abolish and obliterate it."[39] The god delivers fewer oracles now than before because there has been a depopulation of Greece. Whereas two prophetic priestesses (with one held in reserve) were once required to meet the demand for oracles, now one priestess suffices. Although this explanation of the decrease in oracular activity at Delphi is feasible, another character in *De defectu oraculorum*, Lamprias, retorts with a caricature of this viewpoint:

> Certainly it is foolish and childish in the extreme to imagine that the god himself after the manner of the ventriloquists . . . enters into the bodies of his prophets and prompts their utterances, employing their mouths and voices as instruments.[40]

This is not at all what Ammonius has in mind, but Lamprias's interpretation reveals how easily Ammonius's view can be distorted. It would have been precarious, therefore, for Josephus to adopt prima facie the biblical view that God is directly responsible for opening the ass's mouth and putting a word in Balaam's mouth. This view, and the crude misinterpretation to which it is liable, does not comport with a God who is "perfect and blessed, self-sufficing . . . the beginning, the middle, and the end of all things. By His works and bounties He is plainly seen . . . but His form and magnitude surpass our powers of description."[41]

Lamprias presents his own view, based upon the Stoic theory of secondary causes, that a vapor rose from the ground and inspired the Delphic priestess: changes in sun and earth led to the cessation of this vapor, resulting in the obsolescence of oracles.[42] Although this theory is rationalistic

---

39. Plutarch, *Def. orac.* 413E (Lacy and Einarson, LCL).

40. Plutarch, *Def. orac.* 414E (Lacy and Einarson, LCL).

41. Josephus, *Ag. Ap.* 2.190 (Thackeray, LCL).

42. On the theory of the vapors, see Fontenrose, *Delphic Oracle*; Parke and Wormell, *History*, 19–26; Flacelière, *Plutarque*, 42–46.

on the lips of Lamprias, its popular interpretation was quite the opposite, tending instead toward a sexual interpretation. In a first-century CE account, Lucan uncritically blended the possession of the Sybil with the inspiration of the Delphic priestess by the vapor or breath of the god Apollo, identifying the vapor itself with Apollo and describing vividly the Delphic priestess's struggle to avoid his penetration:

> And her bosom for the first time drew in the divine power, which the inspiration of the rock, still active after so many centuries, forced upon her. At last Apollo mastered the breast of the Delphian priestess; as fully as ever in the past, he forced his way into her body, driving out her former thoughts.[43]

The prevalence of this sexual interpretation is evident in the writings of Origen and John Chrysostom, who ridiculed Delphic inspiration because the vapor was said to enter the priestess through her genitals as she sat on the tripod above the vapor.[44] Once again, were Josephus to identify the divine spirit with the vapor at Delphi, he would face the potential misconstrual of inspiration as sexual penetration.[45] This view does not comport with the God of the Jews who, as Josephus wrote in the proemium to his *Antiquities*, "possesses the very perfection of virtue."[46]

Josephus's adoption of the view espoused by Cleombrotus has the unique advantage of avoiding the crude and direct involvement of the God of the Jews in the process of inspiration.[47] The preservation of the gods'

43. Lucan, *De bello civili* 5.163-67 (Duff, LCL).

44. Origen, *Cels.* 3.25; Chrysostom *Hom. 1 Cor.* 29.1 (PG 61:242). Verbeke discussed the prevalence of this view, which he considered characteristic also of Pseudo-Longinus (see *Subl.* 13.2) (*Évolution*, 269-71).

45. Two other pieces of evidence suggest that Josephus did not accept the vapor theory espoused by Lamprias. First, according to Cicero and Plutarch, the vapor provides the initial impetus of inspiration but not the words themselves which the priestess utters. In contrast, Josephus attributed the "languages and words" themselves to the divine spirit (*Ant.* 4.119). Second, despite Lamprias's reference to the vapor as τὸ δὲ μαντικὸν ῥεῦμα καὶ πνεῦμα θειότατον ("but the prophetic current and breath is most divine") (Plutarch, *Def. orac.* 432D [Lacy and Einarson, LCL]), Strabo's reference to it as πνεῦμα ἐνθουσιαστικόν ("breath that inspires a divine frenzy") (*Geogr.* 9.3.5 [Jones, LCL]), and Dio Chrysostom's observation that it fills the priestess (ἐμπιμπλαμένη τοῦ πνεύματος) (*Hab.* 72.12), the vapor remains a natural phenomenon that putatively ascended from the earth through the chasm, over which the Delphic priestess sat upon her tripod. Josephus gave no indication that such a natural vapor approaches the ass and conquers Balaam. On the contrary, he identified the divine spirit with an angel.

46. Josephus, *Ant.* 1.23 (Thackeray, LCL).

47. The worst distortion of this view occurs in Lamprias's summary, in which he merely reduces these demigods to "overseers, watchmen, and guardians of this tempered constitution, as if it were a kind of harmony, slackening here and tightening there

transcendence is, according to Cleombrotus, the reason for this interpretation in the first place. In *De defectu oraculorum*, Lamprias, caricaturing Ammonius's view of inspiration as a kind of ventriloquism, insists that a god who directly inspires is "entangled in men's needs" and "prodigal with his majesty," and fails to "observe the dignity and greatness of his preeminence."[48] Cleombrotus responds by contending that "those persons have resolved more and greater perplexities who have set the race of demigods midway between gods and men, and have discovered a force to draw [them] together, in a way, and to unite our common fellowship."[49] By attributing inspiration to an angelic spirit, rather than to a vapor or directly to God, Josephus was able to preserve God's influence and the association between God and humankind without entangling God in human needs.

By adopting the interpretation espoused by Cleombrotus, Josephus was also able to claim for the Jews a mode of inspiration that was associated with Delphi, the most ancient and auspicious of Greek oracular shrines.[50] Josephus was, of course, familiar with the Delphic shrine and its oracles. In a discussion of Moses as legislator, he cited the Greeks, who traced their laws "to Apollo and his oracle at Delphi."[51] He even described the table in the tabernacle by comparing it "to those at Delphi."[52] It is not a messenger of Apollo, however, who appears to the ass and conquers Balaam, but the divine messenger of the God of the Jews.

Another significant antecedent lies behind Cleombrotus's attribution of inspiration to daemonic beings. In *De Iside et Osiride*, Plutarch explicitly traced the association of mediating beings with oracles to Plato: "Plato calls this class of beings an interpretative and ministering class, midway between gods and men, in that they convey thither the prayers and petitions of men, and thence they bring hither the oracles and the gifts of good things."[53] In the *Symposium* (202E), Plato identified love as δαίμων μέγας, that is, one of these daemonic beings who mediate between the divine and human worlds

---

on occasion, taking from it its too distracting and disturbing elements and incorporating those that are painless and harmless to the users" (Plutarch, *Def. orac.* 436F–437A [Lacy and Einarson, LCL]).

48. Plutarch, *Def. orac.* 414E (Lacy and Einarson, LCL).

49. Plutarch, *Def. orac.* 415A (Lacy and Einarson, LCL).

50. On myths associated with the discovery of Delphi, see Parke and Wormell, *History*, 3–16. For a detailed analysis of the Apollo myth, see Fontenrose, *Python*.

51. Josephus, *Ag. Ap.* 2.162 (Thackeray, LCL).

52. Josephus, *Ant.* 3.139 (Thackeray, LCL). It is difficult to verify Josephus's comparison because it is not possible to ascertain exactly the furnishings of the Delphic site. See Parke and Wormell, *History*, 28–30.

53. Plutarch, *Is. Os.* 361C (Babbitt, LCL).

(καὶ γὰρ πᾶν τὸ δαιμόνιον μεταξύ ἐστι θεοῦ τε καὶ θνητοῦ). He continued to describe them as

> interpreting and transporting human things to the gods and divine things to men; entreaties and sacrifices from below, and ordinances and requitals from above: being midway between, it makes each to supplement the other, so that the whole is combined in one. Through it are conveyed all divination and priestcraft concerning sacrifice and ritual and incantations, and all soothsaying and sorcery. God with man does not mingle: but the spiritual is the means of all society and converse of men with gods and of gods with men, whether waking or sleeping.[54]

Josephus was aware of the appeal that a theory traceable to Plato held for his readers.[55] He was careful to note the similarity between Moses's and Plato's views of God (*Ag. Ap.* 2.168) and even went so far as to suggest that Plato followed the example of Moses in two points: the prescription of the study of laws and the precautions against the random mixing of foreigners (*Ag. Ap.* 2.257–58). By adopting the position represented by Cleombrotus, Josephus was in fact adopting a position that originated with Plato. The apologetic force of this maneuver must not be underestimated. Josephus claimed an important theory of a philosopher preeminent in Greco-Roman culture and incorporated the idea of this mode of inspiration into his own history of the Jews.

CONCLUSION

Friedrich Büchsel proffered in *Der Geist Gottes im Neuen Testament*—which remains the most thorough analysis of Josephus's interpretation of the divine spirit—a word of caution: "Josephus is a historian ... a thinker Josephus is not. One cannot expect original conceptions from Josephus."[56] Our analysis of the debut of the divine spirit in the *Antiquities* has, I hope, put this misjudgment of Josephus to rest.

Josephus was confronted with a thorny biblical text about a talking ass and an inspired seer who, although responsible for the fall of Israel to Midian, had received the divine spirit. Avoiding the tale altogether was probably not an option, for it provided to first-century Jews a cherished oracle about

---

54. Plato, *Symp.* 202E–3A (Lamb, LCL).

55. On the popularity of Plato in the Hellenistic period, see Hadas, "Plato in Hellenistic Fusion"; Hadas, *Hellenistic Culture*, 72–82.

56. "Josephus ist Historiker ... Denker ist Josephus nicht. Eigentümliche Anschauungen hat man bei Josephus nicht zu erwarten" (Büchsel, *Geist Gottes*, 94).

the preeminence of Israel, as indicated by the detailed descriptions and discussions of it in Liber antiquitatum biblicarum, the writings of Philo, and rabbinic literature. Nor was recounting the biblical story at face value an option, with its assertions that God without mediation opened the ass's mouth and put a word in Balaam's mouth, given Josephus's desire to present an acceptable, respectable history to his readers. Josephus's own ambivalence regarding the tale of the talking ass is evident in his concluding formula, which gives the reader freedom to think whatever he or she wishes.

Josephus chose to retain and rework this story. His version shows him to be a creative thinker who lived at a critical point of encounter between Jewish tradition and Greco-Roman culture. He deftly preserved the substance of Balaam's oracle, emphasizing the preeminence of Israel and, in the story's final lines, praising Moses (*Ant.* 4.157–158). At the same time, he transformed the potentially embarrassing story of Balaam and the ass into a credible tale in the eyes of his non-Jewish readers by adopting a method of inspiration that provided a popular explanation—traceable directly to Plato—of the most ancient and revered oracle in the Greco-Roman world.

9

The Angelic Spirit in Early Judaism

Several Israelite and early Jewish literary texts present רוח or πνεῦμα as an angelic being that exists and acts both in relation to and independently of God. The purpose of this chapter is to traverse the landscape of Israel and early Judaism diachronically, beginning with the earliest preexilic Israelite texts, pausing at length in the postexilic period, and concluding with early Jewish translations and texts of the Greco-Roman era prior to 135 CE, in order to sketch possible foregrounds for conceptions of the divine spirit in the Fourth Gospel, the Shepherd of Hermas, and the Ascension of Isaiah, three relatively early Christian texts in which the divine spirit can arguably be interpreted as an angelic being.[1]

I. PREEXILIC ISRAEL: THE CANONICAL FORMER PROPHETS

A. Saul and David

A constellation of references to the spirit of God enfolds the narrative of Saul's rise and demise in 1 Samuel (10:6, 10; 11:6; 16:13–23; 18:10; 19:9; 19:20, 23–24). This cycle of narratives is marked by a pronounced use of

---

1. Due to the length of this chapter and time constraints on readers of the Society of Biblical Literature seminar papers, I pared notes to a minimum. Alternative interpretations in secondary literature, in particular, are not cited unless they require refutation.

repetition, which suggests an identity between the natures of the spirit that first rushes upon Saul and the evil spirit that torments him.

10:6	וצלחה עליך רוח יהוה והתנבית
10:10	ותצלח עליו רוח אלהים ויתנבא
11:6	ותצלח רוח־אלהים על־שאול . . . ויחר אפו מאד
16:13	ותצלח רוח־יהוה אל־דוד מהיום ההוא ומעלה
16:14a	ורוח יהוה סרה מעם שאול
16:14b	ובעתתו רוח־רעה מאת־יהוה
16:15	רוח־אלהים רעה מבעתך
16:16	בהיות עליך רוח־אלהים רעה
16:23a	בהיות רוח־אלהים אל־שאול
16:23b	וסרה מעליו רוח הרעה
18:10	ותצלח רוח אלהים רעה אל־שאול ויתנבא
19:9	ותהי רוח יהוה רעה אל־שאול
19:20	ותהי על־מלאכי שאול רוח אלהים ויתנבאו גמ־המה
19:23	ותהי עליו גם־הוא רוח אלהים וילך הלוך ויתנבא עד־באו

In these numerous references to רוחות, several parallels in vocabulary unify the portraits of the good and evil spirits. First, the most distinctive is the repeated references to both spirits as "spirit of God" (רוח אלהים) in 10:10; 11:6; 16:15, 16, 23a; 18:10; 19:20, 23, or "spirit of Yahweh" in 10:6; 16:13; 16:14a (cf. 16:14b); 19:9. Second, both spirits "rush upon" (צלח) Saul in 10:6, 10; 11:6; 16:13; 18:10. Third, both spirits can have the same effect, depicted by the same verb, נבא, in the *hithpael*, in 10:6, 10 (cf. 10:13); 18:10; 19:20, 23. Fourth, both spirits are said to depart (סור) from Saul in 16:14, 23b. The unreserved use of similar vocabulary to describe both spirits, their activities, and their effects suggests that they are understood as similar beings. What distinguishes these two spirits of God is not their differing natures but rather that one is evil (רעה). When the spirit of God departs Saul, another spirit, similar but evil, torments him.

The similarity between these spirits is evident as well in the mirror images provided by Saul's first (10:6, 10) and last prophetic experiences (19:20, 23–24). In both, the "spirit of God" brings about an experience of "prophesying." In the former, this prophesying accompanies Saul's transformation into another person (10:6), but in the latter, such prophesying issues in Saul's spending the night in an undignified state of nakedness. This difference led Ralph W. Klein to suggest that, in the latter context, "the spirit may have been the evil spirit from God previously referred to (cf. 16:14)."[2]

This interpretation, though unusual, is not without exegetical support. First, the preceding instance of Saul's "prophesying" took place when the evil spirit of God rushed upon him (18:10). Second, the idiom employed to describe the spirit's presence in 1 Sam 19:19-23, היה על, is employed otherwise in this narrative only of the *evil* spirit (16:16, 23; 19:9). Third, each of the seven prior references, from 16:14 to 19:9, is to the evil spirit, and its presence is so established that in 16:23 it can be described simply as "spirit of God," without the adjective, "evil." To these may be added the more general observation that the appearance in 1 Sam 19 of the evil rather than good spirit of God would accentuate, by means of contrastive parallel with 1 Sam 10, the irony of Saul's rise and demise: although Saul prophesies both at the beginning and end of his reign, the source of his experiences are as different as night and day.

The spirits of God in 1 Sam 10-19, then, are angelic—or demonic— beings. The narrator provides no clues that the spirits are of different natures, that the evil spirit of God is a demon but the good spirit of God is God's breath, essence, or power poured out like water. On the contrary, the two spirits are described similarly, participate in similar actions, and can produce similar effects. They are in fact so similar that one cannot finally be certain which of the two thwarted the plans of Saul and his messengers.

In addition to these literary observations, some Babylonian cuneiform inscriptions that depict exorcisms also illuminate the nature of the spirits in 1 Sam 10-19. The relevance of exorcism texts to the Saul cycle of stories is hardly surprising, for the highest concentration of references to spirits in 1 Sam 10-19 occurs in 16:13-23, in which David functions as royal musician cum exorcist. One such Babylonian inscription reads:

> When I draw near unto the sick man,
> When I lay my hand on the head of the sick man,
> May a kindly Spirit, a kindly Guardian stand at my side.
> Whether thou art an evil Spirit or an evil Demon,
> Or an evil Ghost or an evil Devil ...
> Be thou removed from before me,
> Out of the house go forth![3]

As in 1 Sam 16:13-23, this Babylonian account refers to the good or kindly spirit that accompanies the exorcist and the evil spirit that must leave the

---

2. Klein, *1 Samuel*, 198.

3. Thompson, *Devils and Evil Spirits*, 1:17, tablet 3.150-58. Cf. 1:19-23, tablet 3.179-203.

person possessed. Moreover, this person may be the king. The Babylonian exorcist pleads:

> May a kindly Spirit, a kindly Guardian,
> Enter the house.
> May no evil Spirit or evil Demon,
> Or evil Ghost or evil Devil,
> Or evil God or evil Fiend,
> Draw nigh unto the king.
> By Heaven be ye exorcised! By Earth be ye exorcised![4]

Although these Babylonian exorcism texts cannot be construed as direct influences on 1 Sam 10–19, they suggest nonetheless that the interpretation of the good and evil spirits of God in 1 Sam 10–19 as coordinate independent spirit beings is at home in an ancient world in which guardian spirits were called upon and evil spirits exorcised.

B. Micaiah ben Imlah and the Prophets of Ahab

Four related depictions of spirits occur in a story that recounts the opposition between the prophets of Ahab, led by Zedekiah, who support Ahab's upcoming battle at Ramoth-Gilead, and Micaiah ben Imlah, who stands alone in opposing Ahab's military plans.

The first reference is the clearest depiction of God's spirit as an independent being. To substantiate his view that Ahab will be killed and his army defeated, Micaiah relates a vision in which the prophets of Ahab are depicted as lying. Yahweh is on the throne, surrounded by the entire host of heaven (כל־צבא השמים). This scenario suggests the presence of the angelic host that gather around God, as in Isa 6 or Ps 103:19–22:

> The LORD has established his throne in the heavens,
> and his kingdom rules over all.
> Bless the LORD, O you his angels [מלאכיו],
> you mighty ones who do his bidding,
> obedient to his spoken word.
> Bless the LORD, all his hosts [כל־צבאיו],
> his ministers that do his will.
> Bless the LORD, all his works,
> in all places of his dominion.
> Bless the LORD, O my soul.

---

4. Thompson, *Devils and Evil Spirits*, 1:111–13, tablet 16.306–13.

The spirit that comes forth from among the heavenly host is portrayed as an independent being: standing in the presence of Yahweh; conversing with Yahweh; volunteering for the task of deceiving Ahab; and responding when God asks, "How?" with a specific plan. Moreover, the use of masculine verbs to describe the spirit's activity points to its personal nature, as in Job 4:15—5:1, where a spirit (ורוח) glides (יחלף), stands (יעמד), and is heard to say: "Even in his servants he [God] puts no trust, and his angels [ובמלאכיו] he charges with error."[5]

The second and third references to the divine spirit (1 Kgs 22:22-23) are to "a lying spirit in the mouth of all the prophets":

... רוח שקר בפי כל־נביאיו
ועתה הנה נתן יהוה רוח שקר בפי כל־נביאיך אלה

The unusual expression—a spirit in the mouth—is due to the influence of Deut 18, which contains the kernel of the issue at stake in 1 Kgs 22, namely, the distinction between true and false prophecy. Micaiah's prior avowal to speak only what Yahweh would say to him (22:14) identifies him as a true prophet, according to the standard of Deut 18:18, even as the subsequent fulfilment of Micaiah's prophecy in 1 Kgs 22:29-40 echoes the single reliable criterion offered in Deuteronomy for discerning the presence of true and false prophets, that is, (non-)fulfilment of a prediction (18:21-22). What the prophets of Ahab experience, in contrast, is the opposite of the experience of the true prophet of Deuteronomy:

| Deut 18:18 | ונתתי דברי בפיו |
| 1 Kgs 22:23 | נתן יהוה רוח שקר בפי |

While the true prophet (Micaiah) receives the words of God in his mouth, the prophets of Ahab receive a lying spirit in their mouths.

The explanation of why the spirit should become a "lying spirit" rather than "lying words" can also be made on the basis of Deut 18:18: God ultimately is the source of prophets' words. The angelic spirit of Micaiah's vision cannot determine those words; it can be only the mediary through which God communicates those words to the prophets of Ahab. Thus it volunteers its services as deceptive divine mediator—a lying spirit—to dupe Ahab into tragedy.

---

5. Gray extends his interpretation beyond the narrative clues of the text when he claims that the spirit here is "an emanation, or extension, of the divine personality, and so may be personified. We may see here the gem of the conception of the Holy Spirit as a person of the Godhead, though at a very primitive level" (*I & II Kings*, 452-53).

The fourth reference to the spirit (1 Kgs 22:24) is proffered not by Micaiah or the spirit within the vision but by Zedekiah, a false prophet, who challenges Micaiah's authority: "Where [NRSV: Which way] did the spirit of the LORD pass from me to you?" The crucial word in this indictment for understanding the nature of the spirit is the verb, עבר (to cross over),[6] for it recalls the transference of the spirit of God from Saul to David—the only other instance in the Hebrew Bible in which the spirit of God is purported to have moved in toto from one person to another.[7] This close and unique parallel between 1 Kgs 22:24 and 1 Sam 16:13-23 confirms the presence of similar conceptions of the spirit in both passages. The spirit of Yahweh in this final reference of 1 Kgs 22 ought then to be interpreted as an angelic being, not unlike the spirit of God in Micaiah's vision, which can transfer its habitation from one person to another.

C. The Spirit and the Judges

The story of Saul and David also illuminates the canonical book of Judges, in which only laconic, formulaic references to the spirit occur. A consistent use of the same formulae throughout the books of Judges and 1 Samuel points to an underlying consistent conception of the spirit of God as an angelic (or demonic) being.

Twice in the biblical book of Judges the advent of the spirit is depicted by the verb היה followed by the preposition על:

| 3:10 (Othniel) | ותהי עליו רוח־יהוה |
| 11:29 (Jephthah) | ותהי על־יפתח רוח יהוה |

In the story of Saul and David, precisely this formula is employed to depict the tormenting attack on Saul by the evil spirit (1 Sam 19:9), as well as the overcoming of Saul and his messengers by the (good or evil) spirit (19:20, 23).[8] The presence of this formula in a more detailed text, 1 Sam 16-19, where the spirits are angelic or demonic beings, permits the inference that

---

6. More generally it denotes movement, e.g., in 1 Kgs 22:36, where a shout crosses over in the camp.

7. The notion of transference is preserved in 2 Chr 18:23. In Num 11, rather than being transferred, the spirit that is upon Moses is apportioned to the Israelite leaders. In the narratives of Moses/Joshua (Deut 34:9) and Elijah/Elisha (2 Kgs 2:7-18), the spirit is bequeathed to a successor only at the point of death or assumption.

8. The related use of the verb היה in the infinitive construct (בהיות) portrays the attack of the evil spirit of God (1 Sam 16:16, 23).

the spirit in laconic texts, Judg 3:10 and 11:29, ought to be interpreted analogously as angelic beings that come upon individual human beings.

The same inference is possible also for three references in the Samson cycle, in which the formula ותצלח עליו רוח יהוה recurs (Judg 14:6, 19; 15:14). In the story of Saul and David, precisely this formula depicts the presence of both good and evil spirits of God (1 Sam 10:10; 11:6; 16:13; 18:10; cf. 10:6 in the perfect tense). This consistency of vocabulary in both the Samson and Saul cycles suggests that the spirit that "rushes upon" Samson ought to be regarded as an angelic being that consists of the same nature as the spirits in the story of Saul.

There is an additional clue in Judg 13:25, where the spirit begins to trouble Samson. The locales named, Zorah and Eshtaol, form a narrative inclusio to the Samson cycle: the spirit of Yahweh *began* to trouble Samson "between Zorah and Eshtaol" (13:25), that is, where Samson would eventually be *buried*, "between Zorah and Eshtaol in the tomb of his father Manoah" (16:31). This region between Zorah and Eshtaol, the family cemetery, is precisely that region where one might have expected the appearance of spirits or ghosts.[9] The first appearance of the spirit of Yahweh—understood as an independent spirit—would very naturally transpire at the family burial ground.

The use of the metaphor of clothing (רוח יהוה לבשה) to describe the spirit's possession of Gideon (Judg 6:34) is also consistent with the interpretation of the spirit as an angelic or demonic being that characterizes the books of Judges, 1 Samuel, and 1 Kings. This metaphor depicts spirit possession in an incantation from the Assyro-Babylonian cuneiform inscriptions to which we already referred, in which possession by an evil demon is described similarly:

> Or an evil demon that envelopeth the man
> As it were with a coverlet,
> Or an evil demon that enshroudeth[10] the man
> As it were with a sack.[11]

For Gideon, of course, the spirit is benign and the effects beneficent; the mode of possession, however, is analogous.

The final reference to a spirit in Judges (9:23) is to an evil spirit sent by God (וישלח אלהים רוח רעה) between Abimelech and the lords of Shechem. Once again, this spirit ought to be understood not generally as

---

9. See Langton, *Good and Evil Spirits*, 98, 100–116.
10. See Thompson, *Devils and Evil Spirits*, 1:183, reverse of tablet H, line 10.
11. See Thompson, *Devils and Evil Spirits*, 1:133, tablet B, lines 38–41.

an "atmosphere of enmity" but specifically as an angelic emissary sent to create enmity, for its closest counterpart, the "evil spirit" that torments Saul, is such an evil emissary of God.

Moreover, analogous preexilic references to a "spirit of whoredom" in the prophecies of Hosea provide evidence that spirits were regarded as the cause of communal disruptions. Twice Hosea attributes Israel's idolatry to this spirit:

| 4:12 | כי רוח זנונים התעה |
| 5:4 | כי רוח זנונים בקרבם |

Another indictment of idolatry in the intervening context provides muted but not insignificant insight into the nature of this "spirit of whoredom":

| 4:19 | צרר רוח אותה בכנפיה |

As in Hos 4:12 and 5:4, the word רוח occurs in 4:19 alongside a form of the root זנה (הזנו הזנה in v. 18). Although רוח is translated in NEB, JB, and NRSV by "wind," certainly the personification of רוח with a reference to its wings, in a context bracketed by references to a "spirit of whoredom," suggests something more than mere meteorology.[12] In light of Pss 18:11 and 104:3,[13] which contain explicit parallels between the cherub or chariot on which God rides and the "wings of the wind" (על־כנפי־רוח), the metaphor of wings in Hos 4:19 ought also to be understood as an indication of the angelic nature of the spirit.

The evil spirits of Judg 9:23 and Hos 4–5, then, are evil angelic presences that wreak havoc on communities. In Judg 9:23, God sends an evil spirit to render neighboring peoples enemies. In Hos 4–5, a spirit of whoredom leads Israel astray into idolatry. The function of these spirits, in fact, is similar to the lying spirit of 1 Kgs 22 that deludes King Ahab and his army.[14]

---

12. As in 1 Kgs 22, the deceiver or seducer is characterized by the masculine gender, indicating that רוח may not be an abstract atmosphere or inanimate phenomenon but an independent being capable of deception.

13. Ps 104:3 continues with the assertion that God makes spirits/winds (רוחות) to be angels (מלאכיו).

14. Volz includes the רוח which, it was supposed, lifted Elijah, according to 1 Kgs 18:12 and 2 Kgs 2:16, in the category of the daemonic *rûaḥ*, which is thought of as an independent person—in this instance, a storm daemon (*Geist Gottes*, 3–4).

II. POSTEXILIC ISRAEL: THE SPIRIT AND THE EXODUS[15]

A. Isaiah 63:7-14

Isaiah 63:7-14 refers to the spirit in a context replete with allusions to the exodus, wilderness wanderings, and conquest. An initial reference to the מלאך פניו (63:9) that delivered Israel is followed by three references to the spirit:

63:10	והמה מרו ועצבו את־רוח קדשו
63:11	איה השם בקרבו את־רוח קדשו
63:14	רוח יהוה תניחנו

The first question this hymn raises is the identification of the angel of God's presence. The Pentateuch contains references to a tradition of the angel that led Israel. First, prior to the parting of the sea, the angel of God and the pillar of cloud moved from in front of (i.e., leading) Israel to a position behind Israel to protect them from Egypt (Exod 14:19). Second, at the conclusion of the so-called book of the covenant, God promises:

> I am going to send an angel in front of you, to guard you on the way and to bring you to the place that I have prepared. Be attentive to him and listen to his voice; do not rebel against him, for he will not pardon your transgression; for my name is in him. But if you listen attentively to his voice and do all that I say, then I will be an enemy to your enemies and a foe to your foes. When my angel goes in front of you, and brings you to the Amorites, the Hittites ... (Exod 23:20-23)

Third, Moses refers to the angelic deliverer in a message sent to the king of Edom to request safe passage through Edom: "And when we cried to the LORD, he heard our voice, and sent an angel and brought us out of Egypt" (Num 20:16). These texts are glimpses of a tradition or a collection of traditions according to which the angel of God led Israel from exodus to conquest.

Alongside this tradition is another according to which God's "presence" went with Israel. God promises Moses, "My presence [פני] will go with you, and I will give you rest" (Exod 33:14), to which Moses retorts, "If your presence will not go, do not carry us up from here" (33:15). The Deuteronomist recalls a similar tradition:

---

15. I worked out the thesis of this section fully in *Holy Spirit before Christianity*.

And because he loved your ancestors, he chose their descendants after them. He brought you out of Egypt with his own presence [בפניו], by his great power, driving out before you nations greater and mightier than yourselves. (Deut 4:37–38)

These two traditions—God's angel and presence—do not remain distinct in their canonical context. In Exod 23:22, for instance, there is an explicit correlation between listening attentively to the voice of the *angel* and doing all that *God* says. Just prior to the promise of God's *presence* in Exod 33:14–15, God twice promises Moses an *angel*: "But now go, lead the people to the place about which I have spoken to you; see, my angel [מלאכי] shall go in front of you" (32:34). Shortly after the reference to God's presence in Exod 33:14–15, God orders Moses to leave, repeating the promise of 32:34: "I will send an angel [מלאך] before you, and I will drive out the Canaanites, the Amorites" (33:2).

The expression מלאך פניו, in Isa 63:9, in a context shaped by the exodus tradition, reflects the amalgamation of traditions of God's accompanying presence and angel. So too do the three references to רוח in Isa 63:10–14, which arise equally out of reflection upon God's presence in the miraculous deliverance of Israel from Egypt to Canaan.

The most influential biblical text can be pinpointed with even more accuracy. The theme of rebellion against God's holy spirit is introduced in Isa 63:10 with the verb מרה, with God's holy spirit as its object. The occurrence of this verb in an exodus context comprises an allusion to Exod 23:21, in which God urges Israel not to rebel against the angel that leads them: אל־תמר בו. The holy spirit of Isa 63:10 is, therefore, the angel of Exod 23:21 and, concomitantly, the angel of the presence of Isa 63:9.

Another illuminating allusion to the tradition of the guiding presence of the exodus occurs at the close of this hymn, in Isa 63:14, in which the spirit of Yahweh gives Israel rest (תניחנו). This provision of rest is precisely what God promises Moses in a context dedicated to the assurance of God's presence with Moses (Exod 33:14):

ויאמר פני ילכו והנחתי לך

This allusion to Exod 33:14 explains the unique attribution of rest to the spirit of Yahweh in Isa 63:14.

In summary, multiple allusions in Isa 63:9–10 to a tradition of the angelic presence of God (מרה; מלאך פניו), alongside an allusion to God's presence of Exod 33:14 in Isa 63:14 (נוח), indicate that the angel of God's presence and the (holy) spirit (of Yahweh) of Isa 63:7–14 are one and the same angelic presence of God that delivered Israel from Egypt to Canaan.

The angel who had delivered Israel from captivity was a spirit devoted ultimately to completing the process begun in Egypt by granting Israel rest in Canaan.

B. Haggai 2:5

The allusions to Exodus in Isa 63:7-14 are not entirely isolated, for they are matched by an oracle of Haggai, delivered in 520 BCE, in which the promise of the spirit is set in the context of the exodus:

> Yet now take courage, O Zerubbabel, says the LORD; take courage, O Joshua, son of Jehozadak, the high priest; take courage, all you people of the land, says the LORD; work, for I am with you, says the LORD of hosts, according to the promise that I made you when you came out of Egypt: my spirit stands in your midst. Do not fear.

There is no promise in the exodus tradition of the spirit understood in impersonal terms as something to be poured (e.g., Isa 32:14-15; 44:1-3; Ezek 39:28-29; Joel 3:1-2) or used to anoint a leader (e.g., Isa 11:1-2; 42:1; 59:21; 61:1-2) or placed within to renew a people (e.g., Ezek 36:26-27). In contrast, as we have seen, there is the distinct promise of God's angel to lead Israel (Exod 23:20-23; 32:34; 33:2). Haggai's exhortation is a reaffirmation of the presence of God's angelic spirit in the postexilic community's midst.

This interpretation is borne out by the choice of the verb עמד (to stand) to depict the spirit's presence. The specific context of the departure from Egypt in which Haggai sets the promise of the spirit's standing in Israel's midst evokes the image of the pillar of cloud that stood in the midst of the Israelites and which was closely associated with the angel of God. The first canonical reference to the angel of God, in fact, occurs in Exod 14:19, in which both this angel and the cloud move from the front of the camp to the rear in order to separate the Israelites from the Egyptians. In this context, both the noun עמוד (pillar) and the verb עמד (to stand) appear. Subsequently, the cloud is said to take its stand at the tent of meeting (Exod 33:9-10; Num 12:5), and the presence of the pillars of cloud and fire are identified with the presence of Yahweh in the midst of the people (Exod 13:21-22; Num 14:14; Deut 1:33).

The most plausible context for interpreting Haggai's recollection of God's promise of the spirit in Israel's midst, therefore, is the promise of the angelic presence, which, as we have seen, the author of Isa 63:7-14 referred to, as well as God's holy spirit and the spirit of Yahweh.

C. Nehemiah 9:20

Yet another reference to the spirit in the context of the exodus, wilderness wanderings, and conquest occurs in Neh 9:20:

> You gave your good spirit to instruct them, and did not withhold your manna from their mouths, and gave them water for their thirst.

This reference occurs in the context of Neh 9:19-25, which, following an account of Israelite rebellion (9:16-18), reiterates the elements of Neh 9:12-15:

the pillars of cloud and fire	9:12	&	19
good laws or instruction	9:13-14	&	20a
physical provision of manna and water	9:15a	&	20b-21
promise and possession of the land	9:15b	&	22-25

This repetition produces a parallel between the giving of Torah in the wilderness (9:13-14) and the giving of the spirit in the wilderness (9:20).

The nature of the relationship between Torah and spirit[16] is clarified in Neh 9:20 by means of the verb להשכילם (to instruct [them]). The nominal and verbal forms of the root, שׂכל, occur in Neh 8 in conjunction with the interpretation of Torah. On the first day of the seventh month, "they read from the book, from the law of God, with interpretation. *They gave the sense* [ושׂום שׂכל], so that the people understood the reading" (8:8). On the following day, "the heads of the ancestral houses of all the people, with the priests and the Levites, came together to the scribe Ezra *in order to study the words of the law* [ולהשׂכיל אל־דברי התורה]" (8:13). The association of this word with the study and interpretation of Torah in Neh 8 suggests that the good spirit of Neh 9:20 proffers as well instruction of Torah. Alongside the gift of the Torah, then, came the gift of the good spirit for interpreting Torah.

Although the vocabulary and literary structure of Neh 9 do not illuminate precisely the nature of the spirit, the relationship of the gifts of Torah and spirit does suggest a plausible foreground in the exodus-conquest traditions, which proved indispensable for interpreting Isa 63:7-14 and Hag 2:5. Three alternative interpretations of this tradition are plausible, each with its own implications for understanding the nature of the spirit in Neh 9:20.

First, if Neh 9:19-21 contains allusions predominantly to Exodus, then the spirit ought to be interpreted as the angelic presence of Exod 14:19,

---

16. The literary symmetry explains the reference to the spirit as "good": just as God (addressed in the second person) gave (ותתן) at Sinai "good commands" (מצות טובים), so God also gave (נתת) God's "*good* spirit" (רוחך הטובה).

32:34, 33:2, and 33:14-15, which we discerned in Isa 63 and Hag 2. Specific allusions to Exodus are, however, scant. The verb נחה, used in Neh 9:19 to depict the leading of the pillar of cloud, occurs similarly in Exod 13:21-22. Additionally, the purpose of the pillar of fire is expressed identically in Neh 9:19 and Exod 13:21: להאיר להם. However, because this infinitive construct occurs in relation to the pillar in Ps 105:39, one of the psalms that rehearses Israelite history, the expression in Neh 9 may be attributed to common liturgical interpretations of the pillar of fire without conscious allusion to the particular tradition of Exodus.

Second, if Neh 9:19-21 contains allusions predominantly to Numbers, then the spirit ought to be interpreted as the non-angelic spirit of Num 11, in which the spirit that is on Moses is divided among the elders, who prophesy. This possibility is not altogether unlikely, for the context of the impartation of the spirit in Num 11 includes the manna (11:1-9), the pillars are mentioned in 14:14, and the incident of the miraculous water occurs in Num 20:2-13. Nor is the use of the verb נתן to describe the impartation of the spirit in both Neh 9:20 and Num 11:25 incidental, although in Numbers the image is different, and the spirit is placed "upon" (על) the elders. More compelling is the reference to water, not in Neh 9:21 but earlier in 9:15, where the source is called a "stone" (סלע). This word occurs throughout Num 20 but not in Exodus or Deuteronomy of the miraculous source of water. However, the same word occurs in Ps 78:16, which, like Ps 105, belongs to a group of psalms devoted to retelling Israel's past; once again, then, the choice of this particular word may be due to a common liturgical tradition rather than to a conscious allusion to the tradition found in Numbers.

Third, if the preponderance of allusions in Neh 9:19-21 is to Deuteronomy, then we are relatively clueless about the nature of the spirit for, apart from Deut 4:37, which possibly depicts the presence and great strength of God as angelic sources of deliverance from Egypt, Deuteronomy makes no mention of the angel or spirit. Yet the weight of allusions in Neh 9:19-21 is to this canonical book. The assertion in Neh 9:21 that for forty years in the wilderness "they lacked nothing; their clothes did not wear out and their feet did not swell" is based upon Deut 8:4 (cf. 29:4), employing in common even the verbs בלה and בצק. The clause in Neh 9:19, immediately prior to the mention of the good spirit, אשר ילכו־בה, echoes Deut 1:33, while the two clauses that follow, in which the manna and miraculous water are mentioned *together* in quick succession, may be influenced by Deut 8:15-16, in which they are mentioned in equally quick succession, though in reverse order.[17]

---

17. The designation "bread of heaven" to describe manna in Neh 9:15, which

In summary, the sorts of allusion that proved invaluable for ascertaining the nature of the spirit in Isa 63:7–14 and Hag 2:5 do not finally lead to a conclusion about the nature of the spirit in Neh 9:20. Moreover, the liturgical vocabulary of Neh 9, which it shares with texts such as Pss 104:39–41, 78:16, 24 renders it difficult precisely to determine which tradition underlies Neh 9:20.[18]

III. GRECO-ROMAN JUDAISM

A. Septuagint

Although F. Büchsel averred that the LXX translation "in dieser Untersuchung über den Geist Gottes näher einzugehen, lohnt wenig,"[19] there are indeed several instances in which LXX translations provide intimations that the spirit continued to be interpreted as an angelic being in the Greco-Roman period. Though scattered, these instances can be taken in their canonical order.

1. Judges 13:24–25

The verb "to trouble" (פעם) is translated naturally by ταράσσω in Gen 41:8, Ps 76:4, and Dan 2:1, and by ἐκινήθη in Dan 2:3. The verb is translated suitably by ἐξέστη in θ Dan 2:1, 3. In contrast, the verb פעם is translated unexpectedly in Judg 13:24–25 by the verb συμπορεύομαι (to accompany).

---

parallels 9:20bc, may be derived from Deut 8:3, in which the provision of manna stands in a position parallel to the contention that God "humbled you by letting you hunger, then by feeding you with manna . . . in order to make you understand that one does not live by bread alone, but by every word that comes from the mouth of the LORD." More likely is the expression due to common liturgical usage, for Ps 78:24–25 describes manna as the grain of heaven and the bread of angels.

18. Volz adds other texts that may be included, though he is not certain about what he calls their "hypostatic nature": (1) Zech 4:6; (2) Isa 34:16 (cf. Zech 6:8); (3) Ps 143:10 (cf. Zech 13:2) (*Geist Gottes*, 153–56). He interprets the reference in Ps 104:29–30 as a hypostatized cosmic spirit, not completely independent but the organ through which God creates (*Geist Gottes*, 156–57). We may add as well some observations about 1–2 Chronicles. To depict the onset of the spirit, the author employs older formulae: (1) The spirit clothes (לבש) in 1 Chr 12:19 and 2 Chr 24:20, as it had Gideon in Judg 6:34. (2) The spirit is upon (היה על) in 2 Chr 15:1–2 and 20:13–15, just as the evil spirit (1 Sam 16:16, 23; cf. 19:9 with אל) and the evil or good spirit (19:20, 23) were upon Saul, and as the spirit was upon Othniel (Judg 3:10) and Jephthah (11:29). Whether these similarities are evidence that the Chronicler understood the spirit in a manner similar to the author of 1 Samuel as an angelic or demonic spirit of God is not certain.

19. Büchsel, *Geist Gottes*, 73.

This Greek verb is employed in LXX of Joshua and Judges of the gathering around of leading warriors (Josh 10:24), of Jephthah's accompanying the elders of Gilead (Judg 11:8), and in Codex Alexandrinus (Vaticanus has only πορεύω) of the going out of the daughters of Israel to mourn the death of Jephthah's daughter (11:40). The occurrence of this verb in Judg 13:25 (Vaticanus has συνεκπορεύομαι) is indeed disquieting, for it departs from other translations of פעם in the LXX by suggesting that the spirit of Yahweh began to accompany rather than to trouble Samson from this point in time. Such a translation indicates the presence of the belief in the Greco-Roman era that a spirit of God could be present by accompanying rather than possessing someone. Moreover, this translation corroborates the interpretation of the spirit in Judges that was proffered earlier, namely, that the spirit is conceived of as an angelic being, which, in the case of Samson, began its interaction with him in the vicinity of his family burial ground—precisely where a reader in antiquity might expect spirit activity.

2. 1 Kings 22:19–24

William R. Schoemaker observed that the absence of the definite article in the LXX translation of 1 Kgs 22:21 suggests that the spirit is "one among many spirits surrounding the throne of God."[20] A related translation, noted Schoemaker, characterizes Num 16:22 and 27:16 LXX, in which the Hebrew "God of the spirits (breath) *of* all flesh" is translated by LXX as "God of the spirits *and* of all flesh." In the Hebrew, רוח refers to human life and breath; πνεύματα in LXX refers "most likely to the unembodied spirits who act as God's messengers."[21]

To Schoemaker's observation we may append another concerning 1 Kgs 22:24. Zedekiah in the Hebrew asks how the spirit of Yahweh *crossed over* from him to speak with Micaiah: "What way did the spirit of Yahweh cross over from with me to speak (with) you?" The Septuagint, by omitting the verb עבר, alters entirely the conception of the spirit in this text. The initial Hebrew words אי זה, with the verb עבר, denote "Which (way) did it cross." Without the verb עבר, the initial words אי זה [22] refer not to the way of crossing but to the spirit: "Which spirit" or "What sort of spirit" (ποῖον πνεῦμα κυρίου). This question in LXX, as opposed to MT, presupposes a multiplicity—or at least a duplicity!—of spirits, including at least the spirit

---

20. Schoemaker, "Use of רוּחַ," 37.

21. Schoemaker, "Use of רוּחַ," 37–38.

22. These words are translated consistently in 1 Samuel–2 Kings LXX by ποῖος (2 Sam 15:2; 1 Kgs 13:12; 2 Kgs 3:8), often interpreted as "which way?".

in the divine council and a lying spirit. One may, of course, postulate that the Hebrew verb עבר was lacking in the *Vorlage* used by the LXX translators, but this scenario seems unlikely since this verb was present in the *Vorlage* utilized by the author of 2 Chronicles, who actually clarified any potential ambiguity with the addition of דרך, "Which *way* did the spirit of Yahweh cross over?" (18:23). This was the *Vorlage* of the LXX, which translates 2 Chr 18:23 with the words ποίᾳ τῇ ὁδῷ. The LXX translation of 1 Kgs 22:24, then, constitutes evidence that Greco-Roman interpreters saw in 1 Kgs 22:19-23 a multiplicity of spirits of Yahweh: "Which spirit?"

3. Isaiah 63:9-14

The first reference to the angel of the presence and the final reference to the spirit of Yahweh in this hymn are significant. Isaiah 63:9a MT reads:

לֹא צָר וּמַלְאַךְ פָּנָיו הוֹשִׁיעָם

The Septuagint translates:

οὐ πρέσβυς οὐδὲ ἄγγελος ἀλλ᾽ αὐτὸς κύριος ἔσωσεν αὐτούς

This translation requires pointing צָר as צִר and inserting the adversative conjunction ἀλλά: "Not an emissary (ambassador) or an angel but his [God's] presence saved them." This forceful contrast between God and an emissary has a polemical edge, which suggests that a quite divergent view existed in the Greco-Roman period, according to which an angel had delivered Israel from Egypt. In Isa 63:9 LXX, in contrast, God delivered Israel.

Startling indeed, in view of this polemical tone, is the presence of the view that an angelic spirit did lead Israel according to Isa 63:14 LXX:

κατέβη πνεῦμα παρὰ κυρίου καὶ ὡδήγησεν αὐτούς

Two characteristics of this LXX translation are significant. First, LXX takes the verb תרד with what follows (רוח) rather than with what precedes (כבהמה בבקעה); thus the spirit, not the cattle, descends.

Second, the spirit is not רוח יהוה but πνεῦμα παρὰ κυρίου. In the LXX, in which the expression πνεῦμα κυρίου occurs frequently,[23] the preposition παρά often signals an independent רוח. In Num 11:31 LXX, a wind went out from (παρά) Yahweh and brought quails. In 2 Chr 18:23, Zedekiah depicts the movement of the spirit from himself to Micaiah with the words παρ᾽

---

23. E.g., Num 11:29; 1 Sam 10:6; 11:6; 16:13-23; 2 Sam 23:2; 1 Kgs 18:12; 22:24; 2 Kgs 2:16; 2 Chr 15:1; 20:14.

ἐμοῦ τοῦ λαλῆσαι πρὸς σέ.[24] The connotation of separation is particularly evident in Isa 57:16 LXX. The Hebrew reads:

כי־רוח מלפני יעטוף ונשמות אני עשיתי

According to the Hebrew text, God will not remain angry forever because people to whom God gives life would become utterly' wearied by God's anger. The Septuagint translates עטף unusually by ἐξέρχομαι, perhaps because of the presence of מן in מלפני: πνεῦμα γὰρ παρ' ἐμοῦ ἐξελεύσεται καὶ πνοὴν πᾶσαν ἐγὼ ἐποίησα, i.e., (a) spirit will go out from God, for God made every breath.[25]

Taken together, these elements suggest that the LXX translator understood Isa 63:14 to refer to a spirit that descended from Yahweh in order to lead the people of Israel to Canaan. This dual action of descent and leading evokes images of the pillar of cloud, which descended at the tent (Exod 33:9) and in which God descended (e.g., Num 11:25; 12:5), although this cloud is never in the canonical text referred to as רוח. The reference may be to the angelic presence of God, as we have suggested as well for the Hebrew text of Isa 63:7–14, although its descent is only implicit in God's sending; presumably God must send it from on high, from which God is said intermittently to descend (e.g., Exod 24:16; Num 11:17).

4. Micah 2:7, 11; 3:8; Haggai 2:5

Micah 2:11 begins: לו־איש הלך רוח ושקר כזב. The words רוח ושקר ought to be translated "wind and lie" or, more idiomatically, "empty falsehoods." The LXX, however, interprets these words as a reference to a lying spirit. This translation of רוח ושקר by πνεῦμα ψεῦδος is probably influenced by 1 Kgs 22:22-23 and 2 Chr 18:21-22, which contain references to a πνεῦμα ψευδές. The personal nature of the spirit is accentuated further in Mic 2:11 LXX, where this lying spirit is not put in the mouth of the prophets but stands in the midst of Israel and lets drip wine and intoxicating drink:

πνεῦμα ἔστησεν ψεῦδος ἐστάλαξέν σοι εἰς οἶνον καὶ μέθυσμα

---

24. The prepositional phrase is employed with respect to human life in Isa 38:12, where despair in the presence of death is depicted by the image of the cutting off of a beam of a weaver, preceded by the words τὸ πνεῦμα μου παρ' ἐμοὶ ἐγένετο.

25. The reference, which is now to God's spirit, not to human spirits, appears to be eschatological, for the words πνεῦμα γὰρ παρ' ἐμοῦ ἐξελεύσεται parallel Isa 51:4 LXX: ὅτι νόμος παρ' ἐμοῦ ἐξελεύσεται καὶ ἡ κρίσις μου εἰς φῶς ἐθνῶν.

The central figure in Mic 2:11 LXX, then, is a false spirit that has taken its stand and made Israel drunk.

This portrayal parallels Hag 2:5 LXX, in which the spirit as an angelic presence stands in the midst of Israel:

| Hag 2:5 | καὶ τὸ πνεῦμά μου ἐφέστηκεν ἐν μέσῳ ὑμῶν |
| Mic 2:11 | πνεῦμα ἔστησεν ψεῦδος |

Haggai 2:5 LXX (consonant with its Hebrew *Vorlage*) encourages Israel by depicting the angelic spirit of the exodus standing in Israel's midst. Micah 2:11 LXX indicts Israel by depicting the false spirit standing in Israel's midst.

This reference to a demonic false spirit in Mic 2:11 LXX may have implications for the interpretation of the spirit in Mic 2:7 and 3:8 LXX, both of which diverge, though in differing measures, from the Hebrew. Although Mic 2:7 indicts the house of Jacob for cutting short God's "patience" (הקצר רוח יהוה), LXX translates:

οἶκος Ιακωβ παρώργισεν πνεῦμα κυρίου

Once again, the translation is far from idiomatic, so that רוח is translated as God's spirit.

Whether one ought to interpret Mic 2:7 LXX as a reference to God's spirit, understood as that component of God which, as in a human, can be grieved, or as an angelic spirit that is treated contemptuously depends upon the weight one gives to two factors.

First, the closest counterpart to Mic 2:7 LXX is Isa 63:10, according to which Israel disobeyed and grieved מרו (παρώξυναν) God's angelic presence. If the understanding of the spirit in Mic 2:7 approximates its closest parallel, then the spirit that is grieved is, as in Isa 63:10 (and Exod 23:21), God's angelic presence in Israel.

Second, because Mic 2:7 and 2:11 belong to the same prophetic oracle, they interpret one another. If they are interpreted in relation to one another, then the spirit of Yahweh in Mic 2:7 LXX ought to be understood as the angelic counterpart to the evil demonic spirit of Mic 2:11 LXX. This interpretative contrast is indeed appealing: Israel has spurned Yahweh's own angelic spirit (2:7) and prefers instead a false spirit, which stands in its midst and makes them drunk (2:11).

In light of the LXX translators' willingness to introduce spirits in Mic 2:7 and 2:11, the symmetrical contrast between a spirit of Yahweh (2:7) and a false spirit (2:11), together with the parallel with Isa 63:10, tilts the balance in favor of interpreting Mic 2:7 LXX as a reference to an angelic spirit.

The divine spirit is again the focus in Mic 3:8 LXX. In the Hebrew, the spirit of Yahweh is one of the elements, alongside power, justice, and strength, with which the prophet claims to be filled:

ואולם אנכי מלאתי כח את־רוח יהוה ומשפט וגבורה

In the LXX, in contrast, the prophet is filled by power, justice, and strength, but not by the spirit:

ἐὰν μὴ ἐγὼ ἐμπλήσω ἰσχὺν ἐν πνεύματι κυρίου καὶ κρίματος καὶ δυναστείας

The claim to being filled with the spirit of Yahweh was altogether acceptable; in Isa 11:2–3, for instance, the verbs ἀναπαύομαι and ἐμπίμπλημι depict the presence of God's spirit. Instead, the translator of Mic 3:8 describes the spirit as the means or person by which the prophet is filled with power and justice. This modification is not minor, for it alters the conception of the spirit from that which is imbued to that by means of which the prophet is imbued with power and justice.

On the basis of the interpretation of spirits in Mic 2:7 and 11 LXX, it is not improbable that the spirit in Mic 3:8 LXX is understood as an angelic presence. According to the LXX, Israel grieved God's true angelic presence (2:7; cf. Isa 63:10), by which true prophets are filled with power, justice, and might (3:8), and listened instead to a false spirit that stood among them and made them drunk (2:11).

B. Judith 16:14; Assumption of Moses; 2 Baruch 21:4; 23:5

Certain poetic passages in the Hebrew Bible suggest that God's רוח is responsible for creation. In these texts, God's breath, by word (Gen 1) or inbreathing (Gen 2), is instrumental in creation. For example, Elihu states:

> The רוח of God has made me,
> and the breath of the Almighty [ונשמת שדי] gives me life.
> (Job 33:4)

In Ps 33:6, the psalmist claims:

> By the word of Yahweh the heavens were made,
> and all their host by the רוח of his mouth.

In Ps 104:29–30, the psalmist praises God's creative power:

> When you hide your face, they are dismayed;
> when you take away their breath,

they die and return to the dust.
When you send forth your רוח, they are created,
and you renew the face of the ground.[26]

In similar later texts, this spirit seems perhaps to have taken on a life of its own. Judith 16:14, in particular, transforms Ps 104:30a (Ps 103:30a LXX) in this way. The psalm reads:

ἐξαποστελεῖς τὸ πνεῦμά σου καὶ κτισθήσονται

The corresponding line, Jdt 16:14c, reads:

ἀπέστειλας τὸ πνεῦμά σου καὶ ᾠκοδόμησεν

As Volz observed, the spirit in Ps 104 is still presented as the organ through which God creates. In Jdt 16, in contrast, the spirit is the subject of the verb, "build." It is no longer a vehicle through which the creation is built but the subject that builds.

Noteworthy as well are three pseudepigraphical texts, to which Volz called attention.[27] In 2 Bar. 21:4 and 23:5, the spirit may be an independent being that creates. In 21:4, Baruch prays,

> O hear me, you who created the earth, the one who fixed the firmament by the word and fastened the height of heaven by the spirit, the one who in the beginning of the world called that which did not yet exist and they obeyed you.

In 23:5, the spirit and the realm of death may be personified: "For my spirit creates the living, and the realm of death receives the dead." I am not sure at all that these references present the spirit as other than the means by which God creates: by the breath that produces word (Gen 1), God created the heavens (2 Bar. 21:4), and by divine inbreathing (Gen 2), God creates humankind (2 Bar. 23:5).

The third text Volz noted occurs in a citation by Gelasius of the Assumption of Moses. During a conversation between the archangel Michael and the devil, Michael claims:

ἀπὸ γὰρ πνεύματος ἁγίου αὐτοῦ πάντες ἐκτίσθημεν.
καὶ πάλιν λέγει
ἀπὸ προσώπου τοῦ θεοῦ ἐξῆλθε τὸ πνεῦμα αὐτοῦ καὶ ὁ κόσμος ἐγένετο

---

26. See also Job 26:12-14.
27. Volz, *Geist Gottes*, 157-58.

This claim may suggest, as Volz contends, "die hier ausgesprochene Überordnung der Geisthypostase über die Engel."²⁸ Volz's interpretation is plausible, particularly since the reference is not merely to spirit or breath but to "holy spirit." This interpretation is not, however, altogether certain. Unlike Jdt 16:14, in which the divine spirit is the subject of a verb (ᾠκοδόμησεν), in this citation, God, not the spirit, may be the implied subject of ἐκτίσθημεν, and the spirit may be the means, not the subject, by which ὁ κόσμος ἐγένετο. Mention of God's face, in fact, may imply that God's holy breath—by word or inbreathing—was the means by which the angelic and physical worlds were created.

Although, among these texts, Jdt 16:14 alone definitively portrays the creative spirit as an independent being, the other texts leave open the possibility that the spirit was regarded as an independent subject responsible for creation. In 2 Bar. 23:5, for instance, the spirit actually creates the living, while in the citation by Gelasius, the attribution of creation to the holy spirit of God rather than to the breath of God permits the interpretation espoused by Volz of the holy spirit as creator.

C. The Two Spirits

The thorniest question this chapter addresses is whether the two spirits of 1QS 3–4 are to be interpreted primarily as spirits instilled in human beings or as cosmic spirits that influence human beings. If the spirits are cosmic beings, then the Qumran scrolls provide a salutary example of the belief that God's spirit was believed to be an angelic presence. However, although an enormous amount of scholarship has attended this question—much of it exceptionally good—there still exists no *consensus communis*. Consequently, the following discussion is a distillation of what appear to me to be the most compelling arguments for both sides of the debate.

1. The Two Spirits and Iranian Influence

The early discussions of K. G. Kuhn and A. Dupont-Sommer postulated Iranian influence to explain the two spirits in 1QS 3–4.²⁹ The similarities between 1QS 3–4 and the Gāthās of Zarathustra are indeed striking. 1QS 3.17b-21 introduces the discussion of the two spirits:

---

28. Volz, *Geist Gottes*, 158.
29. Kuhn, "Sektenschrift und iranische Religion"; Dupont-Sommer, "Instruction sur deux Esprits."

> He [God] created man to rule the world and placed within him two spirits so that he would walk with them until the moment of his visitation: they are the spirits of truth and of deceit. In the hand of the Prince of Lights is dominion over all the sons of justice; they walk on paths of light. And in the hand of the Angel of Darkness is total dominion over the sons of deceit; they walk on paths of darkness.[30]

To this corresponds Yasna 30.2–3 of the Gāthās:

> Listen with your ears to the best of things. Reflect with a clear mind . . . upon the two choices of decision, being aware to declare yourselves to Him before the great retribution. Yes, there are two fundamental spirits, twins which are renowned to be in conflict. In thought and in word, in action, they are two: the good and the bad. And between these two, the beneficent have correctly chosen, not the maleficent.

Similar is Yasna 45.2:

> Yes, I shall speak of the two fundamental spirits of existence, of which the virtuous one would have thus spoken to the evil one: "Neither our thoughts nor teachings nor intentions, neither our preferences nor words, neither our actions nor conceptions nor our souls are in accord."[31]

The singular advantage of this interpretation of 1QS 3–4 as a product of Iranian influence is that it elucidates the emergence of *two* opposing *spirits* in early Judaism, for, despite the presence of dualism in the Hebrew Bible—which Herbert G. May cited to explain the dualism of 1QS 3–4 without appeal to Iranian religion[32]—the Hebrew Bible contains no explicit reference to *two* opposing *spirits*. This crucial element, absent from the Hebrew Bible, is central to Iranian dualism.

Although acceptance of this influence does not a priori demand that the two spirits be understood as two cosmic entities—the quotations from the Gāthās cited above maintain a strong emphasis upon human will—the tendency of those who espouse Iranian influence has been to identify the spirits as cosmic entities. This interpretation, therefore, permits the "spirits" to be identified with the cosmic beings, "angels of light and darkness," of 1QS 3–4.

---

30. Translations of DSS by García Martínez, *Dead Sea Scrolls Translated* (1st ed.).

31. Translations by Insler, *Gāthās of Zarathustra*, 33, 75. For a description of the good spirit, see Yasna 47.

32. May, "Cosmological Reference," 7–14.

2. The Two Spirits as Human Dispositions

P. Wernberg-Møller challenged this interpretation of the two spirits as cosmic beings, contending instead that they are to be understood as two dispositions within a human being, the precursor of the rabbinic concept of the two יצרים. From this perspective, the focus of 1QS 3–4 is not two cosmic spirits, each with its entourage, divided into the children of light and the children of darkness. On the contrary, the focus of 1QS 3–4 is the variety of human spirits produced by the struggle between truth and perversity *within* the human heart.[33]

Five of Wernberg-Møller's exegetical observations deserve mention. (1) 1QS 3.14 refers not to "two kinds" of spirits but to "all kinds" of spirits: "concerning all the ranks of their spirits." In other words, human beings are distinguished from one another on the basis of a variety of spiritual states and not because they belong to one of two mutually exclusive groups. In fact, the number "two" occurs only in 3.18.[34] The strength of this observation is deepened by A. Sekki, who observes that the clearest analogy to the conception "their spirits" is 1QS 2.20, where the expression refers to the varieties of spiritual perfection of priests, which are the basis for their rank in the community.[35] (2) 1QS 3.18, which mentions the placement of two spirits in human beings, alludes to Gen 2:7, which relates the inbreathing of the spirit into a human, not the creation of a cosmic spirit.[36] (3) 1QS 3.13—4.26 presents no strict dualism but rather a framework in which God is always stronger than the angel of darkness. Once again, the focus is not upon two equal and opposed cosmic spirits.[37] (4) The lists in 1QS 4.2–14, which contrast "the spirit of meekness, of patience, generous compassion, eternal goodness" with "the spirit of deceit," do not refer to two cosmic spirits with their respective realms of morality. Rather, each human, both within and outside the Qumran community, exhibits in varying measure the characteristics of these spirits, and it is the mixture of these characteristics that determines "all the ranks of their spirits" (1QS 3.14). The exegetical basis for this inference is that the sons of truth are referred to twice in the first list, but the sons of perversion are not referred to at all in either list. The intent of these contrasting lists, therefore, is not to distinguish between the children of light, who exhibit the characteristics of the good spirit alone,

---

33. Wernberg-Møller, "Reconsideration of Two Spirits," 418–34.
34. Wernberg-Møller, "Reconsideration of Two Spirits," 419–20.
35. Sekki, *Meaning of Ruaḥ*, 195. See also 1QS 4.16; 4.24.
36. Wernberg-Møller, "Reconsideration of Two Spirits," 422.
37. Wernberg-Møller, "Reconsideration of Two Spirits," 425–27.

and the children of darkness, who exhibit the characteristics of the spirit of deceit, for the latter group does not even come into the picture.[38] (5) 1QS 4.17-18 describes a fierce struggle, and 4.23-25 locates this struggle in the human heart: "Until now the spirits of truth and of injustice feud in the heart of man and they walk in wisdom or in folly." The nature of this struggle determines the particular share one has in the spirits of truth and perversion. Once again, the gradations of one's individual share form the basis for the varieties of "all the ranks of their spirits" (3.14) that members of the community exhibit.[39]

A. Sekki has modified and strengthened Wernberg-Møller's position by maintaining Wernberg-Møller's interpretation of the two spirits as human dispositions while, unlike his predecessor, embracing as well the cosmic context that permeates 1QS 3-4. According to Sekki, three different interpretations of רוח coexist in 1QS 3.13—4.26. (1) The use of the feminine gender in the expression רוחות האמת והעול signals a reference to human dispositions (3.18-19). (2) The use of the masculine gender in the similar expression רוחי אמת ועול signals a reference to the good and evil spirits that fill the cosmos. (3) The spirit of holiness or spirit of truth (4.21) is an awaited eschatological reality.

The cornerstone of Sekki's approach is the observation that the gender of the רוחות in 1QS 3.18-19 is female. In contrast, throughout the remainder of the Qumran literature, references to angelic beings as "spirits" occur with relative consistency in the male gender. Therefore, the two spirits in 1QS 3.18-19, as well as "the spirits of light and of darkness" in 3.25, ought to be interpreted as human dispositions and distinguished from the two angels (e.g., of truth and darkness) in 3.20-25. When the author of 1QS 3-4 refers to human dispositions in a cosmic context, therefore, he employs the female gender of רוח.

Conversely, when רוח signifies an angelic being, the author employs the male gender, as in 1QS 4.23: רוחי אמת ועול. These spirits are to be understood as angelic and demonic beings respectively and distinguished from the two dispositions of 1QS 3.18-19.

According to Sekki, the author of this essay on the two spirits allows these two interpretations to coexist in order to teach that "the pious must deal not only with their own sinful nature but also with the problem of demonic attack."[40] Sekki explains:

---

38. Wernberg-Møller, "Reconsideration of Two Spirits," 429-31.
39. Wernberg-Møller, "Reconsideration of Two Spirits," 433.
40. Sekki, *Meaning of Ruaḥ*, 211. See also 4QShir[a] 1, 6, in which the demons attempt to destroy the heart of the faithful.

The feminine gender shows that the author's intent is not to describe personal, angelic beings which exist alongside of man, but to show that the dispositions which spiritually define man are not merely individual or personal matters but are intimately related to a cosmic good and cosmic evil which transcend man. A refusal of those outside the community to follow sectarian law . . . shows that their innermost religious life, i.e., their religious identity as human beings, has its primary source in a great cosmic Well of Darkness (3:19).[41]

Alongside these references to two human dispositions and a multiplicity of angelic and demonic beings, the author of 1QS 3.13—4.26 refers as well to the singular spirit of God as the "spirit of holiness" and the "spirit of truth" (4.21) in an eschatological context replete with allusions to Isa 44:3, Joel 3:1, and Ezek 36:25-27. The connection of "spirit of holiness," which refers unequivocally to God's spirit, and "spirit of truth," which refers to a human disposition in 1QS 3.18-19, is perplexing. Sekki clarifies:

The author tries to reinterpret the traditional view of the sect that God through His Spirit will deliver His people from sin in the last days by describing the eschatological רוח קודש as the רוח אמת of 3:18/19. In this way the author indicates that the "holy Spirit" which will come from God in the future is really none other than the good spirituality given to the sectarian at his creation.[42]

In 1QS 3-4, therefore, רוח refers to human spirits, angelic and demonic spirits, and the spirit of holiness or truth. The two spirits are human dispositions, not cosmic spirits, although they are continually influenced by cosmic powers. The holy spirit, though it shares a similar nature with the human spirits of truth, remains an awaited eschatological reality.

3. The Two Spirits as Angelic Beings

The positions espoused by Wernberg-Møller and Sekki are not without weaknesses. These inadequacies reopen the door again to an interpretation of the two spirits as cosmic or angelic beings.

First, Wernberg-Møller is compelled to interpret the word תולדות in 3.18-19 as human "natures," although, as May observed, in a context replete with creation imagery, the allusion is to Gen 2:4, which concludes a creation

---

41. Sekki, *Meaning of Ruaḥ*, 202.
42. Sekki, *Meaning of Ruaḥ*, 217-18.

narrative, Gen 1, which is cosmic in scope.[43] The more natural meaning, "generations," is therefore preferable to human "natures."

Second, James H. Charlesworth has noted that 1QS 3.18 is not about the placement of two spirits *within* human beings—which Wernberg-Møller interpreted as an allusion to Gen 2:7—but the allotment of two spirits *for* human beings to follow. 1QS 3.18 reads וישם לו (as in 2 Sam 12:20) and not וישם בו. In this interpretation, human beings situate themselves in either of the two spirits; the two spirits are not situated within a human being.[44]

Third, Charlesworth has argued that various designations ought to be interpreted as synonyms. References to the spirit of truth (1QS 3.18-19), the prince of lights (3.20), God's angel of truth (3.24), and the spirit of light (3.25) should not be distinguished from one another but, on the contrary, interpreted as synonyms, particularly when they appear in a unified context characterized by an overall distinction between light and darkness, truth and falsehood. Analogously, various names for God—God of Israel, knowledge, and vengeance—are "alternative names of the same reality" rather than references to three distinct gods.[45] Similarly, the children of light (3.13, 24, 25) ought to be identified with the children of truth (4.5-6).

These observations suggest that the focus of 1QS 3.18-25 may be two angelic spirits, designated variously as the Prince of Lights and Angel of Darkness (3.20-21), or "spirits of light and of darkness" (3.25). Generations (תולדות in 3.18-19) of human beings are distinguished on the basis of the spirit in which they choose to walk (3.20; 4.24), on the basis of whether the spirit of truth or the spirit of injustice is winning the battle within each human heart (4.23).

4. The Testaments of the Twelve Patriarchs

A few significant references to the two spirits appear in these testaments. The foundation for the conception of the two ways is laid out in T. Ash. 1:3-4:

> God has granted two ways to the sons of men, two mind-sets [διαβούλια], two lines of action, two models, and two goals. Accordingly, everything is in pairs, the one over against the other. The two ways are good and evil; concerning them are two dispositions [διαβούλια] within our breasts that choose between them.[46]

43. May, "Cosmological Reference," 1-2.
44. Charlesworth, "Critical Comparison," 396.
45. Charlesworth, "Critical Comparison," 391.
46. Translations from Kee, "Testaments of Twelve Patriarchs"; alternative

A diatribe on the two-faced person follows, in which it becomes clear, as in 1QS 3–4, that there is no middle ground, for the two-faced are said to please Beliar (3.1-2). In fact, the two-faced are doubly punished because "they imitate the spirits of error and join in the struggle against mankind" (6.2; cf. 1QS 3.20-25). In the end, the two-faced cannot evade a display of their evil:

> For the ultimate end of human beings displays their righteousness, since they are made known to [or recognize] the angels of the Lord and Beliar. For when the evil soul departs, it is harassed by the evil spirit which it served through its desires and evil works. But if anyone is peaceful with joy he comes to know the angel of peace and enters eternal life.

These foundational texts share the perspective of 1QS 3–4 with respect to the influence of angels of God, the struggle of the spirits of error under the dominion of Satan against humankind, and the absence of a via media for moral action. What T. Ash. lacks, however, is a precise reference to the two spirits.

This we discover in T. Jud. 20:1-3, 5:

> So understand, my children, that two spirits await an opportunity with [or devote themselves to] humanity: the spirit of truth and the spirit of error. In between is the conscience [or spirit] of the mind which inclines as it will. The things of truth and the things of error are written in the affections of man, each one of whom the Lord knows . . . And the spirit of truth testifies to all things and brings all accusations.

Unambiguous in this text is the presentation of the two spirits as angelic beings that stand apart from humankind; the two spirits are not here two human dispositions. Not entirely clear in this text, however, is whether the two spirits are two cosmic leaders or whether each person has his or her own respective angel and demon between which he or she must choose. The Greek text is ambiguous: δύο πνεύματα σχολάζουσι τῷ ἀνθρώπῳ, τὸ τῆς ἀληθείας καὶ τὸ τῆς πλάνης. καὶ μέσον ἐστὶ τὸ τῆς συνέσεως τοῦ νοός, οὗ ἐὰν θέλῃ κλῖναι. In relation to 1QS 3–4, then, it is not altogether clear whether the two spirits ought to be identified with the Prince of Lights and Angel of Darkness or if they are two among the multiplicity of angelic and demonic spirits charged with influencing humankind in 1QS 3.18-25.

A third significant text is T. Gad 4:7:

---

translations in brackets from Hollander and Jonge, *Testaments of Twelve Patriarchs*.

> For among all men the spirit of hatred works by Satan through human frailty for the death of mankind; but the spirit of love works by the Law of God through forbearance for the salvation of mankind.

In this text, ambiguity once again rears its head. The two spirits could refer to hateful or loving human spirits, to loving angelic and hateful demonic spirits, or to the Angel of Darkness and Prince of Light. The last option is unlikely because, by depicting the spirit of hatred as Satan's coworker with the verb συνέργω, T. Gad 4:7 appears to distinguish Satan from the spirit of hatred.[47]

5. A Concluding Reflection on the Two Spirits

In the end, we arrive at an impasse about the nature of the two spirits. That good scholarship on both sides of this debate should end at an impasse is not surprising in light of the data being examined. Ancient thinkers do not share our penchant for creating discrete units of meaning—wind, breath, angel, spirit of prophecy.

On the contrary, the newness of Zoroaster's teaching was "his apprehension of primeval unity in the sphere of the divine," with the result that the expression "Bounteous Spirit" in the Gāthās at some times represents the power in Ahura Mazda himself, through which he thinks or perceives or acts, and at other times an independent divinity who hypostatizes this power.[48] And the Stoics, of course, regarded πνεῦμα as the unifying substance of the cosmos.[49] Balbus, in Cicero's *Nat. d.* 2.19, claims that the world order is "maintained in unison by a single divine and all-pervading spirit."[50] In the writings of Qumran, the scenario is not altogether different, for the designations "holy spirit" or "spirit of holiness" describe equally God's spirit (e.g., 1QS 8.16; 1QH 7.6; 9.32), angelic spirits (e.g., 1QH 8.12), and the human spirit (CD 5.11-12; 7.3-4). Is it surprising that it should be so difficult to determine whether the two spirits are human or angelic?

---

47. See further Seitz, "Two Spirits in Man," for a discussion of relevant biblical texts, the Dead Sea Scrolls, the Testaments of the Twelve Patriarchs, and the Shepherd of Hermas.

48. Boyce and Grenet, *Zoroastrianism*, 193. The Bounteous Spirit is also one of the seven lesser deities who became guardian each of one creation: dominion in the sky; devotion in the earth; health in the water; good thought in the cattle; the bounteous spirit in the just person; and justice or truth in fire. See Boyce, "Persian Religion," 1:286.

49. On the rational and divine nature of the spirit, see Plotinus, *Enn.* 4.7.4; Lactantius, *Inst.* 1; *De falsa religione* 5.

50. See also Alexander of Aphrodisias, *Mixt.* 216.14-17.

D. The Angelic Spirit According to Josephus and Philo[51]

1. The Tale of Balaam

In the biblical tale of Balaam, Balak king of Midian sent for Balaam to receive from him an oracle that would ensure military victory. While travelling to meet Balak, an angel confronted Balaam, the seer, who ironically did not at first see the angel, while his ass did. Although the angel then commanded Balaam to say only what the angel would command (Num 22:35), Balaam's oracles are attributed also to God (Num 22:20, 38; 23:4-5, 12, 16, 26; 24:13) and the spirit of God (24:2 and 23:7 LXX).

Philo dispels this ambiguity by attributing inspiration to the angel and the prophetic spirit—but not God. In an expanded version of Num 22:35, the angel predicted:

> I shall prompt the needful words without your mind's consent, and direct your organs of speech as justice and convenience require. I shall guide the reins of speech, and, though you understand it not, employ your tongue for each prophetic utterance. (*Mos.* 1.274)

This prediction was fulfilled when Balaam "advanced outside, and straightway became possessed, and there fell upon him the truly prophetic spirit which banished utterly from his soul his art of wizardry" (*Mos.* 1.277). Philo creates this integral relationship between the prediction of the angel and its fulfilment by the divine spirit by omitting the intervening references to God in Num 22:38 and 23:5. Such an alteration results in the interpretation of *the divine spirit as an angel*. While according to Num 22-24, God placed a word in Balaam's mouth, in Philo's version, the angel who promised to prompt Balaam's words, direct his vocal organs, guide the reins of speech, and employ his tongue actually accomplished this when it reappeared, identified as the prophetic spirit. The prediction of the angel in *Mos.* 1.274 and its accomplishment by the prophetic spirit in *Mos.* 1.277 describe the same event, the former prospectively and the latter retrospectively.

Philo confirms this identification of the angel with the prophetic spirit by means of a crucial exegetical modification. According to Num 23:5, God was the source of Balaam's oracle. Philo, however, substitutes for this direct reference to God (Num 23:5) an oblique reference to "another." That this

---

51. This section presents briefly and summarily what I have argued in substantial detail elsewhere. Included in this volume are "Debut of the Divine Spirit," "Prophetic Spirit as an Angel," and "Inspiration and Divine Spirit." Not included in this volume are "Josephus' Interpretation" and "Two Types."

"other" is the angel is evident in the repetition of the verb θεσπίζειν in *Mos.* 1.274 and 1.277. The angel had claimed that it would prophesy (θεσπίζων) by using Balaam's tongue without his understanding; now Balaam prophesied (θεσπίζει) by means of "another" who "cast into" him what he should say.

According to Philo's version of Balaam's inspiration, then, an inspiring angelic spirit displaced Balaam's rational faculties and utilized his vocal organs to produce a prophetic utterance. This portrayal of the spirit as an angel and its method of inspiring Balaam are strikingly similar to Josephus's version of Balaam.

Josephus omits all biblical references to the divine spirit prior to the tale of the ass; the delay of the introduction of the divine spirit to this point results in the identification of the divine spirit with the angel. Josephus carefully draws a parallel between the approach of the *divine angel* and the ass's perception of the *divine spirit*:

> But on the road an angel of God confronted him [ἀγγέλου θείου προσβαλόντος αὐτῷ] in a narrow place ... and the ass whereon Balaam rode, conscious of the divine spirit approaching her [συνεῖσα τοῦ θείου πνεύματος ὑπαντῶντος]. (*Ant.* 4.108)

The manner in which Balaam is inspired by this angelic spirit is proffered by Balaam himself in response to Balak's accusations:

> Thinkest thou that it rests with us at all to be silent or to speak on such themes as these, when we are possessed by the spirit of God? For that spirit gives utterance to such language and words as it will, whereof we are all unconscious. (*Ant.* 4.119; cf. 4.121)

Balaam explains that the divine spirit takes hold (λάβῃ) and lets loose sounds and words (φωνὰς ... λόγους ... ἀφίησιν); it utilizes (λάβῃ ... ἀφίησιν) the seer's mouth to produce the sounds and words it wills. For Balaam, this experience entails the loss of rationality. He is not in himself (οὐκ ὢν ἐν ἑαυτῷ) (*Ant.* 4.118); he becomes unconscious (οὐδὲν ἡμῶν εἰδότων) (4.119); and he no longer possesses his faculties (οὐδὲν γὰρ ἐν ἡμῖν ἔτι φθάσαντος εἰσελθεῖν ἐκείνου ἡμέτερον) (4.122).

As in Philo's version, in Josephus's version of the tale of Balaam, the divine spirit is an angelic being that utilizes the mouth of the mantic to produce the words and sounds of its choosing. Balaam's rational faculties are rendered inactive by the invading presence of the divine spirit.

These interpretations, as I have detailed elsewhere, reflect the influence of the explanation of Delphic inspiration propounded by Cleombrotus in Plutarch's *De defectu oraculorum*. Cleombrotus attributes the obsolescence of oracles at Delphi to the departure of the mediating demons, the divine messengers:

> Let this statement be ventured for us, following the lead of many others before us, that coincidently with the total defection of the guardian spirits [δαιμονίοις] assigned to the oracles and prophetic shrines, occurs the defection of the oracles themselves; and when the spirits flee or go to another place, the oracles themselves lose their power. (418D; cf. 431B)

The passivity of the speaker is expressed by the simile of musical instruments: when the daemons return, "the oracles, like musical instruments, become articulate, since those who can put them to use are present and in charge of them" (418D).

The two elements of inspiration, the presence of an angelic being and the passivity of the mantic, which characterize Cleombrotus's interpretation, are present as well in Philo's and Josephus's interpretations of the tale of Balaam, both of whom identify the angel of Num 22:35 with the spirit of Num 24:2 and stress the passivity of Balaam in the spirit's presence.

2. The Divine Spirit and Socrates's Daemon

Plutarch's *De genio Socratis* contains an illuminating discussion of the nature and power of Socrates's inspiring sign or genius.[52] Simmias, the central spokesperson of the dialogue, explains that Socrates received this communication because of the exemplary purity of his mind:

> Socrates [asserts Simmias] had an understanding which, being pure and free from passion, and commingling with the body but little, for necessary ends, was so sensitive and delicate as to respond at once to what reached him. What reached him, one would conjecture, was not spoken language, but the unuttered

---

52. Plato referred to this phenomenon vaguely as τὸ δαιμόνιον (*Euthyphr.* 3B; *Apol.* 40A; *Apol.* 31D), as Socrates's "customary sign" (*Phaedr.* 242C; see also *Euthyd.* 272E). Xenophon, in order to defend Socrates against the charge that he rejected the gods of the state, went so far as to include Socrates's daemon alongside acceptable forms of divination such as augury (*Mem.* 1.1.4), and to include it alongside the state gods (1.1.5). The anonymous second-century BCE author of *Theages* took his cue from Plato's *Phaedr.* 242C and identified it as a voice (128D-29D). In the subsequent, successive centuries, the nature of Socrates's genius was taken up by Cicero (*Div.* 1.122-24); by Plutarch (*Gen. Socr.* 580B-82C; 588B-89F); and by Maximus of Tyre, who devoted the eighth of forty-one exhortations to the question, "What is the daemon of Socrates?" (*Orationes*).

> words of a daemon, making voiceless contact with his intelligence by their sense alone. (*Gen. Socr.* 588D–E)

Socrates was not alone in this experience but belonged to the race of daemonic persons who receive similar communications. Later, Simmias continues:

> The messages of daemons pass through all other people, but find an echo in those only whose character is untroubled and soul unruffled, the very people in fact we call holy and daemonic. In popular belief, on the other hand, it is only in sleep that people receive inspiration from on high; and the notion that they are so influenced when awake and in full possession of their faculties is accounted strange and incredible. (*Gen. Socr.* 589D)

Still later in the discussion, Simmias relates the myth of Timarchus of Chaeroneia, in which τά δαιμόνια are daemonic beings who communicate directly with the minds of daemonic people. Timarchus, hoping to learn the nature of Socrates's sign, descended into a crypt and had a vision in which he saw a variety of stars, some trembling above the great abyss, others sinking, and others shooting up from the abyss. A voice explained to Timarchus, "You see the daemons themselves" (*Gen. Socr.* 591D). The orderly daemons are connected to "souls which good nurture and training had made submissive to the rein" (592A). From these souls, "which from their very beginning and birth are docile to the rein and obedient to their daemon, comes the race of diviners and of people inspired" (592C).

Discernible in this fascinating discussion are three elements from one vein of first-century interpretations of Socrates's daemon. First, the daemon of Socrates and the daemons that guide daemonic persons are not divinity understood in general terms—as the word δαιμόνιον might be interpreted—but independent daemonic beings. Second, the process of communication presupposes the highest level of rational awareness. And third, daemons communicate intelligently only with people of exceptional virtue, people of the daemonic race.

These observations bring us to Josephus's Daniel. According to Josephus's *Ant.* 10.239, Baltasares (the biblical Belshazzar) tells Daniel that he has learned of him "and his wisdom and of the divine spirit that attended him and how he alone was fully able to discover things which were not within the understanding of others." This paraphrase preserves the biblical association of the divine spirit with the wisdom that distinguishes Daniel from his peers.

This paraphrase is a significant departure from the references to the divine spirit in Dan 5:11-14 that underlie it. Three times Dan 5 asserts that Daniel had the divine spirit *within* him.[53] Josephus instead writes that the divine spirit *accompanied* Daniel: ὅτι τὸ θεῖον αὐτῷ πνεῦμα συμπάρεστι. This alteration signals that Josephus is ill at ease with the biblical point of view. The divine spirit does not, according to Josephus, indwell Daniel; rather it accompanies him.[54]

Josephus's unease is evident further in his paraphrase of Dan 6:4. Like Dan 5, Dan 6:4 attributes Daniel's distinction from his peers to the excellent spirit *within* him: ὅτι πνεῦμα περισσὸν ἐν αὐτῷ. Josephus's paraphrase qualifies this assertion by the addition of a participle, πεπιστευμένος, and the omission of the word πνεῦμα.

> And so Daniel, being held in such great honour and such dazzling favour by Darius and being the only one associated with him in all matters because he was believed to have the divine spirit in him, became a prey to envy.

The key addition in Josephus's version is πεπιστευμένος: Daniel was *believed* to have had the divine within him. The key omission in Josephus's version is πνεῦμα. The spirit's presence is implied, in light of the earlier reference to it in Josephus's paraphrase of Dan 5:11-14, but its presence is muted. With these exegetical adaptations, Josephus avoids making any kind of dogmatic statement to the effect that a divine spirit actually did indwell Daniel.

The introduction of the verbs συμπάρεστι and πεπιστευμένος indicates Josephus's departure from the interpretation of the divine spirit presented by Dan 5-6. Josephus chooses instead to impress upon his readers that Daniel possessed the highest of virtues and wisdom because the divine spirit *accompanied* him.

We can pinpoint more accurately the mode of inspiration presupposed in Josephus's exegetical adaptations by taking a sideways glance at Josephus's other writings. In his *Jewish War*, Josephus explains John Hyrcanus's gift of prophecy in this way: "For the daemon was in his company so that he was ignorant of nothing which was to take place" (ὡμίλει γὰρ αὐτῷ τὸ δαιμόνιον).[55] This attribution of prophetic inspiration to an accompany-

---

53. In θ Dan 5, the queen says, ἔστιν ἀνὴρ . . . ἐν ᾧ πνεῦμα θεοῦ (5:11) and ὅτι πνεῦμα περισσὸν ἐν αὐτῷ (5:12). Consequently, the king says to Daniel, ἤκουσα περὶ σοῦ ὅτι πνεῦμα θεοῦ ἐν σοί (5:14).

54. See also Judg 13:24-25 LXX, which we have already discussed.

55. Josephus, *J.W.* 1.69. The word "daemon" (τὸ δαιμόνιον) has a wide range of meanings, encompassing the divine, the Satanic or daemonic, or a divine sign, such

ing divine presence neatly parallels Josephus's alterations of Dan 5-6. The prophetic gifts of Daniel and John Hyrcanus, according to Josephus, ought not to be attributed to a divine presence within but to an accompanying divine presence without.[56]

The precise nature of this accompanying presence is apparent in Josephus's own version of Socrates's inspiration, which he proffers in *Ag. Ap.* 2.262-64. Of John Hyrcanus, we saw, Josephus writes, ὡμίλει γὰρ αὐτῷ τὸ δαιμόνιον.[57] Of Socrates, Josephus writes, τι δαιμόνιον αὐτῷ σημαίνειν. Josephus's use of the indefinite pronoun, τι, indicates in shorthand that he understands the word δαιμόνιον in a manner extraordinarily similar to his contemporary, Plutarch, who attributes the inspiration of Socrates to "the unuttered words of a daemon"—that is, as an independent spiritual being.

The scenario of inspiration associated with Daniel, John Hyrcanus, and Socrates, therefore, is unified. In all three instances, an accompanying divine being inspires a person of exceptional character. Josephus's refusal to accept the biblical view that the divine spirit inhabited Daniel can be explained by his clear preference for the view that the divine spirit that

---

as an earthquake. In the *Jewish War* and the *Antiquities*, Josephus populates the world with daemonic and angelic beings. For example, Herod attributes the virtuous action of his son Alexander to his being "guided by good daemons" (δαιμόνων ἀγαθῶν ἔτυχεν) (*Ant.* 16.210). Therefore, Josephus may intend to present John Hyrcanus as living in concourse with the daemonic world. Such a view was commonplace in the Greco-Roman era. Cicero, for instance, attributes to Posidonius the view that some dreams occur because "the air is full of immortal souls, already clearly stamped, as it were, with the marks of truth" (*Div.* 1.64).

56. The difference in vocabulary between θεῖον πνεῦμα in Josephus's version of Daniel and δαιμόνιον in his description of John Hyrcanus can be attributed to Josephus's adherence to his biblical source in the *Antiquities*, a *Vorlage* by which he was not constricted in describing John Hyrcanus.

57. The word in *J.W.* 1.69 could mean more generally that John Hyrcanus was gifted with prophecy because God associated with him. Such an interpretation might be supported by Josephus's substitution of "Deity" (τὸ θεῖον) for "daemonic" (τὸ δαιμόνιον) in *Ant* 13.300, written nearly a quarter century later: "For the Deity was with him [συνῆν γὰρ αὐτῷ τὸ θεῖον] and enabled him to foresee and foretell the future." Two other alterations, however, suggest rather that Josephus, in the later version of the *Antiquities*, attempts to generalize the presence of the deity to include all three offices of John Hyrcanus—national rule, high priest, and prophecy—rather than limiting the presence of the deity to Hyrcanus's prophetic abilities. First, in the later version of the two sons that John Hyrcanus was said to predict, Josephus omits the verb "prophesied" (προεφήτευσεν), which appears in the earlier version of *Jewish War*. The two sons, Aristobulus and Antigonus, are national leaders, so Hyrcanus's foreknowledge is related as much to his role as king as it is to his function as prophet. Second, Josephus's attempt to include all three offices under the sway of God explains his preference in the later version for the verb "was with" (συνῆν), rather than the earlier verb, "associated with" (ὡμίλει), which connotes more personal communication and concourse.

accompanied Daniel was a daemonic being that, in a manner parallel to Socrates and John Hyrcanus, remained in close association with Daniel.

A comparable coalescence of conceptions characterizes an exegetical expansion of Exod 16, Moses's discernment of the Sabbath, in which Philo interrupts the narrative to explain the nature of Moses's inspiration:

> Moses, when he heard of this and also actually saw it, was awestruck and, guided by what was not so much surmise as God-sent inspiration, made announcement of the sabbath. I need hardly say that conjectures of this kind are closely akin to prophecies. For the mind could not have made so straight an aim if there was not also the divine spirit guiding it to the truth itself. (*Mos.* 2.265)

Philo carefully affirms in this commentary that Moses's prophetic possession entailed the sharpening of his rational capacities. The "God-sent inspiration" of the divine spirit did not displace reason, as in the case of typical prophetic inspiration, as Philo understands it, but instead guided Moses's mind intact to the truth. The two most significant words that Philo employs in this text to explain Moses's prophetic ability, "conjecture" (εἰκασία) and "guide" (ποδηγετέω)—occur elsewhere in Philo's writings exclusively in association with the rational processes of the human mind. The presence of these words, εἰκασία and ποδηγετέω, to explain Moses's inspiration signals the attribution of the highest achievement of human intellect to the divine spirit.

We can pinpoint even more accurately the model of inspiration Philo presupposes by turning to his autobiographical reflections, which he proffers in *Somn.* 2.251–52, where Philo interrupts his praise of the vision-seeking mind, "the mind which is eager to see all things and never even in its dreams has a wish for faction and turmoil," with a reference to the invisible voice that he hears:

> I hear once more the voice of the invisible spirit, the familiar secret tenant, saying, "Friend, it would seem that there is a matter great and precious of which thou knowest nothing, and this I will ungrudgingly shew thee, for many other well-timed lessons have I given thee."

As in *Mos.* 2.265, the divine spirit here is the essential ingredient of inspiration. Here, in *De somniis*, this divine spirit is depicted as a person who addresses Philo as friend. As in *Mos.* 2.265, the process that leads to this knowledge is rational. The verb here, ἀναδιδάσκειν, indicates that Philo's experience is primarily one of being taught. Indeed, the instruction of the divine spirit is directed toward the human mind (διάνοια), when it is "eager to see all things and never even in its dreams has a wish for faction and turmoil."

One reason Philo's account of his experience is so interesting is that it resonates with Socrates's experience, as it is interpreted by Plato and Plutarch. First of all, Max Pohlenz long ago suggested that Philo's use of the word εἰωθός to describe the recurrent presence of the divine spirit is a distinct allusion to Socrates's daemon.[58] According to Plato, Socrates referred to "the customary [εἰωθυῖα] prophetic inspiration of the daemon" (*Apol.* 40A), or "the daemonic and customary sign" (*Phaedr.* 242B), or "my customary daemonic sign" (*Euthyd.* 272E). Second, Philo's description of the process by which the divine spirit speaks as an echo (ὑπηχεῖ δέ μοι) corresponds to Simmias's belief, explained in Plutarch's *De genio Socratis*, that the "messages of daemons . . . find an echo" (ἐνηχοῦσι) in some people (*Gen. Socr.* 589D). Third, Philo's description of the receptive mind as free from faction and turmoil corresponds to Simmias's contention that daemonic language can be heard only by those whose souls are untroubled and unruffled. Philo describes his own mind as free of turmoil (ταραχῆς); Simmias accuses the ignorant of being in turmoil, a state from which Socrates was free (τὴν ἐν αὐτοῖς ἀναρμοστίαν καὶ ταραχὴν ἧς ἀπήλλακτο Σωκράτης) (*Gen. Socr.* 589E).

The implication of these parallels is extraordinary: even as the ultimate source of Socrates's inspiration was a customary daemonic communication that echoed within his untroubled soul, so the ultimate source of Philo's exegetical insight is the customary communication of the divine spirit that echoes within his untroubled mind.

Once again, then, Josephus and Philo proffer independent instances in which the divine spirit is interpreted as an angelic being who accompanies and inspires people. The model presupposed in this exegetical transformation can be ascertained from Plutarch's *De genio Socratis*, in which daemonic beings inspire the minds of the daemonic race.

IV. CONCLUSION

This journey on the wings of the wind, so to speak, through corpora of Israelite and early Jewish literature, is now at an end. Its termination is, of course, provisional. Other texts (not least those included by Paul Volz in his study but relegated in the present study to notes) might profitably have been included in a more extensive analysis. For instance, we might discuss D. J. Harrington's translation of the anarthrous Latin, *spiritus sanctus*, in LAB 28.6 to refer not to *the* holy spirit but to "a holy spirit," which "came

---

58. Pohlenz, "Philon von Alexandreia," 473.

upon Kenaz and dwelled in him and put him in ecstasy, and he began to prophesy."[59] Or we might explore the reference to "the holy spirit, the angel of Phoibos" in the Greek Magical Papyri 3.289. The texts included in the present analysis serve nonetheless to provide a suitable foundation for discussion of the angelic spirit in the Fourth Gospel, the Shepherd of Hermas, and the Ascension of Isaiah.

In preparation for that discussion, one essential observation may be drawn: conceptions of the spirit of God are frequently related to the interpretation of רוח as an angel or, conversely, the spirit is often *not* conceptualized as "die nach außen projizierte Abstraktion des inneren Wesens Gottes."[60]

In the major periods of Israelite and early Jewish history—preexilic, postexilic, and Greco-Roman—the spirit of God is identified as an angelic being and contrasted with a demonic being. The spirit of God can be contrasted with an evil spirit (1 Sam 10–19; Mic 2:7, 11 LXX), included among the angelic host (1 Kgs 22), and identified with the angelic presence of God in the exodus tradition (Isa 63:7–14; Hag 2:5) or the angel of Balaam's tale (Josephus, *Ant.* 4.108; Philo, *Mos.* 1.274, 277). Discussions of the spirit of God in early Judaism and Christianity, therefore, ought to consider that interpretations of the spirit as an angelic presence are not necessarily the product of a growing hypostatization of the inner spirit or breath of God, as appears to be the case in texts such as Jdt 16:14; the רוח or πνεῦμα of God could also be, and often was, interpreted as an angelic emissary of God.

---

59. Harrington, "Pseudo-Philo," 2:341.
60. Volz, *Geist Gottes*, 169.

10

Retrospect and Prospect

RETROSPECT

A variety of interpretations of the spirit have emerged in the course of this study. Though we now must inspect the most conspicuous of them individually, I do so reluctantly, for it is preeminently the combination of colors and not the dissection of distinctive hues that confounds the rainbow gazer. Still, this is a responsibility incumbent upon the author of a book, at least a book of this sort. We revisit, therefore, in this retrospect the various interpretations of the spirit that emerged in first-century Judaism. To facilitate this review, most subtopics are patterned after the methodological steps that have unfolded throughout most of this book, that is, the identification of exegetical movements followed by analysis of the relevant general and specific milieux that serve ultimately to explain these exegetical movements.

The Spirit and the Human Spirit

Pseudo-Philo's ascription of the human spirit to Balaam would be inordinately ordinary, hardly worth mention, were it not for the extraordinary transformation of the spirit that occurs in his version of the story of Balaam. Pseudo-Philo was presented with a simple formula, "the spirit of God came upon him [Balaam]," which appears undeniably to portray Balaam as the recipient of that spirit that, on momentous occasions, inspires oracular utterances of particular import. In this instance, Balaam succeeded in offering one of Scripture's greatest testimonies to the stellar place of Israel among the nations. Not so in LAB 18, where, by expending considerable exegetical energy, Pseudo-Philo not only denied Balaam that spirit which inspires prophetic trades but also portrayed him as one who lost, by obeying a foreign king, even the spirit that gives life to all people. The exegetical movements required to complete this transformation are worth recalling.

First, in an otherwise abbreviated account, Pseudo-Philo introduced several references, by way of allusion and citation, to Genesis into Balaam's story (Gen 12:3; 18:17; 22:17; 32:24–27). In this context, he introduced an echo of Gen 6:3; Balaam stated clearly that Balak "does not realize that the spirit that is given to us is given for a time" (LAB 18.3). With the introduction of this allusion to Gen 6:3, the spirit could begin to be understood less as the prophetic spirit which comes upon one in extraordinary moments than as the living breath, the spirit "given to us"—all human beings—for a limited time.

The second exegetical movement, though related to the first, is even more noteworthy. Pseudo-Philo contradicted Num 24:2 by recording that "the spirit did not abide in him." Moreover, the verb used, *permaneō*, echoes Gen 6:3 rather than Num 24:2, of which it is the paraphrase (LAB 18.10). This second allusion to Gen 6:3 in LAB 18 is less innocuous than the first, for this time the allusion *contradicts the biblical text*.

Third, Pseudo-Philo articulated the implicit association between this spirit and death that the two allusions to Gen 6:3 had evoked. Balaam lamented, "I am restrained in my speech and cannot say what I see with my eyes, because there is little left of the holy spirit that abides in me. For I know that, because I have been persuaded by Balak, I have lessened the time of my life. And behold my remaining hour" (LAB 18.11). The interpretation of the spirit as life breath, which Pseudo-Philo expended considerable exegetical energy to create through allusions to Gen 6:3 in LAB 18.3 and 18.10, would seem to obtain here as well.

To lay claim to the conviction that the energizing breath within is the divine breath is to remain comfortably within the parameters of the biblical purview. The "breath of life" is the vital force in all beings, human and beast (Gen 6:17; 7:15). It is coterminous with life, as Job in the face of death acknowledged:

> As long as my breath is in me
> and the spirit of God is in my nostrils,

> my lips will not speak falsehood,
>> and my tongue will not utter deceit. (Job 27:3–4)

The psalmist, in reflecting upon creation, realized that God gives that same breath to the beasts:

> When you hide your face,
> they [nonhuman created beings] are dismayed;
> when you take away their breath,
> they die and return to their dust.
> When you send forth your spirit, they are created;
> and you renew the face of the ground. (Ps 104:29–30)

This conception of the spirit persisted into the Greco-Roman era. In the context of a reflection upon "the God of heaven ... who makes everything upon the earth, and created everything by his word," one Palestinian author asked, "Why do you worship those who have no spirit in them?" (Jub. 12:5). In the Testament of Reuben, the first of seven spirits given to human beings at creation "is the spirit of life, with which a human is created as a composite being" (2:4). Similarly for Philo is a human being "a composite one made up of earthly substance and of Divine breath" (*Opif.* 135). Elsewhere, Philo queried of Gen 2:7 "why God deemed the earthly and body-loving mind worthy of divine breath at all" (*Leg.* 1.33).

What presumably cannot be explained by this milieu, however, is the application of the words "the holy spirit" to the human spirit—although this is precisely the interpretation demanded by the allusions to Gen 6:3, the denial of the spirit to Balaam, and the association of the loss of this spirit with impending death. Nor can the designation be explained satisfactorily by its biblical antecedents, Isa 63:10 and Ps 51:13, or by the Greek translation of Ps 51 and Seneca's forty-first letter to Lucilius.

Valuable precedent for this conception of the holy spirit can be discerned preeminently in the manuscripts of the Qumran sectaries. The expression "defiling his holy spirit" in CD 5.11 and 7.4 is analogous to "defiling one's soul" in CD 12.11–13. Furthermore, the biblical sources of these texts are Lev 11:43 and 20:25, in which one can "defile one's soul." From the perspective of the Damascus Document, Balaam's contention that "there is little left of the holy spirit that abides in me" in LAB 18 constitutes his recognition that his self, his life breath, has diminished to the point of death. Therefore, admitted Balaam, "I have lessened the time of my life. And behold my remaining hour."

The transformation Num 22–24 undergoes in LAB 18 is remarkable. The spirit of God of the biblical account appears clearly to be something that came upon Balaam at a particular moment and caused him to prophesy blessings on Israel's behalf. Pseudo-Philo, however, was determined to deny such inspiration by the holy spirit to Balaam, whom he portrayed as the architect of the plan to seduce Israel by means of Midianite women (LAB 18.13-14). Consequently, he interpreted the spirit of Num 24:2 as the human spirit of Gen 6:3, referring to "the holy spirit" to depict the life Balaam forfeited through disobedience or, in vocabulary characteristic of the Damascus Document, to display to his readers what happens to the person who "defiles his or her holy spirit" through obedience to foreigners rather than to God.

The Spirit and Extraordinary Power

On some occasions in the course of this study, we have encountered interpretations in which the nature of the spirit is not altogether clear, but the effects are. Within the diversity of those effects, one salient characteristic is the awesome, transforming power of that spirit.

The Spirit and the Military Hero

In Pseudo-Philo's version of Gideon's military feats, Gideon's reception of the spirit resulted in an immediate rout of the Philistines: "And as soon as Gideon heard these words, he put on the spirit of the Lord and was strengthened and said to the three hundred men, 'Rise up, let each one of you gird on his sword, because the Midianites have been delivered into our hands'" (LAB 36.2). This association between the spirit and the ensuing battle was accomplished through an important exegetical movement. In Judg 6, Gideon's reception of the spirit and the rout of the Midianites are separated by intervening stories about the gathering of the Abiezrites, the setting out of fleece, and the reduction of the soldiers to three hundred. By omitting all three intervening stories, Pseudo-Philo juxtaposed Gideon's reception of the spirit with the battle. The resulting impact was an emphasis upon the power of the spirit as the impetus for battle.

If the emphasis upon the spirit's power was accomplished by *omission* in the story of Gideon, it was achieved by extensive exegetical *expansion* in the tale of Kenaz, where it was spun from the lackluster biblical formula "And the spirit of the LORD was upon him." Around this expression, Pseudo-Philo clustered other expressions related to the spirit's power (LAB 27.9-10). He echoed Gideon's reception of the spirit in Judg 6:34 with the verb "clothed." He described the spirit as "the spirit of power" and connected this description with a second occurrence of the verb "clothed," recalling again the story of Gideon's rout of the Midianites by the impetus of the spirit. Finally, from the story of Saul's initial reception of the spirit in 1 Sam 10:6, he extracted the words "was changed into another person" and applied them to Kenaz's military prowess. By expanding Judg 3:10 in relation to Judg 6:34 and 1 Sam 10:6, and by adding the genitival phrase "of power," Pseudo-Philo transformed the colorless formula "the spirit of the LORD was upon him" into an impressive affirmation of the spirit's power in a military context.

The Spirit and the Prophet

The equally ordinary, formulaic words "Joshua son of Nun was full of the spirit of wisdom" Pseudo-Philo wove with other biblical threads into a vivid tapestry of inspiration. These words from Deut 34:9 (the spirit) were conjoined with expressions from 1 Sam 10:6 (transformation into another person) and Judg 6:34 (clothing). But that does not encompass the entirety of Joshua's experience, for, when he took up the garments that symbolized the spirit, Joshua's "mind was afire and his spirit was moved, and he said to the people . . ." (LAB 20.3). Despite numerous biblical instances of terror, emotional agitation, and trembling, which constituted a significant slice of the milieu that shaped Pseudo-Philo's beliefs about the spirit, we may still ask where the specific biblical precedent is for Pseudo-Philo's attribution of Joshua's inflamed mind and agitated spirit to the divine spirit.

Analogously, the formulaic biblical expression "The spirit of the LORD came upon him" (Judg 3:10) would provide the smoldering embers from which Pseudo-Philo would fan the flames of prophetic inspiration in his central character: the holy spirit leaped upon Kenaz, indwelt him, altered the state of his mind (probably by elevating it), with the result that he began to prophesy (LAB 28.6) and to obtain a cosmic vision, after which his mind was restored (28.10). Once again, the whole of this unified portrait cannot be explained satisfactorily by the sum of its biblical parts. Although other biblical judges and Saul could receive the spirit in much the same way, and although Nebuchadnezzar too had his sense returned to him, though he had lost it because of pride rather than the spirit's work, one may justifiably ask where the biblical precedent lies for the whole of Kenaz's experience, with the spirit's leaping, indwelling, lifting of Kenaz to view the future, and effecting an experience that necessitated the return of sense.

What is more, Kenaz could not remember what he had seen (18.10), just as Saul sometime later could not recall what he had heard (62.2). Where is the biblical precedent for this detail, which actually runs counter to the biblical tradition, according to which prophets were charged to remember precisely what they heard in order to communicate these words and visions to the people of God?

Although biblical precedent for the view of the spirit as the source of powerful prophetic revelations is sufficiently ample to provide a relevant milieu for apprehending Pseudo-Philo's extravagant exegetical movements, it is not adequate to explain these other particulars of Pseudo-Philo's portraits, all of which can be neatly cut from the cloth of Cicero's *De divinatione* and Plutarch's *De defectu oraculorum*, as well as from a complementary trajectory of references from other Jewish and Greco-Roman sources. Quintus, Cicero's Stoic spokesperson, contended that the prophetic frenzy of inspiration occurs "when the soul withdraws itself from the body and is violently stimulated by a divine impulse" (*Div.* 1.66). The ascent of the mind entails equally disturbing effects: "Those then, whose souls, spurning their bodies, take wings and fly abroad—inflamed and aroused by a sort of passion these people, I say, certainly see the things which they foretell in their prophecies" (1.114). What stimulates these experiences is some external impulse: "Such souls do not cling to the body and are kindled by many different influences ... certain vocal tones ... groves and forests ... rivers and seas ... certain subterranean vapours which had the effect of inspiring persons to utter oracles" (1.114). In these two passages of *De divinatione*, inflammation and agitation, ascent of the disembodied soul, and the necessity of an external impulse characterize inspiration.

These elements characterize as well Plutarch's discussions of inspiration in *De defectu oraculorum*, where the catalysts of inspiration are external forces upon the body that cause the soul to withdraw, to become agitated, and to foresee the future. Of these external forces, "the prophetic current and breath is most divine" (432D). Under the influence of this prophetic πνεῦμα "the soul becomes hot and fiery" (432F).

Precisely these details characterize prophetic inspiration in Liber antiquitatum biblicarum, where an external impulse—the spirit—both clothed Joshua, causing him to become inflamed and agitated, and leaped upon Kenaz, causing his mind to foresee far into the future. Moreover, the detail that Kenaz and Saul could not recollect their experiences probably recalls Plato's contention that inspired poets did not know what they were saying (*Apol.* 22C and *Meno* 99C). This conviction was later misinterpreted to mean that inspired folk could not remember what they had said. Awareness of this view spanned more than half a millennium, from Jewish literature of the late first century, in 4 Ezra 14, where Ezra claims, "My spirit retained its memory," to the writings of Aelius Aristides, Pseudo-Justinus, John Cassian, and the author of the late prologue to the Sibylline Oracles.

The work of the spirit in prophetic inspiration, therefore, is sufficient to dislodge the soul from the body. It leaps and clothes. It produces inflammation and agitation, loss of consciousness, a vision of the future, and the inability to recollect the prophetic experience. The spirit in Liber antiquitatum biblicarum is a power like none other, able both to inspire the military might of Gideon and Kenaz and to disturb the human soul to its core in prophetic ecstasy—though Pseudo-Philo painted these vivid portraits of military and prophetic inspiration with hues from two distinct palettes, respectively, biblical and Greco-Roman.

The Spirit and the Ideal Ruler

Even Pseudo-Philo's extensive assimilation of Greco-Roman conceptions of prophecy appears conservative in comparison with Philo's depiction of Abraham, of whom it could be said, "whenever he was possessed, everything in him changed to something better, eyes, complexion, stature, carriage, movements, voice. For the divine spirit which was breathed upon him from on high made its lodging in his soul, and invested his body with singular beauty, his voice with persuasiveness, and his hearers with understanding" (*Virt.* 217–18). The exegetical point of departure for this description is Gen 23:6, in which the Hittites said to Abraham, "You are a king among us." The biblical speech that prompted Philo to this celebration of Abraham's rhetorical preeminence is Abraham's unremarkable request to buy a field in Machpelah for burial caves.

The catalyst for Philo's praise of Abraham lies no doubt elsewhere, in a milieu that prized the very attributes Philo ascribed to this noble ancestor. The association of inward and outward beauty that characterizes Abraham, Adam, and Moses in the writings of Philo (e.g., *Opif.* 136; *Mos.* 2.69, 272) owes far less to exegetical interests than to the thoughts of Plato and his interpreters on the ideal ruler (e.g., *Resp.* 7.535A). The emphasis Philo placed upon rhetorical prowess is integrally related to Greco-Roman discussions, such as Dio Chrysostom's, who stated "that a statesman needs experience and training in public speaking and in eloquence" (*Dic. exercit.* 2).

Most important, however, was the conviction that both king and orator be recognized for virtue. Quintilian contended that the orator demonstrate "not merely the possession of exceptional gifts of speech, but of all the excellences of character as well" (*Inst.*, bk. 1, preface, 9), while Dio Chrysostom emphasized that the king be "a man of good mind and heart" who is "to begin with, happy and wise himself" (*3 Regn.* 39). Abraham was king, not because of any "outward state . . . mere commoner that he was, but because of his greatness of soul" (*Virt.* 216). It was not, therefore, training in rhetoric or even natural abilities that rendered Abraham capable of persuasion but the greatness of his soul that permitted "the divine spirit which was breathed upon him from on high" to make "its lodging in his soul" (*Virt.* 217). This spirit in turn caused Abraham's body to be beautiful, his voice to be persuasive, and his hearers to understand. Small wonder that he "was regarded as a king by those in whose midst he settled" (*Virt.* 218)!

The spirit, then, was believed to provide the power capable of transforming someone ordinary into an orator, a commoner into a king. Nothing escaped this transformation, as Philo observed, for "whenever he was possessed, everything in him changed to something better" (*Virt.* 217).

The Spirit and the Philosopher

With an equally slender exegetical underpinning, Philo described the role of the spirit in the ascent of the philosopher's mind. The biblical text that Philo purported to interpret is Gen 9:20: "Noah began to be a husbandman, tilling the ground, and he planted a vineyard." This text led Philo to Plato's *Tim.* 90A, in which the soul is "not an earthly but a heavenly plant." The basis for Philo's discussion of philosophical ascent, therefore, is allegedly Gen 9:20 but actually *Tim.* 90A; the texts are related by a slender common concern with agriculture.

Platonic discussions of the ascent of the mind, based primarily upon Plato's *Phaedr.* 246A–53C, comprised the milieu of Philo's discussion in *Plant.* 18–24. In fact, Philo was indebted to this Platonic text for many descriptions of the mind's ascent—of ascent in general in *Opif.* 69–71, of Philo's own ascent in *Spec.* 3.1–6, and of Moses's ascent in *Gig.* 50–55. Furthermore, the similarities between these descriptions and Middle and Neoplatonic descriptions of ascent are so palpable that one could forgivably mistake discussions of philosophical ascent in Plutarch's *Platonic Questions*, Maximus of Tyre's *Philosophumena*, and Plotinus's *Enneades* for Philo's *Plant.* 18–26.

With the exception of one element! Philo could have concluded his description of ascent in *Plant.* 18–24 without the slightest nod to the spirit, for his discussion begins with Plato's *Tim.* 90A, is permeated by allusions to the *Phaedrus*, and has more in common with Platonic philosophers than with Gen 9. Even a description of the rational soul as a coinage of the divine and invisible spirit would appear to confirm that the mind is capable of ascent. Nonetheless, at just that point where the discussion could conclude with a reference to Plato's notion of recollection, to Plutarch's "faculty of reason," to Maximus of Tyre's "self," or to Plotinus's "intellect"—all of which were deemed adequate to cause the mind to ascend—Philo introduced the divine spirit. According to *Plant.* 18–26, the ascent of the mind takes place only with the overpowering aid of the divine spirit.

Despite his overwhelming indebtedness to Platonism for this discussion, therefore, Philo neither jettisoned the spirit nor judged it peripheral. On the contrary, in *Plant.* 18–26, he ascribed to the spirit, and to the spirit alone, the requisite power for philosophical ascent. Although "those who crave wisdom and knowledge with insatiable persistence are said in the Sacred Oracles to have been called upwards [Lev 1:1]" (*Plant.* 23), and although those who received God's "down-breathing [Gen 2:7] should be called up to Him," and although this is "so with the mind of the genuine philosopher" (24), who "suffers from no weight of downward pressure towards the objects dear to the body and to earth" (25)—although all of these descriptions appear to render the spirit superfluous, for Philo the spirit alone has the unleashed force capable of producing such ascent:

> For when trees are whirled up, roots and all, into the air by hurricanes and tornadoes, and heavily laden ships of large tonnage are snatched up out of mid-ocean, as though objects of very little weight, and lakes and rivers are borne aloft, and earth's hollows are left empty by the water as it is drawn up by a tangle of violently eddying winds, it is strange if a light substance like the mind is not rendered buoyant and raised to the utmost height by the native force of the Divine spirit, overcoming as it does in its boundless might all powers that are here below. (*Plant.* 24)

The spirit is a hurricane's gales, a tornado's winds, drawing philosophical minds upward in its train. It is ultimately not recollection or intellect that causes the mind to ascend but the violent winds of the spirit that sever the mind from its earthly home and lead it upward.

The Spirit and Cosmic Unity

The Spirit and the Temple

In recasting the biblical version of the dedication of the temple (1 Kgs 8), Josephus excluded references to enemies and war, concluding Solomon's prayer, not with the hope that "all the peoples of the earth may know that the LORD is God; there is no other" (1 Kgs 8:60), but with the hope that all people would realize that the Jews "are not inhumane by nature nor unfriendly to those who are not of our country, but wish that all people equally should receive aid from Thee and enjoy Thy blessings" (*Ant.* 8.117).

These exegetical movements reflect Josephus's unwillingness to embrace a milieu in which the Jews were subject to unfounded libels. His *Contra Apionem*, written slightly later than the *Antiquities*, evinces Josephus's dedication to dispelling the libel of Jewish misanthropy. He proffered a brief account of the Jewish constitution—theocracy—to demonstrate that the Jewish law code is intended "to promote piety, friendly relations with each other, and humanity towards the world at large, besides justice, hardihood, and contempt of death" (*Ag. Ap.* 2.145). The final categories of his survey of Jewish laws encompass "the equitable treatment of aliens" (2.209) and "the duty of sharing," which consists of demonstrating "consideration even to declared enemies" (2.211). Josephus's penchant for promoting the philanthropic nature of the Jews suggests what a difficulty he confronted when he was compelled to interpret in a milieu defined in part by anti-Jewish sentiment the biblical version of Solomon's dedication of the temple, in which the chosenness of Israel, the centrality of the temple, and the conviction that "the LORD is God; there is no other" feature so prominently.

Libels current in this milieu explain as well why Josephus garnished his version of the dedication of the temple with Stoic vocabulary. The introduction of Stoic epistemology (the conceptions of impression and opinion) served to undermine the priests' false "opinion" that God would permanently dwell in the temple. Stoic theology replaced the biblical emphasis on God's unique relation to Israel; God is said instead to move "through all of" creation. The introduction of Stoic cosmology mitigated Jewish exclusivism, for nothing was capable of expressing cosmic unity better than the Stoic conception of πνεῦμα, the cohesive element of cosmic συμπαθεία. A request for a portion of the spirit was fulfilled when fire leaped from air, when the two constituent components of πνεῦμα, understood from a Stoic perspective, appeared.

Josephus's recasting of 1 Kgs 8, then, is the product both of Josephus's resistance to a milieu of malignancy toward the Jews and of the predominance of Stoicism in his era. With shrewd deftness, he transformed 1 Kgs 8 very nearly into a Stoic tract in order to refute his opponents' libels on their own grounds.

The Spirit and the Sage

If Pseudo-Philo capably transformed the prophetic inspiration of Balaam into impending death by means of allusions to Gen 6:3—"My spirit shall not abide forever among human beings, because they are flesh"—Philo ably transformed Gen 6:3 from a statement about life and death into sapiential inspiration. Although their commonplace exegetical movements were largely the same—interpreting one biblical text by means of another—the results were entirely different.

Philo interpreted Gen 6:3 in relation to Exod 31:3 to include the spirit as one of four elements that expressed the skill of Bezalel: πνεῦμα θεῖον, wisdom, understanding, and knowledge (*Gig.* 23). From Exod 31:3, Philo turned to another biblical text, Num 11:17, "I will take of the spirit that is on thee and lay it upon the seventy elders," stripped however of its emphasis upon prophesying. Together, Exod 31:3 and Num 11:17 led Philo to a detailed description of the nature of the spirit of Gen 6:3 understood as an endowment that does not remain permanently with humankind:

> But as it is, the spirit which is on him is the wise, the divine, the excellent spirit, susceptible of neither severance nor division, diffused in its fullness everywhere and through all things, the spirit which helps, but suffers no hurt, which though it be shared with others or added to others suffers no diminution in understanding and knowledge and wisdom. (*Gig.* 27)

This definition of the spirit is more than the product of a loose application of *gezerah shawah*. In Philo's version, for example, the divine spirit does *not fill Bezalel alone but the entire cosmos*. This definition comprises nothing less than an explosion of Stoic vocabulary culled from Philo's Greco-Roman milieu.

This exegetical expansion represents an Alexandrian wisdom tradition in which the author of the Wisdom of Solomon could also be included, for he wrote similarly, "Because the spirit of the Lord has filled the world" (1:7). Cicero's Balbus, in *Nat. d.* 2.19, claimed similarly that the world order is "maintained in unison by a single divine and all-pervading spirit." Alexander of Aphrodisias summarized the perspective of Chrysippus similarly: "He assumes that the whole material world is unified by a spirit [πνεῦμα] which wholly pervades it [διήκοτος] and by which the universe is made coherent and kept together and is made intercommunicating [συμπαθές]" (*Mixt.* 216.14–17).

While this definition indicates how wholeheartedly Philo presumably was willing to embrace Stoicism, it also demonstrates the point at which that embrace ended. The context into which Philo set this stoicized definition of the spirit is intended primarily to inculcate one lesson: the spirit is an ephemeral supplement, which, for most people, infrequently inspires insight. The spirit is not what each human possesses from birth to death. The divine spirit that engenders wisdom such as Bezalel's is not the human soul, which Epictetus described as "parts and portions of God's being" (1.14.6), and Cicero, quoting Chrysippus, as "a small fragment of that which is perfect" (*Nat. d.* 2.37). In contrast to the perspective of Stoicism, according to which the human soul is inherently inspired by virtue of its character as πνεῦμα, Philo contended that the cosmic πνεῦμα is a supplement that temporarily imparts wisdom when it comes upon human beings. For all people, with the exception of Moses, wisdom is not the permanent character of human life but a temporary experience induced by the infrequent presence of the divine spirit.

Therefore, one does not live, with Seneca, "in accordance with his own nature" (*Ep.* 41.9) but in expectation of fleeting moments of sapiential inspiration. This indeed is the lesson of Gen 6:3: "And so though the divine spirit may stay awhile in the soul it cannot abide there, as we have said" (*Gig.* 28). Even Moses, who alone exhibited a permanent endowment of wisdom, did not do so because of his own soul, purified though it was. Philo extrapolated once again from Gen 6:3 that Moses "has ever the divine spirit at his side, taking the lead in every journey of righteousness, but from those others, as I have said, it quickly separates itself, from those to whose span of life he has also set a term of a hundred and twenty years" (*Gig.* 55). It was not Moses's spirit but the spirit at his side that led him in his journey as leader of all.

The Spirit and Angelic Presence

In the literary corpora of Josephus and Philo we have discerned as well interpretations of the spirit as an angelic being. In a variety of contexts, and through a variety of exegetical movements, the spirit was portrayed as an angelic being that could quench mental control and enhance intellectual insight. Although both effects of the angelic spirit are discernible in the biblical and Platonic milieux of Philo and Josephus, the particular combination of angelic presence with either loss of mental control or the enhancement of the mind could be pinpointed to two dialogues of a single first-century popularizer, Plutarch.

An Invading Angel

Philo confronted an exegetical conundrum in the character of Balaam, whom he consistently portrayed as the worst of wizards in contrast with true prophets (e.g., *Mut.* 202; *Deus* 181; *Conf.* 66, 159; *Migr.* 113; *Cher.* 32). Balaam hardly exemplified Philo's conviction that inspiration is contingent upon the possession of wisdom, justice, and goodness (*Her.* 259). Though Josephus's antipathy toward Balaam is less obvious, the preservation of one reference to the spirit, and the addition of two others, despite his tendency to omit such references elsewhere, suggests that for Josephus, as well, this was a story worth including, but certainly not in its biblical form.

Both Philo and Josephus undertook exegetical movements intended to identify the "angel" of Num 22:35 with the "spirit" of Num 24:2 (or 23:7 LXX). Philo did so by relating the prediction of the *angel*, that it would "prompt the needful words without your mind's consent" (*Mos.* 1.274), with its fulfillment by the *prophetic spirit*, which "fell upon him" and "banished utterly from his soul his art of wizardry" (1.277). Josephus's identification occurs at the outset of the story, at the angel's debut. When "an *angel of God* confronted" Balaam, the ass turned aside, "conscious of the *divine spirit* approaching her" (*Ant.* 4.108).

These exegetical movements (and I recall here only the most unconcealed) are complemented by others, in which Balaam's experience was made to consist of the loss of mental control. Philo's angel predicted: "I shall prompt the needful words without your mind's consent, and direct your organs of speech as justice and convenience require. I shall guide the reins of speech, and, though you understand it not, employ your tongue for each prophetic utterance" (*Mos.* 1.274). As a result, Balaam "became possessed, and there fell upon him the truly prophetic spirit which banished utterly from his soul his art of wizardry ... Then he returned, and ... spake these oracles as one repeating the words which another had put into his mouth (*Mos.* 1.277). Balaam's experience prior to his second oracle was similar: "He was suddenly possessed, and, understanding nothing, his reason as it were roaming, uttered these prophetic words which were put into his mouth" (1.283).

Josephus's interpretation is analogous, though he followed his own historiographical techniques by introducing it in Balaam's speech and a narrative aside. Josephus's summary of Balaam's first oracle clarifies the nature of Balaam's inspiration: "Such was the inspired utterance of one who was no longer his own master but was overruled by the divine spirit to deliver it" (*Ant.* 4.118). Balaam's speech contains the profession: "that spirit gives utterance to such language and words as it will, whereof we are all unconscious" (4.119) and "nothing within us, once He [τὸ θεῖον] has gained prior entry, is any more our own" (4.121).

Although they expressed their concurrence through sharply different exegetical movements, Philo and Josephus wrote in unison on the angelic nature of the inspiring spirit and the process by which this spirit caused Balaam to lose control of his own mental faculties. These two elements of their shared interpretation find ample precedent in a milieu comprised of biblical, Platonic, and Greco-Roman interpretations of inspiration.

Israelite literature supplied narratives in which the spirit may have been construed as an angel, such as the story of Saul. Less in evidence, though not altogether missing, are texts expressing the conviction that prophetic inspiration was believed to be the product of the loss of mental control. Never, however, are these two interpretative strands combined in Israelite literature, with perhaps the exception of the story of Saul, although notably absent from that narrative is oracular speech, an integral element of Philo's and Josephus's versions of Balaam.

During the Greco-Roman era, the translators of the Septuagint preserved those texts and included some others in which רוח is portrayed as an angel (good or evil). This translation provides evidence that the identification of the divine spirit as an angel persisted into the Greco-Roman era, although this identification did not give rise to the association of an angelic spirit with oracular speech in such a way as to explain the interpretations of Philo and Josephus any more than its Hebrew *Vorlage* could.

Plato, whom Josephus and Philo cited, discussed both elements. Socrates confirmed that "the greatest of blessings come to us through madness, when it is sent as a gift of the gods" (*Phaedr.* 244A) and that a poet writes only when "he has been inspired and put out of his senses, and his mind is no longer in him" (*Ion* 534B). Diotima, one of Socrates's companions in the *Symposium*, supplied the complementary strand by presenting angels as mediating beings, "interpreting and transporting human things to the gods and divine things to people; entreaties and sacrifices from below, and ordinances and requitals from above: being midway between" (202E). But these are separate discussions, independent of one another.

That combination—the details and particulars that serve to explain the exegetical movements of Philo and Josephus—could be pinpointed to *De defectu oraculorum*, a treatise on Delphic inspiration written by Josephus's contemporary, Plutarch. One of the interlocutors, Cleombrotus, suggested:

> Let this statement be ventured for us, following the lead of many others before us, that coincidently with the total defection of the guardian spirits assigned to the oracles and prophetic shrines,

occurs the defection of the oracles themselves; and when the spirits flee or go to another place, the oracles themselves lose their power. (418C–D)

Daemonic beings are here responsible for oracular activity at Delphi. In the interpretations of Cleombrotus, Philo, and Josephus, then, inspiration transpires at the approach of an angelic or daemonic spirit.

Furthermore, the processes of inspiration are similar, involving full surrender to the approaching presence. Cleombrotus expressed the passivity of the prophet by employing the simile of the musical instrument. Similarly, Philo and Josephus portrayed Balaam as a passive instrument whose vocal chords were instruments for the words of the divine spirit. The process is similar to ventriloquism, an interpretation of prophecy that Lamprias, Cleombrotus's companion in *De defectu oraculorum*, maligned (431B).

The discussion of Delphic inspiration in *De defectu oraculorum*, therefore, contains the essential elements that serve to explain the particular exegetical movements Philo and Josephus undertook in their interpretations of Balaam's inspiration. To trace this interpretation of the invasive inspiration of Balaam to a first-century Greco-Roman treatise is *not* to suggest that Philo and Josephus were impervious to the influence of other literary sources. On the contrary, Philo's and Josephus's milieux contained the elements that would coalesce in Cleombrotus's explanation of why Delphic activity had decreased. Biblical and Platonic texts supplied what Hengel called "the relevant spiritual milieu."[1] But the "details" and "particulars" could be located more accurately in a single, summary treatise of the first-century Greco-Roman popularizer, Plutarch, which he devoted to the nature of Delphic inspiration.

A Customary Friend

In an analogous study of Josephus's presentation of Daniel, Philo's discussions of Moses and Joseph, and some of Philo's autobiographical reflections on his own allegorical exegesis, a variety of exegetical movements converged to suggest the emergence of a common understanding of the spirit as an angelic presence that leads the mind intact to the truth. For Josephus, these exegetical movements were largely negative, indications of his unease with the biblical version of Daniel. His substitution of the verb "accompany" for the biblical contention that the spirit dwelt within Daniel (*Ant.* 10.239;

---

1. Hengel, *Judaism and Hellenism*, 1:217.

Dan 5:11, 12, 14) suggests uneasiness with the notion that the spirit indwelt Daniel. His addition of the participle πεπιστευμένος (was believed) evinces a reluctance once again to affirm the divine presence within Daniel (Dan 6:4): "And so Daniel, being held in such great honour and such dazzling favour by Darius and being the only one associated with him in all matters because he was believed to have the divine spirit [τὸ θεῖον] in him, became a prey to envy" (*Ant.* 10.250). Such exegetical movements reveal an interpretation of the spirit as an accompanying presence that inspires the sage "to discover things which were not within the understanding of others" (10.239).

Philo's depiction of Moses's inspiration by the angelic spirit was far more complex and protracted because it represents the convergence of two streams in his depiction of Moses's peculiar experience of inspiration. This convergence is encapsulated in Philo's confusing introductory definition of the third sort of oracles, which "are spoken by Moses in his own person, when possessed by God and carried away out of himself" (*Mos.* 2.188). This description of Moses contains two incongruous parts. One is Moses's speaking in his own person; the other is Moses's being carried out of himself by inspired possession.

The second part of this definition, which consists of Moses's being carried away, Philo illustrated several times by replacing the biblical word "[Moses] said" with vivid descriptions of prophetic possession. For example, in his paraphrase of Exod 14:13-14, in which Moses "said [εἶπεν] to the people" that they should be courageous and watch God's salvation at the Red Sea, Philo wrote: "The prophet . . . was taken out of himself by divine possession and uttered these inspired words" (*Mos.* 2.250). The phrase οὐκέτ' ὢν ἐν ἑαυτῷ, which constitutes according to Philo the sine qua non of inspiration, unites Moses with the race of prophets, whose experience in turn mirrors Platonic perceptions of prophetic inspiration.

The first part of this definition, according to which Moses spoke in his own person, suggests a very different form of inspiration, the nature of which is encapsulated in *Mos.* 2.264-65, where Philo interpreted Moses's prediction of the Sabbath: "Moses, when he heard of this and also actually saw it, was awestruck and, guided by what was not so much surmise as God-sent inspiration, made announcement of the sabbath. I need hardly say that conjectures of this kind are closely akin to prophecies. For the mind could not have made so straight an aim if there was not also the divine spirit guiding it to the truth itself." We observed that the two words εἰκασία and ποδηγετέω Philo employed elsewhere in association with the conscious processes of the human mind.

According to the presentation of inspiration in *Mos.* 2.264-65, Moses received God's own knowledge: "God has given to him of his own power of foreknowledge and by this he will reveal future events" (2.190). This clarifies the meaning of Philo's contention that Moses spoke "in his own person." Despite the pervasive vocabulary of inspiration in *Mos.* 2.191–92, Moses was not—like Balaam and the race of prophets—a mindless channel of divine oracles but a unique prophet who possessed God's own foreknowledge with mind intact.

One counterpart to this fascinating description of Moses's inspiration is Philo's much simpler explanation of Joseph's ability to interpret dreams, in which Philo drew a parallel between the spirit of God and "the promptings of the divine voice" (*Ios.* 110, 116). The presence of a mind intact is evident in the subsequent remark of Pharaoh, in which he acknowledged Joseph to be a "man of prudence and sense" (117).

This identification of spirit and voice characterizes as well Philo's autobiographical reflections on allegorical interpretation in *Somn.* 2.252: "I hear once more the voice of the invisible spirit, the familiar secret tenant, saying, 'Friend, it would seem that there is a matter great and precious of which thou knowest nothing, and this I will ungrudgingly shew thee, for many other well-timed lessons have I given thee.'" References in this reflection to teaching and to the human mind suggest a mode of interpretation in which the mind remains intact. In this respect, Moses's prophetic abilities, Joseph's divinatory abilities, and Philo's interpretative abilities parallel one another.

All of these exegetical movements converge in their attribution of various forms of insight to a mind guided by the spirit. In each case, a mind intact and open is prompted or directed to see things otherwise unknowable. Not ecstasy, therefore, but heightened intellectual insight was the means by which Moses and interpreters were believed to approach the truth.

Once again, the relevant spiritual milieu of these interpretations was extensive. The spirit was associated in Israelite and early Jewish literature with many of Israel's leading figures, in such a way that there is little indication of a loss of mental control. Joseph, Bezalel, Enoch, Jacob, Rebekkah, et al. attained foreknowledge, skill, and insight through their reception of the spirit. The Israelite leader par excellence, the messianic servant, was also believed to possess wisdom by virtue of the spirit, according to sources as early as Isaiah in the eighth century BCE and as late as the Psalms of Solomon and Testaments of the Twelve Patriarchs in the first century BCE or CE. Moreover, the impetus toward relating inspiration by the spirit to the interpretation of written texts arose in the postexilic period in Neh 9 and continued well into the Greco-Roman era among such segments of Judaism as the Qumran sectaries, extending even to the end of the first century or beginning of the second century CE in 4 Ezra 14. Philo and Josephus, then, lived in a Jewish milieu suited to understanding the working of the spirit as guidance of the engaged mind.

The particulars and details, however, that shaped Philo's descriptions of Moses, Joseph, and himself as interpreter (and perhaps Josephus's interpretation of Daniel, though this is evident more by negation and therefore more elusively) could not be explained entirely by these elements of their milieu. For this level of detail, two discussions of Socrates's *daemonion* in Plutarch's dialogue, *De genio Socratis*, prove invaluable. Socrates's inspiration could be attributed to daemons—which Philo identified with angels—who communicated with "unuttered words . . . voiceless contact with his intelligence by their sense alone" (*Gen. Socr.* 588D-E). Simmias explains: "The messages of daemons pass through all other people, but find an echo in those only whose character is untroubled and soul unruffled, the very people in fact we call holy and daemonic" (589D). When Philo referred to the "customary secret tenant" who taught him the allegorical meaning of the biblical text, when he described the spirit as that which guided Moses's mind to the truth, when he identified the voice Joseph heard with the divine spirit, he adopted a mode of inspiration no less esteemed than Delphic inspiration because it was associated in Greco-Roman circles with the auspicious figure of Socrates.

This interpretation, though not exploited to the same extent, was familiar as well to Josephus, who referred explicitly to the daemon of Socrates in a discussion of the Athenians' unwillingness to tolerate anything about the gods contrary to their laws: "On what other ground was Socrates put to death? He never sought to betray his city to the enemy, he robbed no temple. No; because he used to swear strange oaths and give out . . . that he received communications from a certain daemon, he was therefore condemned to die by drinking hemlock" (*Ag. Ap.* 2.263-64). With the indefinite pronoun τι, Josephus indicated that he understood the word δαιμόνιον to refer to a specific daemonic being.

Summary

This retrospect has provided a modest glimpse of the creativity and diversity that characterized interpretations of the spirit in the first century CE. That diversity was garnered during the first century from a variety of sources. Consequently, the ensuing highlights cannot be neatly distinguished from one another, and several may characterize a single first-century biblical interpretation.

- Interpretations could arise from the juxtaposition of one biblical text with a related text, e.g., Pseudo-Philo's depictions of military might (LAB 27, 36); Philo's interpretation of Gen 6:3 in light of Exod 31 and Num 11.

- Interpretations could reflect an Israelite and early Jewish milieu that encompassed several prior centuries, e.g., the angelic spirit and 1 Sam 10, 19; the association of the spirit and wisdom; the attribution of inspired interpretation to the spirit (from Neh 9 to 4 Ezra 14).

- Interpretations could equally reflect a milieu that encompassed several prior centuries of Greek and Greco-Roman thought, e.g., Stoic conceptions in Josephus's version of 1 Kgs 8 and Philo's interpretation of Gen 6:3 (*Gig.* 23–27); Philo's depiction of Abraham and discussions of the ideal ruler, from Plato to Dio Chrysostom.

- Interpretations could arise primarily as a response to other conceptions and interpretations, e.g., Philo's attribution of the mind's ascent to the spirit (*Plant.* 18–24) in a context otherwise rife with Platonic vocabulary and conceptions.

- Interpretations could reflect particular *Jewish* conceptions during the Greco-Roman era, e.g., Pseudo-Philo's depiction of the human spirit as the holy spirit and the "holy spirit" in the Damascus Document (LAB 18); Philo's interpretation of Gen 6:3 and the cosmic (*Stoic*) spirit of the Alexandrian wisdom tradition (*Gig.* 23–27).

- Interpretations could be traced to particular *non-Jewish* conceptions of the Greco-Roman era, e.g., Pseudo-Philo's portrayals of prophetic inspiration and popular depictions of prophetic inspiration in Cicero's *De divinatione* and Plutarch's *De defectu oraculorum*; Philo's and Josephus's interpretations of the spirit in Balaam's inspiration and the explanation of Delphic inspiration in Plutarch's *De defectu oraculorum* as the work of daemonic beings or as ventriloquism; Philo's interpretations of Moses's inspiration, and his own, and discussions of Socrates's *daemonion* in Plutarch's *De genio Socratis*.

PROSPECT

Because Timarchus's vision in the crypt of Trophonius "more resembles a myth or fiction than an argument," demurred Simmias, "I had better perhaps leave [it] untold" (*Gen. Socr.* 589F). With Simmias, I am hesitant to stray from the parameters and method to which I have adhered in this study. One rationale for my reservation is the apprehension that these implications, because they are relevant in varying degrees to New Testament studies, will overshadow the detailed analyses of early Judaism which comprise the substance of this book. To isolate these implications from those analyses would be to violate the very fiber of this book, which is an exploration of early Judaism in its own right. Nevertheless, Simmias was not permitted the luxury of reticence. Theocritus responded, "Do no such thing . . . but let us have it; for myths, too, despite the loose manner in which they do so, have a way of reaching the truth." Despite my reservations, then, I have decided to pull up anchor and to drift into a few tributaries in the hope that these implications may "have a way of reaching the truth."

Because this chapter is intended not as a summary but as a glimpse of the implications of this book, it is perhaps judicious to express two caveats about this concluding discussion. First, I shall introduce in this chapter ancient texts that have not been analyzed in this book. These texts are intended to provide additional, sometimes corroborative, data concerning conclusions at which other scholars and I have arrived. I do not proffer novel interpretations of any of these texts. My aim in introducing these is quite simply to clarify and broaden the discussion. Second, I regard these implications as suggestive rather than exhaustive, as catalysts identified to foster further discussion. Much more could be written, both in notes and text, but I have limited each of the three following discussions to provide the foci for what I consider to be desiderata that arise from this study of the spirit in first-century Judaism.

The Spirit and Individual Authors

In the previous retrospect, what became so apparent is that a diversity of portraits of the spirit coexist in the biblical interpretations of these three authors. We noted how a single text, Num 24:2, for instance, could be transformed in fundamentally different ways, either into the life-giving human spirit, by Pseudo-Philo, or into an invading angel, by Philo and Josephus. If we just turn this research slightly, as one might rotate a prism, so as to view each author individually, another important aspect of first-century Jewish conceptions of the spirit will emerge: *it is generally the case that each author is able to embrace multiple conceptions of the spirit that may appear to us to be inconsistent.*

Each of these biblical interpreters preserves an astounding *variety of effects* of the spirit's presence. Those effects of the spirit in the writings of Philo are uncommonly numerous. The divine spirit: inspires an ecstatic experience akin to poetic ecstasy that issues in writing (*Migr.* 34–35); employs prophets as channels akin to musical instruments (*Spec.* 1.65; 4.49; *Her.* 259–66); ousts Balaam's skill in artificial divination and employs his vocal organs as channels (*Mos.* 1.273–84); inspires the philosophical ascent of the mind (*Spec.* 3.1–6; *Plant.* 18–26; *Gig.* 29–31; 53–54); inspires the exegete through instruction directed toward the conscious mind (*Somn.* 2.252; *Cher.* 27–29) and similarly prompts the interpretation of dreams (*Ios.* 110–16); directs Moses's mind to the truth while he is inspired to become a prophet in the strict sense (*Mos.* 2.187–92); and transforms Abraham so that he can become the ideal ruler who displays both inward and outward beauty and who masters rhetorical skill (*Virt.* 217–19). Moreover, the spirit represents knowledge and wisdom; though it permeates the cosmos, it can still be placed temporarily upon the sage (*Gig.* 23–27).

The assortment of the spirit's effects in Josephus's *Antiquities* is impressively expansive as well, particularly since such a breadth of effects can be garnered from relatively few references. The spirit: invades Balaam, ousts his consciousness, and speaks through him (*Ant.* 4.102–130); migrates from Saul to David, causing David to begin prophesying (6.166); either drives Saul to Samuel physically or drives him mad,[2] as it had Balaam (6.222–623); emerges as fire from air, a portion of the unifying Stoic spirit, leaping upon the altar and consuming the sacrifice (8.114, 118); and accompanies rather than indwelling Daniel (10.239, 250).

No less diverse are the effects of the spirit in Pseudo-Philo's Liber antiquitatum biblicarum. These effects are depicted in various ways: reception of a dream (Miriam in 9.10); inflammation of mind and agitation of spirit (Joshua in 20.2–3); transformation into another person to utter a prophecy (Joshua in 20.2–3) or to fight a battle (Gideon in 36.2); the attainment of wisdom and understanding (Joshua in 20.2–3); the ability to predict the death of an enemy (Deborah in 31.9); the capacity to praise the works of God that bring about Israelite victory (Deborah in 32.14); the elevation, loss, and subsequent awakening of the mind, *sensus* (Kenaz in 28.6, 10); and the inability to recollect what was seen or said under inspiration (Kenaz in 28.10 and Saul in 62.2).

---

2. On these alternatives, see Levison, "Josephus' Interpretation," 246–47.

Philo, Josephus, and Pseudo-Philo also allow a dramatic diversity of natures to accrue to the spirit. Philo adapts the nature of the spirit to the exigencies of context. The spirit that ousts Balaam's art of wizardry and squelches his consciousness is an angel (*Mos.* 1.274, 277). It is an angel as well, akin to Socrates's *daemonion*, when it guides the mind of Moses to the truth (*Mos.* 2.264-65), grants Joseph the interpretation of Pharaoh's dream (*Ios.* 110, 116), and leads Philo himself to the allegorical level of biblical interpretation (*Somn.* 2.252; see *Cher.* 27-29). When it raises the philosopher's mind, however, the spirit is a violent metaphorical wind, like a tornado (*Plant.* 23-24; see *Spec.* 3.1-6). As the spirit of wisdom, it is comparable, even identical to, the Stoic spirit, for it is "diffused in its fullness everywhere and through all things" (*Gig.* 27).

Philo exhibits little preference for a single understanding of the spirit's nature. Rather, he ascribes to it whatever nature best fits the contextual cogency of his argument. This assessment is evident in *De gigantibus*. A Stoic interpretation dominates Philo's early discussion of Gen 6:3 (*Gig.* 23-31). At the conclusion of his interpretation of Gen 6:3 (*Gig.* 55), Philo's description of the spirit as remaining ever at Moses's side, guiding him in an ascent to learn the mysteries of God, has far more in common with the angelic spirit that in *Mos.* 2.265 guides Moses's mind to the truth than it does with the spirit of wisdom, defined in Stoic terms at the beginning of his interpretation of Gen 6:3. *De gigantibus*, then, reveals the facility with which Philo interprets a biblical text within a unified discussion in a single treatise to produce disparate conceptions of the nature of the spirit.

Josephus's *Antiquities* exhibits a similar complementarity with respect to the spirit's nature. At its debut, the spirit is identified as the angel that approaches Balaam: "But on the road an angel of God confronted him . . . and the ass . . . conscious of the divine spirit approaching her" (*Ant.* 4.108). In contrast, the spirit makes its appearance at the dedication of the temple as fire from air, that is, as the Stoic spirit that provides cosmic unity. This disjuncture between the portrayals of the spirit as angel and cosmic *pneuma* reveals how overriding Josephus's apologetic aims may become. When Josephus attempts to distance God from the inspiration of a foreign seer of dubious character, he presents the spirit as a mediating angel, like the daemons that inspire oracular utterances at Delphi. When Josephus labors to portray the Jews as philanthropic and humane, rather than misanthropic and exclusive, he adopts Stoic conceptions to present the spirit as the unifying principle of the cosmos. As we observed with respect to Philo, particular contexts, specific arguments, and definite aims inevitably shape the contours of the spirit's nature, resulting in the simultaneous embrace of conceptions that appear inconsistent.

Because the Liber antiquitatum biblicarum may be a Latin translation of a Hebrew *Vorlage* through an intermediate Greek translation, it is difficult to ascertain with precision the nature of the spirit in each case. For instance, does *spiritus sanctus* signify "a holy spirit" or "the holy spirit" in LAB 28.6? This translational obstacle, however, does not obfuscate Pseudo-Philo's apparent willingness to interpret a similar Hebrew expression in different ways. The Hebrew depiction of the inspiration of Balaam and Kenaz (Othniel) was probably similar: "The spirit came upon Balaam/Kenaz." Pseudo-Philo conveys the nature of that spirit in two dramatically different ways. The holy spirit of Balaam is his own spirit, his life breath, which he is about to forfeit. The holy spirit that inspires Kenaz is a divine force compelling him temporarily to ascend in a prophetic vision of the future. These divergent interpretations reveal how freely this Palestinian biblical interpreter contraverts the biblical text in order to enhance the inspiration accorded a key Israelite figure and to undermine the inspiration of a foreign seer who plotted the demise of Israel. The holy spirit is understood, on the one hand, as the human spirit and, on the other, as a divine power.

The writings of first-century biblical interpreters, therefore, exhibit enormous creativity and diversity with respect to the *effects* and the *nature* of the spirit, depending upon their contextual needs. Philo, Josephus, and Pseudo-Philo are not alone among Israelite and early Jewish authors in recording divergent views of the spirit. In so-called Third Isaiah, for example, the "spirit of the LORD" can be set upon a savior figure as an anointing (Isa 61:1; see Isa 11:1–9), or it can be an angelic presence, not unlike the angel of the presence which led the people following the exodus (Isa 63:14; see Exod 23:20–21), depending upon whether the dominant interpretative tradition is the messianic servant or the exodus-wilderness narratives.

A similar scenario is evident in the Community Rule (1QS) 3–4, where two quite different interpretations of the spirit are intertwined. In 1QS 3.13—4.16, the two spirits of truth and deceit are either human spirits set in people or angelic and demonic beings that have their respective entourages of good and bad spirits. Thus one reads that God "created 'man' to rule the world and placed within [or for][3] him two spirits so that he would walk with them until the moment of his visitation: they are the spirits of truth and of deceit" (1QS 3.17b–19). Or, "Until now the spirits of truth and of injustice feud in the human heart and they walk in wisdom or in folly" (1QS 4.23c–24a). These spirits either are at war with one another to control human destiny or coexist at war within the human soul. Toward the conclusion of this section on the two spirits, the imagery changes, so that the spirit

---

3. On this translation, see Charlesworth, "Critical Comparison," 396–97.

is portrayed, possibly under the influence of Ezek 36:25–27, as an agent of purification. What differentiates this text so clearly from the discussion of the two spirits is that the spirit is itself sprinkled on the faithful—an image quite incompatible with the nature of the two spirits, which are conceived either as human dispositions or as angelic beings:

> Meanwhile, God will refine, with his truth, all human deeds, and will purify for himself the human configuration, ripping out all spirit of deceit from the innermost part of his flesh, and cleansing him with the spirit of holiness from every irreverent deed. He will sprinkle over him the spirit of truth like lustral water (in order to cleanse him) from all the abhorrences of deceit and from the defilement of the unclean spirit. (1QS 4.20b–22a)

This interpretation of the spirit of truth or spirit of holiness as a cleansing agent that can be sprinkled on the faithful diverges from the interpretation of the spirit of truth as either an angelic being or human disposition. Yet both are intertwined within the same topical section of the Community Rule.[4]

The patent lesson of this portion of our study is that, *in light of the diversity of conceptions that coexist within the writings of individual first-century authors or within a single ancient document, it is ill-advised to attempt to ascertain for each first-century author one dominant conception of the spirit.* The effect of failing to account for this observation can be illustrated by D. Hill's attempt to legitimate the association Josephus establishes between the priestly and prophetic dimensions. Hill appeals to the spirit's presence at the dedication of the temple: "All this reflects the sacral and cultic associations of prophecy in Israel . . . [the temple] at its dedication, received a portion of the divine spirit . . . which, for Josephus as for the rabbis, was pre-eminently the spirit of prophecy."[5] Hill assumes that the spirit is always the spirit of prophecy, so that a reference to the spirit in a cultic context carries the association with prophecy, despite the absence of a reference to prophecy in that context. Our study has indicated that this attempt to interpret one text in light of others that have in common with it only a reference to the spirit is ill-advised, for these first-century biblical interpreters allow a variety of interpretations to coexist. With respect to *Ant.* 8.114, to which Hill appeals, we have seen already that the spirit is associated here less with prophecy than with cosmic unity and Jewish philanthropy.

Just as it may be inadvisable to assume consistency vis-à-vis the spirit, so *is it inappropriate to assume that a lack of consistency is an indication*

---

4. See also 1QS 3.6b–9b.
5. Hill, *New Testament Prophecy*, 30.

of multiple sources or origins. The importance of this point can again be made by illustration. Studies of the Paraclete in the Fourth Gospel have not without evidence noted the disparity between the spirit in the first thirteen chapters and the Paraclete in the Farewell Discourses. On the basis of these observations, some scholars distinguish the spirit and the Paraclete from one another. H. Windisch's discussion is an instructive example of this approach:

> The fourth evangelist has not left his reader in doubt as to the identity of the (other) Paraclete: it is the Holy Spirit. No matter what one may think about the integrity of the Paraclete sayings, it is certain . . . that the Spirit and the Paraclete are originally two very different figures. The Spirit is, according to his nature, power, an incomprehensible being that suddenly enters into man and imparts to him impulses and insights which lift him above his human existence. The Paraclete is a concrete heavenly person, a kind of angel, and when he appears on earth, it is as an emissary from God, as an angel in human form.[6]

Divergent effects and natures, according to Windisch, indicate different origins.

The validity of Windisch's inference that "the Spirit and the Paraclete are originally two very different figures" is seriously undermined by the realization that first-century authors embraced what may appear to us to be incompatible conceptions of the spirit. Philo's description of philosophical ascent, in which "the mind is rendered buoyant and raised to the utmost height by the native force of the Divine spirit" (*Plant.* 18–24), bears an uncanny resemblance to Windisch's depiction of the holy spirit as "an incomprehensible being that suddenly enters into man and imparts to him impulses and insights which lift him above his human existence." Similarly does Philo's characterization of the spirit as an angelic being, akin to Socrates's *daemonion* in *Mos.* 2.264–65, *Ios.* 110–16, and *Somn.* 2.252, exhibit an extraordinary affinity to Windisch's description of the paraclete as "a concrete heavenly person, a kind of angel." Philo embraces both portraits, not because he conjoins two originally different figures, but because contextual requirements compel him to adopt varying characterizations of the spirit. Is the author of the Fourth Gospel not capable of an analogous embrace of complementarity for contextual reasons?

R. Brown, in response to an approach such as Windisch's, accords a similar value to consistency. By observing of the Fourth Gospel that "the combination of these diverse features into a consistent picture and the

---

6. Windisch, *Spirit-Paraclete in Fourth Gospel*, 20.

reshaping of the concept of the Holy Spirit according to that picture are what have given us the Johannine presentation of the Paraclete,"[7] Brown too espouses the assumption that first-century authors adhered to a consistent conception of the spirit. We have noted, however, that this sort of consistency does not characterize first-century literature about the spirit. Josephus holds to apparently inconsistent conceptions of the spirit both as a cosmic force at the temple dedication and as an angel in the tale of Balaam. Philo allows even more disparate conceptions to coexist; in addition to being construed as angel or hurricane wind, the spirit is also wisdom and cosmic unity. Pseudo-Philo designates Balaam's life-breath and the power that indwells Kenaz—two very different entities—with the same words, "holy spirit." Therefore, Brown's attempt to demonstrate "first of all, that the Johannine picture of the Paraclete is not inconsistent with what is said in the Gospel itself and in other NT books about the Holy Spirit,"[8] though it may provide an essential corrective to theories such as Windisch's, does not acknowledge the writings of other first-century authors who attributed to the spirit an apparently inconsistent collection of natures and an array of assorted effects.

This analysis, therefore, has a twofold implication vis-à-vis diversity. It demonstrates, on the one hand, that consistent conceptions of the spirit cannot be assumed, as does Hill, for an ancient author or document. It demonstrates, on the other hand, that diversity and disparity of conceptions ought not to be construed, as do Windisch and Brown, as indications of differing sources or origins. Disparities can be explained by the exigencies of context and exegetical conundrums; it is superfluous to postulate a variety of origins for authors who seem not only to have tolerated but also to have embraced diversity.

The Spirit and Prophecy

Among the effects of the spirit, prophecy is the most pervasive. According to Philo, Balaam became possessed when "there fell upon him the truly prophetic spirit which banished utterly from his soul his art of wizardry" (*Mos.* 1.277). The experience of this false diviner is characteristic as well of the prophetic race: "This is what regularly befalls the fellowship of the prophets. The mind is evicted at the arrival of the divine Spirit, but when that departs the mind returns to its tenancy" (*Her.* 265; see *Spec.* 1.65; 4.49; *QG* 3.9). Moses, too, cannot be excluded from this prophetic race, for he too

7. Brown, *Gospel According to John*, 1139.
8. Brown, *Gospel According to John*, 1139.

spoke "when possessed by God and carried away out of himself" because he experienced "that divine possession in virtue of which he is chiefly and in the strict sense considered a prophet" (*Mos.* 2.188, 191).

Josephus also closely associates the work of the spirit with prophecy. On some occasions, Josephus adds references to prophecy in contexts that focus upon the effects of the spirit. For example, while 1 Sam 16:13 recounts that "the spirit of the LORD came mightily upon David from that day forward," Josephus relates that David, "when the divine spirit had removed to him, began to prophesy" (*Ant.* 6.166). While Zedekiah, the false prophet, asks Micaiah in 1 Kgs 22:24 LXX, "What sort of spirit of the Lord speaks in you?," Josephus explicitly relates the spirit to prophecy: "But you shall know whether he is really a true prophet and has the power of the divine spirit" (*Ant.* 8.408). Although he reduces the number of references to the spirit in his version of the book of Daniel, he does nonetheless preserve a reference to the spirit *and* emphasize Daniel's place as "one of the greatest prophets" (10.266). On other occasions, Josephus preserves the element of prophecy that is already included in a biblical narrative, such as in the story of Saul's pursuit of David. Saul's soldiers, upon encountering Samuel and the prophets, "were themselves possessed by the spirit of God and began to prophesy." Samuel himself then "caused him [Saul] too to prophesy" (6.222–23). Further, Josephus uncharacteristically adds references to the spirit in his version of the Balaam story. Although he does not designate Balaam a prophet—Balaam was too ambiguous a figure to be included alongside the likes of Daniel—he nonetheless colors Balaam's inspiration with hues drawn from the palette of prophetic inspiration at Delphi. In a variety of ways, then, Josephus underscores the attribution of prophecy to the spirit.

This association between the spirit and prophecy is evident as well in the Liber antiquitatum biblicarum. In extra-biblical additions, the spirit comes upon Miriam to be the recipient of a dream in which the birth of Moses is predicted (9.10), while Deborah is said explicitly to have predicted Sisera's demise by the inspiration of the spirit (31.9). Pseudo-Philo also creates de novo the association of prophecy and the spirit in a biblical text, Judg 3:9–10, in which the spirit is associated only with judging Israel: "And when they had sat down, a holy spirit came upon Kenaz . . . and he began to prophesy" (LAB 28.6). The authenticity of Kenaz's prophetic experience is confirmed by his inability to recollect what he had said or seen—an element of prophetic inspiration in Greco-Roman interpretations of Plato's view of prophetic inspiration (28.10). The attentiveness of Pseudo-Philo is evident, furthermore, in his interpretation of Deut 34:9, where an explicit reference to the spirit of wisdom is thoughtfully supplemented by allusions to 1 Sam 10:6 and Judg 6:34, other biblical texts that refer to the spirit. Pseudo-Philo combines these allusions with other effects upon Joshua—a mind afire and an agitated spirit—which correspond to popular Greco-Roman conceptions of prophetic experiences. Even in a highly abbreviated account of Saul's pursuit of David, Pseudo-Philo preserves the explicit association of prophecy and the spirit: "And (a) spirit abided in Saul, and he prophesied." Confirmation of his experience, like Kenaz's, is evident in his inability "to know what he had prophesied" (LAB 62.2).

Philo, Josephus, and Pseudo-Philo, therefore, espouse the association of prophecy and the spirit in creative and thoughtful ways that both preserve biblical attributions of prophecy to the spirit and create that association even where biblical texts do not. Theirs is not merely a tacit acceptance of an ancient conception; these authors are themselves part of the creative process that develops and deepens the association of the spirit and prophecy.

These first-century interpretations constitute only a portion of the rich patchwork of early Judaism, in which this association of the spirit with prophecy was affirmed. The postexilic author of the book of Nehemiah had already incorporated a prayer in which God is said to have been patient with Israel for many years and to have "warned them by your spirit through the prophets" (9:30). This conviction is echoed by the Qumran sectarians: "This is the study of the law which he commanded through the hand of Moses, in order to act in compliance with all that has been revealed from age to age, and according to what the prophets have revealed through his holy spirit" (1QS 8.15-16). In the book of Jubilees, "a spirit of truth descended upon the mouth" of Rebekkah so that she could bless her children (25:14), and Jacob blessed Levi and Judah when "a spirit of prophecy came down upon his mouth" (31:12). In the Enoch cycle of literature, Enoch commands, "Now, my son Methuselah, (please) summon all your brothers on my behalf, and gather together to me all the sons of your mother; for a voice calls me, and the spirit is poured over me so that I may show you everything that shall happen to you forever" (1 En. 91:1). In a humorous portion of the Testament of Abraham, in which the archangel Michael cannot find the resources to convince Abraham that he will die, God says to Michael: "And I shall send my holy spirit upon his son Isaac, and I shall thrust the mention of his death into Isaac's heart, so that he will see his father's death in a dream" (T. Ab. 4:8).

This association of prophecy and the spirit is evident as well in early rabbinic literature. For example, in Mekilta de-Rabbi Ishmael, tractate Shirata 10.58-73, a discussion transpires concerning where in Torah Miriam is said to have been a prophetess.[9] The biblical text quoted, Exod 2:1–3, contains no such indication: "'There went a man of the house of Levi and took to wife . . . and the woman conceived, and bore a son . . . And when she could no longer hide him,' etc." The editors appeal to two other details to explain her prophetic role. In the first, prior to the quotation of Exod 2:1–3, Miriam predicts explicitly that her father will "beget a son who will arise and save Israel from the hands of the Egyptians." Her prophetic conviction is subsequently confirmed by appeal to the ensuing verse, Exod 2:4: "But she still held on to her prophecy, as it is said: 'And his sister stood afar off, to know what would be done to him.'"

The interpretation of Exod 2:4 becomes particularly significant for ascertaining the association of the spirit and prophecy, for proof of Miriam's prophetic role is based, not upon the discernment of *prophecy* in this verse, but in the discernment of the presence of the *holy spirit* in this verse. Thus proof of the holy spirit constitutes proof of Miriam's prophetic role. The hermeneutical principle employed to demonstrate the presence of the holy spirit in Exod 2:4 is *gezerah shawah*, an argument from analogy drawn from two passages with the same expression. Accordingly, four expressions in Exod 2:4 are related to the same expression in other verses from which the presence of the holy spirit can be inferred. For example, the expression "afar off" in Exod 2:4 is said to suggest the holy spirit's presence because in Jer 31:2 it is said, "From afar the Lord appeared to me."[10] What is significant from the perspective of our study is how unquestionably Miriam's prophecy is demonstrated by appeal, not to prophecy, but to the holy spirit's (i.e., the lord's) presence.[11]

---

9. Miriam has a prophetic dream inspired by the holy spirit in LAB 9.10.

10. Translation mine. Three other expressions from Exod 2:4 are interpreted similarly in Shirata 10.58–73: (1) "Standing" suggests the presence of the holy spirit because in three verses where the verb "to stand" occurs, the Lord is present: "I saw the Lord standing beside the altar" (Amos 9:1); "And the Lord came and stood" (1 Sam 3:10); (The Lord says to Moses,) "Call Joshua and stand" (Deut 31:14). (2) "To know" suggests the presence of the holy spirit because it is said in Isa 11:9, "For the earth shall be full of the knowledge of the Lord" (cf. Hab 2:14). (3) "What would be done" suggests the presence of the holy spirit because in Amos 3:7 it is said, "For the Lord will do nothing, but He revealeth His counsel unto His servants the prophets."

11. A similar application of *gezerah shawah* in the context of an explanation of Exod 12:1 demonstrates once again that the association of prophecy and the spirit could be assumed in some rabbinic interpretation (Lauterbach, *Mekilta de-Rabbi Ishmael*, tractate Pisḥa 1.148–66). The complaint of Jeremiah's scribe, Baruch, in Jer 45:3 is quoted, "I am weary with my groaning and I find no rest." This is taken to mean that Baruch, in contrast to other disciples—Joshua the disciple of Moses and Elisha the disciple of Elijah—has not received the holy spirit. Jeremiah 45:3, of course, does not indicate Baruch's failure to receive the holy spirit at all. But the presence of the holy spirit is inferred from the word "rest" (מנוחה): "'Rest' here means prophecy, as it says, 'And the spirit rested upon them' (Num 11:26), and again, 'the spirit of Elijah rested upon

This collection of early Jewish texts that espouse an association between the spirit and prophecy would seem to support the conclusions of scholars such as G. F. Moore, who writes, "The Holy Spirit is the Spirit of prophecy"[12]; or G. W. H. Lampe, who claims, "In the main, the Spirit continues to be thought of as being, pre-eminently, the Spirit of prophecy"[13]; or D. Hill, who interprets Josephus on the basis of the assumption that the spirit "for Josephus as for the rabbis, was pre-eminently the spirit of prophecy."[14] The study we have undertaken, while confirming these statements, has made crystal clear as well that these statements are accurate only if the qualifying statements, "in the main" and "pre-eminently," be taken seriously. There are many other instances in which the presence of the spirit does not effect an experience of prophecy.

This is no more evident than in *De gigantibus*, where the influence of Stoicism upon Philo's exegesis results in a detailed description that is, although built upon the foundation of an explicit citation of Num 11:17,

---

Elisha' (2 Kgs 2:15), and again, 'And the spirit of the LORD will rest in him' (Isa 11:2)" (*Pisḥa* 1.154–56). In each text, an explicit reference to the spirit is accompanied by an implicit reference to prophecy in the word "rest" (though in Num 11:26, prophesying appears in the immediate context). The interpretative flow of this passage is instructive: (1) Two disciples, Joshua and Elisha, had the spirit. (2) Baruch complains that he does not. (3) Jeremiah 45:3 is quoted as biblical proof of his complaint. (4) "Rest" in Jer 45:3 is interpreted as prophecy—thus what Baruch lacks, at first identified as the spirit, is now identified as prophecy. (5) The principle of *gezerah shawah* is applied, and each analogous text does not contain an explicit reference to prophecy but to the spirit which rested. The flow of this passage, from references to the spirit to prophecy and back to the spirit, reveals the assumption that prophecy and spirit are interchangeable.

In Mekilta de-Rabbi Ishmael, tractate Pisḥa 1.42–76, the question arises concerning prophets with whom God spoke "outside of the land of Palestine" (1.58–59). This is a problem because it has already been established that "before the land of Israel had been especially chosen, all lands were suitable for divine revelations; after the land of Israel had been chosen, all other lands were eliminated" (1.42–44). One explanation of this conundrum is that God spoke to these prophets outside of Israel "only because of the merit of the fathers" (1.60). Another is that God spoke only "at a pure spot, near water" (1.64). Still another is that God had already spoken to these prophets inside the land. Subsequently, God's presence everywhere is acknowledged, as the quotation of Ps 139:7–10a indicates, beginning with "Wither shall I go from Thy spirit" (tractate Pisḥa 1.74–75). Here the presence of the spirit is inferred within a discussion of prophecy. On this passage, see the discussion of Davies, "Reflections on the Spirit."

With respect to the Targumim, Schäfer observes that the expression "spirit of prophecy" occurs consistently in Targum Onkelos, while in Targum Pseudo-Jonathan, the expression "holy spirit" occurs fifteen times and "spirit of prophecy" eleven times ("Termini 'Heiliger Geist'").

12. Cited with approbation by Barrett, *Holy Spirit*, 108–9.
13. Lampe, "Holy Spirit," *IDB* 2:630.
14. Hill, *New Testament Prophecy*, 30.

surprisingly void of any reference to prophecy: "But as it is, the spirit which is on him [Moses] is the wise, the divine, the excellent spirit, susceptible of neither severance nor division, diffused in its fullness everywhere and through all things, the spirit which ... though it be shared ... suffers no diminution in understanding and knowledge and wisdom" (*Gig.* 24-27). Philo's reservation about Platonism, moreover, results in the association of the spirit with the ascent of the philosopher's mind (*Plant.* 18-24). Even the powerful persuasive abilities of Abraham, which could be attributed to a prophetic experience, are presented as a transformation into an ideal king— with vocabulary far more at home in the world of Greco-Roman conceptions of the ideal ruler than in Philo's perceptions of prophetic phenomena (*Virt.* 217-19). Philo's own allegorical interpretation of Scripture is the product of his mind's ascent (*Spec.* 3.1-6), and the customary tenant that teaches him bears a striking resemblance to Socrates's inspiring *daemonion* (*Somn.* 2.252) and thus to the angelic spirit that guides Moses's mind to the truth (*Mos.* 2.265).

Josephus, like Philo, interprets the spirit along the lines of the cosmic spirit of Stoicism in his version of the dedication of the temple (*Ant.* 8.114, 118). This is the only instance in Josephus's writings in which the spirit is unrelated to a prophetic experience.

Liber antiquitatum biblicarum also contains references to the spirit unrelated to prophecy. In a creative reinterpretation of Gen 6:3, God says, "And I will reveal to him [Moses] my Law and statutes and judgments, and I will burn an eternal light for him, because I thought of him in the days of old, saying, 'My spirit will not be a mediator among these people forever, because they are flesh and their days will be 120 years'" (LAB 9.8). Then of course there is the inspiration of Kenaz (27.9-10) and Gideon (36.2) in preparation for military routs. Moreover, Deborah is exhorted to "let the grace of the holy spirit awaken" in her so that she may sing praises to God (LAB 33.14). Deborah's experience of the spirit ought to be distinguished from prophetic experiences because, throughout the Liber antiquitatum biblicarum, prophesying under the influence of the spirit consistently involves prediction rather than praise.

Philo, Josephus, and Pseudo-Philo constitute but a slender thread in a tapestry whose textures encompass far more than prophetic inspiration. Once again, we may illustrate with a pastiche of early Jewish texts how much more widely than prophecy the effects of the spirit were believed by Jews of the Greco-Roman era to extend.

The spirit is associated with creation. The influence of Gen 1:2 is apparent in 2 Bar. 21:4, Baruch's address to God: "you who created the earth, the one who fixed the firmament by the word and fastened the height of heaven by the spirit." God responds to this prayer in 23:5, "For my spirit creates the living." Ezra in 4 Ezra 6:39 similarly recalls the earliest creative activity of God: "And then the Spirit was hovering, and darkness and silence embraced everything; the sound of a human voice was not yet there. Then you commanded that a ray of light be brought forth." In Jdt 16:14, it is Gen 2:7 and 2:22,[15] mediated through Ps 104:29–30, that influences the depiction of the spirit's relation to creation. Judith praises God,

> Let all your creatures serve you,
> for you spoke, and they were made,
> You sent forth your spirit, and it formed them;
> there is none that can resist your voice.

The spirit's function vis-à-vis creation is not only to grant life but also to convict wrongdoers. A representative of the Alexandrian wisdom tradition can contend that the ungodly will be punished "because the spirit of the Lord has filled the world, and that which holds all things together knows what is said" (Wis 1:7). In the words of the sibyl composed by another Egyptian author,

> The earth itself will also drink
>   of the blood of the dying; wild beasts will be sated with flesh.
> God himself, the great eternal one, told me
>   to prophesy all these things. These things will not go unfulfilled.
> Nor is anything left unaccomplished that he so much as puts
>   in mind
> for the spirit of God which knows no falsehood is throughout
>   the world. (Sib. Or. 3.696–701)

In many other early Jewish texts, the spirit is related to human purity and cleansing. Rabbi Nehemiah, in Mekilta de-Rabbi Ishmael, tractate Beshallaḥ 7.134–36, associates obedience with reception of the spirit: "For as a reward for the faith with which Israel believed in God, the Holy Spirit rested upon them. R. Nehemiah says: Whence can you prove that whosoever accepts even one single commandment with true faith is deserving of having the Holy Spirit rest upon him." In the Testaments of the Twelve Patriarchs, Benjamin attributes sexual purity to the spirit: "He has no pollution in his heart, because upon him is resting the spirit of God" (T. Benj. 8:3). The Community Rule evinces the conviction that the spirit is integrally related to purification: "By the spirit of holiness which links him with the truth he is cleansed of all his sins. And by the spirit of uprightness and of humility his sin is atoned" (1QS 3.7b–8a). In the eschatological future, the

---

15. See Levison, "Judith 16:14."

spirit will once again purify the child of light, "cleansing him with the spirit of holiness from every irreverent deed. He will sprinkle over him the spirit of truth like lustral water" (1QS 4.21).

The association of purity with the spirit in the context of community initiation is apparent as well in the Qumran hymns, particularly if H.-W. Kuhn's study of initiatory language in the hymns holds true, according to which certain vocabulary can be understood to indicate drawing near to God through the community, such as in 1QH 14.13-14:

> In your kindness toward humankind
> you have enlarged his share with the spirit of your holiness.
> Thus, you make me approach your intelligence,
> and to the degree that I approach
> my fervour against all those who act wickedly
> and (against) people of guile increases;
> for everyone who approaches you,
> does not defy your orders.

The sixteenth hymn, though fragmentary and obtuse at several points, is particularly rich with such language:

> To be strengthened by the spirit of holiness,
> to adhere to the truth of your covenant,
> to serve you in truth, with a perfect heart ... (16.15)
> You have resolved, in fact, to take pity ...
> to show me favour by the spirit of your compassion
> and by the splendour of your glory ... (16.16-17)
> I know that no-one besides you is just.
> I have appeased your face[16] by the spirit which you have given me,
> to lavish your favour on your servant for [ever,]
> to purify me with your holy spirit,
> to approach your will according to the extent of your kindnesses. (16.19-20)[17]

Far from the shores of the Dead Sea—and with much less vehemence—the spirit was also associated with entrance into a life of faith. In the romantic tale Joseph and Aseneth, Aseneth, daughter of Pentephres (the biblical Potiphar), is converted to Judaism. In this story, Joseph places his hand upon her head and prays,

> And renew her by your spirit,

---

16. The phrase ואחלה פניך is difficult to understand.

17. Kuhn, *Enderwartung*, 117-39. Kuhn discerns initiation language as well in 1QH 12.11-12; 13.19; 14.13.

> and form her anew by your hidden hand,
> and make her alive again by your life,
> and let her eat your bread of life,
> and drink your cup of blessing,
> and number her among your people. (8:9)

Subsequently, Aseneth is led by a heavenly man to a room with a marvelous honeycomb. He says to her, "Happy are you, Aseneth, because the ineffable mysteries of the Most High have been revealed to you, and happy (are) all who attach themselves to the Lord God in repentance, because they will eat from this comb. For this comb is (full of the) spirit of life" (16:14). Finally, at a climactic moment, "Joseph put his arms around her, and Aseneth (put hers) around Joseph, and they kissed each other for a long time and both came to life in their spirit. And Joseph kissed Aseneth and gave her spirit of life, and he kissed her the second time and gave her spirit of wisdom, and he kissed her the third time and gave her spirit of truth" (19:10-11). In this lovely romance, then, as in the poetry of the Qumran sectarians, the spirit purifies and draws people into the sphere of the faithful.

This process of purification takes on a communal character in 1QS 9.3-4: "When these exist in Israel in accordance with these rules in order to establish the spirit of holiness in truth eternal, in order to atone for the fault of the transgression and for the guilt of sin and for the approval for the earth, without the flesh of burnt offerings." Similarly, in Jub. 1:20-21, Moses echoes Ps 51, adapting it to a communal setting, when he intercedes for Israel, "O Lord, let your mercy be lifted up upon your people, and create for them an upright spirit . . . Create a pure heart and a holy spirit for them. And do not let them be ensnared by their sin henceforth and forever." God responds (Jub. 1:22-25) in turn by echoing Ps 51 and Ezek 11:19-20: "And I shall create for them a holy spirit, and I shall purify them so that they will not turn away from following me from that day and forever. And their souls will cleave to me and to all my commandments" (1:23).

Although these references to the spirit in relation to experiences other than prophecy certainly do not exhaust the rich reservoir that characterized early Judaism, they do indicate unequivocally that the identification of the spirit as "the spirit of prophecy" can be made only with the awareness of just how deeply convictions concerning the spirit were enmeshed in other spheres of life, from creation to new creation. This observation ought to engender reservation about the assumption of studies such as R. Menzies's, in which Menzies attempts to reconstruct early Christian pneumatology by attributing one dominant effect of the spirit to primitive Christianity, another to Judaism, and another to Luke: "Whereas the primitive church, following in the footsteps of Jesus, broadened the functions traditionally ascribed to the Spirit in first-century Judaism and thus presented the Spirit as the source of miracle-working power, Luke retained the traditional Jewish understanding of the Spirit as the source of special insight and inspired speech."[18] Many associations of the spirit, such as Pseudo-Philo's with military might, Philo's with the ascent of the philosophical mind, the Qumran sectarians' with purification and initiation, and Judith's with creation, burst the boundary artificially created by granting such a notion as the spirit of prophecy all-encompassing scope.

Another inference to be drawn from our study is that it is unwise to marginalize any particular form of prophecy. D. Hill, for instance, contends, "In Philo's writings we find either an acute hellenisation of the Jewish concept of prophecy, or a hellenistic view of prophecy justified on a biblical basis: whichever view of the matter we take, it must be admitted that it certainly represents a significant departure from what is reflected in other extant Jewish literature of the general period."[19] M. M. B. Turner, following a judicious survey of non-rabbinic Judaism, contends: "In all this there is a predictable, though not massive, shift in emphasis towards the Spirit of prophecy as the source of 'wisdom', whether communicated or infused. We also have quite prominent cases of 'invasive' charismatic speech, though it is notable that the clearest cases (in Philo and Josephus) are heavily marked by the language of divine possession, or of mantic prophetism (cf. Plato, *Phaedrus* 244a–45c; *Ion* 533d–34e), and to that extent cannot safely be regarded as conveying a *typically Jewish* notion of the Spirit of prophecy."[20]

There is little need to rehearse the Greco-Roman elements of Pseudo-Philo's Liber antiquitatum biblicarum, but we ought nonetheless to recall how vividly his descriptions of Joshua's inflamed mind and agitated spirit, Kenaz's ascent, and the inability of Saul and Kenaz to recall what they heard and saw bear the marks of popular Greco-Roman conceptions of prophetic inspiration. If Philo in Alexandrian Egypt and Josephus in Rome are accompanied by Pseudo-Philo in Palestine in the process of assimilating Greco-Roman conceptions of prophecy, then one must question the usefulness of a description such as "typically Jewish" and ask further whether these conceptions of prophecy, which exhibit close affinities with Greco-Roman conceptions of inspiration, ought to be shunted aside as a "significant departure" from putatively typical forms of Judaism. Moreover, Hill's contention concerning Christian prophecy, that "there will be few scholars,

---

18. Menzies, *Early Christian Pneumatology*, 279.
19. Hill, *New Testament Prophecy*, 33.
20. Turner, "Spirit of Prophecy," 85; emphasis original.

if any, who will wish to claim that prophetic phenomena in Greek and Roman religion provide *primary* evidence for the understanding of Christian prophecy,"[21] ought perhaps to be revisited in light of the Greco-Roman elements which permeate, not only diaspora Jewish literature, but also a first-century Palestinian example of rewritten Bible composed in Hebrew.

The Spirit and Charismatic Exegesis

D. Aune traces the expression *charismatic exegesis* to H. L. Ginsberg who, in conversation with W. Brownlee, coined it in the 1950s to describe the sort of biblical interpretation employed in the Habakkuk commentary by the Qumran sectarians.[22] During the next decade, D. Georgi broadened the application of this expression by locating the matrix of such inspired exegesis in the synagogue, where "*the medium of Jewish propaganda was the synagogue worship and the exegesis of the law presented there.*"[23] Travelling Jewish leaders who were not tied to any particular synagogue would undertake this teaching in local synagogues. Such leaders were expected to show tricks, for "public attention was typically aroused by extraordinary, often ecstatic performances."[24] For the clearest window into this arena of Jewish life, Georgi turned to Philo, who according to Georgi identifies prophecy and interpretation: "*Interpreters of the Bible, the exegetes, are therefore for Philo the prophets of the present.* They are capable of setting free the spirit bottled up in the composition of holy scripture . . . Insofar as they themselves did not create the text which is to be interpreted, the source of the spirit, they are subordinated to it. But insofar as the spirit speaks through their exegesis, they are quite equal to the prophets of old. The spirit has not vanished; it has merely modified itself."[25]

While Georgi mined Philo's writings to locate charismatic exegesis in the synagogue, M. Hengel garnered an impressive array of writings[26] as evidence of this phenomenon outside the synagogue, leading to the conclusion that "the Spirit was less effective at that time through direct inspiration. The influence of the Spirit was more frequently felt via the charismatic interpretation of Scripture. The formation of the canon did not necessarily have to result in a cessation of prophecy. On the contrary, only someone who was

---

21. Hill, *New Testament Prophecy*, 9; emphasis original.
22. Aune, "Charismatic Exegesis," 126.
23. Georgi, *Opponents of Paul*, 84; emphasis original. See 181–83n59.
24. Georgi, *Opponents of Paul*, 101.
25. Georgi, *Opponents of Paul*, 111; emphasis original.
26. Hengel, *Zealots*, 235–36.

filled with the Spirit could really adequately interpret the words of Holy Scripture which were inspired by God, but were often very obscure."[27] This phenomenon played a crucial role, according to Josephus's *Jewish War*, in the war against Rome. The ambiguous messianic prophecy to which Josephus refers in *J.W.* 6.312–313, which incited the Jews to rebellion because it predicted the rise of a leader whom Josephus identified with Vespasian, illustrates the need for inspired exegesis: "The underlying scriptural text could not be immediately understood: it had first to be interpreted by the σοφοί. This presupposes a prophetic charism on the part of the interpreter."[28] In the last battle for the temple, observes Hengel, allegedly inspired prophecies and counter-prophecies arose, *each of them biblically based*. Josephus urged trust in God by appealing to the divine rescue from the siege of Sennacherib, while others demanded resistance to Rome by appealing to prophecies such as Zech 12:2–6 and 14:2–5.[29]

In a less known but significant study, H.-P. Müller argued that "die archaische Gestalt einer mantischen Weisheit hat sich in der Apokalyptik fortgesetzt."[30] Müller observed first of all that the word חכם occurs in both the biblical and postbiblical traditions in relation to mantic powers or supernatural knowledge. Thus, the sage receives knowledge through various forms of inspiration. The quintessential sage in this respect is Joseph, who was educated, possessed the spirit of God, and could know even more than the Egyptian diviners.[31] In the Greco-Roman era, observed Müller, Daniel was the quintessential sage who possessed inspired knowledge: "Die Weisheit des Daniel von Kapitel ii, iv und v ist also wirklich rein mantischer Art; anders als Joseph hat er mit der Bildungsweisheit nichts zu tun."[32]

When, a few years later, D. Patte examined this topic, he arrived at a similar assessment of biblical interpretation in apocalyptic circles: "For the Jewish Apocalyptic circles the concept of inspiration involved a use of Scripture . . . We can describe this inspiration as the work of the creative imagination of a man permeated with Scripture." This creative imagination "came to a very large extent from Scripture. We should add: from Scripture as read in the writer's milieu, that is, in the Jewish Palestinian milieu of that time. Thus some of the associations which allowed them to tally various biblical texts with it, imposed themselves on the Apocalyptists because of

---

27. Hengel, *Zealots*, 234.
28. Hengel, *Zealots*, 237.
29. Hengel, *Zealots*, 240–44.
30. Müller, "Mantische Weisheit und Apokalyptik," 271.
31. Müller, "Mantische Weisheit und Apokalyptik," 271–75.
32. Müller, "Mantische Weisheit und Apokalyptik," 277; see 275–80.

the way the texts were used in the Synagogal readings, or in other circumstances which lie for the most part, beyond any possible investigation."[33]

Within a decade of Ginsberg's coining of the expression "charismatic exegesis," then, this phenomenon had been located, not only at Qumran, but also in the synagogue, in the Palestinian Jewish populace at large, particularly the Zealots, and in apocalyptic Judaism.

When Aune revisited the topic of charismatic exegesis and the Qumran sectarians, he reflected, "Though there is ample evidence that the Qumran Community believed *that* God revealed the truth to them, there is precious little evidence to suggest *how* they thought that the Spirit revealed truth."[34] This uncertainty about the process of charismatic exegesis mirrors prior analyses. Georgi ultimately did not explain *how* charismatic exegesis transpired when he wrote, "In spite of varied evaluations of pneumatic details, there was a consensus that possession of the spirit was necessary and real, and also that the interpretation of the law was the most important spiritual function."[35] Hengel could not pinpoint *how* Zealot prophecy occurred:

> The Old Testament formed the point of departure for its "prophesying" and was applied in an authoritative and charismatic way to concrete situations in the eschatological present. It is not possible to know from Josephus' works to what extent this prophecy took an ecstatic form. It is, however, possible to assume, on the evidence provided by certain contemporary parallels, that the ecstatic form of prophesying was not completely unknown to the Zealots.[36]

Nor could Patte determine whether the biblical material in apocalyptic literature arose "either in a conscious intellectual effort or unconsciously ... in a psychical experience or in the very process of writing."[37] Therefore, scholars who have attended to the topic of charismatic or inspired exegesis have not adequately determined *how* that inspiration was believed to take place.

In chapter 8 of *The Spirit in First-Century Judaism*, I highlighted several biblical and postbiblical texts that may prove integral to dispelling the uncertainty that surrounds this issue of charismatic exegesis. I acknowledged

---

33. Patte, *Early Jewish Hermeneutic*, 201. He continues, "Thus it is not surprising to find a continuity, as G. Vermes has shown, between the traditional biblical interpretations in classical Judaism and in Apocalyptic literature."
34. Aune, "Charismatic Exegesis," 128.
35. Georgi, *Opponents of Paul*, 112.
36. Hengel, *Zealots*, 244-45.
37. Patte, *Early Jewish Hermeneutic*, 182-83.

that Ezra 9:20, Josephus's *J. W.* 3.351–353, and passages from Qumran, such as 1QH 12.11–13, evince the conviction that knowledge requires inspiration without delineating *how* that inspiration was believed to occur. Other texts, however, do shed indispensable light on the nature of that inspiration.

The explicit conviction of 4 Ezra 14 is that Ezra's mind is inspired in a wakeful state to write ninety-four books. Prior to this inspiration, Ezra is given the promise that the lamp of understanding, *lucernam intellectus*, will remain lit throughout his experience. The process itself begins as he drinks the cup given to him, as his heart pours forth understanding (*intellectum*), and as wisdom (*sapientia*) increases within him. Following his experience, it is said that these ninety-four books contain "the spring of understanding [*intellectus*], the fountain of wisdom [*sapientiae*], and the river of knowledge [*scientiae*]" (14:47). The impression that Ezra is inspired without the onset of ecstasy is confirmed by the significant detail that Ezra's understanding and wisdom overflowed *because* (*nam*) his own spirit retained its memory (*nam spiritus meus conservabat memoriam*). This assertion that Ezra retains his memory distinguishes Ezra's experience from those ecstatic prophets who cannot recall what they said (according to Pseudo-Philo [LAB 28.10; 62.2], Aelius Aristides, Pseudo-Justinus, John Cassian, and the author of the late prologue to the Sibylline Oracles). From start to finish, then, Ezra composes ninety-four books by means of a form of inspiration that magnifies his scribal abilities.

We wrested further insight from Philo's autobiographical reflections on his role as allegorical interpreter. Several of those details ought now to be recalled. First, in *Spec.* 3.1–2 and 3.5–6, Philo draws an evocative correspondence between the ascent of his mind under possession of the spirit and his ability to interpret Torah allegorically. These correspondences between the ascents of Philo or Moses and Philo's ability to interpret Torah suggest that Philo regards inspired exegesis as a process in which the mind awake is inspired by the spirit.

Second, in *Somn.* 2.252, the spirit is the source of the solution to a biblical conundrum. In this autobiographical reflection, Philo lets the reader know that the immediate task is to solve an exegetical dilemma, such as why the biblical text refers to two, rather than to one, Cherubim; that the spirit teaches (ἀναδιδάσκειν) him; and that this teaching is directed toward his mind (διάνοια). *De somniis* 2.252, moreover, can be related to similar descriptions of experiences in which Philo's mind is inspired while he appears to be conscious, including *Cher.* 27–29, *Somn.* 1.164–65, and *Fug.* 53–58.

Third, the ways in which Philo depicts the spirit's guidance of Moses's mind in *Mos.* 2.264–65 and his own mind in *Somn.* 2.252 reflect a similar experience in which mental faculties are illuminated rather than obviated. The resemblance of these descriptions to discussions of Socrates's *daemonion* in *De genio Socratis*, moreover, substantiates the conviction that inspiration entails intellectual illumination. The guidance of Moses's mind to the truth and the instruction of Philo's mind by the spirit correspond to the first-century CE Greco-Roman conviction that inspiration, in the case of extraordinary people such as Socrates, transpires when "the messages of daemons pass through all other people, but find an echo in those only whose character is untroubled and soul unruffled, the very people in fact we call holy and daemonic" (*Gen. Socr.* 589D). This exposé of Socrates's inspiration contains conceptions that correspond to Philo's reflections in *Somn.* 2.252. First, Philo employs the adjective "customary" of the spirit, and Socrates's *daemonion* was frequently designated similarly as "customary." Second, Plutarch's Simmias contends that daemonic language can be heard only by those whose souls are untroubled and unruffled, and Philo calls his own mind untroubled. Third, the image of an echo, ὑπηχεῖ δέ μοι, is similar to Plutarch's explanation of how the language of daemons is communicated: the "messages of daemons pass through all other people, but find an echo [ἐνηχοῦσι] in those only whose character is untroubled and soul unruffled." There are, then, striking similarities between the form of inspiration that was associated with Socrates and experienced by Philo. This sort of inspiration demands the most alert and attuned of minds. In contrast, according to Plutarch's Simmias, "In popular belief, on the other hand, it is only in sleep that people receive inspiration from on high; and the notion that they are so influenced when awake and in full possession of their faculties is accounted strange and incredible" (*Gen. Socr.* 589D).

Therefore, a mode of inspired writing and exegesis to which intellectual faculties are requisite characterizes 4 Ezra 14 and the writings of Philo Judaeus. Alongside these, we ought to include as well Ben Sira, who gives no credence to those who allegedly attain knowledge through divination, omens, and dreams (Sir 34:5); instead, he praises the person who learns inductively through travel and study (34:9; 39:4). It would be unlikely, then, for him to claim for a sage a mode of inspiration by the "spirit of understanding" that obviates intellectual faculties. Not by means of ecstasy does Ben Sira "pour forth words of wisdom of his own," but by means of mediation and learning (Sir 39:6–8a).

These piquant observations from antiquity concerning the necessity of inspiration for the process of interpretation provide an apt conclusion to this study. It is not merely conceptions of the spirit within ancient writings that are riveting, with all of their fascinating permutations and contextual transformations. Equally compelling, and of no less significance, are perceptions and reminiscences concerning the process by which the spirit was believed to lead to a more adequate comprehension of those ancient writings. For, with Philo, many of us yearn to peer into the sacred texts of antiquity.[38]

---

38. Philo, *Spec.* 3.6.

Bibliography

Amir, Yehoshua. "Authority and Interpretation of Scripture in the Writings of Philo." In *Mikra: Text, Translation, Reading and Interpretation of the Hebrew Bible in Ancient Judaism and Early Christianity*, edited by Martin J. Mulder, 421–53. CRINT 2.1. Philadelphia: Fortress, 1988.

Arnim, Hans von. *Plutarch über Dämonen und Mantik*. Verhandelingen der Koninklijke Akademie van Wetenschappen 22. Amsterdam: Müller, 1921.

Aune, David E. "Charismatic Exegesis in Early Judaism and Early Christianity." In *The Pseudepigrapha and Early Biblical Interpretation*, edited by James H. Charlesworth and Craig A. Evans, 126–50. JSPSup 14. SSEJC 2. Sheffield: JSOT Press, 1993.

———. *Prophecy in Early Christianity and the Ancient Mediterranean World*. 1983. Reprint, Eugene, OR: Wipf & Stock, 2003.

Barrett, C. K. *The Holy Spirit and the Gospel Tradition*. 1947. Reprint, Eugene, OR: Wipf & Stock, 2011.

Barton, John. *Oracles of God: Perceptions of Ancient Prophecy in Israel after the Exile*. New York: Oxford University Press, 1986.

Baskin, Judith Reesa. "Reflections of Attitudes towards the Gentiles in Jewish and Christian Exegesis of Jethro, Balaam and Job." PhD diss., Yale University, 1976.

Berchman, Robert M. "Arcana Mundi: Magic and Divination in the *De Somniis* of Philo of Alexandria." In *Society of Biblical Literature 1987 Seminar Papers*, edited by Kent Harold Richards, 403–28. SBLSPS 26. Atlanta: Scholars, 1987.

———. "Arcana Mundi: Prophecy and Divination in the *Vita Mosis* of Philo of Alexandria." In *Society of Biblical Literature 1988 Seminar Papers*, edited by David J. Lull, 385–423. SBLSPS 27. Atlanta: Scholars, 1988.

Best, Ernest. "The Use and Non-Use of Pneuma by Josephus." *NovT* 3 (1959) 218–25.

Betz, Otto. "Die Bileamtradition und die biblische Lehre von der Inspiration." In *Religion im Erbe Ägyptens: Beiträge zur spätantiken Religionsgeschichte zu Ehren Alexander Böhlig*, edited by Manfred Görg, 18–53. Wiesbaden: Harrassowitz, 1988.

———. *Offenbarung und Schriftforschung in der Qumransekte*. WUNT 6. Tübingen: Mohr Siebeck, 1960.

Bockmuehl, Marcus N. A. *Revelation and Mystery: Ancient Judaism and Pauline Christianity*. WUNT 36. Tübingen: Mohr Siebeck, 1990.

Borgen, Peder. "Heavenly Ascent in Philo: An Examination of Selected Passages." In *The Pseudepigrapha and Early Biblical Interpretation*, edited by James H. Charlesworth and Craig A. Evans, 246–68. JSPSup 14. SSEJC 2. Sheffield: JSOT Press, 1993.

Bouché-Leclercq, Auguste. *Histoire de la divination dans l'antiquité*. 4 vols. 1879. Reprint, Aalen: Scientia, 1978.

Bousset, William. "Die Himmelsreise der Seele." *AR* 4 (1901) 136–69, 229–73.

Boyce, Mary. "Persian Religion in the Achaemenid Age." In *The Cambridge History of Judaism*, edited by W. D. Davies and Louis Finkelstein, 1:279–307. Cambridge: Cambridge University Press, 1984.

———. "Zoroaster, Zoroastrianism." In *ABD* 6:1168–74.

Boyce, Mary, and Frantz Grenet, with a contribution by Roger Beck. *Zoroastrianism under Macedonian and Roman Rule*. Vol. 3 of *A History of Zoroastrianism*. Handbuch der Orientalistik I.1.2.2. Leiden: Brill, 1991.

Brown, Raymond E. *The Gospel According to John*. AB 29A. Garden City, NY: Doubleday, 1970.

Büchsel, Friedrich. *Der Geist Gottes im Neuen Testament*. Gütersloh: Bertelsmann, 1926.

Burkhardt, Helmut. *Die Inspiration heiliger Schriften bei Philon von Alexandrien*. Monographien und Studienbücher 340. Gießen: Brunnen, 1988.

Centre d'analyse et de documentation patristiques. *Philo d'Alexandrie*. Biblia Patristica Supplément 5. Paris: Centre national de la recherche scientifique, 1982.

Charlesworth, James H. "A Critical Comparison of the Dualism in 1QS III, 13–IV, 26, and the 'Dualism' Contained in the Fourth Gospel." *NTS* 15 (1969) 389–418.

———, ed. *The Old Testament Pseudepigrapha*. 2 vols. New York: Doubleday, 1983.

Chevallier, Max-Alain. *Ancien Testament, Hellénisme et Judaïsme, la tradition synoptique, l'ouvre de Luc*. Vol. 1 of *Souffle de Dieu: Le saint-esprit dans le Nouveau Testament*. Point théologique 26. Paris: Beauchesne, 1978.

Christiansen, Irmgard. *Die Technik der allegorischen Auslegungswissenschaft bei Philon von Alexandrien*. Beiträge zur Geschichte der biblischen Hermeneutik 7. Tübingen: Mohr Siebeck, 1969.

Cleomedis. *De motu circulari corporum caelestium*. Edited by Hermannus Ziegler. Bibliotheca scriptorum Graecorum et Romanorum Teubneriana 1241. Leipzig: Teubner, 1891.

Collins, John J. "A Throne in the Heavens: Apotheosis in Pre-Christian Judaism." In *Death, Ecstasy, and Other Worldly Journeys*, edited by John J. Collins and Michael Fishbane, 41–56. Albany: State University of New York Press, 1995.

Collins, John J., Pieter G. R. de Villiers, and Adela Yarbro Collins, eds. *Apocalypticism and Mysticism in Ancient Judaism and Early Christianity*. Ekstasis 7. Berlin: de Gruyter, 2018.

Conley, Thomas M. *Philo's Rhetoric: Studies in Style, Composition and Exegesis*. Center for Hermeneutical Studies Monograph 1. Berkeley: Center for Hermeneutical Studies, 1987.

Craven, Toni. *Artistry and Faith in the Book of Judith*. SBLDS 70. Chico, CA: Scholars, 1983.

Danby, Herbert. *The Mishnah*. Oxford: Oxford University Press, 1933.

Davies, W. D. *Paul and Rabbinic Judaism: Some Rabbinic Elements in Pauline Theology*. 4th ed. Philadelphia: Fortress, 1980.

———. "Reflections on the Spirit in the Mekilta: A Suggestion." *Journal of the Ancient Near Eastern Society of Columbia University (Gaster Festschrift)* 5 (1973) 95–105.

Dean-Otting, Miriam. *Heavenly Journeys: A Study of the Motif in Hellenistic Jewish Literature.* Judentum und Umwelt 8. Frankfurt: Lang, 1984.
Des Places, Édouard. *Jamblique: Les mystères d'Égypte.* Paris: Belles Lettres, 1966.
Dietzfelbinger, Christian. *Pseudo-Philo: Antiquitates Biblicae.* JSHRZ 2.2. Gütersloh: Mohn, 1975.
Dodds, E. R. *The Greeks and the Irrational.* Sather Classical Lectures 25. Berkeley: University of California Press, 1951.
Duchesne-Guillemin, Jacques. "Le Zervanisme et les manuscrits de la Mer Morte." *Indo-Iranian Journal* 1 (1957) 96–99.
Duhaime, Jean. "Les voies des deux Esprits (1QS iv 2–14): Une analyse structurelle." *RevQ* 19 (2000) 349–67.
Dunn, James D. G. *Baptism in the Holy Spirit: A Re-Examination of the New Testament Teaching on the Gift of the Spirit in Relation to Pentecostalism Today.* Philadelphia: Westminster, 1970.
———. *Christology in the Making: A New Testament Inquiry into the Origins of the Doctrine of the Incarnation.* Philadelphia: Westminster, 1980.
Dupont-Sommer, André. *The Dead Sea Scrolls: A Preliminary Survey.* Oxford: Blackwell, 1952.
———. "L'instruction sur les deux Esprits dans le *Manuel de Discipline.*" *RHR* 142 (1952) 5–35.
Eltester, Friedrich Wilhelm. *Eikon im Neuen Testament.* BZNW 23. Berlin: Töppelmann, 1958.
Euripides. *Euripides.* Translated by Arthur S. Way. 4 vols. LCL. Cambridge, MA: Harvard University Press, 1978–80.
Faye, Eugene de. *L'ambiance philosophique.* Vol. 2 of *Origène: Sa vie, son oeuvre, sa pensée.* Paris: Leroux, 1927.
Fee, Gordon D. *God's Empowering Presence: The Holy Spirit in the Letters of Paul.* Peabody, MA: Hendrickson, 1994.
Feldman, Louis H. "How Much Hellenism in Jewish Palestine?" *HUCA* 57 (1986) 83–111.
———. *Josephus and Modern Scholarship, 1938–1980.* Berlin: de Gruyter, 1984.
———. "Josephus' *Jewish Antiquities* and Pseudo-Philo's *Biblical Antiquities.*" In *Josephus, the Bible, and History,* edited by Louis H. Feldman and Gohei Hata, 59–80. Leiden: Brill, 1989.
———. "Josephus' Portrait of Balaam." *SPhiloA* 5 (1993) 48–83.
———. "Josephus' Portrait of Moses: Part Three." *JQR* 83 (1993) 301–30.
———. "Josephus' Portrait of Noah and Its Parallels in Philo, Pseudo-Philo's *Biblical Antiquities,* and Rabbinic Midrashim." *PAAJR* 55 (1988) 31–57.
———. "Josephus' Portrait of Saul." *HUCA* 53 (1982) 45–99.
———. "Josephus' Version of Samson." *JSJ* 19 (1988) 171–214.
———. "Pro-Jewish Intimations in Anti-Jewish Remarks Cited in Josephus' *Against Apion.*" *JQR* 78 (1988) 187–251.
———. "Prophets and Prophecy in Josephus." *JTS* 41 (1990) 386–422.
———. "Use, Authority and Exegesis of Mikra in the Writings of Josephus." In *The Literature of the Jewish People in the Period of the Second Temple and the Talmud,* edited by Martin-Jan Mulder, 1:455–518. CRINT 2.1. Philadelphia: Fortress, 1988.
Flacelière, Robert. *Plutarque: Sur la disparition des oracles.* Paris: Belles Lettres, 1947.
Foerster, Werner. "Der Heilige Geist im Spätjudentum." *NTS* 8 (1962) 117–34.

Fontenrose, Joseph. *The Delphic Oracle: Its Responses and Operations.* Berkeley: University of California Press, 1978.

———. *Python: A Study of Delphic Myth and Its Origins.* Berkeley: University of California Press, 1959.

Gammie, John G. "Spatial and Ethical Dualism in Jewish Wisdom and Apocalyptic Literature." *JBL* 93 (1974) 356–85.

García Martínez, Florentino. *The Dead Sea Scrolls Translated: The Qumran Texts in English.* Translated by Wilfred G. E. Watson. Leiden: Brill, 1994.

———. *The Dead Sea Scrolls Translated: The Qumran Texts in English.* 2nd ed. Translated by Wilfred G. E. Watson. Leiden: Brill, 1996.

Georgi, Dieter. *The Opponents of Paul in Second Corinthians.* Philadelphia: Fortress, 1986.

Goldin, Judah. "The Magic of Magic and Superstition." In *Aspects of Religious Propaganda in Judaism and Early Christianity*, edited by Elisabeth Schüssler Fiorenza, 115–47. Notre Dame: University of Notre Dame Press, 1976.

Goldstein, Jonathan A. *I Maccabees.* AB 41. Garden City, NY: Doubleday, 1976.

Goodenough, E. R. *By Light, Light: The Mystic Gospel of Hellenistic Judaism.* New Haven: Yale University Press, 1935.

———. *The Politics of Philo Judaeus: Practice and Theory.* New Haven: Yale University Press, 1938.

Gray, John. *I & II Kings: A Commentary.* 2nd ed. OTL. Philadelphia: Westminster, 1970.

———. *The Legacy of Canaan.* 2nd ed. VTSup 5. Leiden: Brill, 1965.

Gray, Rebecca. *Prophetic Figures in Late Second Temple Jewish Palestine: The Evidence from Josephus.* New York: Oxford University Press, 1993.

Greenspahn, Frederick E. "Why Prophecy Ceased." *JBL* 108 (1989) 37–49.

Gunkel, Hermann. *The Influence of the Holy Spirit: The Popular View of the Apostolic Age and the Teaching of the Apostle Paul.* Translated by Roy A. Harrisville and Philip A. Quanbeck II. Minneapolis: Fortress, 1979.

Hadas, Moses. *Hellenistic Culture: Fusion and Diffusion.* New York: Columbia University, 1959.

———. "Plato in Hellenistic Fusion." *Journal of the History of Ideas* 19 (1958) 3–13.

Hare, Douglas R. A. "The Lives of the Prophets." In *OTP* 2:379–99.

Harrington, Daniel J. "The Biblical Text of Pseudo-Philo's *Liber Antiquitatum Biblicarum.*" *CBQ* 33 (1971) 1–17.

———. "The Original Language of Pseudo-Philo's *Liber Antiquitatum Biblicarum.*" *HTR* 63 (1970) 503–14.

———. "Pseudo-Philo." In *OTP* 2:297–377.

Hay, David. "Philo's View of Himself as an Exegete: Inspired, but Not Authoritative." *SPhiloA* 3 (1991) 40–52.

Hengel, Martin. *Judaism and Hellenism: Studies in Their Encounter in Palestine during the Early Hellenistic Period.* Translated by John Bowden. 2 vols. Philadelphia: Fortress, 1974.

———. *The Zealots: Investigations into the Jewish Freedom Movement in the Period from Herod I until 70 A.D.* Translated by David Smith. Edinburgh: T. & T. Clark, 1989.

Hengel, Martin, with Christoph Markschies. *The "Hellenization" of Judaea in the First Century after Christ.* Translated by John Bowden. 1989. Reprint, Eugene, OR: Wipf & Stock, 2003.

Hill, David. *New Testament Prophecy.* Atlanta: John Knox, 1979.

Himmelfarb, Martha. *Ascent to Heaven in Jewish and Christian Apocalypses.* New York: Oxford University Press, 1993.
Hobein, Hermann, ed. *Maximi Tyrii: Philosophumena.* Leipzig: Teubner, 1910.
Hollander, Harm, and Marinus de Jonge. *The Testaments of the Twelve Patriarchs: A Commentary.* SVTP 8. Leiden: Brill, 1985.
Horn, Friedrich Wilhelm. *Das Angeld des Geistes: Studien zur paulinischen Pneumatologie.* FRLANT 154. Göttingen: Vandenhoeck & Ruprecht, 1992.
———. "Holy Spirit." In *ABD* 3:260–80.
Insler, S. *The Gāthās of Zarathustra.* Textes et mémoires 1. Acta Iranica 8. Leiden: Brill, 1975.
Isaacs, Marie E. *The Concept of Spirit: A Study of Pneuma in Hellenistic Judaism and Its Bearing on the New Testament.* Heythrop Monographs 1. London: Heythrop College Press, 1976.
James, Montague Rhodes. *The Biblical Antiquities of Philo.* New York: Ktav, 1971.
Jeremias, Joachim. *New Testament Theology.* New York: Scribner, 1971.
Jervell, Jacob. *Imago Dei: Gen 1, 26 f. im Spätjudentum, in der Gnosis und in den paulinischen Briefen.* Göttingen: Vandenhoeck & Ruprecht, 1960.
Jobling, David. "'And Have Dominion . . .': The Interpretation of Genesis 1, 28 in Philo Judaeus." *JSJ* 8 (1977) 50–82.
Josephus. *Jewish Antiquities.* Translated by H. St. J. Thackeray. Vol. 1, bks. 1–3. LCL 242. Cambridge: Harvard University Press, 1930.
———. *Jewish Antiquities.* Translated by H. St. J. Thackeray and Ralph Marcus. Vol. 2, bks. 4–6. LCL 490. Cambridge: Harvard University Press, 1930.
———. *The Jewish War.* Translated by H. St. J. Thackeray. Vol. 1, bks. 1–2. LCL 203. Cambridge: Harvard University Press, 1927.
———. *The Life. Against Apion.* Translated by H. St. J. Thackeray. LCL 186. Cambridge: Harvard University Press, 1926.
Kee, H. C. "Testaments of the Twelve Patriarchs." In *OTP* 1:775–828.
Kennedy, George A. *The Art of Rhetoric in the Roman World: 300 B.C.–A.D. 300.* Princeton: Princeton University Press, 1972.
Kirkpatrick, A. F. *The Book of Psalms.* Cambridge: Cambridge University Press, 1902.
Klein, Ralph W. *1 Samuel.* WBC 10. Waco: Word, 1983.
Kuhn, Heinz-Wolfgang. *Enderwartung und gegenwärtiges Heil: Untersuchungen zu den Gemeindeliedern von Qumran mit einem Anhang über Eschatologie und Gegenwart in der Verkündigung Jesu.* SUNT 4. Göttingen: Vandenhoeck & Ruprecht, 1966.
Kuhn, Karl Georg. "Die in Palästina gefundenen hebräischen Texte und das Neue Testament." *ZTK* 47 (1950) 192–211.
———. "Die Sektenschrift und die iranische Religion." *ZTK* 49 (1952) 296–316.
Lampe, G. W. H. "Holy Spirit." In *IDB* 2:626–39.
Langton, Edward. *Good and Evil Spirits: A Study of the Jewish and Christian Doctrine, Its Origin and Development.* 1942. Reprint, Eugene, OR: Wipf & Stock, 2014.
Laurentin, A. "Le pneuma dans la doctrine de Philo." *ETL* 27 (1951) 390–437.
Lauterbach, Jacob Zallel. *Mekilta de-Rabbi Ishmael: A Critical Edition on the Basis of the Manuscripts and Early Editions with an English Translation, Introduction and Notes.* 3 vols. Philadelphia: Jewish Publication Society of America, 1933–35.
Leaney, A. R. C. *The Rule of Qumran and Its Meaning: Introduction, Translation and Commentary.* NTL. Philadelphia: Westminster, 1966.

Leisegang, Hans. *Der heilige Geist: Das Wesen und Werden der mystisch-intuitiven Erkenntnis in der Philosophie und Religion der Griechen.* Darmstadt: Wissenschaftliche Buchgesellschaft, 1967.

Leivestad, Ragnar. "Das Dogma von der prophetenlosen Zeit." NTS 19 (1973) 288–99.

Levison, John R. "The Debut of the Divine Spirit in Josephus's *Antiquities.*" HTR 87 (1994) 123–38.

———. *Filled with the Spirit.* Grand Rapids: Eerdmans, 2009.

———. *The Holy Spirit before Christianity.* Waco: Baylor University Press, 2019.

———. "Inspiration and the Divine Spirit in the Writings of Philo Judaeus." JSJ 26 (1995) 271–323.

———. "Josephus' Interpretation of the Divine Spirit." JJS 47 (1996) 234–55.

———. "Judith 16:14 and the Creation of Woman." JBL 114 (1995) 467–69.

———. *Portraits of Adam in Early Judaism: From Sirach to 2 Baruch.* JSPSup 1. Sheffield: JSOT Press, 1988.

———. "Prophetic Inspiration in Pseudo-Philo's *Liber Antiquitatum Biblicarum.*" JQR 85 (1995) 297–329.

———. "The Prophetic Spirit as an Angel According to Philo." HTR 88 (1995) 189–207.

———. *The Spirit in First-Century Judaism.* AGJU 29. Leiden: Brill, 1997.

———. "Two Types of Ecstatic Prophecy According to Philo Judaeus." SPhiloA 6 (1994) 83–89.

Lewy, Hans. *Sobria Ebrietas: Untersuchungen zur Geschichte der antiken Mystik.* BZNW 9. Giessen: Töppelmann, 1929.

Lichtenberger, Hermann. *Studien zum Menschenbild in Texten der Qumrangemeinde.* SUNT 15. Göttingen: Vandenhoeck & Ruprecht, 1980.

Lindblom, J. *Prophecy in Ancient Israel.* Philadelphia: Muhlenberg, 1962.

Linforth, Ivan M. "The Corybantic Rites in Plato." *University of California Publications in Classical Philology* 13 (1945) 121–62.

Lucan. *The Civil War (Pharsalia).* Translated by J. D. Duff. LCL 220. Cambridge: Harvard University Press, 1928.

Lucas, F. L. *Euripides and His Influence.* Boston: Jones, 1923.

Manns, Frédéric. *Le symbole eau-esprit dans le Judaisme ancient.* Jerusalem: Franciscan, 1983.

Marcovich, Miroslav, ed. *Pseudo-Iustinus: Cohortatio ad Graecos, de Monarchia, Oratio ad Graecos.* PTS 32. Berlin: de Gruyter, 1990.

Marmorstein, A. "The Holy Spirit in Rabbinic Legend." In *Studies in Jewish Theology*, edited by J. Rabbinowitz and M. S. Lew, 122–44. New York: Oxford University Press, 1950.

May, Herbert G. "Cosmological Reference in the Qumran Doctrine of the Two Spirits and in Old Testament Imagery." JBL 82 (1963) 1–14.

Méasson, Anita. *Du char ailé de Zeus à l'arche d'alliance: Images et mythes platoniciens chez Philon d'Alexandrie.* Paris: Études augustiniennes, 1986.

Meeks, Wayne A. *The Prophet-King: Moses Traditions and the Johannine Christology.* NovTSup 14. Leiden: Brill, 1967.

Mendels, Doron. "Pseudo-Philo's *Biblical Antiquities*, the 'Fourth Philosophy,' and the Political Messianism of the First Century C.E." In *The Messiah: Developments in Earliest Judaism and Christianity*, edited by James H. Charlesworth, 261–75. Minneapolis: Fortress, 1992.

Menzies, Robert P. *The Development of Early Christian Pneumatology with Special Reference to Luke-Acts*. Sheffield: JSOT Press, 1991.

Mesch, Eckardt. *Hans Leisegang: Leben und Werk*. Erlangen: Palm & Enke, 1999.

Meyer, Rudolph. "Prophecy and Prophets." In *TDNT* 6 (1968) 812–27.

Meyers, Eric M. "The Crisis of the Mid-Fifth Century B.C.E., Second Zechariah and the 'End' of Prophecy." In *Pomegranates and Golden Bells: Studies in Biblical, Jewish, and Near Eastern Ritual, Law, and Literature in Honor of Jacob Milgrom*, edited by David P. Wright et al., 713–23. Winona Lake, IN: Eisenbrauns, 1995.

Moore, Carey A. *Judith: A New Translation with Introduction and Commentary*. AB 40. Garden City, NY: Doubleday, 1985.

Müller, Hans-Peter. "Mantische Weisheit und Apokalyptik." In *Congress Volume Uppsala 1971*, edited by P. A. H. de Boer, 268–93. VTSup 22. Leiden: Brill, 1972.

Murphy, Frederick J. *Pseudo-Philo: Rewriting the Bible*. New York: Oxford University Press, 1993.

Neusner, Jacob. *The Tosefta, Translated from the Hebrew: Third Division Nashim (The Order of Women)*. New York: Ktav, 1979.

Niese, Benedict. *Flavii Iosephi opera*. Berlin: Weidmann, 1887.

Nikiprowetsky, Valentin. *Le commentaire de l'écriture chez Philon d'Alexandrie: Son caractère et sa portée; Observations philologiques*. ALGHJ 11. Leiden: Brill, 1977.

Nötscher, Friedrich. *Zur theologischen Terminologie der Qumran-texte*. BBB 10. Bonn: Hanstein, 1956.

Osten-Sacken, Peter von der. *Gott und Belial: Traditionsgeschichtliche Untersuchungen zum Dualismus in den Texten aus Qumran*. SUNT 6. Göttingen: Vandenhoeck & Ruprecht, 1969.

Otzen, Benedikt. "Die neugefundenen hebräischen sektenschriften und die testamente der Zwölf Patriarchen." *ST* 7 (1953) 125–57.

Parke, H. W., and D. E. W. Wormell. *The History*. Vol. 1 of *The Delphic Oracle*. Oxford: Blackwell, 1956.

Parzen, Herbert. "The Ruaḥ Haḳodesh in Tannaitic Literature." *JQR* 20 (1929) 51–76.

Patte, Daniel. *Early Jewish Hermeneutic in Palestine*. SBLDS 22. Missoula, MT: Scholars, 1975.

Pease, Arthur Stanley, ed. *M. Tulli Ciceronis de divinatione*. 2 vols. Urbana: University of Illinois Press, 1920–23.

Philo. *Every Good Man Is Free. On the Contemplative Life. On the Eternity of the World. Against Flaccus. Apology for the Jews. On Providence*. Translated by F. H. Colson. LCL 363. Cambridge: Harvard University Press, 1941.

———. *On Abraham. On Joseph. On Moses*. Translated by F. H. Colson. LCL 289. Cambridge: Harvard University Press, 1935.

———. *On Flight and Finding. On the Change of Names. On Dreams*. Translated by F. H. Colson and G. H. Whitaker. LCL 275. Cambridge: Harvard University Press, 1934.

———. *On the Cherubim. The Sacrifices of Abel and Cain. The Worse Attacks the Better. On the Posterity and Exile of Cain. On the Giants*. Translated by F. H. Colson and G. H. Whitaker. LCL 227. Cambridge: Harvard University Press, 1929.

———. *On the Confusion of Tongues. On the Migration of Abraham. Who Is the Heir of Divine Things? On Mating with the Preliminary Studies*. Translated by F. H. Colson and G. H. Whitaker. LCL 261. Cambridge: Harvard University Press, 1932.

BIBLIOGRAPHY

———. *On the Decalogue. On the Special Laws, Books 1–3*. Translated by F. H. Colson. LCL 320. Cambridge: Harvard University Press, 1937.

———. *On the Embassy to Gaius. General Indexes*. Translated by F. H. Colson. Index by J. W. Earp. LCL 379. Cambridge: Harvard University Press, 1962.

———. *On the Special Laws, Book 4. On the Virtues. On Rewards and Punishments*. Translated by F. H. Colson. LCL 341. Cambridge: Harvard University Press, 1939.

———. *On the Unchangeableness of God. On Husbandry. Concerning Noah's Work as a Planter. On Drunkenness. On Sobriety*. Translated by F. H. Colson and G. H. Whitaker. LCL 247. Cambridge: Harvard University Press, 1930.

———. *Questions on Genesis*. Translated by Ralph Marcus. LCL 380. Cambridge: Harvard University Press, 1953.

Philonenko, Marc. "La doctrine qoumrânienne des deux Esprits: Ses origins iraniennes et ses prolongements dans le judaïsme essénien et le christianisme antique." In *Apocalyptique iranienne et dualisme qoumrânien*, edited by Geo Widengren et al., 163–211. Recherches Intertestamentaires 2. Paris: Andrien Maisonneuve, 1995.

Pichery, Étienne, ed. *Jean Cassien: Conférences I–VII*. SC 42. Paris: Cerf, 1955.

Piñero, Antonio. "A Mediterranean View of Prophetic Inspiration: On the Concept of Inspiration in the *Liber Antiquitatum Biblicarum* by Pseudo-Philo." *Mediterranean Historical Review* 6 (1991) 5–34.

Plato. *Euthyphro. Apology. Crito. Phaedo. Phaedrus*. Translated by Harold North Fowler. LCL 36. Cambridge: Harvard University Press, 1914.

———. *Lysis. Symposium. Gorgias*. Translated by W. R. M. Lamb. LCL 166. Cambridge: Harvard University Press, 1925.

Plutarch. *Isis and Osiris. The E at Delphi. The Oracles at Delphi No Longer Given in Verse. The Obsolescence of Oracles*. Translated by Frank Cole Babbitt. Vol. 5 of *Moralia*. LCL 306. Cambridge: Harvard University Press, 1936.

———. *On Love of Wealth. On Compliancy. On Envy and Hate. On Praising Oneself Inoffensively. On the Delays of the Divine Vengeance. On Fate. On the Sign of Socrates. On Exile. Consolation to His Wife*. Translated by Phillip H. de Lacy and Benedict Einarson. Vol. 7 of *Moralia*. LCL 405. Cambridge: Harvard University Press, 1959.

Pohlenz, Max. "Philon von Alexandreia." *NAWG, Philologisch-historische Klasse* 5 (1942) 409–87.

Pseudo-Philon. *Les Antiquités Bibliques*. Edited by Daniel J. Harrington et al. 2 vols. SC 229–30. Paris: Cerf, 1976.

Qimron, Elisha, and James H. Charlesworth. "Rule of the Community (1QS)." In *The Dead Sea Scrolls: Hebrew, Aramaic and Greek Texts with English Translations*, edited by James H. Charlesworth et al., 1:1–52. PTSDSSP 1. Tübingen: Mohr Siebeck, 1994.

Radice, Roberto. "Observations on the Theory of the Ideas as the Thoughts of God in Philo of Alexandria." In *Heirs of the Septuagint: Philo, Hellenistic Judaism, and Early Christianity*, edited by David T. Runia et al., 126–34. SPhiloA 3. Atlanta: Scholars, 1991.

Reiling, J. *Hermas and Christian Prophecy: A Study of the Eleventh Mandate*. NovTSup 37. Leiden: Brill, 1973.

Roberts, Alexander, and James Donaldson, eds. *The Ante-Nicene Fathers*. 10 vols. 1885. Reprint, Eugene, OR: Wipf & Stock, 2022.

Runia, David T. *On the Creation of the Cosmos: Introduction, Translation and Commentary.* Philo of Alexandria Commentary Series 1. Leiden: Brill, 2001.

———. *Philo of Alexandria and the* Timaeus *of Plato.* Philosophia Antigua 44. Leiden: Brill, 1986.

Sambursky, Samuel. *Physics of the Stoics.* London: Routledge & Kegan Paul, 1959.

Sandmel, Samuel. *Philo's Place in Judaism: A Study of Conceptions of Abraham in Jewish Literature.* Cincinnati: Hebrew Union College Press, 1956.

Schäfer, J. P. "Die Termini 'Heiliger Geist' und 'Geist der Prophetie' in den Targumim und das Verhältnis der Targumim Zueinander." *VT* 20 (1970) 304–14.

Schäfer, Peter. *Die Vorstellung vom heiligen Geist in der rabbinischen Literatur.* SANT 28. Munich: Kösel, 1972.

Schaff, Philip, ed. *The Nicene and Post-Nicene Fathers.* 2nd ser. 14 vols. Peabody, MA: Hendrickson, 1994.

Schlatter, Adolf. *Wie sprach Josephus von Gott?* BFCT 14. Gütersloh: Bertelsmann, 1910.

Schoemaker, William Ross. "The Use of רוּחַ in the Old Testament, and of πνεῦμα in the New Testament: A Lexicographical Study." *JBL* 23 (1904) 13–67.

Schuller, Eileen M., and Carol A. Newsom. *The Hodayot (Thanksgiving Psalms): A Study Edition of 1QH^a.* EJL 36. Atlanta: Society of Biblical Literature, 2012.

Schweizer, Eduard. "Gegenwart des Geistes und eschatologische Hoffnung bei Zarathustra, spätjüdischen Gruppen, Gnostikern und den Zeugen des Neuen Testaments." In *The Background of the New Testament and Its Eschatology: Studies in Honor of Charles Harold Dodd,* edited by W. D. Davies and D. Daube, 482–508. Cambridge: Cambridge University Press, 1956.

———. *The Holy Spirit.* Translated by Reginald H. Fuller and Ilse Fuller. Philadelphia: Fortress, 1980.

Segal, Alan. "Heavenly Ascent in Hellenistic Judaism, Early Christianity and Their Environment." In *ANRW* 23/2:1333–94.

Seitz, Oscar J. F. "Two Spirits in Man: An Essay in Biblical Exegesis." *NTS* 6 (1959) 82–95.

Sekki, Arthur E. *The Meaning of Ruaḥ at Qumran.* SBLDS 110. Atlanta: Scholars, 1989.

Sevenster, J. N. *Do You Know Greek? How Much Greek Could the First Jewish Christians Have Known?* NovTSup 19. Leiden: Brill, 1969.

Sjöberg, Erik. "Neuschöpfung in den Toten-Meer-Rollen." *ST* 9 (1955) 131–36.

———. "πνεῦμα, πνευματικός." In *TDNT* 6 (1968) 368–89.

Smith, Morton. "The Occult in Josephus." In *Josephus, Judaism, and Christianity,* edited by Louis H. Feldman and Gohei Hata, 236–56. Detroit: Wayne State University Press, 1987.

Strabo. *Geography.* Translated by Horace Leonard Jones. Vol. 4, bks. 8–9. LCL 196. Cambridge: Harvard University Press, 1927.

Strack, H. L., and Günter Stemberger. *Introduction to the Talmud and Midrash.* Translated by Marcus Bockmuehl. Edinburgh: T. & T. Clark, 1991.

Sukenik, E. L., ed. *The Dead Sea Scrolls of the Hebrew University.* Jerusalem: Magnes, 1955.

Tabor, James. *Things Unutterable: Paul's Ascent to Paradise in Its Greco-Roman, Judaic, and Early Christian Context.* Lanham, MD: University Press of America, 1986.

Tate, Marvin E. *Psalms 51–100.* WBC 20. Waco, TX: Word, 1990.

Taylor, Thomas. *Iamblichus on the Mysteries of the Egyptians, Chaldeans, and Assyrians.* Chiswick, UK: Wittingham, 1821.

Tcherikover, Victor. "Jewish Apologetic Literature Reconsidered." *Eos* 48 (1956) 169–93.

Thompson, R. Campbell. *The Devils and Evil Spirits of Babylonia: Being Babylonian and Assyrian Incantations against the Demons, Ghouls, Vampires, Hobgoblins, Ghosts, and Kindred Evil Spirits, Which Attack Mankind.* 2 vols. Luzac's Semitic Text and Translation Series 14–15. London: Luzac, 1903.

Tiede, David L. *The Charismatic Figure as Miracle Worker.* SBLDS 1. Missoula, MT: Society of Biblical Literature, 1972.

Tobin, Thomas H. *The Creation of Man: Philo and the History of Interpretation.* CBQMS 14. Washington, DC: Catholic Biblical Association, 1983.

Treves, Marco. "The Two Spirits of the Rule of the Community." *RevQ* 3 (1961) 449–52.

Turner, Max. "The Spirit of Prophecy and the Power of Authoritative Preaching in Luke-Acts: A Question of Origins." *NTS* 38 (1992) 66–88.

Urbach, E. A. "Matay Paseqah Hanevu'ah?" *Tarbiz* 17 (1945–46) 1–11.

Verbeke, Gérard. *L'évolution de la doctrine du pneuma: du Stoïcisme à S. Augustin: Étude philosophique.* Bibliothèque de l'Institut Supérieur de Philosophie, Université de Louvain. Paris: Presse de l'Institut Supérior de Philosophie, 1945.

Volz, Paul. *Der Geist Gottes und die verwandten Erscheinungen im Alten Testament und im anschließenden Judentum.* Tübingen: Mohr Siebeck, 1910.

Vos, J. S. *Traditionsgeschichtliche Untersuchungen zur paulinische Pneumatologie.* Assen: Van Gorcum, 1973.

Wagner, Siegfried. "בָּנָה." In *TDOT* 2 (1975) 166–81.

Wan, Sze-Kar. "Charismatic Exegesis: Philo and Paul Compared." *SPhiloA* 6 (1994) 54–82.

Weaver, Mary Jo. "Πνεῦμα in Philo of Alexandria." PhD diss., University of Notre Dame, 1973.

Wernberg-Møller, Preben. "A Reconsideration of the Two Spirits in the Rule of the Community (1 Q Serek III,13—IV,26)." *RevQ* 11 (1961) 413–41.

Wildberger, Hans. "Der Dualismus in den Qumranschriften." *Asiatische Studien* 8 (1954) 163–77.

Windisch, Hans. *The Spirit-Paraclete in the Fourth Gospel.* Translated by James W. Cox. Facet Books: Biblical Studies. Philadelphia: Fortress, 1968.

Winston, David, and John Dillon. *Two Treatises of Philo of Alexandria: A Commentary on "De gigantibus" and "Quod Deus sit immutabilis."* BJS 25. Chico, CA: Scholars, 1983.

———. "Two Types of Mosaic Prophecy According to Philo." *JSP* 2 (1989) 49–67.

———. "Was Philo a Mystic?" In *Studies in Jewish Mysticism: Proceedings of Regional Conferences Held at the University of California, Los Angeles, and McGill University in April, 1978,* edited by Joseph Dan and Frank Talmage, 15–39. Cambridge, MA: Association for Jewish Studies, 1982.

Wolfson, Harry A. *Philo: Foundations of Religious Philosophy in Judaism, Christianity, and Islam.* 2 vols. Cambridge: Harvard University Press, 1948.

Zimmermann, Frank. "Aids for the Recovery of the Hebrew Original of Judith." *JBL* 57 (1938) 67–74.

Zuckermandel, M. S. *Tosephta: Based on the Erfurt and Vienna Codices, with Parallels and Variants.* 2nd ed. Jerusalem: Bamberger & Wahrmann, 1937.

Index of Modern Authors

Amir, Yehoshua, 147n99
Arnim, Hans von, 185n31
Aune, David E., 3, 4n18, 7n28, 9n31, 20, 148, 149n2, 172, 265, 267

Babbitt, Frank Cole, 131nn16–17, 132n19, 134n29, 184nn25–26, 190n53
Baer, Heinrich von, xxii
Barrett, C. K., 1, 259n12
Barton, John, 3, 4n19, 7n26, 20n62
Baskin, Judith Reesa, 187n38
Berchman, Robert M., 54–55, 175n65
Best, Ernest, 179
Betz, Otto, 44–47, 49, 51–52, 177n1, 187n38
Bockmuehl, Marcus N. A., 57n20
Borgen, Peder, 101n4, 104n11
Bouché-Leclercq, Auguste, 181n15
Bousset, William, 101n4, 104n11
Boyce, Mary, 34n13, 220n48
Brown, Raymond E., 254–55
Brownlee, William, 265
Büchsel, Friedrich, xxii, 20, 61, 96, 191, 206
Burkhardt, Helmut, 54–55, 96, 135n32

Charlesworth, James H., 10n34, 30n, 35n21, 38, 218, 252n
Chevallier, Max-Alain, 149n2
Christiansen, Irmgard, 55

Collins, John J., 100n3, 101n4
Colson, F. H., 130n11, 132nn21–22, 133n24, 133nn27–28, 135n31, 135–36nn33–39, 136–37nn44–48, 137n50, 137–38nn55–62, 139nn65–66, 141n71, 145n, 181n14, 183n21
Conley, Thomas M., 55
Craven, Toni, 26n6

Danby, Herbert, 17n46
Davies, W. D., 1–2, 259n11
Dean-Otting, Miriam, 101n4, 104n11
Des Places, Édouard, 161n39
Dietzfelbinger, Christian, 153n16, 156n26
Dodds, E. R., 172
Duchesne-Guillemin, Jacques, 35n21
Duff, J. D., 189n43
Duhaime, Jean, 52n59
Dunn, James D. G., 2
Dupont-Sommer, André, 31–35, 37–38, 40, 43–44, 52, 213

Einarson, Benedict, 141n70, 142n76, 144nn87–91, 186nn32–33, 188nn39–40, 189n45, 190nn47–49
Eltester, Friedrich Wilhelm, 102n7

Fee, Gordon D., 2

INDEX OF MODERN AUTHORS

Feldman, Louis H., xxi, 1n1, 8n, 9n31, 9n33, 56n17, 66n35, 148n1, 152n15, 158n32, 160n38, 169n, 170, 171n56, 176n, 177n1, 177n3, 181n13, 181n16, 187n36, 187n38
Flacelière, Robert, 146n96, 184, 188n42
Foerster, Werner, 47n48,
Fontenrose, Joseph, 188n42, 190n50
Fowler, Harold North, 143n86

Gammie, John G., 41, 52
García Martínez, Florentino, 30n, 214n30
Georgi, Dieter, 265, 267
Ginsberg, Harold Louis, 265, 267
Goldin, Judah, 176n
Goldstein, Jonathan A., 5n22
Goodenough, E. R., 53–55, 92nn80–81
Gray, John, 26n5, 197n
Gray, Rebecca, 1n1, 7n27, 9nn32–33
Greenspahn, Frederick E., 3, 4n18, 7n29, 9n31, 11, 20
Grenet, Frantz, 220n48
Gunkel, Hermann, xxi–xxiv

Hadas, Moses, 65n32, 160n37, 191n55
Hare, Douglas R. A., 156n25
Harrington, Daniel J., 151n8, 153n16, 156n26, 169n53, 170, 228–29
Hay, David, 55, 61, 80n, 84n69, 95, 142n78
Heinemann, I., xxii
Hengel, Martin, 176n, 244, 265–67
Hill, David, 2, 148, 149n2, 253, 255, 259, 264–65
Himmelfarb, Martha, 101n4
Hobein, Hermann, 114n20, 140n69
Hollander, Harm, 219n
Horn, Friedrich Wilhelm, 2, 5n22, 12n40

Insler, S., 32n7, 214n31
Isaacs, Marie E., 53n1, 54–55

James, Montague Rhodes, 152n15, 153n16, 155–56, 158n32, 169n, 170, 171n, 181n13

Jeremias, Joachim, 2, 156n25
Jervell, Jacob, 102n7
Jobling, David, 102n7
Jones, Horace Leonard, 189n45
Jonge, Marinus de, 219n

Kee, H. C., 218n46
Kennedy, George A., 91n79
Kirkpatrick, A. F., 3n17
Klein, Ralph W., 195
Kuhn, Heinz-Wolfgang, 47–51, 262
Kuhn, Karl Georg, 31–35, 37–38, 40, 43–44, 47, 52, 213

Lacy, Phillip H. de, 141n70, 142n76, 144nn87–91, 186nn32–33, 188nn39–40, 189n45, 190nn47–49
Lamb, W. R. M., 132n18, 191n54
Lampe, G. W. H., 2, 3n14, 259
Langton, Edward, 199n9
Laurentin, A., 53n1, 54–55
Lauterbach, Jacob Zallel, 21n65, 258n11
Leaney, A. R. C., 41, 52
Leisegang, Hans, xxii–xxiii, 53–55
Leivestad, Ragnar, 3, 4n21, 7n28, 20
Levison, John R., xxivn9, 19nn50–51, 25n4, 53n2, 56n17, 57nn21–22, 58n23, 83nn66–68, 93n, 118n24, 130n12, 131n15, 133n26, 134n30, 136n40, 139n65, 141n74, 146n93, 183n20, 250n2, 261n15
Lewy, Hans, 53–55
Lichtenberger, Hermann, 27n, 41–42, 52
Lindblom, J., 66, 151–52, 153n17, 166n48, 182n19
Linforth, Ivan M., 63n30
Lucas, F. L., 168n51

Manns, Frédéric, 149n2
Marcovich, Miroslav, 155n22
Marcus, Ralph, 145n92, 179nn7–8, 180n12, 182nn17–18, 185n28, 187n37
Markschies, Christoph, 176n

282

INDEX OF MODERN AUTHORS

Marmorstein, A., 12–13n41, 19n52
May, Herbert G., 34, 38, 214, 217–18
Méasson, Anita, 69nn38–40, 103n9, 118n23
Meeks, Wayne A., 74n48, 126n
Mendels, Doron, 176n
Menzies, Robert P., 148, 149n2, 263–64
Mesch, Eckardt, xxii
Meyer, Rudolph, 3, 4n18, 7n27, 11n36, 12, 20
Meyers, Eric M., 1n1, 12n39, 22n67
Moore, Carey A., 24n1, 26nn5–6
Moore, George Foot, 1, 259
Müller, Hans-Peter, 266
Murphy, Frederick J., 149, 176n

Neusner, Jacob, 12n39, 13n43, 18
Newsom, Carol A., xvi, 27n
Niese, Benedict, 182n18
Nikiprowetsky, Valentin, 55
Nötscher, Friedrich, 34

Osten-Sacken, Peter von der, 41n39, 49–51
Otzen, Benedikt, 41, 52

Parke, H. W., 188n42, 190n50, 190n52
Parzen, Herbert, 19n52
Patte, Daniel, 266–67
Pease, Arthur Stanley, 158
Philonenko, Marc, 51–52
Pichery, Étienne, 155n23
Piñero, Antonio, 149–50, 171–73, 175
Pohlenz, Max, 84, 142, 228

Qimron, Elisha, 30n

Radice, Roberto, 97n87
Reiling, J., 161n39
Runia, David T., 65n33, 102n6, 103–4, 133n25

Sambursky, Samuel, 53n1, 59n
Sandmel, Samuel, 90n
Schäfer, J. P., 259n11
Schäfer, Peter, 19n52, 20
Schlatter, Adolf, 179
Schoemaker, William Ross, 130n12, 207

Schuller, Eileen M., xvin1, 27n
Schweizer, Eduard, 20, 41, 52
Segal, Alan, 100, 101n4, 119
Seitz, Oscar J. F., 31, 38–40, 43–44, 52, 220n47
Sekki, Arthur E., 27n, 38n32, 42–43, 46n46, 47n48, 52, 130n12, 179n10, 215–17
Sevenster, J. N., 176n
Sjöberg, Erik, 1, 17, 46n46
Smith, Morton, 179
Stemberger, Günter, 11n38
Strack, H. L., 11n38
Sukenik, E. L., xvin, 27n
Swete, Henry Barclay, xxii

Tabor, James, 101n4, 104n11
Tate, Marvin E., 3n17
Taylor, Thomas, 161n39
Tcherikover, Victor, 55n13
Thackeray, H. St. J., 8n, 146n94, 178n5, 179nn7–8, 180nn11–12, 182nn17–18, 185nn28–29, 187n37, 188n41, 189n46, 190nn51–52
Thompson, R. Campbell, 195n3, 196n, 199nn10–11
Tiede, David L., 55n13, 84n69, 92n80, 147n98
Tobin, Thomas H., 53n2
Treves, Marco, 36n22
Turner, Max, 264

Urbach, E. A., 20

Verbeke, Gérard, xxii, 53n1, 54–55, 97, 189n44
Volz, Paul, xxii, xxiv, 128–29, 200n14, 206n18, 212–13, 228, 229n60
Vos, J. S., 1

Wagner, Siegfried, 25n5
Wan, Sze-Kar, 55, 79n58
Way, Arthur S., 181n15
Weaver, Mary Jo, 53n1, 54–55
Wernberg-Møller, Preben, 31, 36–38, 40, 43–44, 47, 52, 215–18

INDEX OF MODERN AUTHORS

Whitaker, G. H., 132nn21–22, 133n24, 133nn27–28, 136n45, 137–38nn56–58, 139nn65–66, 145n, 181n14, 183n21
Wildberger, Hans, 35n20
Windisch, Hans, 254–55
Winston, David, 55, 76n51, 96, 133n25

Wolfson, Harry A., 54–55, 76n51, 97n87, 98, 129, 175
Wormell, D. E. W., 188n42, 190n50, 190n52

Ziegler, Hermannus, 59n
Zimmermann, Frank, 24
Zuckermandel, M. S., 12n39, 13n43

Index of Ancient Documents

HEBREW SCRIPTURES

Genesis

1	45, 211–12, 218
1:1	178n6
1:2	53, 106n15, 260
1:26–27	101, 103–4, 127
1:26	101, 124
1:27	93, 120
2	45, 211–12
2:4	217–18
2:7	25, 36, 53, 60, 92, 112, 114, 120, 127, 215, 218, 232, 261
2:22	25, 26, 261
3:19	25
6:1–4	106
6:2–3	105
6:2	132n20
6:3	58–60, 70, 72, 74, 86, 105–9, 115–116, 178n6, 231–33, 240–41, 248, 251, 260
6:17	231
7:15	231
9	237
9:20	109–10, 115, 237
12:3	231
15:4	120
15:6	120
15:12	58, 63, 133
15:13	58, 133
16	88
16:15	88
16:23	88
16:25–26	88
18:17	231
22:17	231
23:6	236
28:12	133n24
32:24–27	231
32:26	88
41:8	206
41:38	56n14, 138, 178

Exodus

	205
2:1–3	258
2:4	258
12:1	258n11
13:21–22	203, 205
13:21	205
14:13–14	88, 245
14:19	201, 203, 204–5
15:8	178n6
15:10	178n6
16	227
16 (LXX)	136
16:15	135
16:22–23	135

INDEX OF ANCIENT DOCUMENTS

Exodus (continued)

16:23	135
16:25–26	135
18:14	75
19:20	76n52
20:21	76n52
23:20–23	201
23:20–21	252
23:21	210
23:22	202
24:1–2	76n52
24:12	124
24:13–18	76n52
24:16	209
28:3	178n4
31	248
31:3	58–60, 106, 178, 240
31:3 (LXX)	59
32:1—34:35	76n52
32:34	202, 205
33:2	202, 205
33:7	75, 108, 126
33:9–10	203
33:9	209
33:14–15	202, 205
33:14	201, 202
33:15	201
35:31	178
35:31 (LXX)	58n24

Leviticus

1:1	69, 75, 114
11:43	45, 232
20:25	232

Numbers

	205
11	58, 106, 178, 198n7, 205, 248
11:1–9	205
11:4	178n5
11:16 (LXX)	56
11:17	58–59, 106, 209, 240, 259–60
11:17 (LXX)	56
11:18–19	178n5
11:25	205, 209
11:25 (LXX)	56
11:26	258–59n11
11:29 (LXX)	56, 208n
11:31 (LXX)	208
11:34	178n5
11:35	178n5
12:5	203, 209
14:14	203, 205
14:24 (LXX)	56
16:22 (LXX)	207
16:28	88
20	205
20:2–13	205
20:16	201
22–24	57, 59, 130, 168, 177, 180, 182, 187–88, 221, 232
22–23	130
22	168
22:20	130, 179, 221
22:24	207
22:24 (LXX)	207–8
22:28	182
22:35	98, 130, 134, 179, 221, 223, 242
22:35 (LXX)	130
22:38	57, 130, 179, 221
22:41b	169
23:1–6	180
23:4–5	130, 179, 221
23:5	57, 130, 131, 182, 221–22
23:6 (LXX)	182
23:7–10	168–69
23:7 (LXX)	57, 130, 134, 153n16, 169–70, 173, 177n3, 179, 221, 242
23:12	130, 179, 221
23:14–17	180
23:16	57, 130, 179, 182, 221
23:21	202
23:23	180
23:26	130, 179, 221
23:27—24:2	180
24:1–2	180
24:1	180

INDEX OF ANCIENT DOCUMENTS

24:2	98, 130, 135, 153n16, 169–70, 173, 177, 179, 182, 221, 223, 231, 233, 242, 249	3:10	198–99, 206, 234
		5:29–30	171n
		6–8	157n26
		6	233
24:3–4	169–70	6:34	153n16, 156, 164–65, 173, 174, 199, 206, 233–34, 256
24:6	169		
24:13	130, 179, 221		
25:15	57	9:23	199–200
27:16 (LXX)	207	11:8 (LXX)	207
27:18	178	11:29	198–99, 206
28:1	178	11:40 (Alexandrinus)	207
		13:24–25	206–7

Deuteronomy

	205	13:24–25 (LXX)	225n54
1:33	203, 205	13:25 (LXX)	199, 207
4:4	80	14:6	199
4:37–38	201–2	14:19	199
4:37	205	15:14	199
8:3	206n17	16:31	199
8:4	205		
8:15–16	205		

1 Samuel

15:18	57n19		198–99, 206
18	197	3:10	258n10
18:10–11	57n19	10–19	195–96, 229
18:15–18	8	10	152–53, 195, 248
18:18	57, 197	10:5–6	151
18:21–22	197	10:5	152
29:4	205	10:6	151n9, 152, 157, 164–65, 174, 193–94, 199, 234, 256
30:15	80		
30:20	80		
31:14	258n10	10:6 (LXX)	208n
34:9	153n16, 164, 165n, 173, 174, 178, 198n7, 234, 256	10:10–13	151
		10:10	193–94, 199
		10:12	151
34:9a	164	10:13	194
		11:6	193–94, 199

Joshua

		11:6 (LXX)	208n
1	163–64, 174	16–19	198–99
10:24 (LXX)	207	16:13–23	193, 195–96, 198, 208n
		16:13	194, 199, 256

Judges

	198, 199, 207	16:14	31, 38–40, 44, 52, 194
3:9–11	156–58	16:14a	194
3:9–10	256	16:14b	194
3:9	153n16, 156, 173, 174–75	16:15	194
		16:16	194–95, 198n7, 206
		16:23	195, 198n7, 206

287

1 Samuel (continued)

16:23a	194
16:23b	194
18:10	193–95, 199
19	152–53, 195, 248
19:9	193–95, 198, 206
19:18–24	151n9, 152–53, 174
19:19–23	195
19:20–24	151, 153
19:20	193–94, 198, 206
19:23–24	173, 193–94
19:23	194, 198, 206
19:23b	194
19:24	151

2 Samuel

12:20	38n32, 218
15:2 (LXX)	207n22
23:2 (LXX)	208n

1 Kings

	199
8	238–39, 248
8:60	238–39
13:9	153
13:12 (LXX)	207n22
16:14 (LXX)	39
18:12	200n14
18:12 (LXX)	208n
22	197–98, 200, 229
22:14	197
22:19–24	207–8
22:19–23	208
22:21–23	39n33
22:21 (LXX)	207
22:22–23	197
22:22–23 (LXX)	209
22:23	197
22:24	198
22:24 (LXX)	208, 256
22:29–40	197
22:36	198n6

2 Kings

2:7–18	198n7
2:16	200n14
2:16 (LXX)	208n
3:8 (LXX)	207n22

1 Chronicles

	206
12:19	206

2 Chronicles

	206
15:1–2	206
15:1 (LXX)	208n
18:21–22 (LXX)	209
18:23	198n7, 208
18:23 (LXX)	208–9
20:13–15	206
20:14 (LXX)	208n
24:20	206

Ezra

2:63	7

Nehemiah

8	204
8:8	204
8:13	204
9	204–6, 246, 248
9:12–15	204
9:12	204
9:13–14	204
9:15	205
9:15a	204
9:15b	204
9:16–18	204
9:19–25	204
9:19–21	204–5
9:19	204–5
9:20	204–6
9:20a	204
9:20b–21	204
9:20bc	206n17
9:21	205
9:22–25	204
9:30	257

INDEX OF ANCIENT DOCUMENTS

Job

	165n
4:15—5:1	197
4:15-16 (LXX)	130n12
26:12-14	212n26
27:3-4	231-32
33:4	211

Psalms

18:11	200
33:3	25n3
33:6	25, 211
51	263
51 (LXX)	232
51:10	35
51:12-14	35
51:13	232
51:19	35
74	4
74:9	1, 2-4, 11, 12, 22
76:4	206
78:16	205-6
78:24-25	206n17
78:24	206
78:69	25n5
85:11-14	34n18
103:19-22	196
103:30a (LXX)	25, 212
104	26
104:3	200
104:4	179
104:29-30	25, 206, 211-12, 232, 261
104:30	26
104:30a	25, 212
104:30c	26
104:39-41	206
105	205
105:39	205
139:7-10a	259n11
143:10	206
144:9	25n3

Proverbs

	165n

Isaiah

6	196
8:11	153
11	165n
11:1-9	252
11:1-2	203
11:2-3 (LXX)	211
11:2	59, 153n16, 165n
11:9	59, 258n10
21:3	166
32:14-15	203
34:16	206
38:12 (LXX)	209n24
42:1	203
44:1-3	203
44:3	42, 217
48:16	66, 152
51:4 (LXX)	209n25
57:16	209
57:16 (LXX)	209
59:21	203
61:1-2	203, 252
63	205
63:7-14	201-3, 204, 206, 209, 229
63:9-14	208-9
63:9-10	202
63:9	201, 202
63:9 (LXX)	208
63:9a	208
63:9a (LXX)	208
63:10-14	202
63:10	201, 202, 232
63:10 (LXX)	210-11
63:11	201
63:14	201, 202, 209, 252
63:14 (LXX)	208-9

Jeremiah

4:19	166
15:18	166
20	166
20:9	166, 174, 182-83
20:10	166
31:2	258
45:3	258-59n11

Lamentations

2:6	4
2:14	4

Ezekiel

	154
3:10–11	153–54
3:12	66, 73n, 152, 158, 182
3:14	66, 73n, 152, 158, 166, 174, 182
3:18	154n19
8–11	153
8:1–3	158
8:1	153n16, 154n19, 157, 173, 175
8:3	73n, 158
10:2	154n19
10:20–22	154n18
11:5	66, 152, 182
11:19–20	263
12:24	73n, 158
20:1	153n16, 154n19, 157, 173, 175
21:15	166n47
23:20–23	203
32:34	203
33:2	203
36:25–27	35, 42, 217, 253
36:26–27	203
38–39	34
39:28–29	203

Daniel

	2
2:1	206
2:1 (θ)	206
2:3	206
2:3 (θ)	206
4	159, 173–74
4:33	159
4:34	159n33, 173
4:36	159, 173, 183
5–6	225–26
5	225
5:11–14	225
5:11	245
5:11 (θ)	225n53
5:12	245
5:12 (θ)	225n53
5:14	245
5:14 (θ)	225n53
6:4	225, 245
7:2	161n41
7:13–15	161n40
7:15	166
8:15–18	161n40
8:17–18	166
8:27	161n40, 166
10:8–9	161n40, 166
10:15–17	166
10:16–17	161n40

Hosea

4–5	200
4:12	200
4:18	200
4:19	200
5:4	200
9:7	36, 66, 152, 159, 182

Joel

2:28–29	8
3:1–2	203
3:1	42, 217

Amos

3:7	258n10
9:1	258n10
9:6	25n5

Micah

	152
2:7	209–11
2:7 (LXX)	210–11, 229
2:11	209–11
2:11 (LXX)	209–11, 229
3:5–8	66
3:8	209–11
3:8 (LXX)	210–11

Habakkuk

2:14	258n10
3:16	166

Haggai

2	205
2:5	203, 204, 206, 209–11, 229
2:5 (LXX)	210

Zechariah

4:1	161
4:6	206
6:8	206
11:8	18
12:2–6	266
13:2–6	2
13:2	206
14:2–5	266

NEW TESTAMENT

Mark

1:8	2
3:28–29	2

John

	52, 193, 229, 254–55
7:39	2
20:22	2

Acts

19:2	2

2 Corinthians

12:2–4	120

Hebrews

1:7	179

ANCIENT NEAR EASTERN TEXTS

Greek Magical Papyri

3.289	229

DEUTEROCANONICAL WORKS/OLD TESTAMENT APOCRYPHA

Judith

8–16	26
15:12	26
16:4	26
16:11–12	26
16:13–17	26
16:13	25n3, 26
16:14	24–26, 211–13, 229, 261
16:14a	26
16:14b–c	25
16:14c	25, 212
16:18–25	26

1 Maccabees

	2, 5–8
4:6	6n
4:19	6n
4:46	1, 3, 5, 7–8, 11, 12
9:27	1, 3, 5–8, 11, 12, 22
9:29	5
12:10	5
12:21	6
12:22	5n23, 6
14:25	7
14:27–45	7
14:41	1, 3, 5, 7–8, 11, 12
16:24	5n23, 6

Prayer of Azariah

15	1, 3, 4, 11, 12, 22

Sirach/Ecclesiasticus

34:5	269
34:9	269
39:4	269
39:6-8a	269
39:6	59, 65n31

Wisdom of Solomon

1:7	59, 107, 240, 261
7:7	59
9:17	65

OLD TESTAMENT PSEUDEPIGRAPHA

Ascension of Isaiah

193, 229

Assumption of Moses

211-13

2 Baruch

	2, 52
21:4	211-13, 260-61
23:5	211-13, 261
54:15	10n35
85:3	1-3, 10-11, 22
85:9	10
85:10	10
85:12	10

1 Enoch

	2
91:1	257

2 Enoch

2

4 Ezra

	2
6:39	261
9:20	268

14	235-36, 246, 248, 268-69
14:47	268

Joseph and Aseneth

8:9	262-63
16:14	263
19:10-11	263

Jubilees

1:20-21	263
1:22-25	263
1:23	263
12:5	232
25:14	257
31:12	257

Liber Antiquitatum Biblicarum (Pseudo-Philo)

	148-76, 187, 235-36, 250, 252, 264
9.8	260
9.10	154n19, 250, 256, 258n9
9.15	171n
18	169, 230-33, 248
18.2	170
18.3	169, 183, 231
18.4-6	168
18.4	171n
18.7-10	181
18.8	171n
18.9	168
18.10-12	183
18.10	153n16, 169, 231, 234
18.11	153n16, 168, 171n, 231
18.11d-12a	169
18.12	170
18.13-14	233
20.1-3	174
20.1-2	157n26
20.2-3	163-66, 168, 250
20.2	152n14, 153n16, 165, 174

20.3	165–67, 234	3.4–5	167
23.3	171n	3.696–701	261
27	248		
27.5	156n26		
27.7–12	156n26	## Testament of Abraham	
27.7	156n26	4:8	257
27.9–10	19n51, 153n16, 156n26, 164, 233–34, 260	## Testaments of the Twelve Patriarchs	
27.9	153n16, 156, 164		38, 40, 218–20, 246
27.10	152n14, 156, 164–65		
28.4	171n	## Testament of Asher	
28.6–10	159		219
28.6	153n16, 154n19, 157, 170, 228–29, 234, 250, 252, 256	1:3–4	218–19
		1:6–9	40
28.9–10	173		
28.10	159, 161, 234, 250, 256, 268	## Testament of Benjamin	
		6:1	40
28.10a	157	8:3	261
31.1	156n26, 171n		
31.9	250, 256	## Testament of Gad	
32.9	153n16		
32.14	250	4:7	39–40, 219–20
32.16	171n		
33.14	260	## Testament of Judah	
35.6–7	156n26	20:1–3	219
36	248	20:5	219
36.1–2	156n26		
36.2	153n16, 156n26, 164, 233, 250, 260	## Testament of Levi	
37.2	154n19	2:3	59
53.3–4	171n	18:7	59
56.3	171n		
60.1–2	39n34	## Testament of Reuben	
62.2	151–54, 174, 234, 250, 257, 268	2:4	232

Lives of the Prophets

10.9	156n25

Psalms of Solomon

	246

Sibylline Oracles

	236

JOSEPHUS

Antiquitates Judaicae

	177–92, 226n56
1.23	189
1.108	187n37
1.240–41	9n33
2.87	178
2.338	185n29

INDEX OF ANCIENT DOCUMENTS

Antiquitates Judaicae (continued)

2.347–48	187n37
3.81	187n37
3.105	178
3.139	168n52, 190
3.200	178
3.295–99	178n5
4.102–30	178, 180, 250
4.108	19n51, 177, 179, 222, 229, 242, 251
4.109	182n18
4.111	180
4.113–14	180
4.113	180n11
4.118–19	19n51
4.118	88n72, 177, 180, 182, 185, 222, 242
4.119–21	183
4.119	88n72, 177, 181–82, 189n45, 222, 242–43
4.121	88n72, 182n17, 222, 243
4.122	182, 222
4.157–58	184n27, 187, 192
4.165	178
4.311	178
5.182	156n25
6.166	177n2, 250, 256
6.222–23	250, 256
6.222	177n2
6.223	88n72, 177n2
8.108	181n15
8.109	185n29
8.114	19n51, 177n2, 250, 253, 260
8.117	239
8.118	250, 260
8.408	177n2, 256
10.239	177n2, 224–25, 244–45, 250
10.250	245, 250
10.266	256
10.281	187n37
13.5	8
13.299–300	9n33
13.300	226n57
16.210	226n55
17.121	181n15
17.354	187n37
19.141	185n29
20.97–99	9n33

Bellum Judaicum

	183, 225–26n55
1.68–69	9n33
1.69–70	146
1.69	225, 226n57
1.656	185n29
3.351–53	268
6.312–13	266

Contra Apionem

1.37–41	1–3, 8–9, 12, 22
1.37	9
1.40	9
1.41	8–9, 11
2.131	168n52
2.145	239
2.162	168n52, 190
2.168	191
2.190	188
2.211	239
2.257–58	191
2.262–64	226
2.262–63	146
2.263–64	186n33, 247

PHILO

De Abrahamo

	90n, 92n81
73	78n56

De aeternitate mundi

76–77	79–80
76	80
77	80

De Agricultura

104	121

INDEX OF ANCIENT DOCUMENTS

De cherubim
21–29	77, 96
27–29	19n50, 77–85, 86, 97, 98, 139n65, 250–51, 268
27–28	62, 78n58
27	79, 81–82, 143n79
29	80–81
32	57n18, 242
43–47	74n49
48–52	98
48–49	81n
48	74n49, 188n24
49	74n49
69	83n66, 136n43
116	83n66, 137n50

De confusion linguarum
66	57n18, 242
95–97	70n
159	57nn18–19, 83n66, 136n42, 242

De decalogo
18–19	75n51
175	75–76, 85

De Demosthene
22	63n30

De fuga et inventione
21	83n66, 137–38
23–47	71n
53–58	80–83, 85, 96, 98, 139n65, 268
54–55	81
54	81, 85
55	80
186	56, 60

De gigantibus
	109, 259
6–18	132
6	57n22, 105, 132
8	105
12	132
13–15	105
13–14	121
13	121
14	121
16	105
19–57	70, 86
19–55	104–8, 111, 115
19–31	108
19	58, 106
20	106
22–23	53n1
22	106n15
23–31	251
23–29	61
23–27	56, 97, 248, 250
23	58–59, 106, 240
24–27	260
24	58–59, 106, 128n7
25	114–15
26–28	106–7
26	106
27	59, 107, 240, 251
28	60, 86, 107, 241
29–31	70–73, 85, 97, 98, 101, 104, 127, 250
29	60, 72, 107
30–31	108
30	72, 107, 122
31	71–72, 105, 126
50–55	112, 237
50–51	75
53–54	74–77, 81n, 85, 86, 94, 96, 97, 98, 101, 108–9, 126, 250
54	74–75
55	75, 86, 109, 116, 126, 241, 251
56	86
57	86

De Iosepho
107–9	82
110–16	83, 97, 139, 250, 254
110–15	82n63
110	78, 82, 138, 246, 251

De Iosepho (continued)

116	56n14, 82, 138–39, 246, 251
117	138, 246

De migratione Abrahami

23	83n66, 137–38
33–35	63n29
34–35	62–68, 72, 84–85, 96, 98, 250
34	62, 63n29
35	62–65
39	64
40	64–65
84	185n30
86	121n
113	57n18, 242
114	78
191	71n

De mutatione nominum

113	185n30
123	56, 61
178	120
179–80	70n, 104
180	124–25
202–3	57n19
202	57n18, 242

De opificio mundi

22–35	53n1
69–71	70n, 101–4, 107, 112, 115, 125–26, 237
69	114n21, 120, 122, 124
70	83n66, 124, 137n51
71	102, 124
134–48	53n2
135	60, 112, 232
136–50	93
136–38	93
136	93, 236
148	93
150	93

De plantatione

2	109–10
14	57n22, 132
17	69n42, 110
18–26	69–75, 85, 96n85, 97, 98, 101, 104, 109–16, 127, 237–38, 250
18–24	237, 248, 254, 260
18–19	112
18	111n, 112, 120
21	61
22–23	125
22	69–70, 112–13
23–25	72, 122
23–24	251
23	69n41, 114, 238
24–26	71
24–25	69n41, 70, 72, 113
24	69–72, 115, 121, 238
25	71, 120, 125, 238
26–27	58n24
27	116
28	110
65–66	144–45

De posteritate Caini

10	185n30
13–16	76n53
31	83n66, 137n53
80	83n66, 137n49

De praemiis et poenis

2	76n51
25–26	122
26	70n
28–30	122
30	104n13
31–35	122
36–46	122
37	104, 122
39	125–26
50	78, 81n
53–55	89
53	89
55	78, 89–90
84	83n66, 137n52

121–22	70n, 104n12, 124		114n21, 116–19, 122, 127, 237, 250–51, 260
De sacrificiis Abelis et Caini		3.1–2	69n41, 71, 73, 75–76, 95–96, 98, 118, 123–24, 268
13	83n66, 137n50		
		3.1	69–70, 72, 185n30
De somniis		3.2	73, 118
	227	3.3–4	73, 118
1.23	83n66, 136, 139n64	3.3	69, 71
1.141	57n22, 133	3.4–5	72
1.164–65	85, 96, 268	3.4	71, 72n46
1.164–65a	81	3.5–6	69n41, 73–77, 95–96, 98, 118, 268
1.164	78		
1.206	58n24	3.5	71
2.172	185n30	3.6	74, 114n21, 118, 124, 126, 270n
2.225–34	71n		
2.251–52	142, 227	4.48–52	57n19
2.251	139, 142n77	4.49	57n19, 63–64, 67, 84, 96, 98, 106n16, 250, 255
2.252	19n50, 62, 77–84, 85, 86, 96, 97, 98, 128n4, 128n6, 129, 139, 246, 250, 251, 254, 260, 268–69		
		4.50	83n66, 136–37, 139n64
		4.123	53n2, 78n55, 112
		4.132	76n51
De specialibus legibus		*De virtutibus*	
1.32–42	53n2		94
1.36	120–21	55	185n30
1.37	104n12, 121, 125	185	121n
1.38	83n66, 137, 139n64	211–19	86
1.59–65	57n19	211	86
1.63	83n66, 136	214	185n30
1.65	57n19, 63–64, 67, 84, 89–90, 96, 98, 106n16, 250, 255	215	83n66, 138
		216–17	91–92
1.164	81, 85	216	237
1.207	104n12, 121–22, 125	217–19	91–94, 96n85, 97, 98, 250, 260
1.269	83n66, 137, 138n59		
1.315	57n19	217–18	90–91, 236
2.44–45	122–23	217	91–92, 185n30, 237
2.46	125	218	92, 237
2.189	76n51		
2.229–30	123	*De vita contemplativa*	
2.230	125	57	145n92
3.1–6	19n50, 62, 68–77, 81n, 85, 86, 97, 98, 101, 109, 112,	84	185n30

INDEX OF ANCIENT DOCUMENTS

De vita Mosis

	55, 89, 97, 131
1	94
1.1	86
1.57–59	94
1.59	94
1.68	83n66, 137n50
1.263–99	98
1.263–91	183
1.273–84	56, 58–62, 66, 96–97, 129, 250
1.274–83	67
1.274	57–58, 64, 78, 130–31, 183, 221–22, 229, 242, 251
1.277	57–58, 63–64, 84, 130–31, 181, 221–22, 229, 242, 251, 255
1.281	78
1.283	63–64, 183, 242
1.294	83n66, 136
2	98
2.6	79n60
2.69	236
2.187–92	250
2.187–91	135n32
2.187	79, 87, 141
2.188–91	135
2.188	79, 87, 89, 136, 141, 185n30, 245, 255–56
2.190	87, 89, 246
2.191–92	89, 246
2.191	79, 87, 89, 255–56
2.192–220	87n
2.221–33a	87n
2.233b–35	87n
2.246–87	141n73
2.246–57	83, 87
2.246	87
2.250	88, 245
2.258–69	83, 87–88
2.259	88, 135, 185n30
2.263	141, 185n30
2.264–65	82, 135, 245, 251, 254, 268
2.264	83, 88, 135
2.265	82–83, 86, 89, 94, 128n5, 129, 136, 138n63, 139, 141, 227–28, 251, 260
2.268–69	88, 135
2.269	88, 135–36
2.270–74	83, 88
2.270	88, 136
2.272	88, 94, 185n30, 236
2.275–87	83, 88
2.275	88
2.280	88–89
2.291	185n30

Legatio ad Gaium

3.161	112
5	104n13
21	83n66, 136, 139n64
245	78

Legum allegoriae

	71
1.33	232
2.85–86	62n
3.161	60

Quaestiones et solutiones in Exodum

2.29	76n53
2.33	53n2
2.40	124
2.43	76n53
2.44	76n53

Quaestiones et solutiones in Genesin

1.4	53n2
1.90	58n24
2.6	145n92
2.58–59	53n2
3.9	63–64, 84, 88n72, 255

INDEX OF ANCIENT DOCUMENTS

Quis rerum divinarum heres sit

29–30	63n29
55–57	53n2
69	118, 185n30
70	119
98	83n66, 137n50
249–65	67
259–66	96, 250
259	57, 78, 242
264–66	58, 62–64, 106n16, 129
264–65	63–64, 67, 84
265	63–64, 67, 119, 133, 255
266	133

Quod deterius potiori insidari soleat

38	137n50
71	57n18
79–90	104

Quod Deus sit immutabilis

4	185n30
139	185n30
146–47	145n92
181	57n18, 242
182	83n66, 137

Quod omnis probus liber sit

99	121n
123	78n57

Dead Sea Scrolls

CD	49, 233, 248
CD 5.11–12	45, 220
CD 5.11	232
CD 7.3–4	45, 220
CD 7.4	232
CD 12.11–13	232
CD 12.11	45
1QH	27n, 44–45, 47, 49, 51
1QH 4.25	45
1QH 5.21–22	44
1QH 7	48
1QH 7.6	220
1QH 7.16–17	48
1QH 7.25	48
1QH 8.12	220
1QH 8.19–20	49
1QH 9.8–9	48
1QH 9.32	220
1QH 12.11–13	268
1QH 12.11–12	19n49, 59, 262n17
1QH 13.19	19n49, 262n17
1QH 14.11–12	48n52
1QH 14.13–14	262
1QH 14.13	262n17
1QH 14.25	19n49
1QH 15.6–8	46
1QH 15.21–22	50
1QH 16.15	262
1QH 16.16–17	262
1QH 16.19–20	262
1QH 20.11–12	49
1QM	49–51
1QM 1	50
1QS	27, 38, 40, 49, 253
1QS 3–4	31–32, 35, 36, 38, 40–44, 45, 46–51, 213–20, 252
1QS 3.1–2	219
1QS 3.6b–9b	253n4
1QS 3.7b–8a	261
1QS 3.13—4.26	27–32, 41–43, 44, 47, 49, 51, 215–17
1QS 3.13—4.16	252
1QS 3.13—4.14	50–51
1QS 3.13—4.6	37
1QS 3.13	218
1QS 3.14–15	36
1QS 3.14	36–38, 215–16
1QS 3.15—4.19	35
1QS 3.15–19	35
1QS 3.15b—4.1	52n59
1QS 3.16	48, 50
1QS 3.17–19	50
1QS 3.17b–21	213–14
1QS 3.17b–19	252
1QS 3.18–25	218–19
1QS 3.18–19	37, 38n32, 41–42, 45, 46n46, 216–18

Dead Sea Scrolls (continued)

1QS 3.18	32, 36, 38n32, 41–42, 44, 215, 218
1QS 3.19–21	34
1QS 3.19	32n6
1QS 3.20–25	50–51, 216, 219
1QS 3.20–21	218
1QS 3.20	218
1QS 3.21	32n6
1QS 3.22	35
1QS 3.23	36
1QS 3.24–25	32–33
1QS 3.24	36n22, 40, 50, 218
1QS 3.25	42, 216, 218
1QS 4.2–16	45
1QS 4.2–14	37, 52n59, 215
1QS 4.2–6	46
1QS 4.2	33
1QS 4.3	40
1QS 4.4–5	40
1QS 4.5–6	218
1QS 4.6	33
1QS 4.9–11	46
1QS 4.9	39n33
1QS 4.10	40
1QS 4.15–26	50–51, 52n59
1QS 4.15–18	33
1QS 4.15–16	34
1QS 4.16	215n35
1QS 4.17–18	37, 216
1QS 4.18–22	37
1QS 4.18	34
1QS 4.20–23	35, 46n46
1QS 4.20	35, 46
1QS 4.20b–22a	253
1QS 4.21	36, 42, 216–17, 262
1QS 4.23–25	216
1QS 4.23	35, 36n22, 37, 40, 42, 216, 218
1QS 4.23b–24a	252
1QS 4.24–25	48n52
1QS 4.24	215n35, 218
1QS 5.4–5	40
1QS 6.2	219
1QS 8.15–16	257
1QS 8.16	220
1QS 9.3–4	263
1QS 9.15–16	49
1QS 10.21	35n20
1QS 11.21–22	46
1QS 20	38n32
1QShira 1	42n42, 216n40
1QShira 6	42n42, 216n40
Visions of Amram	51

RABBINIC LITERATURE

Mishnah

ʾbot 1.1	17
Soṭah 9.10–15	21
Soṭah 9.12	18–19
Soṭah 9.15	15, 21

Tosefta

Pesaḥim 1.27	20n56
Soṭah 10–15	15–19
Soṭah 10.1—15.7	13
Soṭah 10.1–3	13
Soṭah 10.1	13–15, 17–18, 21, 22
Soṭah 10.5–10	13
Soṭah 11.1–2	13
Soṭah 11.10	13, 18
Soṭah 12.5–6	13
Soṭah 12.5	16
Soṭah 13–15	21
Soṭah 13.2–4	1, 3, 11–12, 13–14, 16–18, 19–23
Soṭah 13.2	14, 15–19
Soṭah 13.3–4	21
Soṭah 13.3	12n41, 17
Soṭah 13.5	15n
Soṭah 13.7	14
Soṭah 14	14
Soṭah 14.3	16
Soṭah 14.8	16
Soṭah 15.2	18–19
Soṭah 15.3–5	14, 15–16
Soṭah 15.3	16

Babylonian Talmud

Baba Batra 12b	152n11
Sanhedrin 11a	2, 21n66

INDEX OF ANCIENT DOCUMENTS

Sanhedrin 11b	21n66
Soṭah 48b	21n66
Soṭah 49ab	2
Yoma 9b	21n66

Jerusalem Talmud

Šebiʿit 9.1	19n55
Soṭah 1.4	19n54
Soṭah 9.17	21–22n66

Targums

Onkelos	259n11
Pseudo-Jonathan	259n11

Leviticus Rabbah

21.8	19n53

Mekilta de-Rabbi Ishmael

Beshallaḥ	21
Beshallaḥ 7	21n65
Beshallaḥ 7.134–36	261
Pisḥa 1.42–76	259n11
Pisḥa 1.42–44	259n11
Pisḥa 1.58–59	259n11
Pisḥa 1.60	259n11
Pisḥa 1.64	259n11
Pisḥa 1.74–75	259n11
Pisḥa 1.148–66	258n11
Pisḥa 1.154–56	258–59n11
Shirata 10.58–73	257–58

Sefer ha-Razim

	176n

GREEK AND ROMAN LITERATURE

Aelius Aristides

In Defense of Oratory

43	154
432C	162
432D	160–62

Alexander of Aphrodisias

De mixtione

216.14–17	59, 107, 220n50, 240
223.6–9	59n

Cicero

De divinatione

158, 166–68, 171, 235, 248

1.1	162n42
1.8–9	149n1
1.11–12	57n19, 130–31
1.34–35	186n34
1.34	57n19
1.63	186n34
1.64–65	186n34
1.64	171, 226n55
1.66–67	187n34
1.66	235
1.80	160n36
1.114	158, 167, 235
1.122–24	140n68, 223n
1.129	161–62, 167
2.3	149n1

De natura deorum

	149n1
2.19	59, 220, 240
2.37	60, 241
2.38	112n

De oratore

1.18	91
3.19–27	91n77

Tusculanae disputationes

5.91	145n92

Cleomedes

De motu circulari

1.1	59n

Dio Chrysostom

De dicendi exercitatione (Or. 18)
2   236

De habitu (Or. 72)
72.12   189n45

De regno iii (Or. 3)
39   236–37

Diogenes Laertius

Lives of Eminent Philosophers
2.25   145n92
7.143   111n

Epictetus

Diatribai (Dissertationes)
1.14.6   60, 112n, 241

Euripides

Iphigenia taurica
16   181n15

Phoenissae
954–58   181n15
1255–58   181n15

Iamblichus

De Mysteriis
    161n39

Lucan

De bello civili
    166–67
5.163–67   88n72, 146n97, 189
5.169–77   167

Maximus of Tyre

Philosophumena
    126, 237–38

Orationes
    223n
3.3   144n91
9.7   144n91

Plato

Apologia
22C   65n33, 154, 235
31D   84n70, 143n83, 143n86, 223n
40A   84n70, 143, 223n, 228

Euthydemus
3B   223n
272E   84n70, 143, 223n, 228

Euthyphro
3B   140n67, 143n86

Ion
533D–36D   65
533D–34E   159
534A   66
534B   65, 67, 88n72, 159nn34–35, 243
534C–D   65, 67, 159–60
536C   66

Meno
99C   65n33, 154, 235

Phaedrus
    103–4, 114, 116, 118n23, 119, 126, 237
128D–29D   223n

242B–C	143n86	*Timaeus*	
242B	84n70, 143, 228	29E	69n39, 118n23
242C	143n86, 223n	41–42	102
244A–B	160	71E	160–62
244A	243	90A	69n42, 110, 237
245A	65, 67		
245C	160n36	**Plotinus**	
246–53	103, 109, 112		
246A–53C	69, 103, 117–18, 237	*Enneades*	
246A–47E	158		126, 237–38
246A	103, 113	1.3.3	115n
246B	69, 118	4.7.4	220n49
246D	103, 113	6.7.36	114n21
246E	103–4		
247A	69, 118	**Plutarch**	
247B–C	70, 113	*Amatorius*	
247B	104	16 (II.758E)	66–67
248A	69, 118	758D–E	160, 167
248D	69n40		
249A	69n40	*De defectu oraculorum*	
249C	69, 74–75, 103–4, 113, 118		68, 98, 131, 133, 135, 140, 146, 149n1, 168, 183–85, 187–88, 222, 235, 244, 248
249D–E	103		
249D	75, 103, 113		
249E	73–74		
251B–C	70		
251C	113	413E	188
251E	113	414E	188, 190
254B	115	415A	190
265B	160	418C–D	57, 131, 184, 243–44
		418D	58, 131, 134, 184, 187, 222–23
Respublica		431A	184n22
3.402D	92	431B	131n16, 184n25, 223, 244
7.535A	92, 236	432D	167–68, 189n45, 235
		432E–F	167n49
Symposium		432F	235
	132	436D–38E	184n22
202E–3A	58, 190–91	436F–37A	189–90n47
202E	57n22, 132, 190, 243		
		De E apud Delphos	
Theaetetus			149n1
128D	143n84		
173C–74A	68–69, 117, 158n31		

INDEX OF ANCIENT DOCUMENTS

De genio Socratis
    83, 141, 149n1, 223, 228, 248, 269
580B–82C   185, 223n
580C–82C   140
580C–D   140–41, 185–86
580C   84n70, 143n85
588B–89F   140, 185, 223n
588D–E   84, 143–44, 223–24, 247
589C–D   162
589D   141, 186, 224, 228, 247, 269
589E–F   84n70, 143n85
589E   142n77, 228
589F–92F   105n
589F   186, 249
591D–92C   186
591D   105n, 144, 224
592A   144, 224
592C   144, 224

De Iside et Osiride
     34–35, 132, 149n1
361C   57n22, 132, 190

De Pythiae oraculis
     149n1, 184n22

Moralia
     166–67

Quaestiones platonicae
     126, 237–38
6   113

Pollux
Onomasticon
1.15   161

Pseudo-Longinus
De sublimitate
13.2   147n97, 189n44

Pseudo-Plato
Theages
     140, 223n
128D–29D   143n86
128D   84n70
128E   143n86

Quintilian
Institutio oratoria
1.preface.9   236
1.9   91
12   91n78

Rhetorica ad Herennium
     91
1.3   91n76
3.19–27   91n76
3.20   91n77

Seneca
Ad Lucilium epistulae morales
41   232
41.5   60
41.9   241

Stobaeus
Eclogues
153.34—154.5   59n

Strabo
Geographica
9.3.5   189n45

Tacitus
Annals
2.54   161n39

Virgil

Aeneid

6.42–102	168

Xenophon

Memorabilia

	143n86
1.1–2	140n67
1.1.2–3	143n86
1.1.4	143n86, 223n
1.1.5	143n86, 223n

EARLY CHRISTIAN LITERATURE

John Cassian

Collationes

	149n1
12	155

JOHN CHRYSOSTOM

Homiliae in epistulam i ad Corinthios

29.1	147n97, 189n44

LACTANTIUS

De falsa religione

5	220n49

Divinarum institutionum libri VII

1	220n49

ORIGEN

Contra Celsum

3.25	148n97, 189n44
6.71	59n

PSEUDO-JUSTINUS

Cohortatio ad Graecos

	149n1, 154
37.2	155
37.3	155

Shepherd of Hermas

38, 40, 193, 220n47, 229

Mandates

3.1	39n33
3.2	39n33
3.4	39n33
5.1.2a	38–39
5.1.3–4	38–39
5.2.8	38–39
6.2.1	39
12.2.2–5	39

ZOROASTRIAN LITERATURE

Gāthās of Zarathustra

31, 33, 213, 220

Yasna

30.2–3	214
30.3–5	32
30.8	33n12
30.10	33n12
31.2	33
31.3	33
31.19	33
43.5	33n12
43.8	33n12
43.12	33
43.15	33n12
44.2	33
44.16	33
45.2	32, 214
46.6	33n12
47	32n7, 214n31

Yasna (continued)

47.6	33
50.5	32
51.9	33

www.ingramcontent.com/pod-product-compliance
Lightning Source LLC
Chambersburg PA
CBHW031900220426
43663CB00006B/707